LIBRARY OF NEW TESTAMENT STUDIES

690

Formerly the Journal for the Study of the New Testament Supplement Series

Editor
Chris Keith

Editorial Board
Dale C. Allison, Lynn H. Cohick, Kylie Crabbe, R. Alan Culpepper,
Craig A. Evans, Jennifer Eyl, Robert Fowler, Juan Hernández Jr.,
John S. Kloppenborg, Michael Labahn, Matthew V. Novenson,
Love L. Sechrest, Robert Wall, Catrin H. Williams, Brittany E. Wilson

Reading the Way, Paul, and "The Jews" in Acts within Judaism

"Among My Own Nation"

Jason F. Moraff

LONDON • NEW YORK • OXFORD • NEW DELHI • SYDNEY

T&T CLARK

Bloomsbury Publishing Plc, 50 Bedford Square, London, WC1B 3DP, UK
Bloomsbury Publishing Inc, 1385 Broadway, New York, NY 10018, USA
Bloomsbury Publishing Ireland, 29 Earlsfort Terrace, Dublin 2, D02 AY28, Ireland

BLOOMSBURY, T&T CLARK and the T&T Clark logo are trademarks of
Bloomsbury Publishing Plc

First published in Great Britain 2024
Paperback edition published in 2025

Copyright © Jason F. Moraff, 2024

Jason F. Moraff has asserted his right under the Copyright, Designs and
Patents Act, 1988, to be identified as Author of this work.

For legal purposes the Acknowledgments on p. xi constitute an extension of
this copyright page.

All rights reserved. No part of this publication may be: i) reproduced or transmitted
in any form, electronic or mechanical, including photocopying, recording or by means
of any information storage or retrieval system without prior permission in writing
from the publishers; or ii) used or reproduced in any way for the training, development
or operation of artificial intelligence (AI) technologies, including generative AI technologies.
The rights holders expressly reserve this publication from the text and data mining
exception as per Article 4(3) of the Digital Single Market Directive (EU) 2019/790.

Bloomsbury Publishing Plc does not have any control over, or responsibility for,
any third-party websites referred to or in this book. All internet addresses given in
this book were correct at the time of going to press. The author and publisher
regret any inconvenience caused if addresses have changed or sites have ceased
to exist, but can accept no responsibility for any such changes.

A catalogue record for this book is available from the British Library.

Library of Congress Cataloging-in-Publication Data
Names: Moraff, Jason F., author.
Title: Reading the Way, Paul, and "the Jews" in Acts within Judaism :
"among my own nation" / by Jason F. Moraff.
Description: London ; New York : T&T Clark, 2023. |
Series: Library of New Testament studies, 2513-8790 ; 690 |
Includes bibliographical references. | Summary: "Jason F. Moraff argues that Acts uses
common Jewish ethnicity and parallel characterization to bind the Way, Paul, and "the
Jews" together into a shared identity as Israel, God's covenant people, on a communal
journey of repentance"-- Provided by publisher.
Identifiers: LCCN 2023021075 | ISBN 9780567712462 (hardback) |
ISBN 9780567712509 (paperback) | ISBN 9780567712479 (ePDF) |
ISBN 9780567712493 (epub)
Subjects: LCSH: Bible. Acts–Criticism, interpretation, etc. | Jews in the New Testament. |
Judaism–Relations–Christianity–Biblical teaching. |
Christianity and other religions–Judaism–Biblical teaching.
Classification: LCC BS2625.52 .M67 2023 | DDC 226.6/06—dc23/eng/20230621
LC record available at https://lccn.loc.gov/2023021075

ISBN:	HB:	978-0-5677-1246-2
	PB:	978-0-5677-1250-9
	ePDF:	978-0-5677-1247-9
	eBook:	978-0-5677-1249-3

Series: Library of New Testament Studies, volume 690
ISSN 2513-8790

Typeset by RefineCatch Limited, Bungay, Suffolk

For product safety related questions contact productsafety@bloomsbury.com.

To find out more about our authors and books visit www.bloomsbury.com and
sign up for our newsletters.

To Dustin Murphy †

וְיֵשׁ אֹהֵב דָּבֵק מֵאָח

Contents

Acknowledgments   xi
Abbreviations   xii

1   "Nothing against My Nation": Acts, Jews, and Judaism   1
    1.1   Framing the Contemporary Debate   2
    1.2   Recent Developments   5
         1.2.1   Contrasted Identities   6
         1.2.2   Interconnected Identities   9
         1.2.3   Reading Acts as Early Jewish Literature   11
         1.2.4   Summary   13
    1.3   Thesis   14
    1.4   Methodology   17
    1.5   Guiding Assumptions about Acts   18
         1.5.1   The Unity of Luke-Acts   18
         1.5.2   Luke's Ethnic Identity   19
         1.5.3   Dating Acts   21
    1.6   Terminological and Translational Issues   21
         1.6.1   Judaism, "within Judaism," and Christianity   21
         1.6.2   Jews, Israel, Gentiles, and the Way   24
         1.6.3   Repentance and/or Conversion   26
         1.6.4   Antisemitism, Anti/Pro-Judaism/Jewish, and Supersessionism   27
    1.7   The Way Ahead   29

2   "I am a Jew": Ancient Ethnicity, Jewish Identity, and Lukan Characterization   31
    2.1   Ancient Ethnic Contours   32
    2.2   Shared Blood: Genealogy, History, and Territory   34
         2.2.1   Kinship in Antiquity   34
         2.2.2   Acts and Jewish Kinship   35
         2.2.3   Acts and Jewish Ancestral History   37
         2.2.4   Acts and "the Region of the Jews"   42
         2.2.5   Summary   42

	2.3	Shared Language	43
		2.3.1 Language and Ethnicity in Antiquity	43
		2.3.2 Acts and "the Hebrew Dialect"	43
	2.4	Common Cult	44
		2.4.1 Gods, Cults, and Ethnicity in Antiquity	44
		2.4.2 Acts and Israel's God	46
		2.4.3 Acts and the Jerusalem Temple	47
		2.4.4 Summary	50
	2.5	Shared Custom	50
		2.5.1 Ancestral Custom and Ethnic Identity in Antiquity	50
		2.5.2 Acts and Jewish Ancestral Custom	51
		2.5.3 Summary	53
	2.6	The Way as Jewish Subgroup	53
		2.6.1 Jewish Subgroups in Josephus	54
		2.6.2 Jewish Subgroups in Acts	55
		2.6.3 The Way's Jewish Exclusivism	58
		2.6.4 Gentile Inclusion and the Jewishness of the Way	59
		2.6.5 Summary	62
	2.7	Conclusion: "I Am a Jew"	62
3	"Like You are Today": Images of the Jews, the Way, and Paul		65
	3.1	Luke's Mixed Picture of the Jews	68
		3.1.1 Differentiating among Jews	68
		3.1.2 Differentiating Jewish Responses	69
		3.1.2.1 Jewish Division in Acts 1–8	69
		3.1.2.2 Jewish Division in Saul/Paul's Ministry	71
		3.1.2.3 Summary	76
		3.1.3 Noble Non-Jesus-Following Jews	77
		3.1.4 Summary: The Jews "in Disagreement with One Another"	79
	3.2	Bumps along the Way	79
		3.2.1 Divergences in the Way	80
		3.2.2 Ignoble Jesus-Followers	85
		3.2.3 Stumbling along the Way	88
		3.2.4 Summary: A Less-than-Ideal Jewish Community	95
	3.3	Paul's Rough Edges	96
		3.3.1 The Divisive Paul	97
		3.3.2 The Temperamental Paul	99
		3.3.3 A Parting of the Ways	102

		3.3.4	Paul and the Holy Spirit	103
		3.3.5	Summary	106
	3.4	Conclusion		107
4	"I Persecuted this Way": Agents of Violence in Acts			109
	4.1	Jewish Violence		111
		4.1.1	Interpretive Guides	111
			4.1.1.1 Simeon: The Fall and Rise of Many in Israel	111
			4.1.1.2 Jesus: Israel Persecuting the Prophets	113
			4.1.1.3 Gamaliel: Fighting against God	115
			4.1.1.4 Stephen: Jealous Brothers and Unjust Israelites	116
			4.1.1.5 Summary	117
		4.1.2	Patterns of Jewish Violence	118
			4.1.2.1 Violence against the Jerusalem Community	118
			4.1.2.2 Violence against Paul	119
		4.1.3	Summary	122
	4.2	Gentile Violence		123
		4.2.1	Arrest and Abuse in Philippi	124
		4.2.2	Riot in Ephesus	125
		4.2.3	Summary	125
	4.3	Paul's Violence		126
		4.3.1	The Quintessential God-fighter	127
		4.3.2	Raising the Persecutor	129
		4.3.3	Apologizing with Violence	131
		4.3.4	Summary	135
	4.4	Conclusion		136
5	"I Could Not See": Israel's Blindness, Paul, and the End of Acts			139
	5.1	Blindness in Luke's Gospel		143
		5.1.1	Establishing the Metaphor: Blindness and Sight in Luke 1–2	143
		5.1.2	Israel, God's Blind Servant	146
		5.1.3	Jesus, God's Servant Who Opens Blind Eyes	147
		5.1.4	Revelation of the Risen Lord	150
		5.1.5	Summary	152
	5.2	Blindness in Acts		153
		5.2.1	Paul's Blindness as Israel's Blindness	153
		5.2.2	Paul's Vocation: "To Open Their Eyes"	155
		5.2.3	Paul and Elymas	157
		5.2.4	Summary	160

	5.3	Blindness at the End of Acts	160
		5.3.1 Paul's Prophetic Posture	161
		5.3.2 Isaianic Expectation amidst Judgment	162
		5.3.3 Paul's Last Word and Actions	164
		Excursus: Turning to the Gentiles	165
		5.3.4 Summary	167
	5.4	Conclusion	168

Conclusion   "Among My Own Nation": Reading the Way, Paul, and "the Jews" in Acts within Judaism   171

Bibliography   175

Acknowledgments

It takes a lot to write a monograph. This one endured a pandemic and the passing of my best friend, Dustin Murphy. Completing it would have been impossible without the support of friends, colleagues, mentors, and family. I am grateful for Tony Amoury Alkhoury, Melanie Dzugan, John Pendleton, and Nick Scott-Blakely. Their friendship was life-giving during a difficult time. Larry McCutcheon and Reed Metcalf have been pillars of love and joy, while also helping me become a better scholar. Nick Scott-Blakely and Tommy Givens were invaluable in helping me refine my thinking about supersessionism. Wil Rogan helped me improve my writing. I am thankful for the encouraging, insightful input of Isaac Oliver, Robert Brawley, Marianne Meye Thompson, and especially Joel B. Green. Joel's guidance throughout the process was invaluable. Thank you to my parents, David and Johanna Moraff, and my sister Elizabeth, for their consistent support. My wife, Anna, provided stability and encouragement amid volatile circumstances. I cannot adequately express my love and appreciation for her. Finally, I am grateful to and for my daughter, Nora. She motivated me to finish this monograph so I could focus on being "dada."

Abbreviations

Abbreviations follow the *SBL Handbook of Style* with the following additions:

AJEC	Ancient Judaism and Early Christianity
Antí	*Antíteses*
ASE	Annali di storia dell'esegesi
BAFCS	The Book of Acts in Its First Century Setting
BBC	Blackwell Bible Commentaries
BCAW	Blackwell Companions to the Ancient World
BCCR	Brill Companions to Classical Reception
Belief	Belief: A Theological Commentary on the Bible
BMSSEC	Baylor-Mohr Siebeck Studies in Early Christianity
BRLJ	Brill Reference Library of Judaism
BU	Biblische Untersuchungen
CBCN	Comentario Bíblico del Continente Nuevo
CHSC	Center for Hellenic Studies Colloquia
COQG	Christian Origins and the Question of God
CsB	Conozca su Biblia
DCLS	Deuterocanonical and Cognate Literature Studies
ECM	Novum Testamentum Graecum: editio critica maior
ESEC	Emory Studies in Early Christianity
EstB	*Estudios Bíblicos*
Glo	*Glotta*
IA	*Israel Affairs*
'Ilu	*'Ilu: Revista de Ciencias de las Religiones*
JDR	*Journal of Disability & Religion*
JECH	*Journal of Early Christian History*
JPT	*Journal of Pentecostal Theology*
JPTSup	Journal of Pentecostal Theology Supplement Series
JSJSup	Supplements to the Journal for the Study of Judaism
JTI	*Journal of Theological Interpretation*
KWJS	Key Words in Jewish Studies
LCBI	Literary Currents in Biblical Interpretation
LNT	Lectura del Nuevo Testamento
MBI	Methods in Biblical Interpretation
MBPS	Mellen Biblical Press Series
Nar	*Narrative*
NSBT	New Studies in Biblical Theology
NTM	New Testament Monographs
NTT	New Testament Theology (Cambridge)
OTM	Oxford Theological Monographs
OWC	Oxford World's Classics

PPS	Popular Patristics Series
RelSocSup	Religion and Society Supplemental Series
SGNT	T&T Clark Study Guides to the New Testament
SJCA	Notre Dame Center for the Study of Judaism and Christianity in Antiquity
SMTFIJS	The S. Mark Taper Foundation Imprint in Jewish Studies
TANZ	Texte und Arbeiten zum neutestamentlichen Zeitalter
TC	Texts@Contexts
TNTC	Tyndale New Testament Commentary
ZECNT	Zondervan Exegetical Commentary on the New Testament

1

"Nothing against My Nation": Acts, Jews, and Judaism

During Paul's final trip to Jerusalem in the Acts of the Apostles, Jews from Asia (οἱ ἀπὸ τῆς Ἀσίας Ἰουδαῖοι) accuse him of "teaching everyone everywhere against the [Jewish] people (κατὰ τοῦ λαοῦ), the Torah, and this place [the temple]" (21:28).[1] This threefold charge leads to Paul's arrest, apologetic speeches, appeal to Caesar, and journey to Rome. To maintain Paul's innocence, Luke must not only refute claims that Paul opposes Torah and temple but also accusations that he teaches against the Jewish people.[2] Scholars have often acknowledged that Luke's Paul affirms Torah and temple in his subsequent defense speeches. Whether Luke's Paul (and thereby the text of Acts itself) teaches against the people, that is, "the Jews" (οἱ Ἰουδαῖοι), remains a more disputed question.[3]

Yet, lack of animosity toward the Jewish people is a central concern of Paul's self-defense before Jewish leaders in Rome:

> Men, brothers (ἀδελφοί), although I myself did *nothing against the people* or the ancestral customs (οὐδὲν ἐναντίον ποιήσας τῷ λαῷ ἢ τοῖς ἔθεσι τοῖς πατρῴοις), I was handed over as a prisoner from Jerusalem into the hands of the Romans. After examining me, they were willing to release me because they found no reason to put me to death. Now, after the Jews (οἱ Ἰουδαῖοι) objected, I was compelled to appeal to Caesar, not that I have anything for which to accuse my nation (ὡς τοῦ ἔθνους μου ἔχων τι κατηγορεῖν). Therefore, for this reason (διὰ ταύτην οὖν τὴν αἰτίαν) I requested to see and to speak with you, because it is on account of (ἕνεκεν) the hope of Israel that I am bound by this chain.
>
> Acts 28:17–19

---

[1] Translations are mine unless otherwise noted.
[2] I use "Luke" to refer to the author of Acts for convenience and style, not due to historical conclusions about the author's identity. For the Gospel text, I use "the Third Gospel," "Luke's Gospel," and "the Gospel of Luke."
[3] Joseph B. Tyson, ed., *Luke-Acts and the Jewish People: Eight Critical Perspectives* (Minneapolis, MN: Augsburg, 1988); idem. *Luke, Judaism, and the Scholars: Critical Approaches to Luke-Acts* (Columbia, SC: University of South Carolina Press, 1999); François Bovon, *Luke the Theologian: Fifty-Five Years of Research*, 2nd ed. (Waco, TX: Baylor University Press, 2006), 364–88, 490–94, 503–64; Christopher Stroup, *The Christians Who Became Jews: Acts of the Apostles and Ethnicity in the Roman City*, Synkrisis (New Haven, CT: Yale University Press, 2020), 17–34; Jason F. Moraff, "Recent Trends in the Study of Jews and Judaism in Luke-Acts," *CBR* 19 (2020): 64–87; cf. W. Ward Gasque, *A History of the Interpretation of the Acts of the Apostles*, 2nd ed. (Eugene, OR: Wipf and Stock, 2000).

At the narrative's conclusion, Paul clarifies that he did not wrong the Jewish people or their tradition. He brings no accusations against his own nation (τοῦ ἔθνους μου), the Jewish people (οἱ Ἰουδαῖοι), before Caesar. They remain Paul's family (ἀδελφοί). In fact, the reason (διὰ ταύτην οὖν τὴν αἰτίαν) he addresses the Roman Jewish leaders is to explain that he suffers in chains *because of* (ἕνεκεν) Israel's national hope (28:20; cf. 26:6–7). Paul neither opposes the Jewish people nor threatens their ancestral ways. He stands with them.

I contend that the Lukan Paul's words reveal Acts' overall posture toward the Jewish people: it views them as family and remains concerned with their ancestral hope. More specifically, I argue that, in its depiction of the Way, Paul, and "the Jews," Acts narrates a conflict within Judaism over the direction of the ancestral tradition. Acts calls all Jews to repent, reorienting themselves and centering the Jewish tradition around Jesus, whom the Way and Paul proclaim as Israel's Lord and Messiah, the fulfillment of Israel's hope. But rather than using "the Jews" as a negative foil to construct Jesus' followers as "true Israel" or replacing the Jewish people as God's people, Acts binds the Way, Paul, and "the Jews" together in a shared identity of *Israel*. Together they sojourn on Israel's communal repentance-journey, the gradual movement from infidelity and ignorance toward greater fidelity to and understanding of what God is doing in Jesus. The Way and Paul—and by implication, the book of Acts—identify with the Jewish people. Indeed, Acts' central characters display how God remains faithful to Israel when they act unfaithfully. In other words, Acts, like Paul, does not teach against the Jewish people; it levies no charge against the Jewish nation. Instead, Acts speaks from among them.

1.1 Framing the Contemporary Debate

Of course, many scholars think Acts, unlike its main character Paul, does bring a charge, if not several, against the Jewish people. Acts, they argue, repudiates the Jewish people.[4] In these readings, Acts constructs "the Jews" as a uniformly negative "other" in contrast to the idealized *ecclesia*. Luke transforms non-Jesus-following Jews into "hermeneutical Jews," literary caricatures that function as an adverse foil in Luke's construction of Christian (read: not Jewish) identity.[5] On the one hand, Acts depicts "the Jews" as increasingly uniform in their rejection of Jesus and his followers. They are

---

[4] E.g., Hans Conzelmann, *The Theology of St. Luke*, trans. Geoffrey Buswell (Philadelphia, PA: Fortress, 1982), 227; Ernst Haenchen, *Acts of the Apostles: A Commentary* (Philadelphia, PA: Westminster John Knox, 1971), 266, 274; Jack T. Sanders, *The Jews in Luke-Acts* (Philadelphia, PA: Fortress, 1987); Jerry Lynn Ray, *Narrative Irony in Luke-Acts: The Paradoxical Interaction of Prophetic Fulfillment and Jewish Rejection*, MBPS 28 (Lewiston, NY: Mellen, 1996), 101–73; Shelly Matthews, *Perfect Martyr: The Stoning of Stephen and the Construction of Christian Identity* (Oxford: Oxford University Press, 2010); Mitzi J. Smith, *Literary Construction of the Other in the Acts of the Apostles: Charismatics, the Jews, and Women*, PTMS 154 (Eugene, OR: Pickwick, 2011), 57–94.

[5] The phrase "hermeneutical Jew" is Jeremy Cohen's. Cohen describes it as how "the Christian idea of Jewish identity crystallized around the theological purpose the Jew served in Christendom; Christians perceived the Jews to be who they were supposed to be, not who they actually were, and related to them accordingly" (*Living Letters of the Law: Ideas of the Jew in Medieval Christianity*, SMTFIJS [Berkeley, CA: University of California Press, 1999], 1).

a violent and contentious group, ignorant of their own Scriptures and traditions. As a result, "the Jews" forfeit their identity as God's people. On the other hand, Luke portrays the Way as faithful to God through Jesus. They are harmonious, peaceful, united, and enlightened. Luke thus reinterprets Israel's Scriptures, history, and practices through Jesus, wresting them away from the Jewish people in order to legitimate the Way—a predominantly gentile movement in Luke's day—as the true people of God. Christopher Stroup provides an apt summary: those who take this view "contend that in Acts the term οἱ Ἰουδαῖοι functions like a *terminus technicus* meaning 'the Jews.' 'The Jews,' on this reading, identify not only those Jews who oppose Christians, but also negatively signify all Jews who do not become Christians."[6] Acts' narration of an originally Jewish movement ultimately explains and justifies how and why Christians superseded Jews as God's people and became the sole, proper inheritors of Israel's tradition.

For such interpreters, the Lukan Paul, the violent persecutor turned champion of the Way, embodies Acts' supersessionism and "anti-Jewish" tendencies by way of his contrast with the rest of "the Jews."[7] Though Paul was like them, he (and Acts) leaves his past behind, "the Jews" included, in favor of the Way and the gentile mission. "The Jews," unlike Paul, persist in their violence, misunderstand their own Scriptures, and continue to reject Jesus and his followers. Therefore, Paul closes the door on their inclusion, sealing their rejection as God's people by the end of the book (28:25–28). Luke thus uses Paul to legitimate the Way as *the* proper interpretation and inheritor of defunct Judaism and its members as the replacement of "the Jews" as God's people. While interpretive specifics differ, the conclusion remains the same: Acts amounts to an early form of gentile Christian supersessionism and anti-Judaism. Luke is "anti-Jewish."[8]

Other readers have reached a diametrically opposed conclusion. Luke, they claim, is "pro-Jewish." This interpretive tradition traces its origins to Jacob Jervell.[9] Jervell read Acts' rhetoric about "the Jews" as internecine quarrel. The Way remains a Jewish movement in Acts. It embodies proper interpretation of the Jewish ancestral tradition in continuity with Judaism without leaving all Jews or Judaism behind. For Jervell and his successors, Luke critiques particular Jewish people or groups and certain understandings of Israel's Scriptures, but his portrait of the Jewish people and Judaism is generally positive. The Jewishness of the Way tempers negative images of Jews and Judaism. Luke refrains from rejecting the Jewish people *in toto* or excluding a future hope for them. They remain the one, albeit divided, people of God.[10]

---

[6] Stroup, *Christians*, 23.
[7] E.g., Sanders, *Jews*, 98–101; Matthews, *Perfect Martyr*, 73–75. "[I]n Acts, Paul emerges as the only Pharisee, and perhaps the only Jew, who displays correct Jewish piety" (Amy-Jill Levine, review of *The Portrayals of the Pharisees in the Gospels and Acts*, by Mary Marshall, *SCJR* 11 (2016): 1–3 [2]).
[8] E.g., Joseph B. Tyson, *Images of Judaism in Luke-Acts* (Columbia, SC: University of South Carolina Press, 1992); John G. Gager, "Where Does Luke's Anti-Judaism Come From?," *ASE* 24 (2007): 31–35; Smith, *Literary Construction*, 57–94; cf. Amy-Jill Levine, "Luke and the Jewish Religion," *Int* 68 (2014): 389–402.
[9] Jacob Jervell, *Luke and the People of God: A New Look at Luke-Acts* (Minneapolis, MN: Augsburg, 1979).
[10] E.g., Robert L. Brawley, *Luke-Acts and the Jews: Conflict, Apology, and Conciliation*, SBLMS 33 (Atlanta, GA: Scholars Press, 1987); David L. Tiede, "'Glory to Thy People Israel': Luke-Acts and the Jews," in *Eight Critical Perspectives*, 21–34. Cf. Jacob Jervell, *Die Apostelgeschichte*, KEK (Göttingen: Vandenhoeck & Ruprecht, 1998), 626–31; Robert C. Tannehill, "Israel in Luke-Acts: A Tragic Story," *JBL* 104 (1985): 69–85, both of whom read the end of Acts with greater terminality for unbelieving Jews.

This "pro-Jewish" camp also finds support in the character of Paul.[11] They argue that Acts paints Paul as a faithful Jew, one whose loyalty to his ancestral polity, despite rumors, is beyond reproach. This Paul is a prophet who calls Israel to repent and join the Way. His critical comments toward the Jewish people are for their sake, not their condemnation or rejection.[12] Paul "turns to the gentiles" after having substantial success preaching to the Jewish people. Some may see the Jews falling short of Paul's expectations for a uniform response to the message about Jesus, yet Paul never abandons them. He stays faithful to them, their future, and their ancestral customs and beliefs.[13] Paul thus personifies Luke's "pro-Jewish" posture.

Since Jervell's work, the final quarter of the twentieth century saw numerous studies examine Luke's view of Jews and Judaism. These works came to variously nuanced yet utterly opposed conclusions. As a result, the Acts of the Apostles, with Paul a central puzzle piece, plays an abstruse role in discussions about the NT and Judaism. It simultaneously sits among or atop lists of the most "pro-Jewish" NT texts and the most "anti-Jewish" ones.[14]

Contemporary debates about Acts' ambivalence toward Jews and Judaism trace their origins to F. C. Baur and the Tübingen School and their attempt to situate Acts in the historical development in Christianity. In their dialectical approach, Acts reflected a second-century "early catholic," irenic synthesis between Petrine/Jewish Christianity and Pauline/Gentile Christianity that resulted from the Marcionite conflict. A Marcionite background helped explain Lukan ambivalence toward Jews and Judaism: Acts retained Jewish Scripture, practices, and communal structures in the *ecclesia* to rebut Marcion, yet took issue with "the Jews" themselves and presents the Way as the true people of God. Put differently, Acts preserves aspects of Judaism but eschews the Jewish people. Acts, therefore, must be a second-century document from the early catholic, gentile Christian church.[15] As such, Acts reflects an anti-Jewish, supersessionist

---

[11] E.g., Jacob Jervell, *The Unknown Paul: Essays on Luke-Acts and Early Christian History* (Minneapolis, MN: Augsburg, 1984); idem, "Paulus in der Apostelgeschichte und die Geschichte des Urchristentums," *NTS* 32 (1986): 378–92; Brawley, *Jews*, 68–83; cf. Joshua W. Jipp, "The Paul of Acts: Proclaimer of the Hope of Israel or Teacher of Apostasy from Moses?," *NovT* 62 (2020): 60–78.

[12] Cf. Jocelyn McWhirter, *Rejected Prophets: Jesus and His Witnesses in Luke-Acts* (Minneapolis, MN: Fortress, 2014), 95–110; David P. Moessner, *Luke the Historian of Israel's Legacy, Theologian of Israel's "Christ": A New Reading of the "Gospel Acts" of Luke*, BZNW 182 (Berlin: de Gruyter, 2016), 201–301; Dulcinea Boesenberg, "Prophetic Rebuke in Acts: Calling for Reform Rather than Rejection of Israel," in *Religion and Reform*, ed. Ronald A. Simkins and Zachary B. Smith, RelSocSup 18 (Omaha, NE: Kripke Center, 2019), 5–19.

[13] Brawley, *Jews*, 75–77; Jervell, *People*, 64, 153–83.

[14] On how both camps tend to formulate Jewish and Christian identities in abstract, essentialist, and binary ways, see Stroup, *Christians*, 17–34; David A. Smith, "Luke, the Jews, and the Politics of Early Christian Identity" (PhD diss., Duke University, Durham, NC, 2018), 23–24; cf. Pamela M. Eisenbaum, "Paul, Polemics, and the Problem of Essentialism," *BibInt* 13 (2005): 224–38. See also Isaac W. Oliver, *Torah Praxis after 70 CE: Reading Matthew and Luke-Acts as Jewish Texts*, WUNT 2/355 (Tübingen: Mohr Siebeck, 2013), 18–32; Arthur Francis Carter, Jr., "Diaspora Acts: Contextualizing a Metanarrative Syntacts," in *Luke-Acts*, ed. James P. Grimshaw, TC (London: Bloomsbury, 2018), 74–103, esp. 94–103, both of whom criticize assumed metanarratives that fund these divergent interpretations.

[15] F. C. Baur, *The Church History of the First Three Centuries*, trans. Allan Menzies (London: Williams and Norgate, 1878), 131–36. See Tyson, *Critical Approaches*, 12–29, for an overview. In fairness, Baur recognized major Jewish elements of Acts more than some of his disciples. On Baur's ongoing

posture even as it claims certain Jewish elements for the (gentile) church. Its vantage point stands outside Judaism.[16]

Subsequent rebuttals of the "anti-Jewish" perspective likewise involved identifying Luke's sociohistorical location. Objections often rested on historical claims that enabled interpreters to identify the portrait of Jews and Judaism as reflecting "intramural conflict." If one locates Luke "within Judaism," as an insider, his critiques of certain Jews become more conciliatory than condemnatory. They amount to sectarian and/or prophetic calls to join a renewal movement centered on Jesus of Nazareth.[17]

The foundational debate Baur initiated continues. When it comes to Acts and Judaism, what scholars see depends on where they think Luke stands. How one understands Luke's social position in relation to the Jewish people, Judaism, Jewish Christianity, and Gentile Christianity fundamentally informs how one interprets Acts. Where one locates Acts sociohistorically vis-à-vis Judaism—where Acts falls on the spectrum of early Judaism and emerging gentile Christianity—invariably informs how one interprets the entire book.[18] Today, the question of the sociohistorical relationship between Acts, Jews, and Judaism is arguably *the* eye of the "storm center" that is Luke-Acts scholarship.[19] And how scholars address that question largely depends on how they understand Luke's portraits of the Way, Paul, and the Jews.

1.2 Recent Developments

The past decade or so has seen renewed attempts at overcoming the *anti-/pro-Jewish* impasse of prior scholarship.[20] Developments owe much to conversations about the

---

influence, see David Lincicum, "F. C. Baur's Place in the Study of Jewish Christianity," in *The Rediscovery of Jewish Christianity: From Toland to Baur*, ed. F. Stanley Jones, HHBS (Atlanta, GA: Society of Biblical Literature, 2012), 137–66; Martin Bauspiess, Christof Landmesser, and David Lincicum, eds., *Ferdinand Christian Baur und die Geschichte des frühen Christentums* (Tübingen: Mohr Siebeck, 2014).

[16] Richard I. Pervo, *Dating Acts: Between the Evangelists and the Apologists* (Sonoma, CA: Polebridge, 2006), 324–30. The thesis that Luke-Acts responds to Marcionism has been revived by Joseph B. Tyson, *Marcion and Luke-Acts: A Defining Struggle* (Columbia, SC: University of South Carolina Press, 2006); Matthews, *Perfect Martyr*, 27–52. See Isaac W. Oliver, "Are Luke and Acts Anti-Marcionite?" in *Wisdom Poured out Like Water: Studies on Jewish and Christian Antiquity in Honor of Gabriele Boccaccini*, ed. J. Harold Ellens, Isaac W. Oliver, Jason von Ehrenkrook, James Waddell, and Jason M. Zurawski, DCLS 38 (Berlin: de Gruyter, 2018), 499–525, for a critique.

[17] Marilyn Salmon, "Insider or Outsider? Luke's Relationship with Judaism," in *Eight Critical Perspectives*, 76–82. For a critique, see Martin Rese, "The Jews in Luke-Acts: Some Second Thoughts," in *The Unity of Luke-Acts*, ed. Jozef Verheyden, BETL 142 (Leuven: Peeters, 1999), 185–201, esp. 188–94.

[18] Levine captures this inevitable circularity wherein "we read a text, identify author and audience on the basis of our reading, and then interpret the text on the basis of this reconstruction" ("Luke," 389). Simply compare Jacob Jervell, *The Theology of the Acts of the Apostles*, NTT (Cambridge: Cambridge University Press, 1996), with Shelly Matthews, *The Acts of the Apostles: An Introduction and Study Guide: Taming the Tongues of Fire*, SGNT 5 (London: T&T Clark, 2017), to see this debate's impact on interpretation.

[19] Willem C. van Unnik, "Luke-Acts: A Storm Center in Contemporary Scholarship," in *Sparsa Collecta*, Part 1, *Evangelia, Paulina, Acta*, NovTSup 9 (Leiden: Brill, 1973), 92–110.

[20] The following is adapted from Moraff, "Recent Trends." Used with permission.

partings of the ways, the gradual divergences (and convergences) between Judaism and Christianity into separate systems of beliefs and ways of life at various times and various places.[21] This research has aided work on Acts and Judaism in two primary, interlinked ways. First, partings of the ways discussions have challenged treating Jewish and Christian identities as binaries. This shift has caused renewed interest in how Luke constructs Jewish and Christian identity, whether through contradistinction or intramural distinction. Second, some now posit that Acts should be read within the matrix of post-70 CE early Jewish literature as a text from a particular genus of Judaism.

1.2.1 Contrasted Identities

Considering the portrait of "the Jews" in Acts is not new. Such studies stand front and center in debates about Acts and Judaism.[22] Mitzi J. Smith and Shelly Matthews have recently reiterated nuanced readings of Acts' portrait of "the Jews" as anti-Jewish. "The Jews," in their view, become a uniform, rhetorical category used by Luke to depict Christian identity in continuity and discontinuity with the Jewish people and their tradition. Both authors highlight the Jewish proclivity toward violence in their treatment of Jesus' followers as a central feature of Luke's "othering" project.[23] To make their cases, Smith and Matthews draw from Lawrence Wills' category of "imperial sociology" to argue that Acts paints "the Jews" as a threat to Roman order due to their tendency toward *stasis*. In other words, they cause civil strife and disorder in the Roman Empire through riots. Acts legitimates the peaceable Way before Rome in contrast to volatile Jewish communities.[24] Jewish and Christian identities are thereby formed in opposition through violent behavior.

For Smith and Matthews, Paul plays a central role in Acts' binary identity construction. For Smith, Paul's threefold "turn to the gentiles" establishes a narrative tension in which Christianity abandons Judaism yet remains in proximity and dialogue

---

[21] For a recent survey of literature and terminology, see Timothy A. Gabrielson, "Parting Ways or Rival Siblings? A Review and Analysis of Metaphors for the Separation of Jews and Christians in Antiquity," *CBR* 19 (2021): 178–204.

[22] E.g., Dixon H. Slingerland, "'The Jews' in the Pauline Portion of Acts," *JAAR* 54 (1986): 305–21; John G. Gager, "Jews, Gentiles, and Synagogues in the Book of Acts," *HTR* 79 (1986): 91–99; Sanders, *Jews*, 37–83; Jon A. Weatherly, "The Jews in Luke-Acts," *TynBul* 40 (1989): 107–17; Augusto Barbi, "The Use and Meaning of (*Hoi*) *Ioudaioi* in Acts," in *Luke and Acts*, ed. Gerald O'Collins and Gilberto Marconi, trans. Matthew J. O'Connell (New York: Paulist, 1993), 123–42. Robert F. O'Toole, "Reflections on Luke's Treatment of Jews in Luke-Acts," *Bib* 74 (1993): 529–55.

[23] Matthews, *Perfect Martyr*, 56–75; Smith, *Literary Construction*, 5–7, 57–94.

[24] Smith, *Literary Construction*, 61–65; Matthews, *Perfect Martyr*, 6, 27–52; cf. Lawrence M. Wills, "The Depiction of the Jews in Acts," *JBL* 110 (1991): 631–54. Wills revised this argument in *Not God's People: Insiders and Outsiders in the Biblical World* (Lanham, MD: Rowman and Littlefield, 2008), 187–200. Cf. Pamela Hedrick, "Fewer Answers and Further Questions: Jews and Gentiles in Acts," *Int* 66 (2012): 294–305; Christopher Mount, "Constructing Paul as a Christian in the Acts of the Apostles," in *Engaging Early Christian History: Reading Acts in the Second Century*, ed. Ruben R. Dupertuis and Todd Penner (London: Routledge, 2014), 141–52. For an evaluation of claims that Acts pursues external legitimation, see J. Andrew Cowan, *The Writings of Luke and the Jewish Roots of the Christian Way: An Examination of the Aims of the First Christian Historian in the Light of Ancient Politics, Ethnography, and Historiography*, LNTS 599 (London: T&T Clark, 2019).

with "the Jews." The *ecclesia* is near to but separate and distinct from them.²⁵ Matthews similarly contends that, "key to Acts' own construction of the two distinct social groups, Jews and Christians, is the sculpting of the former as persecutors and the latter as persecuted. To be a nonbelieving Jew is to inflict violence upon Christians; to be a Christian is to be subject to Jewish violence."²⁶ Indeed, she contends, Paul personifies the movement from one identity, the persecuting Jew, to the other, the persecuted Christian. "Situating Acts" within second-century gentile Christianity further funds and is reinforced by this reading.²⁷ Acts reveals its second-century, non-Jewish context through its characterization of Jews according to Roman fears about stasis. Legitimating Christianity and demonizing the Jews are two sides of the same coin. Acts, Matthews argues, "is not participating in an intramural debate—a debate within a fixed set of walls—but rather working to construct a different set of boundaries and borderlines."²⁸ As literature from the third generation of now predominantly gentile Christianity, Acts provides an early contribution to the partings of the ways.

Two notable issues arise in Smith's and Matthews' arguments. First, their terms are somewhat unclear.²⁹ How Smith delineates *continuity* and *discontinuity* between Judaism and the *ecclesia* is uncertain. Matthews likewise neither defines *anti-Judaism* and *supersessionism* clearly, nor does she identify the criteria for qualifying elements of Acts as supersessionist and anti-Jewish. She seems to assume they are self-evident. For example, Matthews argues that the call for Jews to confess Jesus as the Christ, rather than merely being a call to repent, causes Jews to cross the emerging border lines with Christianity, to convert to something other than Judaism.³⁰ In the evolving world of early Judaism, innovation, divergent interpretations, social isolation, exclusivist claims, and even animosity toward other Jews were anything but uncommon.³¹ Acts' exclusivist claims about Jesus—though they might be considered hegemonic and thereby

---

²⁵ Smith, *Literary Construction*, 8, 59–73, 80, 88; John Eifion Morgan-Wynne, *Paul's Pisidian Antioch Speech (Acts 13)* (Eugene, OR: Wipf and Stock, 2014), 206.

²⁶ Matthews, *Perfect Martyr*, 13.

²⁷ Ibid., 9, 27–52.

²⁸ Ibid., 31–32; cf. 6, 27–52. For a critique of pro-Roman readings of Acts, see C. Kavin Rowe, *World Upside Down: Reading Acts in the Graeco-Roman Age* (Oxford: Oxford University Press, 2009); cf. Carsten Burfeind, "Paulus muß nach Rom: Zur politischen Dimension der Apostelgeschichte," *NTS* 46 (2000): 75–91. Daniel Marguerat, *The First Christian Historian: Writing the "Acts of the Apostles,"* SNTSMS 121 (Cambridge: Cambridge University Press, 2002), 65–84, challenges tendencies to treat Luke's views of Judaism and the Roman Empire as a polarity.

²⁹ On the chronic lack of terminological clarity in discussions of anti-Judaism and supersessionism in NT studies, see Terence L. Donaldson, *Jews and Anti-Judaism in the New Testament: Decision Points and Divergent Interpretations* (Waco, TX: Baylor University Press, 2010), 12–28.

³⁰ Matthews, *Perfect Martyr*, 33; cf. Jipp, "Paul," 78.

³¹ Shemaryahu Talmon, "The Emergence of Jewish Sectarianism in the Early Second Temple Period," in *Ancient Israelite Religion: Essays in Honor of Frank Moore Cross*, ed. Patrick D. Miller, Paul D. Hanson, and S. Dean McBride (Philadelphia, PA: Fortress, 1987), 587–616; Peter Richardson, *Israel in the Apostolic Church*, SNTSMS 10 (Cambridge: Cambridge University Press, 1969), 217–28; John Sietze Bergsma, "Qumran Self-Identity: 'Israel' or 'Judah'?," *DSD* 15 (2008): 172–89; Eyal Regev, "Were the Early Christians Sectarians?," *JBL* 130 (2011): 771–93. On the temple, see Timothy Wardle, *The Jerusalem Temple and Early Christian Identity*, WUNT 2/191 (Tübingen: Mohr Siebeck, 2010); Paula Fredriksen, *When Christians Were Jews: The First Generation* (New Haven, CT: Yale University Press, 2018), 29–42.

problematic—should be reevaluated in this light as to whether they are necessarily anti-Jewish or supersessionist.[32] Matthews presumes more than demonstrates the incompatibility of following Jesus and retaining Jewish identity in Luke's writings and time. The partings of the ways conversation to which Matthews appeals challenges assumptions that commitment to Jesus was a boundary-crossing belief, even if a second-century date for Acts is granted. Despite her acknowledgment that *Christianity* and *Judaism* are not discrete groups at Luke's time, she often treats them as fully formed, already opposed categories.[33]

Second and more significantly, Acts simply does not paint Jews monolithically as negative—that is, contentious, violent, and ignorant—or the Way as uniformly positive—that is, harmonious, peaceable, and enlightened. The identity of Jewish Jesus-followers and "the Jews" overlap to a far greater extent than Smith and Matthews acknowledge. Members of "the Jews" join the Way in Acts in response to Paul's preaching (13:45–46; 18:6; cf. 14:2–5). Numerous Jews who believe in Jesus not only observe Jewish customs but are identified as Jews (e.g., 16:1; 18:2, 24). Paul even self-identifies as a Jew (21:39; 22:3). Matthews, acknowledging this point, claims that, since the Jewish–Christian distinction was in its formative stages, Acts lacked the adequate terminology to describe Christians as "not-Jews."[34] Yet, if Luke sought to distance the Way from the Jews, labeling Jesus-following characters as Jews seems counterproductive. One would expect that Luke simply would not call these characters Jews if he sought to construct Jews and Jesus' followers in opposition, akin to the Gospel of John.[35] Including a common Jewish identity blurs more than establishes boundaries between the Way and Judaism.

Acts also details that members of the Way remain identifiably Jewish to gentiles, even being indistinguishable from other Jews. To non-Jewish observers, the Way is a Jewish group arguing with other Jews about Jewish ancestral customs (e.g., 16:20–21; 18:12–17; 19:23–41; 25:13–21).[36] Beyond that, priests and Pharisees—most notably Paul—retain affiliations with their respective subgroups (αἵρεσις) after joining the Way (e.g., 6:7; 15:1–2; 22:3; 23:6). Participation in the αἵρεσις known as "the Way" (24:5, 14; 28:22) does not preclude ongoing identification with other Jewish subgroups according to Acts.[37] The common identity as Jews, the Way's ongoing fidelity to Jewish praxis and subgroup identity, as well as the repeated use of familial language used in discourse with Jewish people push against interpreting Acts as constructing binary, oppositional Jewish and Christian identities.

---

[32] E.g., Terence L. Donaldson, "Moses Typology and the Sectarian Nature of Early Christian Anti-Judaism: A Study in Acts 7," *JSNT* 12 (1981): 27–52. Of course, conclusions about whether present exclusivism derived from Acts should be classified as anti-Jewish or supersessionist might differ. I limit my evaluation to antiquity in hopes it impacts contemporary conversations.

[33] See the incisive critiques of Arthur Francis Carter, "Diaspora Poetics and (Re)Constructions of Differentness: Conceiving Acts 6.1–8.40 as Diaspora" (PhD diss., Vanderbilt University, Nashville, TN, 2016) 43–79; Stroup, *Christians*, 26–29, respectively.

[34] Matthews, *Perfect Martyr*, 7.

[35] On this point while still reading John as internecine conflict, see Christopher Blumhofer, *The Gospel of John and the Future of Israel*, SNTSMS 177 (Cambridge: Cambridge University Press, 2020).

[36] Jervell, *Apostelgeschichte*, 51; Mount, "Constructing Paul," 142–45; Rowe, *World*, 78, 147.

[37] On αἵρεσις in Josephus, see Albert I. Baumgarten, "Josephus and the Jewish Sects," in *A Companion to Josephus*, BCAW 110 (Malden, MA: Wiley-Blackwell, 2015), 261–72.

Furthermore, the depiction of Jewish violence and Christian innocence in Acts is not clear-cut. Luke never explicitly accuses "the Jews" of *stasis*, as Smith observes. The only group directly accused of (risking) stasis is the Ephesian mob (19:40).[38] Moreover, no Jewish violence arises from locals in certain places like Berea even after some gentiles join the Way (17:10–12). Jews are not a uniquely hostile group for Luke. In the four scenes in Acts 16–19 when members of the Way are forcibly brought before public officials, Jews initiate aggression twice (Thessalonica and Corinth) and gentiles do so twice (Philippi and Ephesus).[39] "Imprisonment and persecutions" await Paul in "every city," not simply from "the Jews" (20:23).

Perhaps more significantly, Paul is accused of causing stasis among the Jews (25:5) and causes stasis to erupt among Jewish groups on two occasions, once within the Way itself (15:1–2; 23:7, 10). Acts repeatedly depicts Paul as the catalyst, the spark that ignites mobs, Jewish and gentile, throughout the Roman world. A Roman even assumes that Paul is the revolutionary known as the Egyptian (21:38–39). If anything, Paul is perceived as a greater societal hazard than "the Jews." It is he and the Way that threaten to "turn the empire upside down" (17:6). To be sure, Luke maintains Paul's innocence and corrects such misconceptions. Such perceptions remain, nevertheless.[40] Paul also has a past chock-full of violence, a point he reiterates in two defense speeches (22:1–7; 26:9–15). Acts simply does not paint the Jews as violent and Paul as peaceful. The narrative is more complex.

1.2.2 Interconnected Identities

Other studies seek to resolve these complexities by positing that Acts participates in intra-Jewish conflict. Acts distinguishes the Jews of the Jesus movement from other Jews without separating the Jesus movement from Judaism and the Jewish people as a whole. The Way becomes an identifiable subgroup of Judaism but does not part from it. These studies identify the Jewishness of Jesus' followers and their interactions with the wider Jewish world as integral to understanding the overall portrait of Jews and Judaism in Acts. Two pillars provide foundations for these views, both of which derive from conversations about the partings of the ways. First, many of these interpreters reject binary identity construction in the ancient Mediterranean world and in the narrative presentation of Acts. Second, because Jewish and Christian identities remained flexible and blurred through the second century, some locate the book of Acts, not only the movement it recounts, within the diverse matrix of early Judaism rather than later gentile Christian attempts to separate from Jews and Judaism.

Using the lens of identity formation, Dulcinea Boesenberg highlights two ways in which Acts links Jewish Jesus-followers to the Jewish world.[41] First, Jesus-following

---

[38] Smith, *Literary Construction*, 65–66.
[39] Robert Tannehill, *The Narrative Unity of Luke-Acts*, 2 vols. (Minneapolis, MN: Fortress, 1986–1990), 2:201–3; Brawley, *Jews*, 80–83. One might add Paul's trial in Athens (per Rowe, *World*, 27–41).
[40] Rowe, *World*, 53–89; Craig S. Keener, "Paul and Sedition: Pauline Apologetic in Acts," *BBR* 22 (2012): 201–24; Loveday Alexander, "Luke's Political Vision," *Int* 66 (2012): 283–93; Jipp, "Paul," 67.
[41] Dulcinea Boesenberg, "Negotiating Identity: The Jewish of the Way in Acts," in *Religion and Identity*, RelSocSup 13 (Omaha, NE: Kripke Center, 2016), 58–75. Boesenberg discusses the role of Torah ("Negotiating Identity," 67–73), but I omit it since others cover it more extensively.

Jews and non-Jesus-following Jews use familial language when speaking to each other. Jesus has not dissolved Jewish kinship bonds. Second, the Way begins as an exclusively and exclusivist Jewish movement where loyalty to Jesus constitutes a group boundary marker. Those Jews who do not join it risk being cut off from Israel (3:23). Nevertheless, this threat remains within the bounds of early Jewish diversity and sectarian exegesis.[42] Acts, for Boesenberg, still paints within the malleable contours of Jewish identity.

Christopher Stroup examines how Acts constructs Jewish and Christian identity in light of ethnic and civic identity formation in Greco-Roman material and textual sources. Stroup uses "ethnic reasoning" to explore how Acts negotiates Jewish identity in the context of the Greco-Roman *polis*.[43] "The author of Acts," Stroup argues,

> uses a connection between gods, people, and place to strategically represent Jewish identity as hybrid in order to identify all Jesus followers, both Jews and non-Jews, as Jewish. At the same time, the writer creates an internal distinction between Jesus followers and other Jews, which privileges 'Christians' as the members of an ideal, unified Jewish community and contrasts them with what are identified as factious, local Jewish 'associations.'[44]

Luke's portrait of other Jewish groups as "factious" reflects an internecine polemical attempt at legitimating the Way as an ideal *Jewish* community within the Roman Empire. Reading through the lens of "imperial sociology," then, need not entail the denigration of all non-Jesus-believing Jews or the Jewish religion as a whole.[45] The link between gods, people, and geography—that is, the interconnected nature of ethnicity and way of life in antiquity—challenges those who argue that the Jewishness of the Jesus movement can be separated from the Jewish people and their ancestral custom as a whole in Acts. Stroup thus undermines tendencies to separate "religion" and "praxis" from ethnicity in the ancient Mediterranean world that often generate binary, essentialist readings of Jews and Christians in Acts.[46]

Joshua Jipp explores how Luke's depiction of a Jewish Paul must factor into evaluations of Acts' view of the Jewish world and its way of life. Acts' portrait of Paul contains more nuance than often acknowledged; Luke's Paul has rough edges. His faithfulness to Jewish ancestral custom in Acts accompanies perceptions that he "is a teacher of apostasy from Moses whose person and message is viewed as a destabilizing

---

[42] Boesenberg, "Negotiating Identity," 61–67.
[43] Stroup draws "ethnic reasoning" from Denise Kimber Buell and defines it as "the rhetoric of peoplehood that ancients used to communicate and convince others about identity" (*Christians*, 5).
[44] Stroup, *Christians*, 2.
[45] Ibid., 71–127. However, Stroup interprets Luke as idealizing the Way as a Jewish movement in part by portraying the flaws of other Jewish communities (*Christians*, 103).
[46] E.g., Randy J. Hedlun, "Rethinking Luke's Purpose: The Effect of First-Century Social Conflict," *JPT* 22 (2013): 226–56. For recent, expansive critiques of using "religion" in studying antiquity, see Brent Nongbri, *Before Religion: A History of a Modern Concept* (New Haven, CT: Yale University Press, 2015); Carlin A. Barton and Daniel Boyarin, *Imagine No Religion: How Modern Abstractions Hide Ancient Realities* (New York: Fordham University Press, 2016); Daniel Boyarin, *Judaism: The Genealogy of a Modern Notion*, KWJS 9 (New Brunswick, NJ: Rutgers University Press, 2018).

threat to the Jewish ancestral way of life."[47] If one does not accept Paul's claims, his message "could be construed as having negative implications for the people of Israel, the Law of Moses, and the sanctity of the Temple."[48] Like Matthews, Jipp acknowledges the serious nature of exclusivist truth claims made by Paul in Acts and their role in developing Christian supersessionism.[49] Jipp reintroduces Paul as a central piece in the Acts-and-Judaism puzzle by incorporating aspects of Paul's characterization beyond Torah observance. Some facets of Paul's character, like his violent past, remain untouched, however.

Overall, Boesenberg, Stroup, and Jipp reinforce David Smith's claim that "the act of differentiation, which is constitutive of identity formation, may involve not only the establishing of *distinction from* the other but also and importantly *connection to* the other."[50] Identity construction is not a zero-sum game for Luke. The Jewishness of Luke's main Jesus-following characters, therefore, should factor into understanding Luke's view of Jews and Judaism. What none of these authors explore, Smith has unpacked in the Third Gospel: Luke interweaves Jesus' followers, including Paul, with the broader Jewish world by means of common flaws and ignorance, as well as through shared ethnicity, practices, and beliefs. The disciples reflect Israel's struggle with unbelief and unfaithfulness to Jesus. Smith's work raises the possibility of exploring how the Way and Paul's imperfections and journey to understand and be faithful to Jesus shed light on this same tension in the wider Jewish world in Acts.[51]

1.2.3 Reading Acts as Early Jewish Literature

Other scholars have advocated resituating Acts within the boundaries of early Judaism. Isaac Oliver stands at the forefront. He reasons that,

> If there was no complete and final separation between Judaism and Christianity before the fourth century CE, then certainly the boundaries between the two remained fluid even after the destruction of the temple in 70, the period when Matthew and Luke most likely composed their works. It is therefore misleading and anachronistic to speak of the Jewish 'background' or Jewish 'roots' when relating early 'Christian' (also an anachronism for the first century) texts of the New Testament to the Judaism of that time. From a historical point of view, there is no Jewish background of the New Testament because this literary corpus contains what were originally Jewish documents.

---

[47] Jipp, "Paul," 67; cf. 61–64. Space constrains Jipp's ability to unpack what about Paul's teachings are "destabilizing" and "absurd, dangerous, and inappropriate" about Paul's "understanding of what constitutes faithfulness to the God of Israel" for these other Jews (62).
[48] Jipp, "Paul," 73. Still, for Acts, such views *misconstrue* Paul's message.
[49] Whether exclusivist claims in Acts necessarily entail "appropriation," especially in light of the early Jewish diversity, remains to be demonstrated (Jipp, "Paul," 78; cf. Stroup, *Christians*, 2).
[50] Smith, "Politics," 27; emphasis original. See also Gerd Baumann, "Grammars of Identity/Alterity: A Structuralist Approach," in *Grammars of Identity/Alterity: A Structural Approach*, ed. Gerd Baumann and André Gingrich (New York: Berghahn Books, 2004), 18–51.
[51] Smith, "Politics," 241–66, 383–84. Also, Carter, "Diaspora Acts," 100–1.

In other words, Oliver frames and interprets Luke-Acts "'simply' as *Jewish* texts."[52] He explores how Luke's view of Torah fits within the diversity of Second Temple *halakhic* reasoning. Oliver recently extended this similar argument regarding Lukan eschatology. Luke, Oliver contends, joins other Jews in mourning the Second Temple's destruction and maintaining hopes for Israel's salvation, including Jerusalem's restoration.[53] Oliver's two volumes powerfully move beyond assertions that the author of Luke-Acts was Jewish—though he does make this claim—to arguing that the *perspective* of Acts belongs among early Jewish literature.[54] A lacuna remains in Oliver's work, however. He recognizes "Luke's polemical treatment of Jews who reject Jesus," yet he does not address it in depth.[55] To be sure, Oliver contextualizes it within early Jewish and Christian contexts and in conversation with Israel's prophetic tradition.[56] Still, Acts' characterization of "the Jews" presents the possibility that Luke upholds Jewish symbols and even eschatological hope while rejecting actual Jews and using them as a negative foil for the Way's identity.

Christfried Böttrich also argues that Acts should be treated as early Jewish literature.[57] Most significantly, he contends that Acts' sharp rhetoric suggests continued proximity within the greater Jewish world rather than a location outside it. Familial fights, Böttrich claims, sound worse. This is a helpful observation, but more work is needed to explicate how to differentiate familial fights from external polemics between opposing groups within a narrative. Still, Böttrich reminds interpreters that harsh rhetoric can occur in-house.

Susan Wendel compares how the scriptural interpretation of Luke-Acts and Justin Martyr impact identity construction of Jesus-followers vis-à-vis Judaism in divergent ways.[58] Luke and Justin, according to Wendel, inherit and develop traditions of scriptural interpretation in early Jewish literature in which "competing forms of exegesis came to play a prominent role in articulating the identity of certain early Jewish groups" through claims of proper understanding.[59] On the one hand, for both Luke-Acts and Justin, Christ-followers are *the* authoritative interpreters of Israel's Scriptures. This knowledge distinguishes insiders and outsiders in the emerging

---

[52] Oliver, *Torah Praxis*, 4; emphasis original. Likewise, Mikeal C. Parsons, *Acts*, Paideia (Grand Rapids, MI: Baker Academic, 2008), 4–7.

[53] Isaac W. Oliver, *Luke's Jewish Eschatology: The National Restoration of Israel in Luke-Acts* (Oxford: Oxford University Press, 2021). Similarly, Mark S. Kinzer, *Jerusalem Crucified, Jerusalem Risen: The Resurrected Messiah, the Jewish People, and the Land of Promise* (Eugene, OR: Cascade, 2018). On the holistic nature of salvation in Luke-Acts, see Timothy W. Reardon, *The Politics of Salvation: Lukan Soteriology, Atonement, and the Victory of Christ*, LNTS 642 (London: T&T Clark, 2021).

[54] Oliver, *Torah Praxis*, 31–32; cf. idem. *Eschatology*, 134–35.

[55] Idem, *Eschatology*, 143.

[56] Ibid., 131–38.

[57] Christfried Böttrich, "Das lukanische Doppelwerk im Kontext frühjüdischer Literatur," ZNW 106 (2015): 151–83. Also, Ulrike Mittmann, "Polemik im eschatologischen Kontext: Israel und die Heiden im lukanischen Doppelwerk," in *Polemik in der frühchristlichen Literatur: Texte und Kontexte*, ed. Oda Wischmeyer and Lorenzo Scornaienchi, BZNW 170 (Berlin: de Gruyter, 2011), 517–42, esp. 523–27.

[58] Susan J. Wendel, *Scriptural Interpretation and Community Self-Definition in Luke-Acts and the Writings of Justin Martyr*, NovTSup 139 (Leiden: Brill, 2011); cf. Matthews, *Perfect Martyr*, 80–97.

[59] Wendel, *Scriptural Interpretation*, 2.

communities. On the other hand, Luke retains a role for the Jewish people, whereas Justin claims Christ-followers have displaced Jews as the inheritors of Israel's promises. Luke's continued concern for a Jewish future challenges claims that Acts reflects a gentile Christianity that has parted from Judaism.[60] Exclusivist claims and drawing of boundaries based on interpretation of Scripture, Wendel reminds, were common in early Judaism. They need not indicate parted ways.

1.2.4 Summary

Thanks to discussions about the partings of the ways, the question about Acts and Judaism is no longer primarily about anti-/pro-Judaism per se but whether Acts reflects a critical insider perspective or an outsider and supersessionist vantage point.[61] Two interlocked barriers continue to impede identifying Acts as early Jewish literature. First and foremost are Luke's seemingly contrastive images of the Way and Paul on the one hand and the Jews on the other. Luke ostensibly uses Jews as a negative foil for constructing the identity of Jesus-followers. For many, this hostile characterization of Jews bears greater resemblance to *Adversus Judaeos* traditions than bickering between early Jewish groups.[62] Second is Lukan exclusivism. Acts depicts the Way as properly understanding the Scriptures while other Jews fail to grasp the fulfillment of their ancestral hopes. The speeches in Acts call Jews to repent by accepting Jesus as the Messiah. For some, such hegemonic claims result from Luke's place within gentile Christianity: Acts summons Jews to convert, that is, to cross the (emerging) boundaries between Judaism and Christianity.[63] As of yet, there are no sustained "Acts within Judaism" engagements with the book's depictions of the Jews and the exclusivist truth claims made by the Way.[64]

Issues about Acts and Judaism converge in the character of Paul. The Paul of Acts articulates and embodies Luke's perspective on the Jewish people.[65] For some, Acts uses its portrait of Paul as faithful to Israel's God as foil contrasted with unfaithful Jews to legitimate the Way. For others, Luke's Paul shows the continued Jewishness of the Way

---

[60] Wendel, *Scriptural Interpretation*, 85–270. For a similar conclusion based on Luke's ongoing concern for the covenantal status of Jews who do not follow Jesus, see Christoph Schaefer, *Die Zukunft Israels bei Lukas: Biblisch-frühjüdische Zukunftsvorstellungen im lukanischen Doppelwerk im Vergleich zu Röm 9–11*, BZNW 190 (Berlin: de Gruyter, 2012).
[61] Salmon, "Insider or Outsider," argued this about thirty-five years ago, though based on identifying the historical author as Jewish.
[62] E.g., Pervo, *Dating Acts*, 324–27; Matthews, *Perfect Martyr*, 27–52. On the development and social matrices of *Adversus Judaeos* traditions, see Paula Fredriksen, "What 'Parting of the Ways'? Jews, Gentiles, and the Ancient Mediterranean City," in *The Ways That Never Parted: Jews and Christians in Late Antiquity and the Early Middle Ages*, ed. Adam H. Becker and Annette Yoshiko Reed, TSAJ 95 (Minneapolis, MN: Fortress, 2007), 35–63, esp. 37–38.
[63] Matthews, *Perfect Martyr*, 33.
[64] Antecedents exist but see Acts as "pro-Jewish"—e.g., Jervell, *People*; Brawley, *Jews*. These studies tend to construe believing Jews and non-believing Jews in binary ways and presume substantial degrees of opposition and social distance between them (Stroup, *Christians*, 29–33; Carter, "Diaspora Acts," 94–103).
[65] Paul is a "reliable character" in Acts. He generally voices the narrative perspective and aims (Tannehill, "Israel," 70–71). Still, even Paul must be measured against the narrative whole.

in solidarity with the Jewish people. Most investigations have centered on Paul's self-identification as a Jew, his Torah observance, or his "turnings to the gentiles."[66] Yet, Paul's commonalities with the Jews go beyond observance and conflict. Luke characterizes them in similar ways as mixed characters. The Jews are not a uniformly negative group, and Paul is an imperfect character throughout Acts. When introduced, Paul is the quintessential "God-fighter" (θεομάχος; 5:39), the consummate agent of violence against the Way (7:58; 8:1, 3; 9:1–2), a point he reiterates on multiple occasions (22:4–5, 19–20; 26:9–11). After joining the Way, Paul provokes comparable hostility from Jews and gentiles alike against himself because of his preaching the message about Jesus he once opposed (e.g., 13:45–14:7, 19–20; 15:1–2; 16:16–24; 17:1–34). Paul endured the same blindness he proclaims on the divided Jewish community even as he ends up in exile with them in Rome (9:1–25; 22:11–15; 28:17–28).[67] These common traits might provide insight for understanding Acts' view of the Jews and would prove invaluable in addressing the hurdles belying framing Acts within Judaism.

1.3 Thesis

I seek to address these impediments by evaluating Acts' depictions of the Way, Paul, and "the Jews." I contend that Luke establishes ongoing connections between the Way, Paul, and the Jewish people through their common Jewishness and similar characterizations. They share Israel's covenantal identity even as the Way exhorts all Jews to accept its interpretation of Israel's tradition. Together they participate in Israel's ongoing repentance-journey, that is, the gradual movement from infidelity and ignorance to greater faithfulness and understanding.[68] For Acts, Jesus is the proper orienting factor for all Israel; the Jewish people and their tradition should be aligned with and toward him. Therefore, some Jews in Israel are going the wrong direction as they resist Jesus. To alter the metaphor slightly, some in Israel make crooked the Way that God seeks to make straight for Israel (cf. Isa 40:3–5). Therefore, they must repent, change directions by turning to Jesus lest they be judged and/or removed from the

---

[66] E.g., Eyal Regev, "Jewish Legal Practice and Piety in the Acts of the Apostles: Apologetics or Identity Marker?," in *Religious Stories in Transformation: Conflict, Revision and Reception*, ed. Alberdina Houtman, Tamar Kadari, Marcel Poorthuis, and Vered Tohar (Leiden: Brill, 2016), 126–43; David J. Rudolph, "Portrait of Paul in Acts 21:17–26," in *The Early Reception of Paul the Second Temple Jew: Text, Narrative and Reception History*, ed. Gabriele Boccaccini and Isaac W. Oliver, LSTS 92 (London: T&T Clark, 2018), 192–205.

[67] Beverly Roberts Gaventa, *From Darkness to Light: Aspects of Conversion in the New Testament*, OBT 20 (Philadelphia, PA: Fortress, 1986), 52–70; Dennis Hamm, "Paul's Blindness and Its Healing: Clues to Symbolic Intent (Acts 9; 22 and 26)," *Bib* 71 (1990): 63–72; Vittorio Fusco, "Luke-Acts and the Future of Israel," *NovT* 38 (1996): 1–17; Mittmann, "Polemik," 523–30; cf. Karl Matthias Schmidt, "Abkehr von der Rückkehr: Aufbau und Theologie der Apostelgeschichte im Kontext des lukanischen Diasporaverständnisses," *NTS* 53 (2007): 406–24.

[68] On the repentance-as-journey metaphor in Luke-Acts, Joel B. Green, *Conversion in Luke-Acts: Divine Action, Human Cognition, and the People of God* (Grand Rapids, MI: Baker Academic, 2015), 87–122.

people.⁶⁹ The Way is not a novel, divergent path, though. It is the path for Israel, albeit refracted through Jesus—the repentance and hope of Israel. Nevertheless, the unfaithful in Israel remain members of God's people for whom the potential for repentance toward Jesus lingers. Paul in particular emerges as a personification of Jewish recalcitrance and the potential all Israel has for reorientation. Luke's Paul demonstrates that even the most aggressive Jewish God-fighters can have their eyes opened by Jesus to see him anew; all can change direction or be reoriented on the repentance-journey.⁷⁰

In short, I argue that Acts, in absolving Paul from charges that he teaches against the Jewish people, defends itself from this same claim (cf. 21:23). Acts, too, has "no charge to bring against my nation" (28:18). Though Acts calls Jews to repent, it neither rejects the Jews, nor uses them as a negative foil, nor transcends the bounds of intra-Jewish polemic and exclusivism. Luke's intertwined portrait of the Way, Paul, and the Jewish people reinforces recent arguments that Acts should be understood from the vantage point of pluriform early Judaism. From a narrative, rhetorical, and theological perspective, Acts reflects an "insider" point of view by using the Jewish images and voices of the Way and Paul, who, like all Israel, struggle with faithfulness, to address Jewish people about Jewish customs and beliefs regarding the Jewish Messiah, Jesus. Acts, through the Way and Paul, continues to identify with the Jewish people.

In arguing this thesis, I address the two aforementioned barriers hindering identifying Acts as Jewish literature. First, I tackle head-on the primary source of purported Lukan anti-Judaism: the rhetorical use and depiction of "the Jews" in Acts. To pursue this goal, I explore the depictions and emerging relations between the Way, Paul, and the wider Jewish world. I demonstrate that the term "the Jews" does not function as a *terminus technicus* and that the Jews are not pictured in a uniformly hostile or ignorant manner. Instead of contrasting them with Jews, Acts identifies the Way and Paul with the Jewish world through shared kinship and ongoing struggles to be faithful to Israel's God. Paul is specifically linked to Jewish violent opposition toward the Way and blindness to God's acts in Jesus. Acts, through the Way and Paul, maintains solidarity with the Jewish nation, even amidst critiques and calls for repentance.

Second, I attempt to read Acts' rhetoric and exclusivism within post-70 CE Judaism. Acts, I contend, participates in internecine disputes about the interpretation and direction of a shared tradition-in-crisis.⁷¹ The Way (and Acts) interprets the Scriptures

---

⁶⁹ For the spatial and directional connotations of *repentance*, see David A. Lambert, *How Repentance Became Biblical: Judaism, Christianity, and the Interpretation of Scripture* (Oxford: Oxford University Press, 2016).

⁷⁰ This is not to say that all Jews will repent or are faithful in Acts. All are called to repent (e.g., 2:38; 13:24; 17:30) and those who fail to do so face judgment, including possible exclusion from the people, for infidelity to Jesus and rejection of his servants (e.g., 3:23; 13:41; 18:6). Israel's covenant identity can remain amidst judgment and the removal of some. Indeed, threats of removal presume participation in God's people. Moreover, "Paul's transformation alongside the presence of non-Christ following Jews encourages interpreters to resist static perceptions of identity or judgement within Acts" (Carter, "Diaspora Acts," 101).

⁷¹ Alasdair C. MacIntyre, *Whose Justice? Which Rationality?* (Notre Dame, IN: University of Notre Dame Press, 1988). My use of these categories is indebted to C. Kavin Rowe, *One True Life: The Stoics and Early Christians as Rival Traditions* (New Haven, CT: Yale University Press, 2016), 1–9, 112–42, 175–258; Blumhofer, *Future*, 28–38. For cautions about exaggerating the impact of 70 CE, see Jonathan Klawans, "Josephus, the Rabbis, and Responses to Catastrophes Ancient and Modern," *JQR*

through Jesus, but their truth claims affirm the constitutive elements of the tradition known as Judaism, including identification with the Jewish people. Therefore, Acts can be said to evince a perspective "within Judaism." The claim that Jesus is Israel's Messiah, the central source of conflict between the Way and the wider Jewish world (9:22; 17:3; 18:5 cf. 5:42; 18:27), does not threaten the Jewish tradition's core or the identity of the people who inhabit its way of life. Rather, the Way is portrayed as the faithful culmination of the ancestral tradition's hopes (2:39; 3:17–26; 13:26–33).[72] Acts depicts Jewish Jesus-followers as a Jewish "inner group," a renewed nucleus of the "in-group" of Israel. They are the faithful among the larger category of Israel, which, in Israel's Scripture (e.g., 1 Kgs 19:15–18; Jer 11:13–21; 23:1–4; Mic 4:6–7) and early Jewish literature (e.g., 1 Macc 1:11–14; 2:19–27; CD 2–5; 4QMMT; 1 Enoch 85–90), consists of faithful and unfaithful members.

In other words, Acts exhibits a reformist, quasi-sectarian position within Judaism insofar as it expects all Jews, their fellow members of the covenant people of Israel, to repent by accepting the message about Jesus as *the* proper understanding of Israel's Scriptures and ancestral customs (2:36–40; 3:17–26; 13:38–41; 28:17–28).[73] Luke presents no *Sonderweg* for Israel apart from Jesus (4:12). Judgment lingers over those who reject the message (3:23; 13:46; 18:6; 28:17–28). Still, the call to repent occurs among and for the sake of Jewish-Israelites, who retain their status as "insiders" among God's covenant people (13:38–41; 22:1; 23:5; 24:14–16, 21; 26:22–23; cf. 18:12–17). Luke's exclusivist perspective might be considered problematic for modern readers, to be sure. Regardless, such an exclusivist outlook is not tantamount to "teaching against the people" and, therefore, does not move Acts outside the contours of early Judaism. Acts reflects a posture toward the wider Jewish world comparable to other early Jewish subgroups.[74] The narrative provides an intramural call to repentance without wholesale rejection or replacement of the Jewish people in favor of gentile "outsiders," though its language lends itself to later supersessionist perspectives.[75]

---

100 (2010): 278–309; Daniel R. Schwartz and Zeev Weiss, eds., *Was 70 CE a Watershed in Jewish History?: On Jews and Judaism before and after the Destruction of the Second Temple*, AJEC 78 (Leiden: Brill, 2012).

[72] "To occupy a position whereby a new belief is (purportedly) true in contrast to an old belief is to take up and embody an argument: I claim that my new way of understanding our tradition and living it out overcomes the challenges of the past in a way that maintains continuity with our basic convictions" (Blumhofer, *Future*, 29). Gentile outsiders unsurprisingly perceive the conflict as debates about Jewish ancestral tradition (18:14–15; 25:19). Rowe, *World*, 77–78; Mittmann, "Polemik," 523–27; Böttrich, "Lukanische Doppelwerk," 159–62.

[73] On "reformist" subgroups or sects, see Baumgarten, "Jewish Sects," 261–65; Regev, "Early Christians," 772–81. I use "quasi-sectarian" since, unlike the Qumran community, the Way maintains some fellowship with other Jewish groups and institutions (cf. 2:36; 18:5–8; 21:17–26; 28:17–22). Acts allows for diversity within how Jewish ancestral custom is lived out, evinced by continuing subgroup affiliations within the Way (6:7; 15:1–2).

[74] The Qumran sect saw itself as the core of Israel's initial restoration yet expected all Jews to join their group as the greater realization of Israel's eschatological renewal (Bergsma, "Qumran," 176–78, 187–89; Jason A. Staples, *The Idea of "Israel" in Second Temple Judaism: A New Theory of People, Exile, and Jewish Identity* [Cambridge: Cambridge University Press, 2021], 259–89). On early Jewish sectarianism and the language of "inner group" or being faithful Israel within larger (unfaithful) Israel, see Talmon, "Sectarianism," 601–10; Richardson, *Israel*, 217–28; Regev, "Early Christians," 781–93; idem. "New Religious Movements," 486.

[75] Tiede, "Glory," 21; Oliver, *Torah Praxis*, 18–32; Stroup, *Christians*, 3, 31; Jipp, "Paul," 78.

1.4 Methodology

As my primary concern is to examine how the final form of Acts, which presents itself as a narrative (1:1–4; cf. Luke 1:1–4), depicts the Way, Paul, "the Jews," and their interrelationship, I use a narrative approach. I seek to understand Acts as a literary creation.[76] Three main features are of particular interest. First, I highlight Lukan characterization, how Luke gradually depicts and constructs his characters in relation to others within the story-world as the text progresses in a linear fashion. Character development builds cumulatively, and expectations are constantly revised.[77] Second, at points, I examine the effect of Lukan intertextuality, specifically how he uses Israel's Scriptures and his Gospel, in developing the portraits of the Way, Paul, and the Jewish people.[78] Third, I focus on rhetorical effect enacted by textual characterization, not authorial intention.[79] As my focus is on the completed form of Acts, I forego questions pertaining to compositional layers, debates about historicity, or attempts to reconstruct a particular historical audience.[80] My concern lies with identifying the narratival, rhetorical, and theological perspective of Acts that emerges through its characterization, voices in speeches, and the interactions among characters.

I do not eschew sociohistorical concerns, however. Acts remains a "cultural product" of the diverse ancient Mediterranean world inhabited by—in Luke's terms—Jews (Ἰουδαῖοι) and gentiles (ἔθνη) in all their diversity.[81] As such, the narrative should be

---

[76] David Herman, *Basic Elements of Narrative* (Malden, MA: Wiley-Blackwell, 2009); Joel B. Green, "The Book of Acts as History/Writing," *LTQ* 37 (2002): 119–27; idem. "Narrative Criticism," in *Methods for Luke*, ed., Joel B. Green, MBI (Cambridge: Cambridge University Press, 2010), 74–112; Michal Beth Dinkler, *Literary Theory and the New Testament*, AYBRL (New Haven, CT: Yale University Press, 2019).

[77] John A. Darr, *On Character Building: The Reader and the Rhetoric of Characterization in Luke-Acts*, LCBI (Louisville, KY: Westminster John Knox, 1992), 16–59; Michal Beth Dinkler, "Building Character on the Road to Emmaus: Lukan Characterization in Contemporary Literary Perspective," *JBL* 136 (2017): 687–706, esp. 694–99; cf. Cornelis Bennema, "Character Reconstruction in the New Testament (1): The Theory," *ExpTim* 127 (2016): 365–74; idem, "Character Reconstruction in the New Testament (2): The Practice," *ExpTim* 127 (2016): 417–29.

[78] In approaching intertextuality, I follow a blend of Robert L. Brawley, *Text to Text Pours Forth Speech: Voices of Scripture in Luke-Acts* (Bloomington, IN: Indiana University Press, 1995); Richard B. Hays, *Echoes of Scripture in the Gospels* (Waco, TX: Baylor University Press, 2016), by considering patterns, motifs, type scenes, and structuring devices as well as echoes, allusions, and quotes. See also Kenneth D. Litwak, *Echoes of Scripture in Luke-Acts: Telling the History of God's People Intertextually*, JSNTSup 282 (London: T&T Clark, 2005), 8–30, 47–65.

[79] Michal Beth Dinkler, "New Testament Rhetorical Narratology: An Invitation toward Integration," *BibInt* 24 (2016): 203–28.

[80] I follow the NA28 and Barbara Aland and Holger Strutwolf, eds., *The Acts of the Apostles*, 3 vols., ECM III (Stuttgart: Deutsche Bibelgesellschaft, 1997), as reliable initial texts for Acts. On the text(s) of Acts, see W. A. Strange, *The Problem of the Text of Acts*, SNTSMS 71 (Cambridge: Cambridge University Press, 1991); Eldon Jay Epp, *The Theological Tendency of Codex Bezae Cantabrigiensis in Acts*, SNTSMS 3 (Cambridge: Cambridge University Press, 1966); Tobias Nicklas and Michael Tilly, eds., *The Book of Acts as Church History: Text, Textual Traditions and Ancient Interpretations*, BZNW 120 (Berlin: de Gruyter, 2003). For critiques of audience reconstruction, see Darr, *Character Building*, 23–29; Stephen C. Barton, "Can We Identify the Gospel Audiences?" in *The Gospels for All Christians: Rethinking the Gospel Audiences*, ed. Richard Bauckham (Grand Rapids, MI: Eerdmans, 1998), 173–94.

[81] Green, "Narrative Criticism," 82; Dinkler, *Literary Theory*, 14–43.

read in conversation with "the extratext," that is, "all the skills and knowledge that readers of a particular culture are expected to possess in order to read competently: (1) language; (2) social norms and cultural scripts; (3) classical or canonical literature; (4) literary conventions (e.g., genres, type scenes, standard plots, stock characters) and reading rules (e.g., how to categorize, rank, and process various kinds of textual data); and (5) commonly known historical and geographical facts."[82] Knowledge of this cultural encyclopedia aids in comprehending and filling in the gaps of the narrative. It serves a close reading of the text.

This project incorporates aspects of socio-scientific approaches when relevant, particularly regarding issues about identifying sects and/or subgroups, legitimation of social groups, and (ethnic) identity formation. As Acts' literary construction of characters participates in identity formation within broader sociohistorical contexts, I integrate contemporary works and ancient conceptions of ethnicity and social group dynamics when evaluating Lukan characterization. I presume that identity is flexible and constructed through a complex process of differentiation and connection, though I do not rely on any particular theory or model of identity formation.[83] I similarly assume that "religion" in antiquity should neither be abstracted nor separated from ethnicity, though it is not reducible to it.[84] Examining ancient portraits of Jews and Judaism should engage the concreteness of ancient ethnoreligious traditions, which entailed patterns of being and behaving, not merely beliefs or perspectives. Such considerations seem particularly relevant when exploring conflicts within traditions-in-crisis and between rival traditions.[85] In the end, though, textual evidence takes priority over historical reconstruction and sociological reflection.

1.5 Guiding Assumptions about Acts

1.5.1 The Unity of Luke-Acts

Before delving into the text, a few comments outlining my guiding assumptions about the unity of Luke-Acts, authorship, and dating are in order. I presume a narrative unity

---

[82] Darr, *Character Building*, 22.
[83] For sociological models and approaches to ethnicity and identity in Acts, see Eric D. Barreto, *Ethnic Negotiations: The Function of Race and Ethnicity in Acts 16*, WUNT 2/294 (Tübingen: Mohr Siebeck, 2010), 3–59; David L. Balch, *Contested Ethnicities and Images: Studies in Acts and Art*, WUNT 345 (Tübingen: Mohr Siebeck, 2015); Stroup, *Christians*, 1–8; Smith, "Politics," 24–32. On the difficulties of *ethnicity* in studying early Judaism, see David M. Miller, "Ethnicity Comes of Age: An Overview of Twentieth-Century Terms for Ioudaios," *CBR* 10 (2012): 293–311; idem, "Ethnicity, Religion and the Meaning of Ioudaios in Ancient 'Judaism,'" *CBR* 12 (2014): 216–65; John M. G. Barclay, "'Ἰουδαῖος': Ethnicity, Race, Religion: Identities and Ideologies in Early Jewish and Christian Texts, and in Modern Biblical Interpretation*, ed. David G. Horrell and Katherine M. Hockey (London: Bloomsbury, 2018), 46–58.
[84] Nongbri, *Before Religion*, 25–84; Boyarin, *Judaism*, 1–58.
[85] MacIntyre, *Whose Justice*, 349–403; Rowe, *Life*, 175–258; cf. Pierre Hadot, *What is Ancient Philosophy?*, trans. Michael Chase (Cambridge, MA: Harvard University Press, 2004), on Greco-Roman philosophies as tangible ways of life.

between Acts and the Gospel of Luke.[86] Acts' prologue (1:1–4) provides a simple justification in that it assumes the reader's familiarity with the Third Gospel. Acts presents itself as a sequel. It draws from and expands on themes and motifs established in the Gospel of Luke, amidst elements of development, tension, and even disjunction. In fact, differences between the panes of the diptych should be expected since "tensions and shifts are intrinsic to narrativity."[87] This point alone, regardless of whether Luke and Acts share a common author, legitimates using Luke's Gospel to inform interpretation of Acts.[88] Luke's use of *synkrisis*—rhetorical comparative correlations between characters—illustrates the dialogical interrelationship between Luke-Acts. Characters and events are constructed in comparable ways but are not carbon copies. Each retains their uniqueness, even as the reader recalls similarities.[89] I draw from the Third Gospel when Acts signals to it through verbal links, similar characterizations, and/or comparable settings and scenes. Identifying links between Luke's Gospel and Acts and how they inform Acts, in other words, is a type of intertextuality.[90]

1.5.2 Luke's Ethnic Identity

While I find good reasons to posit a Jewish author of Acts, and my argument lends itself to that conclusion, my reading does not rest on a particular ethnic identity of the historical author or redactor. Due to assumptions about the binary nature of Jewish "insiders" and gentile "outsiders," a certain circularity has characterized discussions about the author's ethnicity and the question of Lukan anti-Judaism: if Luke is a gentile outsider, then he is (more likely to be) anti-Jewish; if he is a Jewish insider, he cannot be anti-Jewish.[91] Two observations challenge these assumptions. First, gentiles like centurions (Luke 7:4–5; Acts 10:1–3) complicate claims that gentiles are necessarily more hostile to Jews. Godfearers are present in Jewish communities, suggesting proximity and interaction between the two groups prior to gentile inclusion among Jesus' followers. One might argue that Godfearers and centurions serve the Lukan strategy to paint gentiles more favorably than Jews to explain their separation from Judaism, but the presence of gentiles who are charitable to and participate in the Jewish world breaks down a simplistic insider–outsider paradigm based on ethnic lines alone.

---

[86] Mikeal C. Parsons and Richard I. Pervo, *Rethinking the Unity of Luke and Acts* (Minneapolis, MN: Fortress Press, 1993); Verheyden, ed., *Unity*; Marguerat, *Christian Historian*, 43–64; Patrick E. Spencer, "The Unity of Luke-Acts: A Four-Bolted Hermeneutical Hinge," *CBR* 5 (2007): 341–66; Andrew F. Gregory and C. Kavin Rowe, eds., *Rethinking the Unity and Reception of Luke and Acts* (Columbia, SC: University of South Carolina Press, 2010); Joel B. Green, "Luke/Acts, or Luke and Acts? A Reaffirmation of Narrative Unity," in *Reading Acts Today: Essays in Honour of Loveday C. A. Alexander*, ed. Steve Walton, LNTS 427 (London: Bloomsbury, 2011), 101–19.

[87] Marguerat, *Christian Historian*, 46, drawing on the work of Stephen Moore.

[88] Cf. Patricia Walters, *The Assumed Authorial Unity of Luke and Acts: A Reassessment of the Evidence*, SNTSMS 145 (Cambridge: Cambridge University Press, 2009).

[89] Marguerat, *Christian Historian*, 56–59. For examples, see Kinzer, *Jerusalem*, 21–56; Smith, "Politics"; David P. Moessner, *Luke the Historian of Israel's Legacy, Theologian of Israel's "Christ": A New Reading of the "Gospel Acts" of Luke*, BZNW 182 (Berlin: de Gruyter, 2016), 238–72, 292–301.

[90] Marguerat, *Christian Historian*, 45–46, 63–64.

[91] E.g., Salmon, "Insider or Outsider," 76–82.

Gentiles, too, can be favorably inclined toward Jews and Judaism. A gentile Luke does not necessarily entail an anti-Jewish Luke.[92]

Second, plenty of early Jewish texts condemn fellow Jews for compromising or abandoning their ancestral customs, even to the point of valorizing violence against these Jews. These texts defend exclusivist truth claims with sharp rhetoric and often view Israel's failure to obey as an underlying reason for their present exilic conditions (e.g., 1 Macc. 2:19–28, 49–70; Josephus, *J.W.* 7.47–53; 4QMMT; CD 1.14–2.1; 1QS 1–3, 8–9).[93] For an example from the Jewish-Christian side, Melito of Sardis, whom some identify as Jewish and would dub the originator of the "Deicide Charge," demonstrates that being Jewish does not remove the potential for anti-Judaism (e.g., *Pasch.* 73–99).[94] Positing a Jewish Luke might not absolve him of anti-Judaism or separating from (at least the rest of) Judaism any more than his portrait of intra-Jewish violence and his exclusivist claims preclude reading him as Jewish. A Jewish Luke might increase the likelihood of his having a conciliatory posture toward the Jewish people, but it does not guarantee it.[95]

As Martin Rese observes, the focus on the ethnic identity of the historical Luke "assumes a postulated fundamental ontological difference between the language of insiders and that of outsiders . . . *Bad words and harsh judgements about a group remain bad words and harsh judgements, whoever makes use of them*."[96] Social position invariably impacts the perception of harsh words, but sharp rhetoric cannot be circumvented simply by appealing to insider versus outsider. Evaluation of textual evidence and rhetorical effect must take interpretive priority. Like Oliver, I strive to demonstrate that the Acts' *perspective* on certain Jews and the Jewish ancestral custom is Jewish; that is, Acts' rhetoric does not transcend or violate the boundaries of variegated early Judaism by rejecting its core tenets, by denying ongoing relationship with the people as a whole, or by self-identifying with something other than Jewishness.[97] My interpretations must be persuasive in their own right, apart from assumptions about the historical author.

---

[92] Cf. the opposing views on Luke and Judaism based on identifying Acts with Godfearers in Tyson, *Images*, 181–88; Craig S. Keener, *Acts: An Exegetical Commentary*, 4 vols. (Grand Rapids, MI: Baker Academic, 2012–2015), 1:402–15.

[93] Talmon, "Sectarianism," 601–10; Richardson, *Israel*, 217–28; Bergsma, "Qumran," 176–89.

[94] Oskar Skarsaune, "Evidence for Jewish Believers in Greek and Latin Patristic Literature," in *Jewish Believers in Jesus: The Early Centuries*, ed. Oskar Skarsaune and Reidar Hvalvik (Peabody, MA: Hendrickson, 2007), 505–67, esp. 516–28; Alistair Stewart-Sykes' comments in Melito of Sardis, *On Pascha: With the Fragments of Melito and Other Material Related to the Quartodecimans*, trans. Alistair Stewart-Sykes, PPS (Crestwood, NY: St. Vladimir's Seminary Press, 2001), 3–4, 25–29. In fairness, Melito never outright condemns "the Jews" but rebukes "Israel," though these might be coterminous. Melito's writings could be calling for repentance rather than repudiation. Such examination is beyond the present scope. Suffice it to say, Melito's rhetoric seems harsher than Luke's.

[95] Amy-Jill Levine, *The Misunderstood Jew: The Church and the Scandal of the Jewish Jesus* (San Francisco, CA: HarperOne, 2006), 110–14.

[96] Rese, "Second Thoughts," 192; emphasis mine.

[97] Oliver, *Torah Praxis*, 31–32; similarly, Parsons, *Acts*, 6–7.

1.5.3 Dating Acts

Questions about dating Acts have a similar circularity and disproportionate influence on debates about Lukan anti-Judaism.[98] On the one hand, an early origin—before the end of the first century—might explain Acts' Jewishness.[99] On the other hand, the later Luke's writings are, the more likely they reflect anti-Jewish posture. For many, Lukan anti-Judaism is a central argument for dating Acts to the first third of the second century.[100] The importance of dating lessens in light of conversations about the partings of the ways, however. A second-century date for Acts no longer *necessarily* suggests that it reflects and legitimates a separation between Christianity and Judaism. A second-century date increases the likelihood that Acts originates within gentile Christianity, but this presumption has been destabilized.[101] I would date Acts to the final quarter of the first century and suspect my thesis reinforces that conclusion, but, as with the ethnic identity of the historical Luke, my claims do not rest on a particular dating.

1.6 Terminological and Translational Issues

1.6.1 Judaism, "within Judaism," and Christianity

Nomenclature remains a hindrance in debates about Acts and Judaism, so it behooves me to delineate my terms and translation choices prior to my analysis.[102] The most problematic categories have been *Judaism* and *Christianity*. They are frequently defined in mutually exclusive, essentialist, and abstract ways, that is, as "religions." *Judaism* means following Torah; *Christianity* means following Jesus. Recent scholarship has challenged such binary and abstract definitions, reiterating that *Jewishness* and *Christian-ness* in antiquity existed on a flexible, multifaceted identity spectrum shaped

---

[98] "Historical facts or facts assumed to be historical are taken up for attacking text interpretations of other exegetes and for defending one's own. This in itself is not a bad thing. We all do it. What concerns me here is the very polemical attempt to condemn other interpretations, an attempt based on a historical presupposition which is, at best, conjecture. As regards the relations between Christians and Jews in the first century, the 'Jewish intramural struggle' is an open historical question which is misused here as a basis for intolerance" (Rese, "Second Thoughts," 190; similarly, Levine, "Luke," 389; Carter, "Diaspora Poetics," 73–79).

[99] E.g., Oliver, "Anti-Marcionite," 499–520. For recent arguments for dating Acts before 70 CE, see Alexander Mittelstaedt, *Lukas als Historiker: Zur Datierung des lukanischen Doppelwerkes*, TANZ 43 (Tübingen: Francke, 2006); Karl L. Armstrong, "A New Plea for an Early Date of Acts," *JGRCJ* 13 (2017): 79–110.

[100] E.g., Pervo, *Dating Acts*, 324–27; Tyson, *Marcion*; Matthews, *Perfect Martyr*, 27–54; Knut Backhaus, "Zur Datierung der Apostelgeschichte: Ein Ordnungsversuch im chronologischen Chaos," *ZNW* 108 (2017): 212–58.

[101] Wendel, *Scriptural Interpretation*, 21–22; Oliver, *Torah Praxis*, 2–5. Matthews' exploration of the Pseudo-Clementines' conciliatory posture toward the Jews reiterates that dating can have little bearing on whether a text is anti-Jewish (*Perfect Martyr*, 91–95).

[102] Günter Wasserberg, *Aus Israels Mitte—Heil für die Welt: Eine narrativ-exegetische Studie zur Theologie des Lukas*, BZNW 92 (Berlin: de Gruyter, 1998), 13–30; Moraff, "Recent Trends," 81–82; cf. Robert A. Kraft, "The Weighing of the Parts: Pivots and Pitfalls in the Study of Early Judaisms and Their Early Christian Offspring," in *Never Parted*, 87–94, esp. 90; John G. Gager, *The Origins of Anti-Semitism: Attitudes toward Judaism in Pagan and Christian Antiquity* (Oxford: Oxford University Press, 1983), 13–34; Donaldson, *Anti-Judaism*, 12–28.

by belief and praxis.¹⁰³ As such, my definitions and evaluation of primary sources maintain an eye toward the concrete, the materiality of the human beings who inhabited these ways of life.

By *Judaism*, then, I mean the ancestral way of life, the tangible practices, customs, and civilization of the people known as Ἰουδαῖοι. I use *Judaism* as coterminous and interchangeable with *Jewish ancestral custom/tradition, Jewish way of life*, and *Jewish civilization*.¹⁰⁴ Second Temple Judaism, though variegated as it navigated the Roman Empire, especially within the diaspora environs, had unifying elements that identified something as a form of *Judaism*.¹⁰⁵ In a more expanded sense, by *Judaism* I mean (1) participation in and identification with the Jewish people (by genealogy or incorporation via conversion), who (2) professed loyalty to Israel's God, the Jewish ancestral deity, (3) through worship in the Jerusalem temple—though, commitment to the temple might be manifest in critique and protest—and (4) faithfulness embodied in the practices of Torah, the Jewish constitution, with all its *halakhic* variations. *Judaism* entails embodying *Jewishness*, that is, doing the kinds of things associated with Jews in antiquity (e.g., *kashrut, Shabbat*, circumcision) and commitment to the kinds of things Jews believed (e.g., the ancestral god, the people, and Israel's sacred texts).¹⁰⁶

Such broad contours allow for diversity, nested identities, hybridity, and disputations about how to interpret and practice the Jewish ancestral tradition within the Roman Empire.¹⁰⁷ These contours permit disagreement, innovation, and refining the tradition's internal logic as new situations arise. Indeed, the disparity of views and innovations evident within early Jewish literature are well documented.¹⁰⁸ These divergent views

---

¹⁰³ Michael L. Satlow, "Defining Judaism: Accounting for 'Religions' in the Study of Religion," *JAAR* 74 (2006): 837–60; Daniel Boyarin, "Semantic Differences; or, 'Judaism'/'Christianity,'" in *Never Parted*, 65–85; idem. *Judaism*, 107–14.

¹⁰⁴ Boyarin has called for abandonment of *Judaism* in the study of antiquity (*Judaism*, 1–30). However, it remains the best way to refer to patterns of belief, behavior, and customs of the Jewish people. See Seth Schwartz, "How Many Judaisms Were There? A Critique of Neusner and Smith on Definition and Mason and Boyarin on Categorization," *JAJ* 2 (2011): 208–38.

¹⁰⁵ I presume degrees of Hellenistic influence on Judaism. John M. G. Barclay, *Jews in the Mediterranean Diaspora: From Alexander to Trajan (323 BCE–117 CE)* (Edinburgh: T&T Clark, 1998); Isaiah Gafni, *Land, Center and Diaspora: Jewish Constructs in Late Antiquity*, JSPSup 21 (Sheffield: Sheffield Academic, 1997); Erich S. Gruen, *The Constructs of Identity in Hellenistic Judaism: Essays on Early Jewish Literature and History*, DCLS 29 (Berlin: de Gruyter, 2016); Jonathan Robert Trotter, *The Jerusalem Temple in Diaspora: Jewish Practice and Thought during the Second Temple Period*, JSJSup 192 (Leiden: Brill, 2019); cf. Carter, "Diaspora Poetics," 459–534; Drew J. Strait, *Hidden Criticism of the Angry Tyrant in Early Judaism and the Acts of the Apostles* (Lanham, MD: Lexington Books, 2019).

¹⁰⁶ Seth Schwartz, *Imperialism and Jewish Society: 200 B.C.E. to 640 CE.* (Princeton, NJ: Princeton University Press, 2009), 49–100; E. P. Sanders, *Judaism: Practice and Belief, 63 BCE–66 CE*, 40th Anniversary Edition (Minneapolis, MN: Fortress, 2016). These contours are malleable, negotiated, and sometimes transgressed. They provide a core and a reliable set of (semi-porous) boundaries for what constitutes being "within Judaism," nonetheless. So, Kraft: "It becomes difficult, for example, to imagine someone, or some group, being at the same time 'Jewish' and uninterested in aspects of ritual law (e.g., circumcision, food restrictions). Were there such people? Of course" ("Weighing," 90).

¹⁰⁷ Barclay, *Mediterranean Diaspora*; Cynthia M. Baker, "'From Every Nation under Heaven': Jewish Ethnicities in the Greco-Roman World," in *Prejudice and Christian Beginnings: Investigating Race, Gender, and Ethnicity in Early Christian Studies*, ed. Laura S. Nasrallah and Elisabeth Schüssler Fiorenza (Minneapolis, MN: Fortress, 2009), 79–99; Gruen, *Constructs*, 7–196.

¹⁰⁸ Schwartz provides a helpful critique of tendencies to exaggerate diversity and sectarianism within early Judaism ("How Many," 208–38).

can be said to remain "within Judaism" when those espousing them continue to identify with/as Jews, and do not reject, fundamentally compromise, or radically redefine the constitutive elements of the ancestral tradition. If innovation reaches a point where it either (1) denies the covenantal relationship between Israel's God and the Jewish people *in toto* or replaces Jews *en masse* with an alternative people, (2) moves away from commitment to the Jewish ancestral deity, (3) denies wholesale the validity of the temple institution—again, critique of the temple institution *as it was practiced* was common—and/or (4) removes the particulars of Torah observance so as to undermine Jewish custom and identity, then it begins to become something other than Judaism.[109] Those who advocate reading Acts within Judaism have assumed the Way's commitment to Israel's God, and others have examined how Luke upholds Torah and temple.[110] The question of whether Acts dissociates from and/or rejects the Jewish people as a whole—at least those Jews outside of the Way—and/or replaces non-Jesus-following Jews with gentiles as God's covenantal people remain the main areas of contention (cf. 21:28). I seek to show that Acts participates in the renegotiation of the Jewish ancestral tradition-in-crisis without rejecting the Jewish people or undermining their covenantal relationship with their God.

What of *Christian* and *Christianity*? Acts has two of the earliest attestations of the term χριστιανός (11:26; 26:28).[111] Since it is not explicitly used for self-designation in Acts and often carries connotations of "non-Jewish" in contemporary parlance, I do not use it to refer to Jesus' followers in Acts.[112] I opt instead for more cumbersome terms like *Jewish/gentile Jesus-follower*. Similarly, instead of *Christianity*, I use the main epithets for the group of Jesus' followers in Acts: the Way and the assembly or *ecclesia*.[113] Eschewing the term *Christianity* when discussing Acts ideally helps avoid contrasting the Way from Judaism simply based on nomenclature and preconceptions.

---

[109] Such movement differentiates between a *subgroup*, a *sect*, and a *cult*. Each moves further from the parent tradition. The first two both adhere to the core elements. A *sect* may innovate more and distance itself spatially depending on if it is *reformist* or *introvertionist*. A *cult* denigrates the parent tradition to move beyond it (Regev, "Early Christians," 771–93; idem, "Early Christianity," 484–93; Baumgarten, "Jewish Sects," 263–65). To be sure, examples of Jews challenging each tenet can be found in antiquity (Fredriksen, "Parting," 35–63). These contours provide a helpful rubric, nevertheless. One might add whether the wider Jewish populace considers members of these groups to be fellow Jews.

[110] See Böttrich, "Lukanische Doppelwerk," 165–68, on reading Lukan Christology within Judaism. On Torah, see Jervell, *Unknown Paul*; Oliver, *Torah Praxis*; Regev, "Legal Practice," 126–43; Kinzer, *Jerusalem*, 160–224; Rudolph, "Portrait of Paul," 192–205. On the temple, see J. Bradley Chance, *Jerusalem, the Temple, and the New Age in Luke-Acts* (Macon, GA: Mercer University Press, 1988); Wardle, *Jerusalem Temple*, esp. 192–205.

[111] Cf. Joseph B. Tyson, "Acts, the 'Parting of the Ways' and the Use of the Term 'Christians,'" in *Bridging between Sister Religions: Studies of Jewish and Christian Scriptures Offered in Honor of Prof. John T. Townsend*, ed. Isaac Kalimi, BRLJ 51 (Leiden: Brill, 2016), 128–40; Carter, "Diaspora Acts," 97–98.

[112] Eisenbaum's comments on Paul apply to Acts: "Since most modern Jews and Christians see belief in Christ as the quintessential boundary marker between Judaism and Christianity, labeling Paul Christian reinforces essentialist definitions of Christianity and Judaism as mutually exclusive, and thus makes claims to Paul's Jewish identity confusing at best, impossible at worst" ("Essentialism," 237).

[113] On labels for the early Jesus movement, see Paul Trebilco, *Self-Designations and Group Identity in the New Testament* (Cambridge: Cambridge University Press, 2014). See Ralph J. Korner, *The Origin and Meaning of Ekklēsia in the Early Jesus Movement* (Leiden: Brill, 2017), on assembly/ecclesia.

1.6.2 Jews, Israel, Gentiles, and the Way

For the much-disputed term Ἰουδαῖοι, I use *Jews* or *Jewish people* instead of *Judean* for three main reasons.[114] First, *Jews* and *Jewish*, despite potential weaknesses, can connote ethnicity, culture, and religion (way of life), especially if one frames *Judaism* as Jewish ancestral custom and civilization. *Judaism* is still an ethnoreligion, that is, a system of belief and practices connected to a particular people known as *Jews*. The term *Jew/Jewish* might carry primarily religious or ethnic terms to many in the modern world, but the ethnic and religious connotations are difficult, if not impossible, to disentangle completely. Similarly, with the advent of the state of Israel, a Jewish nation-state, *Jew/Jewish* increasingly denotes—sometimes problematically—an ongoing geographic link to the land of Judea.[115] Second, diaspora literature like Josephus and Acts often challenges using geography as *the* central criterion for the identity of Ἰουδαῖοι, though it is clearly a factor (e.g., *Ant.* 11.173; 20.43; Acts 2:5, 11; 16:1; 18:2). Kinship and custom also form this people.[116] Third, there are theological and ethical reasons for using *Jew* or *Jewish*. The painful history of Christian antisemitism reminds us of the importance of maintaining the living link between the ancient Ἰουδαῖοι and the modern Jewish people.[117] Given recent rises in antisemitism and my own concerns to address supersessionism in Christian theology, *Jew/Jewish* is my preferred translation of Ἰουδαῖος.

A perennial question is whether Luke redefines *Israel* apart from the Jewish people, at least from those who do not accept Jesus as the Messiah.[118] Jason Staples has recently reexamined the relationship between Israel and Jews in early Jewish literature, concluding that *Israel* is a larger category in which Jews participate. *Israel* refers to the ten northern tribes and/or the twelve tribes who live in covenant with Israel's God while *Jews* refer specifically to the descendants of the southern kingdom of Judah.[119] This seems true in the broader early Jewish world and may underlie Luke's presuppositions as well. However, the two terms overlap substantially within Acts to the point of being difficult to differentiate. Jewish people and only Jewish people in both the land and the diaspora are referred to as *Israel* or *Israelites* by the narrator (5:21), Jewish members of the Way (2:22, 36; 3:12; 5:31; 10:36; 13:16–24), non-Jesus-following Jews (5:35; 21:28), and even Jesus himself (9:15; cf. 26:17, which reads "your

---

[114] Miller, "Ioudaios"; idem, "Comes of Age"; idem, "Religion"; Staples, *Israel*, 11–21; Cynthia M. Baker, *Jew*, KWJS 7 (New Brunswick, NJ: Rutgers University Press, 2017).

[115] For issues and perspectives related to the covenant people *Israel* and the modern nation-state, see J. Kameron Carter, *Race: A Theological Account* (Oxford: Oxford University Press, 2008), 398, 435, 451; G. Tommy Givens, *We the People: Israel and the Catholicity of Jesus* (Minneapolis, MN: Fortress, 2014), 107–76; Adam Gregerman, "Israel as the 'Hermeneutical Jew' in Protestant Statements on the Land and State of Israel: Four Presbyterian Examples," *IA* 23 (2017): 773–93; Kinzer, *Jerusalem*, 240–64.

[116] Barclay, "Ἰουδαῖος," 46–48; Staples, *Israel*, 11–21.

[117] Levine, *Misunderstood*, 160–66; Miller, "Religion," 255–59.

[118] For overviews, see Bovon, *Luke the Theologian*, 350–86, 515–19; José Antonio Jáuregui, "'Israel' y la Iglesia en la Teologia de Lucas," *EstEcl* 61 (1986): 129–49; Maria Neubrand, *Israel, die Völker und die Kirche: Eine exegetische Studie zu Apg. 15*, SBAB 55 (Stuttgart: Katholisches Bibelwerk, 2006), 39–79.

[119] Staples, *Israel*, 25–53. Cf. Paul Spilsbury, *The Image of the Jew in Flavius Josephus' Paraphrase of the Bible*, TSAJ 69 (Tübingen: Mohr Siebeck, 1998), 36–42.

people" instead of *Israel*). Gentiles are differentiated from *Israel* and *Jews* (e.g., 4:27; 13:16; 15:23).[120]

Of course, Jews are threatened with being cut off "from the people," presumably the covenant people of *Israel* (3:23; cf. Deut 18:15–20; Lev 23:29). It remains unclear if that occurs within Acts itself or remains a future judgment, however. Nevertheless, this general threat does not cut the root-connection between the Jewish people and Israel.[121] Israel's Scriptures have long portrayed individuals and swaths of Israelites being removed from the people without entailing a "redefinition" of Israel (e.g., Gen 17:14; Exod 12:15, 19; Deut 31–34; Isa 9:13–17). Similarly, the prophets, especially Isaiah, a guiding text for Luke, often espouse remnant ideologies that refrain from fundamentally redefining the people of God (e.g., Isa 10:20–27; 49:6; 65:1–16; 66:1–6). Remnant views differentiate between faithful and unfaithful Israel, but both remain Israel.[122] That Acts similarly avoids redefining Israel while constructing an "inner group" in Israel and warning other Jews about the threat of judgment is evident in that, at the end of the narrative, the Jews, Paul's brothers, and Israel still stand as parallel conceptions (28:17–18). Such observations permit treating *the Jewish people* and *Israel* as (relatively) coterminous within Acts, though a partitive relationship—Jews as a subset of Israel— might be implicit (cf. Luke 22:30).[123]

I opt for *the gentiles* or *the nations* to translate τὰ ἔθνη and *gentile* to refer to individuals from τὰ ἔθνη. From a Jewish vantage point, τὰ ἔθνη refers to non-Israelite people groups (cf. Num 23:9) and, as such, bears ethnoreligious connotations: gentiles are non-Jewish peoples who practice their respective ancestral customs and follow their people's gods.[124] I distinguish gentiles when pertinent within the narrative. When referring to those gentiles affiliated with Jewish institutions, most notably the

---

[120] The ἔθνος of the Samaritans might be an exception (8:9). They are neither Jews nor gentiles. Acts does not say explicitly that Samaritans (re)join the people Israel, though it might imply or presume their Israelite identity (cf. 2 Macc 5:22–23). See Jervell, *People*, 113–32; David A. Ravens, *Luke and the Restoration of Israel*, JSNTSup 119 (Sheffield: Sheffield Academic, 1995), 72–106; Matthew Chalmers, "Rethinking Luke 10: The Parable of the Good Samaritan Israelite," *JBL* 139 (2020): 543–66; Oliver, *Eschatology*, 120–24. On Samaritans generally, see Staples, *Israel*, 54–84; Timothy Wardle, "Samaritans, Jews, and Christians: Multiple Partings and Multiple Ways," in *The Ways That Often Parted: Essays in Honor of Joel Marcus*, ed., Lori Baron, Jill Hicks-Keeton, and Matthew Thiessen, ECL 24 (Atlanta, GA: SBL Press, 2018), 15–39.

[121] The threat of being cut off "is not a statement about God's disinheritance of Israel but about the removal of some within Israel from Israel's inheritance. The people and their election will endure" (Smith, "Politics," 377; cf. Tiede, "Glory," 25, 34). Further, see Tannehill, *Narrative Unity* 2:56–57; Kinzer, *Jerusalem*, 109–18, 147–56; Oliver, *Eschatology*, 136–38.

[122] Staples, *Israel*, 87–180; *pace* David W. Pao, *Acts and the Isaianic New Exodus*, 2nd ed. (Eugene, OR: Wipf and Stock, 2016). As Joel S. Kaminsky notes, "In the servant passages and the Joseph narrative there are three basic categories of people: the elect of the elect who receive special attention within each text, those belonging to the larger elect group but not specially chosen, and the other nations of the world" (*Yet I Loved Jacob: Reclaiming the Biblical Concept of Election* [Nashville, TN: Abingdon, 2007], 155). Qumran, too, follows the divided-Israel pattern and expects Jews to join their new community as faithful Israel (Bergsma, "Qumran," 172–79).

[123] Suggestive of a partitive relationship is how Anna is "from the tribe of Asher" (Luke 2:36), and Paul's hope is for "the twelve tribes" (Acts 26:7; cf. Luke 22:30). For articulations that *Israel* remains ethnic Israel in Luke-Acts, see Nils A. Dahl, "'A People for His Name' (Acts 15:14)," *NTS* 4 (1958): 319–27; Brawley, *Jews*, 133–54; Neubrand, *Israel*, 108–219; Moessner, *Luke*, 289–301.

[124] Fredriksen, "Parting," 35–63. I translate ἔθνος as *nation* when in reference to Jews/Israel.

synagogue, and adopted elements of Jewish practice short of conversion, I use the term *Godfearer* or *Godfearing gentile*.¹²⁵ Those non-Jews who practice their own ancestral customs and worship a plethora of deities I refer to as *pagan-gentiles*. Such a label seems tautological—from a first-century Jewish perspective, a pagan is a gentile by definition—but remains helpful.

1.6.3 Repentance and/or Conversion

Since the boundaries between Jews and the Jesus movement remain contested space in Acts and in the wider Mediterranean world until the fourth century or so, a few comments on Luke's language of *repentance* and/or *conversion* seem in order. Μετανοέω and ἐπιστρέφω by and large function as equivalents in Luke-Acts. Both entail changes in perspective, behavior, and (re)alignment with God's activities in the world.¹²⁶ A primary issue for translation is whether exclusivist Christological commitment to Jesus necessitates a break with Judaism. *Conversion* in this sense would mean moving to a way of life and self-identification that fundamentally differs from Judaism, which would eventually become known as Christianity.¹²⁷ However, the Christological element of Acts' call to *repentance* need not indicate crossing "religious" boundaries—established or in formation—between oppositional groups. The call for fealty to Jesus can be heard as an internal exhortation to join the Way's interpretation of the Jewish ancestral tradition and Scripture akin to other exclusivist claims within early Judaism (e.g., CD 1.14–2.1; 1QS 1–3, 8–9).¹²⁸ It is a call to realign with the ancestral tradition—at least as understood by the Way—by submitting to Israel's Messiah-Lord (cf. Luke 2:10). For this reason, I translate μετανοέω, ἐπιστρέφω, and related terms as *to repent*

---

¹²⁵ Irina A. Levinskaya, *The Book of Acts in Its Diaspora Setting*, vol. 5 of *BAFCS* (Grand Rapids, MI: Eerdmans, 1996), 51–126; Paula Fredriksen, "'If It Looks like a Duck, and It Quacks like a Duck...': On Not Giving up the Godfearers," in *A Most Reliable Witness: Essays in Honor of Ross Shepard Kraemer*, ed. Susan Ashbrook Harvey, Daniel P. DesRosier, Shira L. Landerr, Jacqueline Z. Pastis, and Daniel Ullucci, BJS 358 (Providence, RI: Brown Judaic Studies, 2015), 25–33; Bruce Chilton, "The Godfearers: From the Gospels to Aphrodisias," in *Partings: How Judaism and Christianity Became Two*, ed. Hershel Shanks (Washington, DC: Biblical Archaeology Society, 2014), 55–72.

¹²⁶ Guy D. Nave, *The Role and Function of Repentance in Luke-Acts*, AcBib 4 (Atlanta, GA: Society of Biblical Literature, 2002), 39–144; David S. Morlan, *Conversion in Luke and Paul: An Exegetical and Theological Exploration*, LNTS 464 (London: T&T Clark, 2013), 80–139. For a corrective to Nave's differentiation between repentance for Jews and Gentiles on lexical grounds (*Repentance*, 223–24), see Green, *Conversion*, 45–53. There is no *lexical* reason to claim that Jews and gentiles are called to different responses to Jesus, though the manifestation of repentance might differ. Both are called to loyalty to Jesus and to conform their behavior accordingly to the respective expectations for Jews and gentiles within the Way. See also Mark J. Boda, *Return to Me: A Biblical Theology of Repentance*, NSBT 35 (Downers Grove, IL: InterVarsity Press, 2015).

¹²⁷ Such is Matthews' concern: "In Acts, however (as in much subsequent Christian literature concerning Jewish depravity), *the language of repentance* is meshed with *the language of conversion,* such that repentance is *not understood as a turning back* toward what has been established but a *turning toward the new*—toward Jesus as Christ and as fulfillment of the Jewish Scriptures" (*Perfect Martyr*, 33; emphasis mine). Such a view reduces *Judaism* and *Christianity* to "religions," abstractions that differ based on belief. To be fair, Matthews argues that Luke's rhetoric reinforces this differentiation in more tangible ways.

¹²⁸ Talmon, "Sectarianism," 601–10; Richardson, *Israel*, 217–28; Bergsma, "Qumran," 176–78, 187–89; Regev, "Early Christians," 781–93.

and *to return*, rather than *to convert*. *Conversion*, in my view, carries too much historical baggage: for a Jew to convert to following Jesus often insinuates a cessation of being Jewish.[129] Thus, I avoid the term.

1.6.4 Antisemitism, Anti/Pro-Judaism/Jewish, and Supersessionism

The main terms used to evaluate Acts' perspective on Jews and Judaism, *antisemitism*, *anti/pro-Judaism/Jewish*, and *supersessionism*, merit brief evaluation.[130] The most notable proponent of using *antisemitism* for Acts is Jack Sanders. Following John Gager, Sanders defines *antisemitism* as systematic hostility toward the Jewish people. He uses this term to challenge attempts to delineate cleanly critiques of ideas and practices from criticisms of people. To critique the Jewish ancestral tradition is to critique the people who inhabit that way of life.[131] Still, *antisemitism* remains anachronistic for studying an ancient text like Acts. It carries modern connotations of genetics, contemporary politics, racial stereotyping, and calls for violence against Jewish people in ways absent in Acts.

Anti/pro-Judaism and *anti/pro-Jewish* have been the most common terms used to evaluate Luke and Judaism.[132] The fundamental problem for the dominant nomenclature is that it inclines the interpreter toward an outsider position. To be *anti* or *pro* often insinuates an external posture more than an internal position. With regard to Luke-Acts, framing the conversation with anti/pro terms seems to presume that Luke-Acts (or the historical Luke) stands outside early Judaism. This is the crux of debate, however. If the contents of Acts evince a perspective that fits within the boundaries of first or early second-century Judaism, then it seems problematic to characterize it as *anti/pro-Judaism/Jewish*. One might conclude that Acts rightly can be labeled *anti-Judaism/Jewish*, the assumptions that underlie these categories should be scrutinized and their application withheld until the final analysis, nevertheless. The category may well become *apropos* after evaluating the evidence but framing the investigation with these terms might predispose one's conclusion.

---

[129] Indeed, what one might consider *conversion* in antiquity entailed ethnic change. Paula Fredriksen, "Mandatory Retirement: Ideas in the Study of Christian Origins Whose Time Has Come to Go," *SR* 35 (2006): 231–46 (on conversion, see 232–37). To be sure, some define *conversion* in a way that avoids this implication (e.g., Green, *Conversion*, 98–99). Nevertheless, the history of Jewish–Christian relations, particularly the legacy of forced conversions, leads me to eschew it in translation. See e.g., James Carroll, *Constantine's Sword: The Church and the Jews* (Boston, MA: Houghton Mifflin, 2001).

[130] See Gager, *Origins*, 13–34; Levine, *Misunderstood Jew*, 87–93; Donaldson, *Anti-Judaism*, 12–28; Wasserberg, *Aus Israels*, 13–30; Stroup, *Christians*, 23–37; Smith, "Politics," 9–24, for extended evaluations. Cf. Benjamin Isaac, *The Invention of Racism in Classical Antiquity* (Princeton, NJ: Princeton University Press, 2004), 481–500; Gruen, *Constructs*, 313–32.

[131] Sanders, *Jews*, xv–xvii; Gager, *Origins*, 8. This observation is particularly astute in light of recent problematizing of *religion* in antiquity.

[132] For a more nuanced taxonomy of anti-Judaism (Jewish, Jewish-Christian, and gentile), see Douglas R. A. Hare, "The Rejection of the Jews in the Synoptic Gospels and Acts," in *Antisemitism and the Foundations of Christianity*, ed. Alan T. Davies (Mahweh, NJ: Paulist, 1979) 27–47 (28–32); cf. the criticisms in Gager, *Origins*, 8–9; Donaldson, *Anti-Judaism*, 17–20.

Supersessionism appears to be the most promising term since it focuses on how Jesus-followers define themselves vis-à-vis the Jewish people. At stake in discussing *supersessionism* is the identity of the people of God, their way of life, and their participation in the covenantal relationship with their ancestral God.[133] Two issues compromise use of the term. First, *supersessionism* is often used in abstraction, focusing mostly on rhetoric and interpretations of Israel's Scriptures to the neglect of concrete, identify-forming practices. Some forms of *supersessionism* are functional in that they erase the Jewish people by annulling their customs and identity markers. Second, *supersessionism* is usually treated as an on-off switch: A text is supersessionist or not.[134] This tendency flattens the complexities of a text like Acts, or most texts for that matter. *Supersessionism* rarely exists in a "pure" form. It is better understood as a spectrum of how Jesus-followers defined themselves vis-à-vis the Jewish people.

Considering these problems, I offer my own working definition: *Supersessionism is the view that Jesus-followers (Jewish and/or Gentile) supplant the Jewish people and their ancestral way of life as the covenantal people of God. Supersessionism* carries the narrow and tangible sense of *replacement* or *displacement*. An "insider group" (i.e., Jews) is replaced by an "outsider group" (i.e., gentiles) or is transformed (i.e., by rejection of the fundamental tenets, vocation, practices, and identity markers of the Jewish people and their tradition). The genealogical people of God are rejected or redefined at a foundational level.[135] My working definition seeks to avoid abstraction by highlighting tangible people and practices, not simply institutions (e.g., *church* and *synagogue*) or beliefs. Though general, it also permits a sliding scale.[136]

---

[133] For Christian attempts at delineating *supersessionism* and its effects, see R. Kendall Soulen, *The God of Israel and Christian Theology* (Minneapolis, MN: Fortress, 1996), 1–106; Craig C. Hill, "Restoring the Kingdom to Israel: Luke-Acts and Christian Supersessionism," in *A Shadow of Glory: Reading the New Testament after the Holocaust*, ed. Tod Linafelt (New York: Routledge, 2002), 185–200; Carter, *Race*; Willie James Jennings, *The Christian Imagination: Theology and the Origins of Race* (New Haven, CT: Yale University Press, 2010), 32–33, 250–88; Givens, *We the People*; Terence L. Donaldson, "Supersessionism and Early Christian Self-Definition," *JJMJS* 3 (2016): 1–32. Central to debates about *supersessionism* is whether exclusivist claims about Jesus are inherently *supersessionist* or can be framed within Judaism.

[134] *Supersessionism* is often used as a "blunt instrument" to attack interpretations perceived as anti-Jewish (Donaldson, *Anti-Judaism*, 25).

[135] As such, *supersessionism* should not be equated with *remnant* or *sectarian* ideologies whereby Israel is divided into faithful and unfaithful groups, individual members of the people of God are cut off, and/or claims to exclusive understanding of Israel's tradition are made. Remnant or sectarian perspectives find their roots in Jewish sacred texts (e.g., Deut 4:25–31; Isa 10:20–23; Ezra 9:10–15) and early Jewish literature (e.g., 4QMMT; CD 1.14–2.1; 1QS 1–3), and ultimately retain the empirical idea of Israel but do so in a way that excludes others of their own kin. Talmon, "Sectarianism," 601–10; Krister Stendahl, "Qumran and Supersessionism—and the Road Not Taken," *PSB* 19 (1998): 134–42; Richardson, *Israel*, 217–28; Bergsma, "Qumran," 176–78, 187–89; Regev, "Early Christians," 781–93; Staples, *Israel*, 85–348. Claims that all early Judaism was supersessionist misses the main issue supersessionism names: the replacement of one people (i.e., Jews) with another (i.e., Christians) by some form or another (e.g., identity erasure, punitive rejection, radical redefinition via "fulfillment").

[136] See Soulen's three categories: economic, punitive, and structural (*God of Israel*, 1–7). Donaldson expands Soulen's types into a fivefold scale: (1) binary oppositions (e.g., Marcion or faithful/true vs. unfaithful/false Israel); (2) replacement with discontinuity (church replaces Israel in totality); (3) replacement with continuity, either through a Jewish remnant or a redefinition of Israel around Jesus; (4) solidarity and mission where all Jews remain God's people but risk being cut off if they do not turn to Jesus; (5) "all Israel will be saved" position, either through Jesus or a parallel covenant ("Supersessionism," 10–32).

According to Terence Donaldson, questions of *supersessionism* boil down to self-definition, extent of social distance, and rhetoric.[137] I evaluate each aspect by examining the depictions of the Way, Paul, and the Jewish people, their interactions, and the resultant rhetorical effect. Analyzing characterization centers on how Luke defines his characters in relation to Jewish people and practices. Looking at group interactions enables assessment of social proximity and distance within the story-world. Speeches illumine all three aspects by exploring how characters identify with and/or distance themselves from their listeners. Together, these scenes inform how the perspective of Acts might be framed vis-à-vis the Jewish people and their tradition.

1.7 The Way Ahead

The following two chapters explore how Luke interweaves the Way, Paul, and the Jews into a common Jewish identity and legacy as Israel. I explore how Acts interconnects the Way, Paul, and the Jews, even as Luke calls Jews to turn to Jesus, to refute claims that Acts uses Jews as a negative foil for Christian identity construction. Instead, they share in Israel's identity and process of repentance. The latter chapters, like Acts, focus on Paul. I examine the *synkrisis* between Paul and the Jewish people, particularly those who oppose him and/or remain unpersuaded by his message, to show Luke's continued expectations of Israel's corporate reorientation toward Jesus. I contend that Luke presents Paul's narrative arc and vocation as representative of Israel. He embodies God's interactions with the Jewish people, namely, how neither fighting against God nor blindness to God's acts in the world are terminal conditions. Those going the wrong way in Israel, Paul exemplifies, can turn (or be turned) to follow the Way.

The subsequent chapter examines how Luke links the Way, Paul, and the Jews through Jewishness. Using the ethnic contours drawn by Herodotus and Josephus, I show how the Way and Paul check all the boxes of Jewishness: kinship bonds, ancestral language, customs, and cult. Notably, Acts brings Paul's Jewish identity forward at the moments in which it is most called into question. Acts leverages Jewishness in ways that identify and establish commonality with the Jewish world. It presents the Way as a Jewish subgroup vying for all Jews to join its interpretation and practice of Israel's ancestral tradition.

Next, I address the claim that Acts negatively depicts "the Jews" to construct positively the identity of Jesus-followers as an idealized community. I contend that Acts blurs the characterizations of the faithful and unfaithful in Israel, though these categories still exist. Rather than being an on-off switch, faithfulness and understanding are a spectrum and a journey. Acts neither depicts "the Jews" as uniformly hostile and ignorant, or the Way and Paul as monolithically faithful and understanding. Instead, groups and individuals in Acts exist on the same path of (attempted) faithfulness to Israel's God. They are mixed characters who struggle with obedience and proper understanding. Many meander and stumble on along the way. Others, including

---

[137] Donaldson, *Anti-Judaism*, 27–28.

members of the Way, go in the wrong direction and risk falling from the path altogether. As such, the Way, non-Jesus-following Jews, and even Paul are at different places on Israel's continued and communal repentance-journey.

Turning to Paul, I challenge arguments that Acts uses violent behavior as means of constructing Jews as a negative other on three fronts. First, Luke's portrait of Jewish violence is variegated. Some Jews in some places are hostile; others are entirely peaceful. Second, Jews are not particularly or uniquely violent in Acts. Gentiles commit violence against Paul, at times without Jewish involvement. Moreover, gentiles persecute Paul *because he is a Jew*. Enduring gentile anti-Jewish threats provides another ironic aspect of solidarity between the Way and the wider Jewish world. Third and most significant is that violence reinforces the *synkrisis* between Paul and those Jews who oppose him with hostility. No Jew enacts more violence than Paul. Acts does not absolve Paul of his violent past. In fact, Paul often defends himself by recounting his prior persecution of the Way in increasingly extreme terms comparable to and even beyond the aggression he faces from other Jews. Paul's own mouth highlights similarities between himself and hostile Jews. Acts leverages Paul's violent behavior to provide further commonality with the Jewish people. Violence can also afford opportunities to repent. Moreover, Paul's narrative arc suggests that Israel's Lord can reorient even the most violent and resistant "God-fighters" within Israel (5:39).

Finally, I make a similar argument using the motif of blindness. I examine Isaiah's influence on the blindness-sight metaphor in Luke-Acts in order to interpret Paul's citation at the conclusion of the narrative. Blindness for Luke as for Isaiah, I contend, is a temporary condition. Moving from blindness to sight and from darkness to light are analogous metaphors for the repentance-journey. However, blindness is a condition that often requires direct intervention from Jesus to be overcome. Jesus proves quite able to open Israel's blind eyes, bringing those in darkness to light (cf. Luke 4:18; 7:21). Jesus' disciples and Paul in particular exemplify Jesus' ability to rectify Jewish lack of sight. The judgment of blindness, in Paul's case, even facilitated his movement toward seeing the light of Jesus. Indeed, Jesus calls Paul to extend this mission to Jews and gentile alike (Acts 26:16–18). When one reaches Acts' conclusion, the blindness-motif in Luke-Acts gives reason for confidence that Jesus might one day heal Israel's blind condition. Paul's last words and acts continue in solidarity with the Jewish people, reaching out and warning of judgment, while still retaining hope for their restoration. At the story's end, Paul (and Acts') self-understanding, social distance, and rhetoric of Paul remain committed to the Jewish people and their ancestral tradition.

2

"I am a Jew": Ancient Ethnicity, Jewish Identity, and Lukan Characterization

The Jewishness of the Way and Paul in Acts is well recognized. Whether Luke wrests Israel's ancestral customs from the Jewish people, or if the Way and Paul's commitment to Jewish life and identity tempers Luke's harsher comments about some Jews remain open questions.[1] This chapter seeks to demonstrate that, when placed within ancient ethnic discourse, Acts leverages the Jewishness of the Way and Paul to establish commonality and solidarity with the wider Jewish world. It depicts them "within Judaism." Acts constructs the Way as a Jewish subgroup (αἵρεσις) that calls all Israel to accept its truth claims about Jesus. Paul is likewise depicted as a faithful Jew. The Way and Paul check all the typical boxes of Jewishness—kinship (including identification with Jewish ancestral history and shared homeland), language, cult, and custom. More significantly, the Jewish credentials of the Way and especially Paul are accentuated at the points when they are most called into question.[2] Their mission and message is for the sake of the Jewish people, their ancestral tradition, and God's promises to them. Even critical comments against other Jews and certain practices resemble other examples of Second Temple Jewish infighting. In other words, Acts reflects and participates in a familial conflict. Shared Jewishness, then, mitigates the rhetorical charge of the phrase "the Jews." The Way, Paul, and the Jews should be interpreted [together].

To make this claim, I use Herodotus primarily to establish the prominent criteria of ethnicity in antiquity and Josephus to specify the constitutive elements of Jewish identity.[3] I place Acts in conversation with the outlines drawn by Herodotus and

---

[1] Cf. Smith, *Literary Other*, 57–94; Jervell, "Paulus," 378–92.
[2] That is, Luke retains perceptions of the Way and Paul as threats to Jewish civilization *in order to refute them* (cf. Jipp, "Paul," 73–78).
[3] Despite the chronological gap with Acts, I use Herodotus as a guide for two reasons. First, he provides the most succinct summary of ancient ethnic criteria. Second, ethnic reasoning among later Greco-Roman authors demonstrates the continued influence and use of Herodotus' categories. As for Josephus, while he presents Judaism to the Romans and therefore might be biased, he remains a Jewish insider who seeks to represent Jewish identity and its engagement with the wider social world in comprehensible terms and in their best light. Put differently, Josephus reflects how some Jews would have described their ancestral tradition to those unfamiliar with it. He gives the most comprehensive single overview—with, of course, his biases—of Judaism and its contours in the first century and, therefore, seems like a natural conversation partner with Acts which also describes Jewish engagements in diaspora environs.

Josephus. Since many, if not all, of these ethnic characteristics have been observed by others, my focus is the contexts in which these elements appear in Acts. What many neglect in noting the Jewishness of the Way and Paul is *when* Luke appeals to their Jewishness. The settings in which these appeals are found suggest that Luke applies Jewish identifiers to the Way and Paul to foster ongoing mutuality. Finally, I address two potential problems for perceiving Acts' depiction of the Way as a subgroup within Judaism: its exclusivism and the inclusion of gentiles.

2.1 Ancient Ethnic Contours

I begin by framing Acts' constructions of ethnicity within the broader ancient world. Two figures provide general guides: the fifth-century historian Herodotus and Luke's (near) contemporary Josephus.[4] Despite the centuries between them, Herodotus, Josephus, and Luke evince the same general dimensions for identifying people groups. Engaging Herodotus and other Greco-Roman authors anchors Acts within a larger world of ethnic reasoning. Examining Josephus helps particularize the criteria for first-century Judaism. Utilizing these ancient authors mitigates imposing contemporary baggage associated with studying *ethnicity* by allowing them to establish the parameters.[5]

Before beginning, it is important to note that *ethnicity* is a polythetic category. Clusters of character traits converge in particular groups, but no single characteristic is *the* essential factor for constituting the ethnic group.[6] Ethnicity was (and is) contingent, negotiated, flexible, porous in boundaries, open to hybridity, and subject to change. Variations, exceptions, and/or violations of specific dimensions are to be expected. Construction of ethnicity also involves "othering"—that is, the construction of self-

---

[4] In using Herodotus and Josephus, I am not suggesting Luke explicitly consulted either, though some have argued for Lukan familiarity with Josephus (e.g., Pervo, *Dating Acts*, 149–99). On Herodotus' influence on Josephus, see Eran Almagor, "'This is What Herodotus Relates': The Presence of Herodotus' Histories in Josephus' Writings," in *The Reception of Herodotus in Antiquity and Beyond*, ed. Jessica Priestley and Vasiliki Zali, BCCR 6 (Leiden: Brill, 2016), 83–100.

[5] For a survey of classical scholarship on ethnicity, see Teresa Morgan, "Society, Identity, and Ethnicity in the Hellenic World," in *Ethnicity, Race, Religion: Identities and Ideologies in Early Jewish and Christian Texts, and in Modern Biblical Interpretation*, ed. David G. Horrell and Katherine M. Hockey (London: Bloomsbury, 2018), 23–45. For expanded explorations, see Jonathan M. Hall, *Ethnic Identity in Greek Antiquity* (Cambridge: Cambridge University Press, 1997); Ray Laurence and Joanne Berry, eds., *Cultural Identity in the Roman Empire* (London: Routledge, 1998); Irad Malkin, ed., *Ancient Perceptions of Greek Ethnicity*, CHSC 5 (Cambridge, MA: Harvard University Press, 2001); Gabriele Cifani, Simon Stoddart, and Skylar Neil, eds., *Landscape, Ethnicity and Identity in the Archaic Mediterranean Area* (Oxford: Oxbow, 2012); Maria Fragoulaki, *Kinship in Thucydides: Intercommunal Ties and Historical Narrative* (Oxford: Oxford University Press, 2014); Louise Revell, *Ways of Being Roman: Discourses of Identity in the Roman West* (Oxford: Oxbow, 2016); Thomas J. Figueira and Carmen Soares, eds., *Ethnicity and Identity in Herodotus* (New York: Routledge, 2020).

[6] Barreto, *Ethnic Negotiations*, 19–20; Revell, *Being Roman*, 26–28; Barclay, "Ἰουδαῖος," 46–58; Stroup, *Christians*, 1–39. Cf. Paula Fredriksen, "God is Jewish, but Gentiles Don't Have to Be: Ethnicity and Eschatology in Paul's Gospel," in *The Message of Paul the Apostle within Second Temple Judaism*, ed. Frantisek Ábel (Minneapolis, MN: Fortress, 2020), 3–19.

identity vis-à-vis the alterity of other groups— but not in an absolute sense. Individuals and groups can have multiple layered identities. Succinctly put, ethnic identity formation navigates similarity *and* difference, distance *and* connection with others.[7] Herodotus and Josephus provide contours, not hard-and-fast boundaries.

Herodotus' dictum about "Greekness (Ἑλληνικός)" provides the clearest sketch of ancient ethnicity: "shared blood (ὅμαιμόν), shared language (ὁμόγλωσσον), temples of the gods (θεῶν ἱδρύματα) and sacrificial customs (θυσίαι ἤθεα) in common (κοινά), and shared habits (ὁμότροπα)" (*Hist.* 8.144.2; cf. 7.9.2; 7.145.2).[8] Particularly significant is the context in which this ethnic appeal appears. Herodotus describes the leveraging of a common ethnic identity to unify the Greeks in opposition to Xerxes. The appeal sought to unite the disparate *polis*-based ethnicities under one common label: "Greek."[9] Herodotus describes how "it would not be good for the Athenians to become traitors" should they refuse to join in resisting the Persians (*Hist.* 8.144.2). Not to identify with and act on behalf of the Greek ethnicity insinuated abandonment of the people and their ways. Appeals to ethnic identities, then, could foster solidarity and action.[10]

Josephus specifies these ethnic elements for Jewishness in the first century. In *Against Apion* alone, Josephus highlights ancestry (2.289), land (1.60; cf. 1.1, 103, 210; 132, 174, 224; 2.277), language (1.167, 319; 2.27), the Jerusalem temple cult (2.193–98), and Torah, Israel's constitution (πολιτεία), which shapes their cultural practices (2.165). Josephus adds the Scriptures, the source of Israel's history, customs, and identity (1.6–56).[11] Like Herodotus, Josephus strategically highlights particular ethnic features. He seeks to defend and valorize the Jewish people (though he lambasts some Jewish individuals and groups) and their ancestral tradition to facilitate Judaism's place in the Roman Empire after the first Jewish revolt. Josephus tries to defend the

---

[7] Baumann, "Grammars," 19–31; Malkin, "Introduction," in *Greek Ethnicity*, 1–28; Jeremy McInerney, "Ethnos and Ethnicity in Early Greeks," in *Greek Ethnicity*, 51–73. For layered ethnicity and hybridity, see Revell, *Being Roman*, 44–65; Robin Osborne, "Landscape, Ethnicity and the Polis," in *Landscape*, 24–32; Baker, "Every Nation," 79–99; Balch, *Contested*, 17–35; Stewart Alden Moore, *Jewish Ethnic Identity and Relations in Hellenistic Egypt: With Walls of Iron?*, JSJSup 171 (Leiden: Brill, 2015); Gruen, *Constructs*, 7–131; Fredriksen, "Parting," 43–54; Kraft, "Weighing," 90.

[8] On how Dionysius of Halicarnassus uses these categories to link Roman identity to the Greeks, see Cowan, *Writings*, 25–56; cf. Balch, *Contested*, 17–52, on Dionysius and Josephus.

[9] "Even this unity [the Hellenic league], however, is necessarily an amalgamation of lower-hierarchy ethnicities, as Herodotus underlines in his roster of the Greek allies at Salamis" (Thomas Figueira, "Language as a Marker of Ethnicity in Herodotus and Contemporaries," in *Ethnicity and Identity*, 43–71 [46]). For similar comments regarding Roman identity, see Andrea Carandini, "Urban Landscapes and Ethnic Identity of Early Rome," in *Landscape*, 5–23.

[10] Brian Hill, "Protocols of Ethnic Specification in Herodotus," in *Ethnicity and Identity*, 72–83. Cf. David M. Goodblatt, *Elements of Ancient Jewish Nationalism* (Cambridge: Cambridge University Press, 2009), 26–27.

[11] Barclay, "Ἰουδαῖος," 48. Josephus' *Antiquities* similarly seeks "to disclose who the Jews were from the beginning (δηλῶσαι τίνες ὄντες ἐξ ἀρχῆς Ἰουδαῖοι)" (1.6). Spilsbury ties together these elements in the *Antiquities*: "[Josephus] insists that the boundaries of the land are not constitutive of Jewish identity. Rather the proper observance of ancestral traditions (here focused on the sole legitimacy of one place of worship) by the descendants of Abraham is. Josephus does not at any point suggest that religious observance without ethnic descent from Abraham constituted 'Jewishness'. His whole narrative is about those who are by birth Hebrews, and his comments reflect on how such people ought to fulfill their heritage wherever they might be living" (*Image*, 188; cf. 217–27).

Jewish ethnicity and tradition-in-crisis from attacks and accusations. He navigates his Roman identity in conversation with and for the sake of his Jewish ethnicity on behalf of his people.[12]

Herodotus and Josephus illustrate the performative power of ethnic negotiations in antiquity. Common ethnic identity—familial ties and history, language, cult, and customs—unifies the people-group with a sense of solidarity toward common ends.[13] Appeals to ethnicity can unify and establish mutuality. Identities were leveraged for different purposes. Readers of Acts, then, should attend to the broader criteria of ethnic formation in Luke's depictions of the Way and Paul beyond Torah observance, important as it is. The contexts in which Luke's ethnic reasoning about Jewishness appears should be considered.

2.2 Shared Blood: Genealogy, History, and Territory

2.2.1 Kinship in Antiquity

Herodotus begins his list with "shared blood" or common descent (real or fictive).[14] While Greeks organized into smaller kinship groups, particularly along the lines of the *polis*, they claimed a common genealogical origin—mythically linked to the eponymous Hellen (*P.W.* 1.3)—that bonded them.[15] Greeks are one family. Their bond runs in the blood. Of course, Herodotus, and later Thucydides, does not reduce kinship to blood.[16] Though not mentioned explicitly, beyond a simple statement of biology, "shared blood" encompasses other elements of kinship, namely, stories of historical origins and links to a common homeland (*Hist.* 1.1.1–2; *P.W.* 1.2.1; cf. *Hist.* 1.56.3; 8.31; 9.122).[17] Therefore, Herodotus observes, Greeks of all varieties should join together to resist common enemies (*Hist.* 7.145.2; cf. *P.W.* 7.57.1–59.1). The appeal to

---

[12] Tessa Rajak, *Josephus: The Historian and His Society* (Philadelphia, PA: Fortress, 1983), 78–104; Spilsbury, *Image*, 10–12; Gottfried Mader, *Josephus and the Politics of Historiography: Apologetic and Impression Management in the* Bellum Judaicum (Leiden: Brill, 2000); Steve Mason, *Josephus and the New Testament*, 2nd ed. (Peabody, MA: Hendrickson, 2002), 55–145. Cf. Cowan, *Writings*, 57–166.

[13] Revell, *Being Roman*, 34–41.

[14] Regarding Herodotus' ethnic jargon, see Christopher P. Jones, "'Εθνος and Γένος in Herodotus," *ClQ* 46 (1996): 315–20; Hall, *Ethnic Identity*, 34–49; Hill, "Protocols," 72–83. On Josephus, specifically Antiquities, see Spilsbury, *Image*, 12–13, 36–40.

[15] Osborne, "Landscape," 24–32; Catherine Morgan, "Ethne, Ethnicity, and Early Greek States, ca. 1200–480 B.C.: An Archaeological Perspective," in *Ancient Perceptions*, 75–112. On Luke's engagement with *polis* identities, see Stroup, *Christians*, 41–126; Matthijs den Dulk, "Aquila and Apollos: Acts 18 in Light of Ancient Ethnic Stereotypes," *JBL* 139 (2020): 177–89.

[16] Jonathan M. Hall, "Contested Ethnicities: Perceptions of Macedonia within Evolving Definitions of Greek Identity," in *Greek Ethnicity*, 159–86. Still, genealogy "seems to be a universal aspect. Even in societies where a way of life seems to be a predominant marker of ethnicity, it too boils down to blood" (Malkin, "Introduction," 10). Cf. Spilsbury, *Image*, 217–27; Paula Fredriksen, *Paul: The Pagans' Apostle* (New Haven, CT: Yale University Press, 2017), 32–38.

[17] Hall, *Ethnic Identity*, 40–51; Irad Malkin, "Greek Ambiguities: Between 'Ancient Hellas' and 'Barbarian Epirus,'" in *Greek Ethnicity*, 187–212; Carandini, "Urban Landscapes," 5–23; Revell, *Being Roman*, 39; Mason, *Josephus*, 37; Gruen, *Constructs*, 8–13.

genealogy—kinship, history, and territory—proves powerful in unifying a diverse people group.[18]

Josephus highlights these same factors in his description of the antiquity of the Jewish γένος (*Ag. Ap.* 2.288–89).[19] He notes that, in contrast to claims that the Jewish people, earlier known as "Hebrews" and "Israelites" (*Ant.* 1.146), were originally from Egypt, "our ancestors (ἡμῶν τοὺς προγόνους)" migrated there and later willingly returned to their ancestral homeland (τὴν οἰκείαν ὑποστρέψαντες γῆν; cf. τὴν πάτριον γῆν in 2.157).[20] Josephus tersely captures the constitutive elements of the Jewish genealogical bond: Jews share a common descent from Abraham (πάτερ ἡμῶν; *Ant.* 1.158; cf. 3.87; 5.97; 5.113; 14.255; cf. Acts 13:26) and, more specifically, owe their name to the tribe of Judah (*Ant.* 11.173). Abraham establishes circumcision as a central identifying practice of his descendants, the Jewish people (2.141–142; cf. 8.262; Herodotus, *Hist.* 2.104).[21] Furthermore, Josephus portrays Israel's foundational narrative, the exodus from Egypt and their return to their ancestral homeland, as formative for the people's identity (*Ag. Ap.* 2.157). Even in diaspora, Jews bear a connection with this land and its historic (recently sacked) capital and greatest city, Jerusalem (*Life* 7; *Ant.* 11.173; cf. Philo, *Legat.* 281–84; *Flaccus* 45).[22] Israel's sacred texts further outline the common Jewish history and identity (*Ant.* 1.4–6; *Ag. Ap.* 1.6–56). Genealogical ties, shared history, and land bound the Jewish people into one family, even as their identities proliferated in diaspora (*Ant.* 4.115–116; cf. Acts 2:1–11; Philo, *Legat.* 281–91; *Flaccus* 46).[23]

2.2.2 Acts and Jewish Kinship

Acts delineates kinship ties between the Jews, the Way, and Paul along these same lines. The Way and Paul affiliate with two prominent identifiers: *Israel* and *Jew*. Peter and Paul address Jews by their historic identity as God's covenant people. They call Jewish listeners "Israelites" (Ἰσραηλῖται; 2:22; 3:12; 13:16; cf. 7:23, 37) and "the house" or

---

[18] "We can detect an interplay at Athens during the 5th century BC between their pan-Hellenic identity and their *polis* identity ... when at war with Persia, Athenian ambassadors stressed their common Greek origin (Hdt. 8.144.2), whereas during the Peloponnesian War, Pericles stressed their Athenian ethnicity in contrast with the Spartans (Thuc. 2.35–46)" (Revell, *Being Roman*, 51).

[19] Barclay, "Ἰουδαῖος," 46–48.

[20] Spilsbury, *Image*, 36–42; Staples, *Israel*, 43–51.

[21] At least for male Jews. Spilsbury, *Image*, 55–62, 84–86. Cf. Matthew Thiessen, *Contesting Conversion: Genealogy, Circumcision, and Identity in Ancient Judaism and Christianity* (Oxford: Oxford University Press, 2011).

[22] Eyal Ben-Eliyahu, "Josephus's Lands: Mining the Evolution in the Depiction of the Land of Israel in the Words of Josephus," *JSP* 26 (2017): 275–304.

[23] To be sure, diaspora complicates the centrality of the land; not all diaspora Jews were burdened by exile or felt the need to return to Judea. Still, diaspora Jews generally remained committed to the land, evinced in tithe and pilgrimage. Policy or conflict in Judea also impacted diaspora Jews (e.g., Josephus, *J.W.* 2.457–486, 559; 7.367–368). Gafni, *Land*; Gruen, *Constructs*, 283–312; Betsy H. Amaru, "Land Theology in Philo and Josephus," in *The Land of Israel: Jewish Perspectives*, ed. Lawrence A. Hoffman, SJCA 6 (Notre Dame, IN: University of Notre Dame Press, 1986), 65–93; Paul Spilsbury, "God and Israel in Josephus: A Patron-Client Relationship," in *Understanding Josephus: Seven Perspectives*, ed. Steve Mason (Sheffield: Sheffield Academic, 1998), 172–91.

"people(s) of Israel" (2:36; 4:10, 27; 9:15).[24] Their message is for this people's sake. Jesus, Peter states, was exalted "in order to give repentance to Israel and forgiveness of sin" (5:31; cf. 1:6; 2:39; 10:36; 13:23–24).[25] This salvific work was appointed "for you," Israelites (3:17–26). According to Luke, in Jesus, Israel's promised Messiah, lies the fulfillment of the promises God made to this people (26:7; 28:17). The identity and mission of Jesus is intertwined with the relationship between Israel and their ancestral deity (cf. Luke 1–2).[26]

The apostles and Paul participate in Israel. The Twelve are numbered as the proleptic representatives of God's reconstitution of Israel as a whole. Their calling, vocation, and future are inherently tied to this people (Acts 1:6, 12–26; 7:8; 26:7; Luke 6:12–16; 22:30).[27] Paul identifies the Jews, Israel, as "my nation (τὸ ἔθνος μου)" (24:17; 26:4; 28:19). Importantly, Paul's statements of identification occur when his loyalty to Israel is questioned. Rather than stirring up the Jewish community in Jerusalem, Paul was bringing alms to his nation (24:17). Before Agrippa, Paul reiterates that the entire Jewish community knows that he was brought up "among my own nation (γενομένην ἐν τῷ ἔθνει μου)" (26:4). He stands on trial for his hope in Israel's ancient promises, the hope of the twelve tribes (26:4–8). Paul comes to Rome with no charge against his own people (28:19). *Au contraire*, he bears chains *because of* Israel's ancestral hopes (28:17–19). The moments in which Paul is perceived as the greatest threat to the nation are when he locates himself among them most clearly.

Luke explicitly identifies some Jesus-following characters as Jews (cf. 21:20). Peter labels himself a Jewish man (ἀνδρὶ Ἰουδαίῳ) in contrast to the "foreigner (ἀλλοφύλῳ)" Cornelius (10:28). Peter dwells among the people whose identity is linked to circumcision (10:45; 11:12; cf. 7:8). Timothy's mother is dubbed a faithful Jewish woman (γυναικὸς Ἰουδαίας πιστῆς; 16:1). Though Timothy's father is Greek, her Jewish identity leads Paul to circumcise Timothy "because of the Jews that were in those places" (16:3). Notably, Paul does so immediately after the Jerusalem Council's decision that gentiles need not be circumcised and become Jews to be saved (15:1–35). Rather than being a missionary strategy or compromise, Paul clarifies Timothy's covenantal place among the Jewish people to other Jews.[28] Luke identifies Aquila as a Jew who, like

---

[24] Gamaliel and the Asian Jews in the temple also identify fellow Jews as "Israelites" (5:37; 21:28). Stephen's speech contains the only references to *Israelites* and the *house of Israel* who are not characters within the narrative of Acts itself (7:23, 37, 42). These Israelites, Moses' brothers who rejected him (7:23), were "a crooked and distorted generation (γενεὰ σκολιὰ καὶ διεστραμμένη)" (LXX Deut 32:5; cf. LXX Ps 77:8) that failed to inherit the Promised Land (cf. τῆς γενεᾶς τῆς σκολιᾶς ταύτης; Acts 2:40; cf. Luke 9:41; 13:8, 10).

[25] The connection between the "house of Israel" (2:14, 36) and forgiveness echoes expectations of Israel's national restoration (e.g., Isa 40:1–2; Jer 3:15–25; 23:5–8; 31:27–37; Ezek 11:14–21; 36–37).

[26] On Jesus' Israelite identity in Luke-Acts, see Smith, "Politics," 67–123.

[27] Michael E. Fuller, *The Restoration of Israel: Israel's Re-Gathering and the Fate of the Nations in Early Jewish Literature and Luke-Acts*, BZNW 138 (Berlin: de Gruyter, 2006); cf. Jervell, *People*, 75–112. The Twelve also contrast with Israel's present failed shepherds (Luke 15:1–6; cf. Jer 23:1–4; Ezek 34; Acts 20:28). Chance, *Jerusalem*, 66–84; Tannehill, *Narrative Unity*, 2:20–24; Joel B. Green, *The Gospel of Luke*, NICNT (Grand Rapids, MI: Eerdmans, 1997), 258–59.

[28] On Timothy's Jewishness and hybridity, see Barreto, *Ethnic Negotiations*, 61–118; Stroup, *Christians*, 70–95. On circumcision in Luke-Acts, see Oliver, *Torah Praxis*, 399–451.

all Roman Jews, was expelled from Rome by Claudius (18:2; cf. *Claud*. 25). This simple comment that explains how Aquila arrived in Corinth highlights his ongoing affiliation with the Jews, even when facing imperial trouble. Apollos is both Jewish and Alexandrian (18:24). He brings his learning to his fellow Jews in Jewish space by proclaiming Jesus in the synagogues (18:26–28). Juxtaposing this Alexandrian Jew with "the Jews" challenges claims that believing Jews are or becoming something other than Jews.[29] Luke simply calls Jewish believers Jews.

The Paul of Acts twice self-identifies as a Jew (21:39; 22:3), a Pharisee at that (23:6; 26:4; cf. 22:3; 28:17). As with his identification with all Israel, Paul refers to himself as such when this people question his loyalty in their historic capital. He corrects the gentile tribune and then the Jewish crowd, stating that he is a Cilician Jew raised in Jerusalem as a Pharisee (21:38–22:3; 23:6; 26:4). Importantly, Paul self-identifies as a Jew *after* facing repeated hostility from diaspora Jews (e.g., 18:12; 20:3). Nothing they have done dissuades him from claiming to be one of their own. Again, Paul leverages his Jewishness with Jews when his faithfulness to Judaism is doubted.[30] By portraying his characters as members of Israel *and* as Jews, Luke binds them with this people's historic *and* present identities. Members of the Way do not usurp Israel's identity, wresting it away from the Jews; they share both identities.

Given this common Jewish-Israelite identity, the Way and Paul unsurprisingly use familial language when interacting with other Jews, Jesus-following or otherwise. Speakers appeal to "our ancestors" before Jews in scenes of persuasion, whether sermonic or apologetic (e.g., 7:11; 13:17, 32; 15:10; 28:17). "Brothers (ἀδελφοί)" is often used among Jews. Jewish Jesus-followers refer to one another as "brother(s)" (1:14–16; 2:37; 6:3; 15:7, 13; 21:20; cf. 11:29; 18:27). They also call non-Jesus-following Jews "brothers." These addresses occur in the so-called missionary speeches (2:28; 3:17; 13:15, 26, 38) and apologetic settings (7:2; 22:1, 5; 23:1, 5–6; 28:17).[31] Jewish Jesus-followers appeal to family when they proclaim Jesus—who was raised up from among these brothers (3:22; cf. 7:37)—or reiterate their fidelity to Jewish hopes and customs. The familial bond between Jews persists up through the end of the narrative. Despite its threats about Jews being cut off from the people or excluded from eternal life (3:23; 13:46), the Way continues to view non-Jesus-following Jews as family. Non-Jesus-following Jews reciprocate, calling Jews from the Way "brothers" (2:37; 13:15; 28:21). These Jews acknowledge that Jesus-following Jews remain within the family of Israel.

2.2.3 Acts and Jewish Ancestral History

Peter, Stephen, and Paul present Israel's ancestral and national history—including self-criticism—as integral to Jewish identity and, concomitantly, the message about Jesus (2:29–36; 3:11–26; 7:2–51; 13:13–41). As Herodotus and Josephus illustrate, appeals to

---

[29] Contra Matthews, *Perfect Martyr*, 7.
[30] On how Luke's Paul leverages his Roman identity, see Barreto, *Ethnic Negotiations*, 139–80.
[31] In contrast, "brothers" is not used in gentile missionary or apologetic settings (14:15; 17:22). The clearest occurrence of "brothers" for an exclusively non-Jewish audience specifies them as "brothers *from the nations*" (15:23). Other times "brothers" refers to mixed groups of believers (15:1, 36; 16:40). Trebilco, *Self-Designations*, 50–53; Boesenberg, "Negotiating Identity," 61–62.

common legacies, particularly in speeches, can explain present circumstances in order to call listeners to action (e.g., *Hist.* 8.144.2–5; Josephus, *J.W.* 5.362–419; *Ant.* 20.165–66).[32] In Israel's Scriptures, the lynchpin of Israel's national history and identity, recounting the people's history functions similarly. Historical recitations often relate historical sins to call Israel to repent (e.g., Pss 77–78; 105–106; Dan 9:1–19; Neh 9:6–37; cf. 4 Ezra 1:5–40; Sir 44–50). Herodotus, Josephus, and Israel's Scriptures provide an additional dimension to the Lukan recitations of Israelite history: the binding of audience and speaker through a common narrative to spark action. In Acts, narrating Israel's history as culminated in Jesus seeks to provoke repentance, (re)alignment with Israel's God.[33] The ancestral history locates Jesus as the fruition of Israel's national hopes. God's act in Jesus—the one who fulfills the promises to Abraham (3:25), the prophet like Moses (3:22; 7:37), David's greater son (2:29–39; 13:33–37; cf. Luke 1:32; 20:41–45)—is incomprehensible without knowledge of and participation in Israel's national narrative.[34] Peter, Stephen, and Paul recount Israel's history to persuade the people to receive Jesus and the fulfillment of the ancestral promises.

Peter's first two sermons prove illustrative. On Pentecost, after describing Jerusalem's role in Jesus' death and his subsequent resurrection, Peter tells his "brothers" that "the patriarch David (τοῦ πατριάρχου Δαυίδ)" foresaw Jesus (2:29–36; cf. 4:25). Peter recounts the oath God made to David that one of his descendants would sit on his throne (2 Sam 7:1–17; 1 Chr 17:1–15). This oath, Peter continues, culminates in the exalted Jesus, Israel's Lord and Messiah (2:32–36; cf. Luke 1:32; 2:4). When the audience asks their "brothers," the apostles (2:37), how to respond, Peter tells them to "repent and be baptized … because the promise is for you, your children, and all those who are far off, as many as the Lord our God might call" (2:39).[35] The ancestral relations bond speaker and listener, calling these Israelites (2:22) to respond to the acts of God in Jesus, David's promised son and Israel's Messiah, and receive the promised Spirit (2:38; cf. 1:4–11; Ezek 36:16–37:28). This Jesus is "king of the Jews" (Luke 23:3, 37–38).

Peter's second speech reiterates the import of his listeners' ancestry in their relationship to the message of Jesus. In the temple, Peter recounts how "the God of Abraham, the God of Isaac, and the God of Jacob, the God of our ancestors" (cf. Exod

---

[32] Klawans, "Catastrophes," 290–303; Viktor Kókai Nagy, "The Speech of Josephus at the Walls of Jerusalem," *BN* 161 (2014): 141–67.

[33] See Moessner, *Luke*, 238–71; Schaefer, *Zukunft*, 33–104, on Deuteronomistic theology and the so-called missionary speeches. On historical recitations and Stephen's speech, see Oda Wischmeyer, "Stephen's Speech before the Sanhedrin against the Background of the Summaries of the History of Israel (Acts 7)," in *History and Identity: How Israel's Later Authors Viewed Its Earlier History*, ed. Núria Calduch-Benages and Jan Liesen, DCLS (Berlin: de Gruyter, 2006), 341–58.

[34] Speeches directed toward pagan gentiles do not refer to Israel's history and relationship with God but start with God as creator (14:15–17; 17:22–34). Festus voices how the message proclaimed by the Way and Paul sounds to pagan-gentile ears that lack this narrative framework: It is insane (μανία; 26:24–26; Rowe, *World*, 84).

[35] Connecting the promises with those present and future generations echoes Moses' (re)establishing the covenant with Israel prior to entering the land (LXX Deut 29:10–15). Peter's appeal to the "God of Abraham, Isaac, and Jacob" and his reference to the covenant in his temple speech reinforces these intertextual links (Acts 3:13, 25; LXX Deut 29:13–14). Given these echoes, "all those who are far off (πᾶσι τοῖς εἰς μακράν)" is possibly a double entendre, referring to diaspora Jews and gentiles (Acts 22:21; cf. Deut 29:21; Zech 6:15).

3:6, 15–16; 4:5; Luke 20:37) exalted Jesus, his servant, whom Jerusalem ignorantly had handed over for death in fulfillment of prophetic expectations (3:13–18).[36] Peter calls his audience to repent so their sins are blotted out and they might receive the times of refreshing, which God promised through the prophets (3:19–21).[37] Peter casts Jesus as the prophet like Moses, warning his audience that those who ignore the prophet will be rooted out from the people (3:22–23; cf. LXX Lev 23:29; Deut 18:15–20; 29:19–21).[38] In spite of this warning, Peter reiterates that his listeners "are sons of the prophets and of the covenant, which God made with your ancestors, saying to Abraham, 'and in your seed all lineages of the earth will be blessed'" (3:25). They remain the descendants, the intended heirs of these promises. Their covenantal identity stays intact, though at risk if they continue to reject the prophet like Moses.[39] The appeal to the ancestors, particularly Abraham and Moses, and to the covenant, reiterates that God's servant Jesus is the one this people, Peter's brothers (3:17), have long awaited. Therefore, they should repent and receive him.

Stephen's speech provides the most extensive recounting of "our ancestor(s)" (7:2, 11–12, 15, 38–39, 44–45). He outlines to his "brothers and fathers" the major formative events of Israel's history. The speech opens with many constitutive elements of Jewish identity: the calling of "our ancestor Abraham," the promise of land, temple worship, the covenant of circumcision, and the births of Isaac, Jacob, and the twelve patriarchs (7:2–8). Familial conflict arises with the Joseph narrative, which then explains how the people ended up in Egypt (7:9–16). "Our ancestors" then suffer in Israel until God raises up Moses on behalf of his own "brothers" (7:23–25). Though initially rejected (7:26–29), Moses returns to lead the people out of Egypt (7:30–38), emerging as their "ruler and redeemer" (7:34). "Our ancestors" rebel, however. They commit idolatry with the golden calf (7:39–43). Stephen next describes the entrance into the land and the

---

[36] On the "servant" motif in Luke-Acts, see Holly Beers, *The Followers of Jesus as the "Servant": Luke's Model from Isaiah for the Disciples in Luke-Acts*, LNTS 535 (London: T&T Clark, 2015).

[37] On Jesus' resurrection and exaltation, the Spirit, and Israel's restoration, see Max Turner, *Power from on High: The Spirit in Israel's Restoration and Witness in Luke-Acts*, JPTSup 9 (Sheffield: Sheffield Academic, 1996), 140–315; Richard Bauckham, "The Restoration of Israel in Luke-Acts," in *Restoration: Old Testament, Jewish, and Christian Perspectives*, ed. James M. Scott (Leiden: Brill, 2001), 435–88; Kevin L. Anderson, *"But God Raised Him from the Dead": The Theology of Jesus' Resurrection in Luke-Acts* (Eugene, OR: Wipf and Stock, 2006), 197–233; Kinzer, *Jerusalem*, 40–56; Brandon D. Crowe, *The Hope of Israel: The Resurrection of Christ in the Acts of the Apostles* (Grand Rapids: Baker Academic, 2020), 32–53. See also Klaus Haacker, "Das Bekenntnis des Paulus zur Hoffnung Israels nach der Apostelgeschichte des Lukas," *NTS* 31 (1985): 437–51; Philip La G. Du Toit, "Reconsidering the Salvation of Israel in Luke-Acts," *JSNT* 43 (2021): 343–69.

[38] Peter's temple sermon also sounds like a call to covenant renewal (e.g., Josh 24:2–28; 2 Chr 34:29–33). At the covenant renewal at Moab, Moses warns that there will be those who will ignore the covenant blessings and curses (that is, they will ignore Moses), and God will single out (διαστελεῖ) these individuals "from all the sons of Israel (ἐκ πάντων υἱῶν Ἰσραήλ)" (LXX Deut 29:21). Renewing the covenant does not preclude the exclusion of some. While the individual's name is "blotted out (ἐξαλείψει)" in Deut 29:20, sins will be blotted out (ἐξαλειφθῆναι) in Acts 3:19. On whether non-Jesus-following Jews are cut off in Acts itself or this is a future threat, see Tannehill, *Narrative Unity*, 2:56–57; Mittmann, "Polemik," 517–18; Schaefer, *Zukunft*, 100–1, 364–65; Kinzer, *Jerusalem*, 109–18.

[39] Threatening their place among the covenant people suggests Peter's listeners currently have a place among God's people as inheritors of the promises that they risk forfeiting. The threat of being "cut off" is hollow otherwise.

founding of the temple by Solomon. Abraham's calling, the exodus, receiving the Torah from Moses, David's kingdom, and Solomon's temple remain constitutive features of Israel's legacy and identity.[40] And Stephen identifies with this people and history. These ancestors, even the unfaithful ones, are his.

In contrast to Peter and Paul who use Israel's history to frame the narrative of Jesus to call the people to repent, Stephen's speech concludes with a rebuke of his hearers. His recitation of Israel's history resembles a covenant lawsuit (e.g., Isa 1:2–20; Jer 2:2–37; Ezek 20:1–32).[41] Stephen famously switches from first-person plural pronouns in his account of Israel's history to second-person plural when he rebukes the leadership (7:51–53). He discusses historic sins of Israel, particularly their tendencies to violate God's instructions (7:39, 53) and to oppose those appointed to lead and deliver Israel (7:9, 35, 51–52). While he is accused of violating temple and Torah, Stephen turns the charges against his opponents. Israel's present leaders reenact Israel's long legacy of rejecting God's chosen instruments of salvation and violating Torah and temple. This shift is often read as initiating the separation of the Way and the Jewish people in Acts.[42]

However, Stephen's change in pronoun use and his rebuke of his listeners need not denote a severing of the familial link or separation from the Jewish people any more than Peter's use of "your ancestors" separates him from God's promises (cf. 2:22–29; 3:17–26). Six factors suggest Stephen's speech evinces internecine conflict rather than Luke's attempt at separating the Way and the Jewish people.[43] First, Stephen identifies Israel's ancestors who strayed from God as his own (7:11, 39, 44). Israel, including the unfaithful like the exodus/wilderness generation, is "our kin (τὸ γένος ἡμῶν)" (7:19; cf. 7:2). Second, Stephen's speech recounts primarily *familial* conflict. Joseph and Moses are rejected by their own brothers (7:9, 25–28, 39).[44] Israelites' wronging their brothers and neighbors is nothing new (7:26–27). The council will repeat this trend with Stephen (as will Paul's Jewish brethren). Third, Joseph and Moses redeem the people who rejected them (7:9–16, 23–38; cf. 7:37). Jesus reenacts this pattern (cf. 2:22–39; 3:17–26; 5:30–31). Fourth, no call to repent is issued, yet Stephen, like Jesus, petitions the Lord to forgive his murderers (7:59–60; Luke 23:34; cf. Isa 2:9; Dan 9:17–19).[45] Fifth, Stephen's

---

[40] Stephen complicates each because of Israel's infidelity (Tannehill, *Narrative Unity*, 2:90).
[41] Brian K. Peterson, "Stephen's Speech as a Modified Prophetic Rîb Formula," *JETS* 57 (2014): 351–69.
[42] Earl J. Richard, "The Polemical Character of the Joseph Episode in Acts 7," *JBL* 98 (1979): 255–67; Matthews, *Perfect Martyr*, 56–79.
[43] Donaldson, "Moses Typology," 31–39; Ravens, *Restoration* 50–71; Tannehill, *Narrative Unity*, 2:80–96; McWhirter, *Rejected*, 104–9.
[44] Contra Richard, nothing indicates that the patriarchs are not true descendants of Abraham ("Polemical," 262). Joseph is counted among "the twelve patriarchs" (7:8).
[45] Contra Matthews, there is no reason to contrast Stephen's prayer for forgiveness with the views of the author (*Perfect Martyr*, 99–127). The Spirit marks Stephen's reliability as a character (7:55). He reflects the narrator's perspective. To be sure, the Spirit's presence reiterates that Israel's leaders again oppose the Spirit (7:51), but opposing the Spirit is not the same as blaspheming the Spirit (cf. Luke 12:10–12). That Saul, one who approved of the murder (8:1), joins the Way suggests some efficacy in Stephen's prayer. Matthews' reading also misrepresents the *Lex Talionis* in early Judaism as vindictive and unyielding (*Perfect Martyr*, 102–3). On the *Lex Talionis*, see James G. Crossley, *The New Testament and Jewish Law: A Guide for the Perplexed* (London: T&T Clark, 2010), 76. On Jesus' prayer for forgiveness, Joshua M. Strahan, *The Limits of a Text: Luke 23:34a as a Case Study in Theological Interpretation*, JTISup 5 (Winona Lake, IN: Eisenbrauns, 2012).

polemic is rooted in the Jewish prophetic legacy. Calling Israel "stiff-necked" (e.g., Exod 32:9; Neh 9:16–17; Jer 17:23; Bar 2:30; Jub. 1:7) and "uncircumcised in heart and ears" (Lev 26:41; Jer 4:4; 6:10; 9:26; 1QS 5.5; Jub. 1:21–22; cf. Deut 10:16) was frequently levied against the people for reenacting ancestral sins (2 Chr 30:6–9). The council ignores and kills the angelic Stephen (6:15), slaying another prophetic figure in violation of Torah (7:38, 52–53; cf. Zech 7:12–14; 2 Chr 24:18–22).[46] Stephen's historical narration confirms Israel's present identity on two fronts. On the one hand, Stephen's oppressors confirm their continuity with Israel's ancestral history by reenacting the pattern of rejecting God's messengers. On the other hand, Stephen stands in this same history as one of God's oft-opposed messengers. Stephen rebukes his brothers, but he is not leaving the family.[47] Jacob's children continue to quarrel.

Next to Stephen, Paul's Pisidian Antioch speech recounts the most Jewish ancestral history (13:16–41). Like Peter's speeches, though, Paul uses it to frame the narrative of Jesus to provoke repentance. Paul's opening address to these "Israelites and those who fear God" describes how "the God of this people Israel chose our ancestors" (13:16–17). He, his Jewish audience, and their children are the current and future heirs to and recipients of God's promises to the ancestors (13:26, 32–33; cf. 2:39; 26:6–7; Deut 29:14–15).[48] Although "our ancestors" might indicate that Paul portrays Jews and gentile Godfearers alike as descendants of Israel, Paul differentiates between "sons of Abraham's kin and those who fear God among you (υἱοὶ γένους Ἀβραὰμ καὶ οἱ ἐν ὑμῖν φοβούμενοι τὸν θεόν)" (13:26). Jews, Jesus-following and not, remain uniquely identified by Abrahamic descent in Acts.[49] The genealogical identifier stands.

Paul also mentions the exodus, the wilderness wanderings, and the conquest of the land (13:17b–20). Though brief, he retains these as foundational for Israel's identity forming narrative. Much of Paul's speech focuses on David's rise to kingship after Saul to set up the appearance of David's promised son and Israel's savior, Jesus (13:20–23, 36–37). Jesus brings about the fulfillment of the ancestral promises and the forgiveness promised by the prophets, including John (13:24–25, 38–39; cf. Ezek 36:22–36; Luke 3:1–17). Paul proclaims to his own family that they should turn lest they fail to heed the warning of the prophets, reenact their ancestors' historic

---

[46] Otto Glombitza, "Zur Charakterisierung des Stephanus in Act 6 und 7," *ZNW* 53 (1962): 238–44.

[47] Contra Peterson, nothing in Stephen's rebuke suggests God has abandoned Israel because they reenact this pattern ("Stephen's Speech," 369). God's faithfulness to the unfaithful people can coexist with the threat for individual Israelites being cut off (Schaefer, *Zukunft*, 100–1; McWhirter, *Rejected*, 104–9; Moessner, *Luke*, 238–71). Paul's pronoun shift in Rome likely functions similarly (28:25): these Roman Jews risk reenacting the behavior of their ancestors (13:40–41). Boesenberg, "Prophetic Rebuke," 9–12.

[48] For reading "to our children" in 13:33, see Daniel Glover, "The Promises Fulfilled for Whose Children? The Problem of the Text of Acts 13:33 in Contemporary Debate," *JBL* 139 (2020): 789–807. Cf. F. F. Bruce, *The Acts of the Apostles: The Greek Text with Introduction and Commentary*, 3rd ed. (Grand Rapids, MI: Eerdmans, 1990), 269; Conzelmann, *Apostelgeschichte*, 85. Contra Glover, the Israel-centric emphasis of Paul's speech, especially its focus on the ancestors, suggests the focus lies with genealogical Israel, and is not "an expansive perspective on 'the people of God'" ("Promises Fulfilled," 804–5).

[49] Of course, Abrahamic descent does not suffice for receiving the ancestral promises, as John the Baptist warns. Abraham's children must live like Abraham; they must "bear fruit worthy of repentance" (Luke 3:8–9; cf. 1:55, 73; 16:19–31; Acts 5:31–32; 6:35; 19:9).

disbelief, and fall into judgment (13:40–41; citing Hab 1:5).⁵⁰ This reiterates a typical message to Israel. Paul retains the kinship bonds and remains in the family. The message is for their sake.

2.2.4 Acts and "the Region of the Jews"

Acts, through the Way and Paul, retains the links to the ancestral Jewish homeland of Judea and mother-city of Jerusalem (8:1; 22:3). Stephen reminds his accusers of God's promise of land to Abraham and his descendants (7:3–7, 45). Peter recounts Jesus' actions in "the region of the Jews and Jerusalem (τῇ χώρᾳ τῶν Ἰουδαίων)" to the gentile Cornelius (10:39). Paul reiterates that God gave the land as Israel's inheritance after the exodus (κατεκληρονόμησεν τὴν γῆν αὐτῶν; 13:19). The apostles maintain a connection with Jerusalem (8:1). Its community and leaders become chief among the Way, most clearly evinced in the Jerusalem Council (15:2, 13; 21:17–26). Paul, though from Tarsus, was raised in Jerusalem (22:3), a point he uses to build credibility before his accusers. By introducing this detail, Paul can better refute claims that he teaches against the city and its temple (21:27–36). Luke affirms the Way's and Paul's continued connections to the Jewish civilization's homeland and central city.⁵¹

2.2.5 Summary

The self-identity that Luke paints for the Way and Paul maintains and associates with the constitutive elements of the Jewish ethnicity delineated by Herodotus and Josephus. Paul and the Way identify with Israel and as Jews in a non-competitive manner; they share these titles with their Jewish-Israelite brothers. Common ancestry, history, and geographic heritage unite them. Luke retains these Jewish kinship bonds. The Way, Paul, and the Jews have, in Herodotus' term, shared blood. To be sure, conflict arises but, as with Israel's ancestors, such arguments and even violence remain within the family. Acts appeals to these familial relations most explicitly in scenes of conflict to frame the Way's proclamation about Jesus as the culmination of Israel's hopes and to defend Paul's continued loyalty to the Jewish people. In retaining and emphasizing kinship, Acts paints and engages in Jewish internecine disputation.

---

[50] Bart J. Koet, *Five Studies on the Interpretation of Scripture in Luke-Acts*, SNTA 14 (Leuven: Peeters, 1989), 105–18; Huub van de Sandt, "The Quotations in Acts 13,32–52 as a Reflection of Luke's LXX Interpretation," *Bib* 75 (1994): 26–58; Anton Deutschmann, *Synagoge und Gemeindebildung: Christliche Gemeinde und Israel am Beispiel von Apg 13,42–52*, BU 30 (Regensburg: Pustet, 2001); Wenxi Zhang, *Paul among Jews: A Study of the Meaning and Significance of Paul's Inaugural Sermon in the Synagogue of Antioch in Pisidia (Acts 13:16–41) for His Missionary Work among the Jews* (Eugene, OR: Wipf and Stock, 2011), 150–58; Reardon, *Politics*, 133–62. Habakkuk 1:5 appears in 1QpHab 2.1–10 referring to those who reject the teacher of righteousness and violate the covenant (Gert J. Steyn, *Septuagint Quotations in the Context of the Petrine and Pauline Speeches of the Acta Apostolorum*, CBET 12 [Kampen: Kok Pharos, 1995], 188–90).

[51] Exploring Jerusalem's ongoing relevance in Acts is beyond the present scope. Loveday Alexander, *Acts in Its Ancient Literary Context*, LNTS 298 (London: T&T Clark, 2007), 69–96; Kinzer, *Jerusalem*, 40–56; Oliver, *Eschatology*, 71–139; Chance, *Jerusalem*, 47–138; Matthew Sleeman, *Geography and the Ascension Narrative in Acts*, SNTSMS 146 (Cambridge: Cambridge University Press, 2013).

2.3 Shared Language

2.3.1 Language and Ethnicity in Antiquity

Common language for Herodotus, as well as Thucydides after him, features centrally in the formation and adoption of Greek ethnic identity (e.g., *Hist.* 1.57–58; 7.9.2; *P.W.* 1.3.3–4).[52] Herodotus asserts that, though they proliferated into various nations, "the Greeks, as it seems to me, have always spoken the same language since they originated" (*Hist.* 1.58.1). A common language provides cohesion and familiarity in contrast to foreigners and invaders who speak in strange tongues (cf. Strabo, *Geogr.* 8.6.6). In fact, Strabo alleges that the category of "barbarian" developed as an onomatopoeia to describe those who spoke non-Greek languages or spoke Greek poorly (*Geogr.* 14.2.28; *Il.* 2.867; *Ant. rom.* 1.89.4). Central to "barbarization (ἐκβαρβαρόω)," losing Greek identity, was the loss of the Greek language (cf. Strabo, *Geogr.* 6.1.2).[53]

While diaspora complicated the importance of language for Jewish identity, its link to the Jewish people persisted. Josephus refers to "the language of the Hebrews" (*J.W.* 6.97; cf. *Ant.* 1.34; 3.252; 6.22; 9.290; 10.8; 11.159) as his "ancestral" or "native language" (*J.W.* 1.3; 5.361; cf. *Ant.* 1.143, 146).[54] He describes Greek as "a foreign and strange language to us" Jews (ἀλλοδαπὴν ἡμῖν καὶ ξένην διαλέκτου; *Ant.* 1.7; cf. *Ag. Ap.* 1.5). At times, Josephus recounts how he struggled to pronounce Greek words because of his native tongue (*Ant.* 20.263–64; cf. 1.128–29). He highlights the ancestral language's use among his compatriots in the revolt (e.g., *J.W.* 5.356; 6.96; cf. 5.272). Retaining their ancestral language was a form of cultural resistance in the face of imperial forces (cf. 2 Macc 7:8, 21, 28).[55] Its centrality dwindled due to their dispersion, but the Jewish ancestral tongue still plays a valuable role in forming and retaining Jewish ethnic identity in a Greek-dominated world.

2.3.2 Acts and "the Hebrew Dialect"

Given its complication by diaspora, that Luke notes that members of the Way, Paul, and even Jesus speak "the Hebrew dialect (τῇ Ἑβραΐδι διαλέκτῳ)" (2:1–14; 21:40; cf. 22:4; 26:14), the Jewish ancestral language, is remarkable.[56] At Pentecost, what shocks the Jewish audience is that these Galileans can speak various diaspora languages (2:8). Implicit is that these Galileans would primarily address the Jewish inhabitants of Jerusalem (2:5; cf. 2:14) in their own language (ἰδίᾳ διαλέκτῳ αὐτῶν; 1:19) rather than diaspora ones. When Peter addresses these Jews in Jerusalem, he likely does so

---

[52] Edward M. Anson, "Greek Ethnicity and the Greek Language," *Glo* 85 (2009): 5–30; Figueira, "Language," 43–71.
[53] Figueira, "Language," 53–55; Dulk, "Acts 18," 183–4.
[54] Whether these refer to Hebrew, Aramaic, or both is ambiguous and of secondary concern (e.g., *J.W.* 1.3; 5.361; *Ant.* 1.34; 3.252; 6.22; 7.67; 9.290; 11.148). Rajak, *Josephus*, 46–64, 174–84, 230–32.
[55] Nehemiah bemoans that half the sons of intermarriages cannot speak the Jewish language (Ἰουδαϊστί; 2 Esd 23:23; Heb. Neh 13:24). For him, loss of language is a tragic result of sin and exile.
[56] As with Josephus, the referent of "the Hebrew dialect" is of secondary concern. Suffice it to say that "the Hebrew dialect" links Paul to the Jewish people through language. For an argument that it is Hebrew, see Oliver, *Eschatology*, 116–17, 207–8n103–4.

in their shared ancestral language (2:14). Reinforcing this notion, the Jerusalem community contains Hebrews (Ἑβραῖος) and Hellenists (Ἑλληνιστής; 6:1), Jews whose primary language differed.[57] In Acts, Jerusalem retains a connection with the ancestral tongue.

Luke incorporates Paul's connection to the Jewish ancestral language in his two defense speeches directed toward Jews about his loyalty to them and their customs: Jerusalem (21:40; 22:2) and before Agrippa (26:14).[58] Being able to speak and comprehend the Hebrew dialect roots the diaspora Jew Paul, who was accused of teaching Jews to abandon (ἀποστασίαν) their ancestral customs (21:21; cf. LXX Jer 2:15; 1 Macc. 1:41–43, 51–52; 2:15), more firmly within Jewish identity.[59] Put differently, Luke appeals to Paul's knowledge of "the Hebrew dialect" when it carries the most weight. The effect of this linguistic link is not lost in Jerusalem. Paul's listeners become increasingly silent (μᾶλλον παρέσχον ἡσυχίαν) when they hear him speaking Hebrew (22:2). Jesus himself, the messianic figure proclaimed by the Way, spoke to Saul/Paul in the Hebrew dialect (26:14). That Israel's Messiah addressed and commissioned Paul in Israel's tongue aids his defense. It reinforces his (and Jesus') continuity with Jewish ancestral hopes (26:4–8), especially the message of the prophets whom God similarly commissioned (26:27). Amidst diaspora and the proliferation of languages among the Jewish people, Acts retains the link with Israel's historic tongue among the Way and the Jews. They speak the same language.

2.4 Common Cult

2.4.1 Gods, Cults, and Ethnicity in Antiquity

Herodotus next highlights temples and common sacrificial customs—that is, shared cultic practices—as integral to Greekness. In antiquity, cult was particularly unifying for ethnic and civic identities. Gods participated in the ethnic groups as progenitors, benefactors, and guardians (cf. *Ant. rom.* 3.22.1–10; 4.14.1–4; 4.22.1–2). They were part of the family. As Paula Fredriksen puts it, "gods, like their cults, ran in the blood."[60] Proper civic duty entailed honoring them by offering sacrifices in the temples and celebrating common festivals for the deities (*P.W.* 1.24.4; *Moralia* 1102A). Good citizens placate the gods. Happy gods meant prosperous cities and unhappy gods led to

---

[57] Carter, "Diaspora Poetics," 477; Craig C. Hill, *Hellenists and Hebrews: Reappraising Division within the Earliest Church* (Minneapolis, MN: Fortress, 1991); Todd C. Penner, *In Praise of Christian Origins: Stephen and the Hellenists in Lukan Apologetic Historiography*, ESEC (New York: T&T Clark, 2004); Staples, *Israel*, 73–80.

[58] While Festus is present, Paul mainly addresses Agrippa since he, as one of Jewish heritage, understands more (26:2, 26–27). Paul does not highlight Hebrew when he addresses the gentile governor Felix. Paul instead emphasizes his innocence of *stasis*, a charge of greater concern to Felix (24:2–22).

[59] Jipp, "Paul," 62.

[60] Fredriksen, *Paul*, 37. Steve Mason, *Josephus, Judea, and Christian Origins: Methods and Categories* (Peabody, MA: Hendrickson, 2009), 162–65; Stroup, *Christians*, 41–127; Rick Strelan, *Paul, Artemis, and the Jews in Ephesus*, BZNW 80 (Berlin: de Gruyter, 1996), 1–125.

disaster (e.g., *Or.* 31.7, 87).⁶¹ Cult—temple, ritual calendar, and sacrifices—was indispensable for forming cohesive ethnic and civic groups.

According to Josephus, the Jewish people likewise had their own cult devoted to a god who participated in their familial unit and was integral to their ethnic identity (*J.W.* 1.25–26). This God was Israel's progenitor, and Israel was God's son (cf. Exod 4:22; Jer 3:19; 31:9; Hos 11:1–4; Tob 13:1–5).⁶² *Israel's* God was attached to and dwelled in— though was not restrained to (Josephus, *Ant.* 2.76–77; 3.179–187; cf. 1 Kgs 8:27–30; Acts 7:48–49)—Israel's ancestral land (Josephus, *Ant.* 8.111–117). God resided in the Jerusalem temple where this god received offerings. There, the people celebrated festivals honoring their deity (*Ant.* 15.248; 4.203–204).⁶³ The Jerusalem temple, like other temples of other peoples, facilitated the familial relationship between Israel and its god and, concomitantly, in forming Jewishness. Unique to Israel, though, was (1) their rejection of worship of other gods (*Ant.* 2.91; 4.201, 180; cf. Deut 6:4), and (2) their claim that their god was above all other deities and would one day be acknowledged by all (Josephus, *Ant.* 1.155; 4.207; 12.265–284; *Ag. Ap.* 2.237; cf. Exod 19:5; Deut 10:17).⁶⁴ Therefore, Israel served—ideally at least —this god alone and only offered sacrifices at the Jerusalem temple: "In no other city let there be either altar or Temple; for God is one and the Hebrew race is one" (Josephus, *Ant.* 4.201; cf. *Ag. Ap.* 2.193; Deut 12:5–14).⁶⁵ Diaspora Jews participated in this centralizing institution through tithes, tax, and pilgrimage. Though scattered throughout the world, devotion to their ancestral god that manifested in loyalty to the cultic system proscribed by their god was integral to Jewish identity.

Nevertheless, ambivalence and even animosity toward the temple system became common in early Judaism. Some contend that most Jewish subgroups emerged from quarrels with the temple establishment.⁶⁶ Critiques were generally twofold. First, they were directed against the priesthood, especially the chief priests, who were seen as corrupt and impure. Therefore, they polluted the temple (CD-B 20; 1QpHab 12).⁶⁷

---

[61] Fredriksen, *Paul*, 32–48, 87–90; idem, "How Jewish Is God? Divine Ethnicity in Paul's Theology," *JBL* 137 (2018): 193–212; Strelan, *Ephesus*, 25–34.

[62] Spilsbury, "God and Israel," 172–91; Marianne Meye Thompson, *The Promise of the Father: Jesus and God in the New Testament* (Louisville, KY: Westminster John Knox, 2000), 35–55.

[63] Jan Willem van Henten, "Josephus, Fifth Evangelist, and Jesus on the Temple," *HTS* 71 (2015): 1–11; Spilsbury, *Image*, 112. Calendrical disputes reiterate the importance of sacred time. Jews disagreed over *how* (or when) to observe the ritual calendar, not *whether* to do so. Stéphane Saulnier, *Calendrical Variations in Second Temple Judaism: New Perspectives on the "Date of the Last Supper" Debate*, JSJSup 159 (Leiden: Brill, 2012).

[64] "In antiquity, all gods exist, and all humans (except perhaps the doughtiest philosophers) knew this ("believed" this) to be the case: the question was what god(s) one showed respect to, and how" (Fredriksen, *Paul*, 216n39; LXX Exod 22:28; *Mos.* 2.26; *Ant.* 3.179–180; cf. Gruen, *Constructs*, 125; Strelan, *Ephesus*, 112–14).

[65] Translated by Spilsbury, *Image*, 112; cf. Lee I. Levine, "Josephus' Description of the Jerusalem Temple: War, Antiquities, and Other Sources," in *Josephus and the History of the Greco-Roman Period: Essays in Memory of Morton Smith*, ed. Fausto Parente and Joseph Sievers (Leiden: Brill, 1994), 233–46.

[66] Wardle, *Jerusalem Temple*, 12, 46–165.

[67] "Defilement of the temple was not seen as an insurmountable problem... The real problem seems to have been when the impurity was not generally recognized" (Wardle, *Jerusalem Temple*, 96); Clemens Thoma, "The High Priesthood in the Judgment of Josephus," in *Josephus, the Bible and History*, ed. Louis H. Feldman and Gôhei Hata (Detroit, MI: Wayne State University Press, 1989), 196–215.

Issues with temple management led the Qumran community to leave Jerusalem and claim their community as God's residing place (1QS 8.5–6; 4QFlorigelium). They were not anti-temple, however (cf. 11QT; 4QMMT). They opposed the way the temple was maintained by the chief priests. Indeed, the Qumran community anticipated a restoration of the Jerusalem temple services (11Q18).[68] Alternative physical temples to Israel's God were established on Mount Gerizim and in Onias, Egypt. These establishments, though, did not reject the importance of cult for worshiping Israel's God but the current Jerusalem temple cult as it was practiced.[69] Second, negativity toward the Second Temple related more to its inferiority to the First Temple (e.g., Ezra 3:10–13) and/or the heavenly or eschatological temple. Emerging apocalyptic perspectives looked beyond the present temple to the future one established by God, made without human hands (e.g., Ezek 40–48; Rev 21:2–4, 22; 1 En. 90:28–34; Jub. 1:17–18, 29; cf. Acts 7:48–50).[70] Nevertheless, the temple cult, even in its imperfect state, remained central to Jewish identity and was a major cause of early Jewish diversity.

2.4.2 Acts and Israel's God

Like Josephus, Luke identifies the God of the Way as "the God of this people Israel (ὁ θεὸς τοῦ λαοῦ τούτου Ἰσραήλ)" who "chose our ancestors" (13:17; cf. Luke 1:16, 68; Acts 3:13). This deity is "the ancestral God (τῷ πατρῴῳ θεῷ)" (24:14). The Jewish people are this God's own (Luke 2:32).[71] Notably, references to the "God of our ancestors" appear in sites of contestation over the message about Jesus, especially Paul's apologies (24:14; cf. 26:6–7). Peter informs the inhabitants and the council of Jerusalem that the ancestral God who chose Abraham and Moses (7:32; 13:17) glorified Jesus (3:13; 5:30). This same God chose Paul as a witness, he tells the angry crowd in the temple (22:14; cf. 9:15). Before Felix in response to the accusations of Tertullus and certain Jews, Paul declares that, "according to the Way, I worship (λατρεύω) the ancestral God, faithful (πιστεύων) to everything written in the Torah and the prophets" (24:14).[72] His way of life is nothing other than Jewish ancestral custom and loyalty to Israel's God. In one fell swoop, Luke highlights Paul's commitment to the familial God, the temple cult, and the Scriptures that delineate Israel's history, identity, and praxis.

The Way honors Israel's cultic calendar. Like Jesus (Luke 4:16), Paul observes the Sabbath. Discussing Jesus' relationship to the Scriptures with other Jews in synagogues is a customary Sabbath activity for Paul (Acts 13:14, 44; 16:13; 17:2; 18:4). Furthermore, that Paul expects to find Jesus-following Jews in the synagogues suggests they continue

---

[68] Lawrence H. Schiffman, "Qumran Temple? The Literary Evidence," *JAJ* 7 (2016): 71–85.
[69] Wardle, *Jerusalem*, 98–165.
[70] Kinzer, *Jerusalem*, 41–76.
[71] Of course, like early Judaism in general, Luke portrays Israel's God as the universal "most-high God" (e.g., Luke 1:32, 35, 76; 8:28; Acts 16:17; 17:24).
[72] λατρεύω commonly refers to cultic worship, especially in the LXX (Barton and Boyarin, *Imagine*, 137, 167; Fredriksen, "Parting," 52; cf. Luke 1:74; 2:37; 4:8; Acts 7:7; 27:23). This valence is likely present since Paul is defending himself against charges of profaning the temple (24:6, 18).

to participate in synagogue life (9:1–2; cf. 1:12; 15:21).⁷³ The Way and Paul also observe major Jewish pilgrim holidays: Pentecost (2:1; 20:16), Passover (20:6), and the Day of Atonement ("the fast," 27:9). Their ritual habits are identifiably Jewish.

2.4.3 Acts and the Jerusalem Temple

As Paul's defense and participation in the pilgrim festivals indicates, Luke depicts the Way's and Paul's engaging in Israel's temple cult and ritual life (2:46; 3:1–10; 5:12–16; 21:17–26; 24:17). Much has been written on the temple in Luke-Acts. Studies often focus on the bottom-line of whether Luke is pro- or anti-temple.⁷⁴ My primary questions attempt to move beyond this binary. First, does Luke's portrait of the temple affirm its role in the Jewish identity of the Way and Paul? Second, do Luke's temple criticisms resemble those of other first-century Jews? The driving issue is whether Luke attacks the temple *qua* the temple or the temple establishment, that is, how the priestly leaders (mis)used the temple.

Unlike certain Jewish sectarian groups like the Qumran community, the Way does not spatially separate from the temple, even amidst its conflicts with the leading priests.⁷⁵ The Way frequents the temple regularly. It is the locus of their preaching, healing, and participation in "the prayers (ταῖς προσευχαῖς)" (2:2, 42, 46; 3:1; 5:42).⁷⁶ When Paul returns to Jerusalem, the temple's centrality for Jesus-followers is evident. The Jerusalem elders tell Paul to quell rumors that he teaches against Torah by contributing to the completion of a Nazirite vow (εὐχήν) of four men (21:17–26; cf. LXX Num 6:1–21), a vow Paul also took (Acts 18:18).⁷⁷ Paul's continued commitment to the Jewish civilization, the elders conclude, can be demonstrated

---

⁷³ Stanley K. Stowers, "The Synagogue in the Theology of Acts," *RestQ* 17 (1974): 129–43; Denis Fortin, "Paul's Observance of the Sabbath in Acts of the Apostles as a Marker of Continuity between Judaism and Early Christianity," *AUSS* 53 (2015): 321–35.

⁷⁴ E.g., Michael Bachmann, *Jerusalem und der Tempel: Die geographisch-theologischen Elemente in der lukanischen Sicht des jüdischen Kultzentrums*, BWANT 109 (Stuttgart: Kohlhammer, 1980); Chance, *Jerusalem*; Brawley, *Jews*, 107–32; Nicholas H. Taylor, "Stephen, the Temple, and Early Christian Eschatology," *RB* 110 (2003): 62–85; Andrés García Serrano, "The Jerusalem Temple According to Luke," *EstB* 71 (2013): 37–56; Gregory R. Lanier, "Luke's Distinctive Use of the Temple: Portraying the Divine Visitation," *JTS* 65 (2014): 433–62; Steve Smith, *The Fate of the Jerusalem Temple in Luke-Acts: An Intertextual Approach to Jesus' Laments over Jerusalem and Stephen's Speech*, LNTS 553 (London: T&T Clark, 2016).

⁷⁵ "If Luke has any animosity towards priests, it is towards the ruling priests in Jerusalem, not towards priests in general." (Rick Strelan, *Luke the Priest: The Authority of the Author of the Third Gospel* [London: Routledge, 2008], 120). Notably, Paul shows respect to the high priest after his initial imprecation (23:3–5).

⁷⁶ The Pentecost event likely occurs in the temple for three main reasons. First, Luke's Gospel refers to the temple as the "house" (Luke 6:4; 11:51; 13:35; 19:46). Second, Pentecost is a pilgrim holiday with prescribed temple sacrifices (Lev 23:15–22). Third, the presence of so many pilgrims who can be baptized immediately suggests an accommodating setting like the temple. Luke's two volumes also place major revelatory events during the daily *tamid* offering (Exod 29:38–40). Dennis Hamm, "The Tamid Service in Luke-Acts: The Cultic Background behind Luke's Theology of Worship (Luke 1:5–25; 18:9–14; 24:50–53; Acts 3:1; 10:3, 30)," *CBQ* 65 (2003): 215–31; Mark S. Kinzer, "Sacrifice, Prayer, and the Holy Spirit: The Tamid Offering in Luke-Acts," in *Wisdom*, 463–75.

⁷⁷ Friedrich Wilhelm Horn, "Paulus, das Nasiräat und die Nasiräer," *NovT* 39 (1997): 117–37; Rudolph, "Luke's Portrait," 192–205.

through participation in the cult. Paul obliges (21:26; 22:17; 24:11–18).[78] His actions attempt to reestablish cohesion with the Jewish nation. Paul recalls this action to reassert his commitment to the temple when challenged. Contra those who accuse him of profaning the temple (21:28; 24:6), Paul was performing a purification ritual (21:26; 24:18). Beyond that, Paul informs his accusers in Jerusalem that he had a vision *in* the temple. He is the kind of pious Jewish-Israelite whom the Lord visits and commissions in the temple (22:17–21; cf. Luke 1:5–23).[79] Paul later reiterates that he came to the temple "to bring alms to my nation and perform offerings" (24:17). His care for the Jewish nation and participation in the temple cult go hand in hand. Luke's Paul worships like a devout Jew.

Stephen's speech voices the primary temple-critique in Acts. His words are quite harsh. Nevertheless, reminiscent of other Jewish internecine disputes about the temple, Stephen's speech attacks the temple as distorted by Israel's leadership, not the temple *qua* the temple. The prophetic quotations (Amos 5:27–27; Isa 66:1–2) suggest that Stephen's critique is that, when coupled with injustice, bloodshed specifically, the temple cult becomes tantamount to idolatry analogous to the Golden Calf (7:39–53; cf. Jer 7:2–33; 4 Ezra 1:25–34).[80] In Amos, God rejected Israel's cultic practices, which God instituted, because of their injustices (5:4–15, 21–22). Israel ignored God's instructions, reproved holy speech (5:10), and mistreated the poor (5:11–12). Likewise, Isaiah lambasts the temple cult because the people are practicing evil (66:3–5). The LXX version makes Isaiah's critique more explicit by addressing "the lawless who sacrifice (ὁ δὲ ἄνομος ὁ θύων)." For these prophets, Israel's deliberate and repeated sins, particularly violence, cause their temple worship to become idolatrous.[81] Therefore, if Stephen's statement that "the Most does not dwell in handmade (χειροποιήτοις) things" implies idolatry (cf. LXX Lev 26:1,10; Isa 2:18; 10:11; 16:12; Dan 5:4, 23; 6:27; Jdt 8:18; Wis 14:8; Acts 7:41; 17:24), it is not necessarily about the temple in and of itself. The issue is the coupling of the temple and wrongdoing. Stephen censures the establishment's corruption of the temple through violation of Torah (like bearing false witness) and practices of injustice (like executing God's messengers). Indeed, in the narrative world, the council reenacts the very behavior Stephen criticizes.

Four details indicate that Stephen's words are not anti-the-temple *qua* the temple. First, Stephen affirms that God's promise to Abraham included the temple ("this place";

---

[78] Paul is the first Jewish character within the narrative—excluding general references to Jewish (Luke 13:1; 22:7) or idolatrous sacrifices (Acts 7:41–42; 14:13, 18; 15:29; 21:25)—to be involved explicitly in offering sacrifices at the temple since Jesus' parents (Luke 2:24).

[79] The shutting of the temple doors (21:30) is likely a sign of judgment (*J.W.* 6.293, 295–96; Chance, *Jerusalem*, 121–22), but it is not the final image of the temple in Acts.

[80] H. Alan Brehm, "Vindicating the Rejected One: Stephen's Speech as a Critique of the Jewish Leaders," in *Early Christian Interpretation of the Scriptures of Israel: Investigations and Proposals*, ed. Craig A. Evans and James A. Sanders (Sheffield: Sheffield Academic, 1997), 266–99; Joel B. Green, "'They Made a Calf': Idolatry and Temple in Acts 7," in *Golden Calf Traditions in Early Judaism, Christianity, and Islam*, ed. Eric F. Mason and Edmondo F. Lupieri (Leiden: Brill, 2018), 132–41.

[81] Parallels with Jer 26 reinforce this reading. Jeremiah warns of coming judgment due to evil deeds, violations of Torah, and ignoring God's prophets (26:3–6). The primary difference, of course, is that the council executes Stephen, shedding innocent blood (26:15), while Jeremiah was spared.

cf. LXX Exod 3:12) as the locus of Israel's worship (Acts 7:7, 33).[82] Stephen acknowledges it as a divinely given institution relevant for Israel's identity and relationship with God. Second, Stephen's primary contrast is not between the mobile tabernacle and Solomon's stationary temple (δέ) but in the clear adversative (ἀλλά) about "handmade things (χειροποιήτοις)" (Acts 7:47–48; cf. 17:24).[83] Jewish thought recognized that the temple could not contain God and still considered it God's dwelling place (e.g., 1 Kgs 8:27–29; 2 Chr 2:5–6; 2 Macc 3:28–39; Josephus, *J.W.* 6.127). Moreover, other early Jewish texts contrasted the inferior "handmade" temple with the heavenly/cosmic or eschatological temple (2 Bar 4:1–6; 4 Ezra 10:25–28; cf. Dan 2:34–35, 44–45; 4 Ezra 13:6–7, 35–36; cf. Philo, *Spec. Laws* 1.66–67; *Mos.* 2.88).[84] Stephen's contrast, then, is likely not about the transcendence of God or the inadequacy of the temple itself. Third, Luke characterizes Stephen's accusers as "false witnesses (μάρτυρας ψευδής)" (cf. LXX Exod 20:16; Deut 5:20). This indicates that, within the narrative, their claims that Stephen speaks against the temple (and Torah) are false (6:13–14). Fourth, Stephen is killed for his heavenly vision, not his speech. His listeners' initial response to his harsh words is anger (7:54; cf. LXX Ps 36:12); they perceive his critique as infuriating but not as blasphemous and warranting death (cf. 6:11). It is not until Stephen describes seeing the exalted Jesus at God's right hand that they move to kill him, indicating that they believe he has now said something that merits execution for blasphemy (7:57–58; cf. Luke 22:67–71). In short, they do not hear Stephen's words as undermining the temple's role as a constitutive element of Israel's tradition as his accusers portend. Instead, Israel's leaders hear his words as targeting them.

Stephen's temple critique, then, is not foreign to the Jewish tradition.[85] Drawing from the prophets, his words sound like other Jewish negative appraisals of the temple as it was being (ab)used by Israel's leaders. Stephen simultaneously affirms God's promise of "this place" and calls the temple God's "house" (Acts 7:7, 46–47) while lambasting its leaders for distorting it to the point of idolatry like their ancestors. His words are not against the temple per se but the leadership's coupling of temple practices with injustice so as to pollute the divinely given institution (cf. 2 Chr 36:14–16).

Luke's narrative contains this same tension overall. The temple is both a place to encounter God (e.g., Luke 1:8–23; 2:22–24, 36–38; 24:53; Acts 2:46–47; 3:1; 21:26; 22:17; 24:18) and a place that Jesus—quoting a text that denounces the assumption that participation in the temple alone would protect the people from judgment even as they practiced injustice (Jer 7:1–29)—calls "a den of robbers" that will be destroyed (Luke

---

[82] "This place" (7:7) is likely a circumlocution for the temple mount (cf. 6:13–14). W. Gil Shin, "Integrated Stories and Israel's Contested Worship Space: Exod 15.17 and Stephen's Retelling of Heilsgeschichte (Acts 7)," *NTS* 64 (2018): 495–513.
[83] That the critique of "the tent of Molech" (τὴν σκηνὴν τοῦ Μολόχ) precedes the initial mention of the tabernacle (7: 43–44) suggests that tents are not inherently better or less susceptible to idolatry than temples. Parallels with Jeremiah's likening of the coming judgment of Jerusalem and its temple to the tent at Shiloh reiterate this point (26:6). Moreover, the tabernacle was "handmade."
[84] Kinzer, *Jerusalem*, 41–76.
[85] Cf. Monica Selvatici, "'The Most High Does Not Dwell in Houses Made with Human Hands': A Study of Possible Hellenistic Jewish Parallels for the Jerusalem Temple as Idolatry in Acts 7:48," *Antí* 10 (2017): 1063–82.

19:45–48; 21:5–6).⁸⁶ Even amidst harsh critique, Stephen does not undermine the importance of the temple for the Jewish ancestral tradition. It remains a central, though often corrupted, part of Israel's national identity.

2.4.4 Summary

Ultimately, Acts maintains the familial, covenantal relationship between Israel's God and the Jewish people. The Way and Paul maintain fidelity to the cultic customs established to honor the relationship with the ancestral deity. Like other early Jewish writings, Acts affirms the temple's prominence in the tradition even amidst criticism of the temple establishment. Despite the temple's corruption, the Way and Paul do not distance themselves from the cult. Ongoing participation in it reflects continued commitment to this central pillar of Judaism. Paul's involvement in a temple ritual importantly reaffirms his fidelity to the Jewish people and tradition. Acts criticizes the temple establishment and explains its destruction. Such criticisms, though, remain at home in the variegated landscape of early Judaism. Indeed, Acts reflects a less sectarian posture than other contemporary Jewish groups; its characters maintain fellowship amidst criticism.

2.5 Shared Custom

2.5.1 Ancestral Custom and Ethnic Identity in Antiquity

Lastly, Herodotus points to common customs, the shared habits that unify and identify the Greeks. Such practices facilitated the formation of Greek identity in contrast to barbarians (*Hist.* 1.60.3; 3.139.1; 7.175.2; cf. Thucydides, *P.W.* 1.5.3–1.6.2). Customs, generally speaking, provide cultural cohesion and strength (*Hist.* 7.101–104): Greekness entails doing Greek things (*Hist.* 1.56–58). One could adopt Greekness by adopting Greek customs (*Hist.* 5.22.2; cf. 2.104.2–3).⁸⁷ In fact, Herodotus and Thucydides highlight the reverse risk of "Medizing" should Greeks submit to Persian rule (*Hist.* 4.144; 7.138–139; 8.30–134; Thucydides, *P.W.* 1.132.1–2; 1.95.5; 3.64.5).⁸⁸ To abandon Greek traditions was to abandon the Greek people.

Josephus emphasizes the importance of common customs for Jewish identity. Torah lies at the heart of Jewish civilization in the land and diaspora (cf. *Ant.* 4.316–331). The Torah, the teachings of Moses, the ultimate lawgiver (*Ant.* 1.18; cf. Philo, *Moses* 2.2–5), forms the Jewish "constitution (πολιτεία)" (*Ant.* 4.198–199; *Ag. Ap.* 2.145, 165, 184, 257).⁸⁹ It shapes and provides solidity in their identity. Therefore, to be Jewish in antiquity is to do Jewish things, to express Jewishness. Jews were known, and sometimes

---

⁸⁶ Green, "Idolatry," 136–39.
⁸⁷ Hall, "Contested Ethnicities," 167–72.
⁸⁸ Mason, *Christian Origins*, 144–49. Of course, Greeks borrowed from other cultures (Rosalind Thomas, "Ethnicity, Genealogy, and Hellenism in Herodotus," in *Ancient Perceptions*, 213–33).
⁸⁹ Spilsbury, *Image*, 13, 94–146; Lucio Troiani, "The πολιτεία of Israel in the Greco-Roman Age," in *Greco-Roman Period*, 11–22.

maligned, for their distinct practices.⁹⁰ Analogous to Greek concerns with "Medizing," some Jews bore reservations about "Hellenizing" (2 Macc 4:10–20; cf. 1 Macc 1:11–15, 43). To abandon Jewish practices in favor of Greek ones was, in essence, to leave the Jewish ethnic group for Greekness (e.g., Josephus, *J.W.* 7. 47–53; cf. 4 Macc 4:26).⁹¹ Jews were thus willing to fight and die out of loyalty to their ancestral laws, their people, and their god (*Ant.* 5.90; 12.271; *Ag. Ap.* 2.218–219, 232–235; cf. 1 Macc 2:27; 2 Macc 7).⁹² Their constitution and its customs were crucial to their peoplehood.

2.5.2 Acts and Jewish Ancestral Custom

Torah observance in Luke-Acts has been long recognized.⁹³ Instead of rehashing this well-worn conversation, my brief comments focus on how Luke reiterates the Way and Paul's Torah piety in sites of negotiation and contention of Jewish identity. For the Way, Luke implicitly affirms Torah for Jewish Jesus-followers when gentiles are incorporated. At the house of Simon the tanner, Peter has a repeated vision of clean and unclean animals that represents God's provision of the "the repentance into life" for the gentiles (10:9–16; 11:4–9).⁹⁴ Although traditionally understood as annulling *kashrut*, the vision pertains to people rather than meat for three reasons.⁹⁵ First, Peter never eats the animals so he avoids violating *kashrut*. Like Ezekiel, Peter objects to God's request for Peter to defile himself (10:14; cf. Ezek 4:9–15). Unlike Ezekiel, for whom God makes concessions but still requires that he carry out the symbolic action, God does not require Peter to eat. God simply corrects him for calling "common" what God has cleansed (ἐκαθάρισεν; 10:15). Second, Peter does not perceive the vision to be about food; rather, like most visions, its significance lies beyond the surface (10:17; cf. Dan 2:29–30; 8:15; 9:21–23). Subsequent interpretations of the vision reiterate that the vision refers only to people (10:28, 34–35; 11:12).⁹⁶ Third, rather than dissolving the clean–unclean and holy–common distinction, God affirms them by *cleansing* the gentiles. God brings gentiles into the sphere of the holy and clean. The arrival of the Holy Spirit

---

⁹⁰ Boyarin, *Judaism*, 34–48; Oliver, *Torah Praxis*, 5–10; Gager, *Origins*, 35–112; Isaac, *Racism*, 481–500; cf. Gruen, *Constructs*, 265–80, 312–32.

⁹¹ Jipp, "Paul," 62. On the flip side, "Judaizing" entailed adopting Jewish practices—circumcision specifically—to become Jewish (cf. Josephus, *Ant.* 11.285). Some in the Greco-Roman world perceived "Judaizing" as a threat since converts would abandon civic cults, risking the wrath of the gods (Fredriksen, *Paul*, 32–48, 87–90; Boyarin, *Judaism*, 48–59; Spilsbury, *Image*, 215). To be sure, the relationship between Judaism and Hellenism was a sliding scale (Barclay, *Mediterranean Diaspora*; Strelan, *Ephesus*, 172–84; Gruen, *Constructs*, 1–131).

⁹² Spilsbury, *Image*, 13, 143, 149.

⁹³ E.g., Jervell, *People of God*, 134–37; George P. Carras, "Observant Jews in the Story of Luke-Acts," in *Unity*, 693–708; Böttrich, "Lukanische Doppelwerk," 173–75; Oliver, *Torah Praxis*; Kinzer, *Jerusalem*, 160–224; cf. Stephen G. Wilson, *Luke and the Law*, SNTSMS 50 (Cambridge: Cambridge University Press, 2005).

⁹⁴ On tanning's irrelevance for purity concerns, see Isaac W. Oliver, "Simon Peter Meets Simon the Tanner: The Ritual Insignificance of Tanning in Ancient Judaism," *NTS* 59 (2013): 50–60.

⁹⁵ For a recent reaffirmation of the traditional reading, see Cowan, *Writings*, 148–49.

⁹⁶ Jason A. Staples, "'Rise, Kill, and Eat': Animals as Nations in Early Jewish Visionary Literature and Acts 10," *JSNT* 42 (2019): 3–17; David B. Woods, "Interpreting Peter's Vision in Acts 10:9–16," *Conspectus* 13 (2012): 171–214; Willie James Jennings, *Acts: A Theological Commentary on the Bible*, Belief (Louisville, KY: Westminster John Knox Press, 2017), 112–18.

affirms their newfound holiness.⁹⁷ Peter affirms his loyalty to Jewish ancestral custom in not violating Torah while gradually acknowledging God's sanctifying actions among the gentiles (11:1–18).

The Jerusalem Council presumes the centrality of Torah for Jewish Jesus-followers when gentiles are included (15:1–21). Undergirding the debate about whether gentiles need to be circumcised and adopt the Torah *in toto* to be saved—that is, whether they need to become Jews—is the assumption that Jewish Jesus-followers continue to practice these things.⁹⁸ The Jerusalem Council rules that gentiles must adopt some modicum of Torah, primarily abstention from idolatry (15:19–29). Gentiles must abandon their ancestral cults and certain practices. They are expected to observe Torah's requirements for gentiles who live in fellowship with Israel (cf. Lev 17–18).⁹⁹ Gentile Jesus-followers are expected to live somewhat "Jewishly," despite not becoming Jews. Torah continues to facilitate Jew-gentile identity and interaction within the nascent Jesus movement.

Paul is more complicated. Luke retains accusations of "apostasy" against Paul. He, some claim, teaches others to abandon Moses, circumcision, and "not to observe the customs (μηδὲ τοῖς ἔθεσιν περιπατεῖν)" (21:21). Acts preserves these conceptions of Paul as *misconceptions*, though. These accusations enable Paul to refute them by affirming his loyalty to the Jewish civilization.¹⁰⁰ Thus, Paul's Torah observance becomes emphatic in his trial scenes. Rather than depicting greater distance between Paul and Jewish tradition, Acts paints his Jewishness with more vivid colors as the story progresses.

After he hears the accusations against him, Paul immediately participates in the Nazirite vow to refute them (21:17–26). Paul verbally defends his loyalty to Moses and the ancestral customs before his Jewish brethren when it continues to be attacked (24:11–21; 25:8–10; 26:4–7; 28:17–18). Not only that, Luke waits to reveal Paul's Pharisaic identity until his fidelity to the people and their tradition is questioned. Paul informs the angry crowd that the famed Gamaliel was his teacher. Therefore, Paul was trained in and adhered to the most precise school of interpretation within the Jewish tradition (κατὰ ἀκρίβειαν τοῦ πατρῴου νόμου; 22:3; cf. Josephus, *J.W.* 1.110; 2.162).

---

97 Contra Böttrich, "Lukanische Doppelwerk," 175. Staples contends that Peter initially conflates the categories of "clean–unclean" and "holy–common," but the heavenly voice leads him to differentiate them, as Torah does ("Rise," 11–14). Cf. David M. Moffitt, "Atonement at the Right Hand: The Sacrificial Significance of Jesus' Exaltation in Acts," *NTS* 62 (2016): 549–68; Thiessen, *Contesting*, 127–37.

98 Richard Bauckham, "James and the Jerusalem Community," in *Jewish Believers in Jesus: The Early Centuries*, ed. Oskar Skarsaune and Reidar Hvalvik (Peabody, MA: Hendrickson, 2007), 55–95; Craig C. Hill, "The Jerusalem Church," in *Jewish Christianity Reconsidered: Rethinking Ancient Groups and Texts*, ed. Matt A. Jackson-McCabe (Minneapolis, MN: Fortress, 2007), 39–56; Oliver, *Torah Praxis*, 445–82. Paul's circumcision of Timothy reaffirms circumcision for Jewish Jesus-followers (16:1–3). Including baptism as an initiation rite, therefore, does not undermine other Jewish identifying rites. Cf. Balch, *Contested*, 102–17.

99 On reading these instructions as the commands for aliens residing in Israel (Lev 17–18), see Thiessen, *Contesting*, 111–47; Stroup, *Christians*, 80–94. On their being a nascent form of the Noahide laws, see Eckhard J. Schnabel, *Acts*, ZECNT (Grand Rapids: Zondervan, 2012), 500; cf. Markus Bockmuehl, *Jewish Law in Gentile Churches: Halakhah and the Beginning of Christian Public Ethics* (Grand Rapids, MI: Baker Academic, 2003), 87–143.

100 Cf. Jipp, "Paul," 62, 73–75.

Such identifications place Paul firmly among those whom the crowd might consider Israel's most faithful. His fidelity goes beyond the average Jewish person. Paul reiterates his Pharisaic legacy and beliefs before the Sanhedrin and Agrippa to claim his innocence and continuity with Israel's hopes (23:6–10; 26:5). Luke's Paul leverages his Pharisaic identity, the crowning jewel of his Jewishness, when it carries the most weight: refuting accusations by demonstrating his ongoing loyalty to Judaism.

2.5.3 Summary

The centrality of the Torah for Jewish identity, including that of the Way and Paul, remains intact in Acts. Even gentiles who join the Way engage in some measure of Torah observance. Some have accused Paul of violating Torah and profaning the temple but Acts undermines such claims by portraying Paul as a faithful Jew, a loyal Pharisee at that. At the narrative's end, Paul can claim for himself and on behalf of the Way unflinching fidelity to the Jewish people and Israel's ancestral traditions (28:17–19). Their continued commitment to Jewish kinship, history, language, land, and way of life marks them as nothing other than Jewish.

2.6 The Way as Jewish Subgroup

Luke's construction of the Way and Paul retains the core dimensions of early Jewish identity. They self-identify as Jews and consider other Jews family. Acts reiterates their ongoing links with Israel's ancestral history/Scripture, land, language, cult, and custom (24:14). The Way and Paul continue to socialize with other Jews, even those with whom they might disagree. In short, Luke portrays the Way as a Jewish group engaging with other Jews about Jewish belief and praxis.

Two potential complications for understanding Luke's portrait of the Way and Paul within Judaism arise, however. First, the Way and Paul make clear exclusivist truth claims. They call all Jews to repent and accept Jesus as Israel's Messiah. This has led many to claim that the Way constitutes "realized," "fulfilled," or "true Judaism," and/or that the Christian movement emerges as the sole inheritors of Israel's tradition. The rest of Judaism becomes defunct.[101] Such exclusivism, however problematic one might consider it to be, can still have a place within the diversity of early Judaism. When compared to Josephus' descriptions of the various Jewish schools (αἵρεσις) and the Qumran community, the Way in Acts appears to be a Jewish reform movement that pursues renewal within Judaism—not an introversionist group seeking separation

---

[101] E.g., Gerhard Lohfink, *Die Sammlung Israels: Eine Untersuchung zur lukanischen Ekklesiologie*, SANT 39 (München: Kösel, 1975), 55; Conzelmann, *Apostelgeschichte*, 148, 158–60; C. K. Barrett, *Acts*, 2 vols., ICC (London: T&T Clark, 1994–1998), 2:1241; cf. 1:283, 2:1103; F. F. Bruce, *The Book of Acts*, 3rd ed., NICNT (Grand Rapids, MI: Eerdmans, 1988) 10, 444; I. Howard Marshall, *The Acts of the Apostles: An Introduction and Commentary*, TNTC (Grand Rapids, MI: Eerdmans, 1996), 28–30; Joseph A. Fitzmyer, *The Acts of the Apostles*, AB (New Haven, CT: Yale University Press, 1998), 735; Carl R. Holladay, *Acts: A Commentary*, NTL (Louisville, KY: Westminster John Knox, 2016), 509.

from the parent tradition.[102] Second, one might argue that the inclusion of gentiles moves the Way beyond the Jewish ancestral tradition. Gentile inclusion has a place within early Jewish thought, though. Indeed, gentiles participated in Jewish institutions prior to the Way's emergence. In continuity with this stream of thought, Acts depicts gentile inclusion as the beginning of the anticipated ingathering of the "eschatological gentiles," members of the nations who come alongside Israel to worship Israel's God.[103]

2.6.1 Jewish Subgroups in Josephus

Josephus again provides a helpful analogue and framework for considering Jewish subgroups in Acts. His writings famously portray the various groups within "the Jewish philosophy" as philosophical schools using the term αἵρεσις (J.W. 2.119–166; Life 10–12; Ant. 13.292–298, 311). He describes the peculiarities of these groups in their beliefs, practices, and relations to other Jews. This final category about social distance between groups—that is, degree of interaction—is particularly relevant for considering the Way's exclusivism. As Josephus reports, some Jewish groups are more insulated than others.[104]

The Essenes "are Jewish kin, but also care for each other more than the others (Ἰουδαῖοι μὲν γένος ὄντες, φιλάλληλοι δὲ καὶ τῶν ἄλλων πλέον)" (J.W. 2.119). They bear the Jewish familial ties but privilege their inner group over others in the family. Although they exercise care and hospitality toward one another, their beliefs and practices tend toward insulation from the wider Jewish populace (e.g., 2.127–133). Initiates, Josephus states, were called "always to hate the unrighteous" (2.139). Other Jews can join the group, despite its rigidity, though not easily. Josephus notes the difficulties of the entrance process (2.138–142). The Essenes also could expel members for egregious sins (2.143–144), even conducting capital punishment for blasphemers of God or Moses (2.145; cf. Acts 6:11). The Essenes maintained relatively strict exclusionary boundaries. Yet, even their boundaries were semi-porous.

In contrast, "the Pharisees care for each other and also practice harmony with the common folk (Φαρισαῖοι μὲν φιλάλληλοί τε καὶ τὴν εἰς τὸ κοινὸν ὁμόνοιαν ἀσκοῦντες)" (J.W. 2.166). Their beliefs and traditions did not preclude concord with other Jews and subgroups. In fact, their traditions developed to advance the faithfulness of all Israel (Ant. 13.296–298). It is unsurprising that they were the most popular school among the general Jewish populace (cf. J.W. 1.571; Ant. 13.298). This, the most precise and respected subgroup, fraternized with Jews of all stripes, welcoming them to adopt their form of the ancestral tradition (J.W. 1.110; 2.162).

By contrast, Josephus reports that the Sadducees were harsh in their practices (τὸ ἦθος ἀγριώτερον) to each other and to strangers (ἀλλοτρίους; J.W. 2.166). They had the support of the wealthy, not the wider populace (Ant. 13.298). The Sadducees stood to some degree at odds with the wider Jewish world. Nevertheless, at least in Acts, the

---

[102] Baumgarten, "Sects," 265; MacIntyre, Whose Justice, 349–403.
[103] "Eschatological gentiles" is from Fredriksen, Paul, 49–60.
[104] Baumgarten, "Sects," 261–65.

Sadducees shared the Sanhedrin with Pharisees (Acts 23:6–9); Sadducees too maintained contact and relations with the Jewish populace and divergent groups.[105]

Josephus also uses αἵρεσις to describe the Fourth Philosophy, a group he detests and blames for the failed revolution (*Ant.* 18:2–6). This group is the most hostile of the subgroups, being the only one that openly harmed their kin. They, Josephus claims, committed atrocities against their fellow Jews (e.g., *J.W.* 4.134; 7.259). In fact, the Sicarii at Masada considered Jews who submitted to Rome to be "foreigners (ἀλλοφύλων . . . διαφέρειν)" and treated them as "enemies (πολεμίοις)" (*J.W.* 7.253–155).[106] For this reason, Josephus thinks the Fourth Philosophy innovates the ancestral tradition in dangerous ways (*Ant.* 18.23). They are, for Josephus, an "intrusive philosophy (φιλοσοφίαν ἐπείσακτον)" (18.9).[107] Nevertheless, the so-called Fourth Philosophy never claimed to be something other than adherence to and defense of the Jewish tradition. Even Josephus, amidst his critiques, frames it as a (deviant) Jewish group.

Josephus illustrates the diversity of Judaism, its subgroups, and its intergroup interactions. Each subgroup, with their unique beliefs and practices, maintained varying degrees of fellowship, exclusivity, and self-identification with other Jews. Each might perceive its form of the Jewish tradition as correct and hoped others would join their movement and/or adhere to their views, none held a monopoly on the tradition, nonetheless. Subgroups might perceive other Jews as unfaithful to the ancestral tradition, but they typically considered them members of Israel.[108] Differences could cause violence in extreme cases. Still, none of the subgroups Josephus highlights, even those with exclusivist demands, claim to be something other than Judaism. Each considered itself acting on behalf of and for the sake of God, the people, and the tradition. Josephus, then, provides criteria for evaluating Luke's portrait of the Way vis-à-vis Judaism. To determine whether the Way remains a Jewish subgroup in Acts—which, in turn, suggests Acts' own posture vis-à-vis Judaism—self-definitions, perceptions of and interactions with Jews outside the group, extent of their exclusivity, and the degree of innovations must be considered.

2.6.2 Jewish Subgroups in Acts

Like Josephus, Luke uses αἵρεσις to identify different Jewish groups. The first two times Acts uses αἵρεσις, it refers to well-established, mainstream subgroups, namely, the Sadducees (5:17) and the Pharisees (15:5). Here, as in Josephus (cf. *Ant.* 13.171, 288, 293), a αἵρεσις simply is a discrete "school," a form of understanding and maintaining the Jewish way of life.[109] These groups, Luke recognizes, maintain different beliefs and

---

[105] Ibid., 265.
[106] Ibid.
[107] Pieter W. van der Horst, "*Philosophia Epeisaktos*: Some Notes on Josephus, *A.J.* 18.9," in *The Jewish Revolt against Rome: Interdisciplinary Perspectives*, ed. Mladen Popovic (Leiden: Brill, 2011), 311–22. Cf. Rajak, *Josephus*, 78–104; Valentin Nikiprowetzky, "Josephus and the Revolutionary Parties," in *Bible and History*, 216–36.
[108] Bergsma, "Qumran," 176–89; Staples, *Israel*, 259–89.
[109] That αἵρεσις insinuates a Jewish subgroup remains valid regardless of whether Luke depicts Judaism as a "philosophical group" (cf. Cowan, *Writings*, 151–54).

particular practices, which sometimes causes conflicts between them (cf. Luke 5:33–38; 11:37–38). Paul cleverly exploits these divergences before the Sanhedrin (Acts 23:7–8). He self-identifies with one group, the Pharisees, in contrast to the other. Paul's membership in the Way, his belief in Jesus' messianic identity, does not preclude ongoing affiliation with Pharisees.

Characters in Acts also label the Way as a Jewish αἵρεσις (24:5, 14; 26:5; 28:22). This is not a self-designation, its application to the Way is still appropriate, however. The Way claims continuity with the ancestral tradition while concomitantly proclaiming to be the tradition's most faithful manifestation. Of course, the Way calls its fellow Jews to join its ranks. Such activity was not novel. The movement does not claim to be discontinuous or separate from the Jewish way of life. Indeed, Jews and gentiles alike perceive the Way as a Jewish group. The Sanhedrin treats the apostles and Paul as internal problems they must address (4:1–21; 6:11–15; 23:26–30). For example, the council flogs the disciples, tacitly acknowledging the movement's place under the council's jurisdiction, that is, within Judaism (5:40). Saul similarly seeks the high priest's approval to pursue members of the Way because he expects to find them in synagogues (9:1–2; 22:5; 26:10–11). The Way is indistinguishable from other Jewish groups to gentile eyes (16:19–24; 19:23–41). As far as imperial leaders can tell, debates between the Way and the Jews are about the Jewish tradition and law (18:13–15; 25:19). Insiders and outsiders alike perceive the Way as a Jewish group discussing Judaism with other Jews.[110]

Significantly, the Way and Paul have more favorable relations with the wider Jewish world than other Jewish groups that Josephus describes. They socialize with Jews with whom they disagree. Unlike the Qumran community, the Way does not dramatically distance themselves to form their own groups and observe their own practices. The Way and Paul, despite some disagreements and conflict, maintain ongoing participation in Israel's ritual life. Entrance into the Way is far easier than with the Essenes (e.g., 2:37–42). Participation in the Way does not preclude affiliating with other Jewish groups. Levites like Barnabas (4:36), priests (6:7), and Pharisees (15:1), including Paul (22:3; 23:6), join the Way and continue to identify with these other groups.[111]

---

[110] As some claim that Χριστιανοί suggests that the Way becomes (or was becoming) something identifiably distinct Judaism (e.g., Tyson, "Christian," 140; Cowan, Writings, 157–58), four observations are apropos: (1) Χριστιανοί is not a self-identification. It is likely given by outsiders. By whom it is given is not clear. (2) The term simply means "Christ-followers" and is given to followers of the one called Christ. "Christian" could simply be an identifier akin to "party of the Nazarenes," which refers to the Jewish subgroup loyal to Jesus of Nazareth (24:5). (3) Although the term might refer to a mixed group initially, if one understands Ἑλληνιστάς (11:20) as Greeks instead of Greek-speaking Jews (cf. 6:1; 9:29), gentile participation need not preclude identifying the Antioch community as Jewish. Diaspora synagogues were mixed (e.g., 13:16, 48). (4) The other instances of "Christian" appear in solidarity with Jewish believers and Judaism. The Antioch community establishes continuity with Jerusalem (11:27–30). The final use appears in the mouth of Agrippa after Paul's expression of solidarity with the Jewish tradition (26:2–8, 22–23). As such, it need not imply an entity distinct *from* Judaism, even as it emerges as an identifiable (sub)group. Cf. Justin Taylor, "Why Were the Disciples First Called 'Christians' at Antioch? (Acts 11, 26)," RevBib 101 (1994): 75–94; Rowe, World, 126–35; Regev, "Early Christians," 790.

[111] Contra Marshall, Acts, 249, who reads Pharisaic believers as former Pharisees.

Unlike the Fourth Philosophy, the Way and Paul do not treat other Jews like foreigners or enemies. Neither does the Way commit violent acts toward other Jews.[112] Like the Pharisees as described by Josephus, the Way is popular among the common people amid tensions with the Sadducees (e.g., 5:13, 17). The Way appears as nothing other than a group within Judaism that, like other Jewish schools, sought to advance the ancestral tradition.

Why, then, might Paul quibble with the designation αἵρεσις for the Way (24:14)?[113] The answer, I suggest, lies in the frequent misconception of *what kind* of αἵρεσις the Way is, namely, whether the movement threatens Rome with revolution.[114] Of course, the primary contention between the Way and the wider Jewish world, Israel's leaders in particular, involves the messianic identity of Jesus (4:1–21; 5:17–40; cf. 13:13–14:7; 21:13; 25:19; 28:23). The repeated concern about or charge against the Way is that they appear to be a potentially revolutionary or seditious messianic movement that threatens the well-being of the Jewish people living under Roman rule (e.g., 24:5–6).[115] The Messiah they preach, in the eyes of some Jewish leaders, misled the nation and, therefore, was executed as "king of the Jews" (Luke 23:1–5, 13–25, 37–38). For the Jerusalem leaders, preaching the resurrection, which was closely associated with Israel's restoration, could easily stir the crowds to revolt (Acts 4:1–3; cf. Luke 19:29–48).[116] Therefore, the chief priests and the Sadducees arrest them in an attempt to silence their preaching (5:17–28). Numerous characters perceive the Way and Paul as insurrectionists. Gamaliel compares the nascent Jesus movement to two failed revolutionary movements led by Theudas and Judas the Galilean (5:35–39).[117] A Roman tribune similarly mistakes Paul for "the Egyptian who stirred up and led four-thousand men of the Sicarii into the wilderness" (21:38). Tertullus levies the title "the group of the Nazoreans (τῆς τῶν Ναζωραίων αἱρέσεως)" against the Way. By referring to the executed messianic claimant, Jesus of Nazareth, Tertullus alludes to their potentially seditious nature (24:1–9; cf. 28:22).

Paul, of course, refutes these charges (21:39; 24:10–22; cf. 26:2–32). Rather than being a seditious movement, "according to the Way (κατὰ τὴν ὁδόν)" describes the particular manner by which Paul worships the ancestral God. He follows the Jewish tradition "in this way (οὕτως)." This suggests that his beliefs and practices, and those of the Way, correspond to the Jewish ancestral religion; it does not deviate from Judaism. It is a form of the tradition in accord with the Scriptures (23:14–15). In other words, Paul does not eschew the label αἵρεσις to deny the Jewishness of the Way; rather, he denies potential revolutionary connotations associated with the Way. It *is* a Jewish messianic movement, but not the seditious variety.

---

[112] Violence and Paul's turns to the gentiles will be addressed in subsequent chapters.
[113] E.g., Conzelmann, *Apostelgeschichte*, 141; Barrett, *Acts*, 2:1104; Marshall, *Acts*, 377; Bruce, *Book of Acts*, 444; Schnabel, *Acts*, 959.
[114] For a foray into Luke-Acts and empire, see David M. Rhoads, David Esterline, and Jae-won Lee, eds., *Luke-Acts and Empire: Essays in Honor of Robert L. Brawley*, PTMS 151 (Eugene, OR: Pickwick, 2011).
[115] Rowe, *World*, 53–89; Keener, "Paul and Sedition," 201–24.
[116] Anderson, *God Raised*; Bauckham, "Restoration"; Oliver, *Eschatology*, 127–31.
[117] Regardless of potential anachronism, including Theudas highlights perceptions of the Way as a violent messianic movement (Keener, *Acts*, 2:1230–37; Rowe, *World*, 71–79).

If Paul sought to distance the Way from its identification as a Jewish αἵρεσις entirely, one would expect a stronger statement than simply "which they call a subgroup (ἣν λέγουσιν αἵρεσιν)" (24:14). Acts could have put an explicit corrective ("which they *wrongly* call a subgroup"), an adversative conjunction ("*although* they call it a subgroup"), or at least a pronoun for emphasis ("which *they* call a subgroup"). As it is, Paul just acknowledges the label without rejecting or adopting it wholesale.[118] Paul's ambivalent response suggests that the label αἵρεσις fits insofar as it identifies the Way as a form of the ancestral tradition. It is inappropriate if coupled with revolutionary connotations (24:13). The Way is not a Fourth Philosophy-type group; it is more akin to the Pharisees and the Sadducees (cf. *Ant.* 18:2–6). Notably, Paul ignores the Roman Jewish leadership's more neutral application of αἵρεσις to the Way (28:22). When applied in this general sense, then, the Way can fairly be labeled as a αἵρεσις, a Jewish subgroup, akin to those described by Josephus.

2.6.3 The Way's Jewish Exclusivism

Identifying the Way as a αἵρεσις alongside Josephus helps contextualize Lukan exclusivism within Judaism. Ongoing proximity and engagement with other Jews, as well as how Jews of all stripes join the Way and still retain subgroup identity, renders the boundaries established by the Way's truth claims more porous; they do not erase the borders. The Way critiques and calls other Jews to repent and join its movement. Acts establishes an inner group within Israel. These boundaries are analogous to those constructed by the competing claims of other early Jewish subgroups.[119] Two observations from Jewish literature outside of Josephus reinforce that Acts' rhetoric reflects and participates in debates about proper interpretation of and adherence to the Jewish tradition. First, critiques and exhortations were common to Israel's sacred texts and early Judaism (e.g., LXX Deut 32:4–9, 19–27; LXX Ps 77:8; *J.W.* 4.163–192). Rebuking Israel for infidelity and warning of judgment, even using appalling rhetoric at times (e.g., Ezek 16; 23; cf. Hos 2), was a time-honored tradition. It frequently explains Israel's present circumstances (Neh 9:5–37; Dan 9:2–19; 2 Bar 41:1–3; 4 Ezra 1:5–40). Acts continues this tradition of prophetic rebuke and exhortation to repent (e.g., 2:40; 3:26; 4:23–31; 6:8–7:60; 13:40–47).[120]

Second, exclusivist claims are common in Israel's tradition. The prophets demand that the people return to sole worship of Israel's God (e.g., Isa 42:8–25; Jer 10:1–25). Often, the Scriptures depict only a remnant of faithful in Israel (e.g., 1 Kgs 17–19; Isa

---

[118] Cf. Brawley, *Jews*, 97–100; Parsons, *Acts*, 328; Cowan, *Writings*, 161–62.

[119] If Luke eschews αἵρεσις due to his exclusivist claims rather than potential revolutionary connotations, the Way could still be read as seeking to unify disparate subgroups *within Judaism*. It need not insinuate that the new movement is something other than the Jewish ancestral tradition. On how post-70 CE Judaism sought to transcend sectarianism and foster unity, see Shaye J. D. Cohen, "The Significance of Yavneh: Pharisees, Rabbis, and the End of Jewish Sectarianism," *HUCA* 55 (1984): 27–53.

[120] "The book of Deuteronomy is even constructed with such a sense of an ending in which Moses' speech, uttered before the fact, announces destruction which verges on the utter annihilation of Israel" (Tiede, "Glory," 25; similarly, Schaefer, *Zukunft*, 33–308; McWhirter, *Rejected*, 11–19).

10:20–23). The Qumran community identifies itself in comparable ways.¹²¹ They are the faithful among Israel and the prolepsis of the renewed people. The rest of Israel must repent, lest they be judged when God condemns the wicked (e.g., CD 1.14–2.1; 1QS 1–3, 8–9; 1QpHab 12). In Acts, the Way similarly emerges as the core of restored Israel. Those outside the movement must repent, lest they be removed from the people (3:23; 13:41–46). Both Qumran and the Way allow one to join and hope that all Israel will one day participate in the restoration of the nation. In the meantime, faithful and unfaithful Jews constitute Israel together.¹²² Beyond that, the Way is less extreme in its exclusivism than the Qumran community. The Way engages in active outreach to unfaithful Israel and actively seeks their incorporation in the renewed people.

When compared to the prophetic critiques of Israel's Scriptures and the diversity of the Second Temple world, specifically the schools described by Josephus and the Qumran community, the Way as Luke paints it appears to be a reformist group adapting the Jewish tradition-in-crisis.¹²³ The Way's exclusivist tendencies, innovations, and exhortations to repentance resemble other Jewish groups of the time who vied for Israel to adhere to their interpretations of the tradition. The Way depicted in Acts does not try to separate from its parent tradition; it speaks from "within Judaism." It is a renewal movement that claims to be the proper understanding of the Jewish way of life and, therefore, invites all Jews to join it lest they face judgment. Still, the Way's exclusivism seeks the good of the people and their tradition through reform. They beckon their fellow Jews to greater commitment to their ancestral customs, albeit a particular way of observing them, and to realign with the activities of their people's God, albeit as interpreted through Jesus, Israel's Messiah.¹²⁴ The movement is *quasi-sectarian*. They are exclusivists, not separatists.

2.6.4 Gentile Inclusion and the Jewishness of the Way

The question of whether large-scale gentile inclusion would push the Way and Acts beyond the borders of Judaism remains—especially if Acts originates from a time when gentiles formed the majority. *En masse* gentile inclusion need not move the Way outside Judaism for two primary reasons. First, incorporation of gentiles in Jewish communal life is not novel. Other peoples were included among or alongside the Israelites since their foundational event, the exodus. The "children of Israel" (בְּנֵי־יִשְׂרָאֵל; οἱ υἱοὶ Ἰσραήλ) emerged from Egypt with a "mixed multitude" (עֵרֶב רַב; ἐπίμικτος πολύς; Exod 12:37–38). Notably, Exodus distinguishes this group from the Israelites (cf. LXX Num 11:4; 2 Esd 13:3; Ezek 30:5).¹²⁵ Israel's Scriptures and other early Jewish

---

¹²¹ See Trebilco, *Self-Designations*, 253–57, for additional comparisons with Qumran.
¹²² Stendahl, "Qumran," 134–42; Bergsma, "Qumran," 176–78, 187–89; Regev, "Early Christians," 781–93; Moessner, *Luke*, 292–301; Staples, *Israel*, 259–89.
¹²³ MacIntyre, *Whose Justice*, 349–403; Regev, "Early Christians," 772–81.
¹²⁴ On how repentance can entail deepening commitment to one's present tradition, see Gaventa, *Darkness*, 9–12; Green, *Conversion*, 45–86.
¹²⁵ To be sure, the mixed multitude likely becomes incorporated into Israel. Nevertheless, the text differentiates between groups. LXX Ezekiel distinguishes "all the multitudes and the sons of the covenant (πάντες οἱ ἐπίμικτοι καὶ τῶν υἱῶν τῆς διαθήκης)." The ἐπίμικτος in Israel were separated under Nehemiah's reforms (2 Esd 13:3). Cf. Gruen, *Constructs*, 95–111.

texts note the participation of aliens in the midst of Israel (e.g., Exod 12:48–49; 20:10; 22:20; 23:9; 23:12) and the incorporation of non-Jews in the house of Israel (e.g., Ruth 1:16–17; Jdt 14:10; Jos. Asen.).[126] The synagogue, according to Acts, too has gentiles in its midst in the form of Godfearers (e.g., 13:16; 14:1; 17:4). Some gentiles participated in early Jewish life and custom to certain degrees.[127] Throughout Jewish history, foreigners dwelt among Israel and Jews and participated variously in their customs without fundamentally altering the identity of the people and their tradition.

Second, some Jews expected a mass turning of the gentiles as part of God's eschatological activities. Certain streams within Israel's Scriptures and early Judaism expected a time when the gentile nations *en masse* would come alongside Israel to worship of Israel's God and learn Torah (e.g., Isa 2:2–4; 42:1–9; 52:7–10; 55:5–9; 56:6–8; LXX Zech 8:20–23; Amos 9:11–15; Mic 4:1–5).[128] In fact, Luke's Jesus relays that the Scriptures foretell the "repentance and forgiveness of sins to all the nations" (μετάνοιαν καὶ ἄφεσιν ἁμαρτιῶν εἰς πάντα τὰ ἔθνη; Luke 24:47). These prophets envision the ingathering of the gentiles *as gentiles*. They neither become Israel nor are integrated into it (e.g., Isa 19:19–25). They worship God as Israel and as the nations, respectively.[129]

It is no surprise, then, that the Jerusalem Council reasons that it is witnessing the anticipated repentance of the gentiles. In response, they uphold ethnic distinctions embedded in the prophetic vision. They acknowledge that God does not distinguish between Jew and gentile in cleansing both through Jesus (15:9).[130] The restoration of David's tent leads to (ὅπως) the inclusion of the nations called by God's name (15:16–17; cf. 3:25). The Jerusalem Council concludes that they are seeing the manifestation of the prophetic expectation of Israel and the nations coming together in common worship of Israel's God (cf. Isa 42:1–9; 49:1–12). In response, the leadership calls

---

[126] Such figures often remain differentiated from genealogical Israel, even as their children are absorbed into the people. For example, Ruth remains "the Moabite" (1:22; 2:2, 21; 4:5, 10). Jon D. Levenson, "The Universal Horizon of Biblical Particularism," in *Ethnicity and the Bible*, ed. Mark G. Brett, BibInt 19 (Leiden: Brill, 1996), 143–69; John Goldingay, *Israel's Faith*, Old Testament Theology 2 (Downers Grove, IL: InterVarsity Press, 2006), 192–209; Matthew Thiessen, "Revisiting the Προσήλυτος in 'the LXX,'" *JBL* 132 (2013): 333–50; Jill Hicks-Keeton, *Arguing with Aseneth: Gentile Access to Israel's "Living God" in Jewish Antiquity* (New York: Oxford University Press, 2018).

[127] Fredriksen, *Paul*, 49–60; idem, "Godfearers," 25–33; J. Andrew Overman, "The God-Fearers: Some Neglected Features," *JSNT* 32 (1988): 17–26; Chilton, "Godfearers," 55–72; Levinskaya, *Diaspora*, 51–126.

[128] Malka Z. Simkovich, *The Making of Jewish Universalism: From Exile to Alexandria* (Lanham, MD: Lexington Books, 2016).

[129] This is not novel to the wider Jewish world: "Exclusive for insiders (Jews in principle should not worship foreign gods), the synagogue was inclusive for outsiders (interested Gentiles were welcomed). Thus pagans *as pagans* could be found together with Jews in the Diaspora synagogue. So too, until 66 CE, could they be found in Jerusalem, in the largest court of the Temple, a house of *avodah/latreia* for Israel, a house of prayer for all the nations" (Fredriksen, "Parting," 52; cf. idem. *Paul*, 73–77; Tannehill, *Narrative Unity*, 2:187–89; contra Pao, *New Exodus*, 123–27). One might object that the movement of Acts is centrifugal while the prophets anticipate a centripetal movement. To this I offer two points: (1) There is centrifugal movement in the prophets. They describe the Word of the Lord going out from Israel to the nations (e.g., Isa 2:1–4; 51:4–6). (2) Acts has centripetal movement in that it repeatedly returns to Jerusalem (9:26; 11:2, 29; 18:22; 19:21; 20:16, 22).

[130] David B. Woods, "Does Acts 15:9 Refute Intra-ecclesial Jew-Gentile Distinction?," *Conspectus* 19 (2015): 105–45; contra Luke Timothy Johnson, *The Acts of the Apostles*, SP (Collegeville, MN: Liturgical Press, 1992), 268.

gentiles to "Judaize" to some degree. They must abandon certain practices and adopt certain Torah practices mandated for aliens with Israel (15:19-21; cf. Lev 17-18). Torah, as anticipated by the prophets, governs gentile practice in this community (Isa 2:2-4).[131] Nevertheless, the Jerusalem Council continues to refer to them as "gentiles" (15:19) and "brothers from the nations" (15:23). Jewish and gentile ethnic identities remain in place. Israel is not redefined.[132] Fredriksen's category of "eschatological gentile," therefore, is an apt category for non-Jewish Jesus-followers in Acts as it depicts the manifestation of a previously hypothetical or anticipated category in Jewish eschatological imaginations (15:14 cf. Isa 45:20-25).[133]

The inclusion of Cornelius and his household illustrate how gentiles are incorporated in Jewish ways while remaining gentiles. Luke introduces Cornelius as the paradigmatic pious Godfearing gentile (εὐσεβὴς καὶ φοβούμενος τὸν θεόν). He gives alms to the Jewish people (τῷ λαῷ) and prays at the proper Jewish times (Acts 10:1-3, 31). The entire Jewish nation speaks well of him (10:22). Luke, through Cornelius, acknowledges the place of gentiles in the wider Jewish world (cf. Luke 7:1-10), and how God impartially receives those among the nations who fear him (10:34-35). Furthermore, the advent of the Spirit demonstrates that God has cleansed Cornelius and his household without their first joining the Jewish *ethnos*. This does not signal the erasure of the Jewish categories of clean-unclean and holy-common but affirms them. The Spirit brings these gentiles into the sphere of the holy. God has cleansed them without their becoming Jews (15:1-29).[134] Therefore, Peter and the Jewish believers still refer to Cornelius and his household as gentiles, albeit those who have been granted repentance unto life (10:45; 11:18).

Cornelius does err at one point, however. He falls at Peter's feet and worships him (πεσὼν ἐπὶ τοὺς πόδας προσεκύνησεν; 10:25). This idolatrous act suggests that Cornelius, like most Godfearers, continued to worship other gods. Peter commands Cornelius to rise since Peter is a mere human (ἐγὼ αὐτὸς ἄνθρωπός εἰμι; 10:26;

---

[131] Thiessen, *Contesting*, 111-47; Boesenberg, "Negotiating," 67-69; Stroup, *Christians*, 80-94; Keener, *Acts*, 3:2279; cf. Holladay, *Acts*, 303-4.

[132] Neubrand, *Israel*, 137-219; cf. Aaron W. White, *The Prophets Agree: The Function of the Book of the Twelve Prophets in Acts*, BibInt 184 (Leiden: Brill, 2020), 179-216. In the context of Amos 9, the prophet notes God's interactions with non-Israelite peoples (9:7-8). Amos recognizes that God works among the nations sometimes independent from Israel.

[133] Fredriksen, *Christians*, 140-43, 154-59. Despite my appreciation for his study, I remain unpersuaded by Stroup's argument that Luke portrays non-Jewish Jesus-followers as converts to Judaism for three reasons. First, Luke never calls gentile Jesus-followers "Jews" or "proselytes." Stroup's claim rests on inferring gentiles are the προσήλυτος of LXX Lev 17-18 alluded to in Acts 15 (*Christians*, 80-81; cf. Thiessen, *Contesting*, 135-36, who observes Luke differentiates προσήλυτοι from Ἰουδαῖοι in 2:11; 13:43). Second, if Acts 15 should be understood as allowing non-circumcised gentiles to be counted as Jewish converts, Paul's circumcision of Timothy seems to contradict this decision. Why deny what was widely recognized as *the* entry rite for males into the Jewish community to all these gentiles save Timothy? It seems more likely that Paul in Acts clarifies Timothy's identity as a Jew (albeit one with a hybrid identity, which is common for Jews in Acts—e.g., 2:5-10; 18:2, 24; 22:25-29). Third, gentiles becoming Jews undermines Paul's concern with (born or converted) Jews and his repeated turning to the gentiles. These turns lose their gravitas if Paul goes to the gentiles in order to make them Jews. On λαός in Acts 15:14, see Dahl, "'A People,'" 319-27; Neubrand, *Israel*, 110-20; Wendel, *Scriptural Interpretation*, 263.

[134] Moffitt, "Atonement," 559-60; Thiessen, *Contesting*, 124-37; Staples, "Rise," 11-14.

cf. 14:8–18).¹³⁵ Idolatrous practices, as Acts clarifies elsewhere, must now be abandoned by gentiles (15:19–21; 17:30–31). They must adopt exclusive worship of Israel's God. This goes beyond typical synagogue expectations for Godfearers. Adopting exclusive commitment to Israel's God was reserved for proselytes and, therefore, was a form of *Judaizing*.¹³⁶ Gentile Jesus-followers like Cornelius, then, were called to assume this uniquely Jewish practice. God calls gentiles to repent and adopt some Torah requirements, even as God grants them life and cleanses them within their gentilic identities.

2.6.5 Summary

Neither the Way's exclusivist truth claims nor the large-scale incorporation of the gentiles compromises the movement's Jewishness. Early Judaism was a diverse world in which various groups made hegemonic assertions about their role as proper interpreters of the ancestral tradition. Some considered themselves to be the sole faithful in Israel.¹³⁷ Others could be violent toward their fellows. Acts' depiction of the Way appears at home in this matrix. The nascent Jesus movement as Luke paints it similarly claims to be the proper understanding of Israel's tradition. However, it is not the most extreme Jewish group in its exclusivism or posture toward other Jews. Members of the Way continue to interact with other Jews and calls Jews to accept their view of the ancestral tradition for the good of their kin and their common way of life.

Similarly, mass inclusion of the gentiles *qua* gentiles was expected by certain strands of Judaism. Indeed, Luke's Jesus notes that this was foretold by Scripture and integral to the apostles' role as witnesses (Luke 24:47–48). Although it takes them a while to realize it, the apostles witness the start of the anticipated ingathering of the nations, in Cornelius and his household. Once again, gentile exclusion affirms the claims made by the Way that Jesus is the one who fulfills Israel's Scriptures and hopes. It further situates them within Judaism. Luke's portrait is of a Jewish subgroup engaging with other Jewish groups about the people's shared practices and expectations.

2.7 Conclusion: "I Am a Jew"

To return to Donaldson's criteria for measuring supersessionism—self-definition, social proximity, and rhetoric—Acts' portrait of the Way and Paul leaves supersessionist or anti-Jewish conclusions wanting.¹³⁸ The Way and Paul *self-identify* with Israel, as Jews, and maintain all things Jewish. Luke labels his characters, including Paul, Jews

---

¹³⁵ Barnabas and Paul face a similar, more extreme situation when the Lycaonians almost sacrifice to them, thinking them to be gods (14:8–18). Echoing Peter's words, they cry "we ourselves are humans (ἐσμεν ὑμῖν ἄνθρωποι)" (14:15). This link suggests Cornelius' action is idolatrous. The Lycaonians' attempt to sacrifice to Barnabas and Paul accounts for the pair's stronger response (contra Gaventa, *Darkness*, 116).

¹³⁶ Fredriksen, "Parting," 51–56; idem, *Paul*, 49–60.

¹³⁷ Wendel, *Scriptural Interpretation*, 29–78.

¹³⁸ Donaldson, *Anti-Judaism*, 28–29.

(10:28; 16:1; 18:2, 24; 21:39; 22:3). Paul and the Way retain connection with Israel's history, language, and land. They uphold Israel's constitution, the Torah. They maintain *social proximity* to other Jews as they express their exclusive loyalty to Israel's God in the temple, though it and some of the people will be judged (Luke 19:41–44; Acts 3:23; 21:30). Importantly, Jewish ethnic identifiers appear when they carry the most weight, that is, in situations when the Way and Paul could easily be construed as opposed to Judaism. Acts' *rhetorical* use of Jewishness establishes commonality between the Way, Paul, and the Jews. Luke, similar to the purposes of Herodotus' famous dictum, leverages common Jewish identity to establish a sense of cohesion and solidarity. In short, Acts paints the Way as an exclusivist Jewish subgroup at home in the matrix of early Judaism. Luke's Paul is nothing but "a Jew" (21:39; 22:3). Their conflicts with "the Jews" are instances of internecine conflicts that were common to early Judaism.

Luke's rhetorical leveraging of the Jewish identities of the Way and Paul caution against treating "the Jews" simply as an "other" in Acts. If Luke sought to other the Jews completely, repeatedly labeling Paul and other characters in Acts as Jews, having them self-identify with the Jewish kinship group and maintain faithfulness with Jewish ancestral custom is counterproductive. This depiction suggests ongoing identification with the Jewish community amidst tension. Still, the Way's truth claims remain committed to the Jewish tradition and are for the sake of Israel (e.g., 3:17–26; 13:16–47). The Way's claims about Jesus' identity and authority do not threaten Judaism any more than Qumran's claims about the Teacher of Righteousness. Acts thus paints an emerging renewal movement that remains in Jewish spaces, retains Jewish identity, and argues with family. The portraits of the Way, Paul, and the Jews appear complementary, not merely contrastive. Jewishness links them together, challenging treating them as binaries.

3

"Like You are Today": Images of the Jews, the Way, and Paul

One of the most prevalent arguments for Lukan anti-Judaism is that Acts paints diametrically opposed portraits of the Way and "the Jews." On the one hand is Luke's supposedly uniformly negative depiction of the Jews. They are, in Luke's construction, ignorant of their own God, Scriptures, and violate their own institutions. The Jews and their synagogues are discordant, stand in total opposition to Jesus and his followers, and are wholly unfaithful to Israel's God. As one scholar puts it, "*the Jews* do not evolve. [They] consistently act the same way, and this consistency gives the impression that they are a predictable and unified group with respect to their response to the Gentile mission as Paul preached it. Thus, Luke characterizes *the Jews* as close-ended characters."[1] On the other hand, Luke allegedly idealizes the Way. It is a harmonious community of model citizens comprised of the faithful who comprehend God's activities. These are the rightful heirs of Israel's tradition. For many, Luke presents the Way as an "ideal, unified Jewish community" in contrast to the "factious, local Jewish 'associations.'"[2] Paul embodies this contrast in his radical transformation from persecutor to persecuted, from infidelity to fidelity. Indeed, some claim Luke idealizes Paul as one of the only, if not the only, faithful Jews in Acts (if Paul even retains Jewish identity at all). Luke's apologetic agenda to legitimize Paul and the emerging Christian movement rests on "othering" Jews.[3]

---

[1] Smith, *Literary Other*, 71–72; cf. Sanders, *Jews*, 75–81.
[2] Stroup, *Christians*, 2. That Stroup, who otherwise attempts to disarm claims that Luke is anti-Jewish or supersessionist, reinforces the oppositional characterization between *ecclesia* and *synagogē* demonstrates the argument's pervasiveness. Similarly, Conzelmann, *Theology*, 137–69; Wills, "Depiction," 647–53; cf. José Fernández Ubiña, "Razones, Contradicciones e Incógnitas de Las Persecuciones Anticristianas: El Testimonio de Lucas-Hechos," *'Ilu* 18 (2007): 27–60.
[3] Levine, review, 2; Gager, "Luke's Anti-Judaism," 34–35. For the claim that Paul rejects his Jewishness in Acts, see, e.g., Richard I. Pervo, *The Making of Paul: Constructions of the Apostle in Early Christianity* (Minneapolis, MN: Fortress, 2010), 10–16. The idealization of the Way, especially Paul, is often an unstated assumption. For example, see John Clayton Lentz, Jr., *Luke's Portrait of Paul*, SNTSMS 77 (Cambridge: Cambridge University Press, 2004). See Joseph B. Tyson, "Wrestling with and for Paul," in *Contemporary Studies in Acts*, ed. Thomas E. Phillips (Macon, GA: Mercer University Press, 2009), 13–28; Luke MacNamara, *My Chosen Instrument: The Characterisation of Paul in Acts 7:58–15:41*, AnBib Dissertationes 215 (Roma: GBPress, 2016), 18–19; Oliver, "Calling," 180–84, for surveys of readings of Luke's Paul.

In these readings, the Way, with Paul as its representative figure, emerges as the sole legitimate inheritors of Israel's ancestral tradition. They remain loyal to Israel's God, in contrast to the Jews. Luke's positive presentation of the Way and Paul and his negative characterization the Jews are two sides of the same anti-Jewish and/or supersessionist coin. Elevating one comes at the expense of the other. The Way and the Jews, as Luke depicts them, become homogenous, flat, stagnant groups; one is good, the other bad. Individual Jews may repent and become Christian, but they are exceptional cases. In this way, Luke establishes the border between the (Christian) faithful and (Jewish) unfaithful based on behavior and understanding.[4]

This chapter challenges binary readings of Luke's characterization of the Way, Paul, and the Jews. I contend that Luke resists painting static, monolithic characters or groups.[5] He neither portrays the Jews as uniformly hostile and ignorant, nor the Way and Paul as unequivocally faithful and completely aligned with God's will. The Way as a whole is not idealized, and the Jewish people are not universally demonized. Some Jesus-following Jews fail to listen to Jesus (and God). Some Jews outside the Way are pious and perceptive of God's activity. Faithful characters progress toward a deepening fidelity to Israel's God and a growing understanding of God's actions in the world. Even Jesus-followers like Peter and Paul sometimes struggle to obey and understand (e.g., Luke 22:31–34). Even for those as villainous as Saul or Bar-Jesus, the potential for repentance or reorientation remains.

To be sure, Luke distinguishes between Jews *within* Israel based on faith in Jesus (e.g., 14:2; 20:38; 26:18), but the general constructions of the faithfulness and understanding of Jesus-following Jews and non-Jesus-following Jews are not binaries.[6] Luke does not separate the act and process of repentance and ongoing (development in) faithfulness. Indeed, John the Baptist's initial message is that those who do not bear "fruits worthy of repentance" will be "cut down and thrown into fire" (Luke 3:7–9; cf. 13:7–9). Fidelity in Israel cannot be *reduced* to acknowledgement of Jesus' messianic identity, though this is *the* central orienting aspect of the repentance-journey in Acts. The journey is ongoing. Therefore, all characters in Acts must be continually measured by Israel's Scriptures, obedience to Jesus and his instructions, and alignment with the Spirit to determine if they are producing fruit worthy of repentance.

Read against this backdrop, Luke's Jewish figures emerge at different places on Israel's communal repentance-journey, exhibiting varying degrees of (un)faithfulness to Israel's God and God's kingdom (cf. Luke 10:11–12).[7] On the one hand, Acts paints a nuanced picture of Jewish responses to the message of Jesus and varied postures toward the Way. Some directly oppose the Way and, as such, move contrary to Israel's way of salvation. These Jewish-Israelites risk "excluding themselves from eternal life" (13:46), that is, removing themselves from Israel and its promised restoration in accordance with the prophets (3:17–21; cf. Luke 3:7–9). Nevertheless, the call to

---

[4] Wills, "Depiction," 647–54; Matthews, *Perfect Martyr*, 6–10, 30–36; Smith, *Literary Other*, 58–65.
[5] Contra Darr, *Character Building*, 38, 44–45, 48–49, whose method I typically appreciate and follow. See Dinkler, "Building Character," 694–99.
[6] Cf. Lohfink, *Sammlung*, 87–89.
[7] Green, *Conversion*, 87–122. Cf. Gaventa, *Darkness*, 92; Smith, "Politics," 187–266.

reorientation on the journey—that is, repentance through acknowledgement of Jesus' messianic identity—remains.[8] Others, though, are not against Jesus and the Way and, therefore, are in some sense "for" them (Luke 9:50). They are further along on the journey, though they have yet to make the primary turn toward Jesus. On the other hand, the Way and Paul grow in faithfulness to their callings and understanding. Some of the Way's own (cf. 4:23) deviate from the Way entirely. Jesus' Jewish followers, like all Jewish-Israelites, risk being cut off from Israel (Acts 3:23; cf. Deut 18:15–20; Lev 23:29). The *ecclesia*, like the entire Jewish world, struggles to comprehend and obey the Lord properly; all move along the path of repentance in one direction or another.

In short, Luke does not construct a "true Israel" in contrast to a "false Israel." Rather, the Jews, the Way, and Paul are all mixed, ambiguous characters. Together, they share the identity of *Israel*, the heirs to the covenant and its promises (e.g., 3:25–26; 13:32–33), and reflect Luke's extension of Israel's history of divided, less-than-ideal responses to God and God's messengers (e.g., Isa 65:1–16; Ezek 20:1–32, 49; Luke 1:16; 2:34–35; 12:49–53). God, of course, continues to use Israel amidst its imperfections to advance God's purposes (cf. Acts 2:23–24; 3:17–18; 4:27–28).[9] In fact, as Gamaliel observed, the Jesus movement would indeed fail if God was not guiding its steps (Acts 5:39). As Luke writes to reinforce Theophilus' confidence in his instruction (Luke 1:4), the flaws of the Way and Paul magnify God's role in the advancement of the movement. The complex, often ambiguous characterizations of oft-considered "faithful" characters undermine claims about the binary, rhetorically charged use of the term and portrait of "the Jews." Instead, this portrait suggests that Acts participates in intra-Jewish conflict. Paul and the Way share Israel's struggle to be faithful to God with their fellow Jews. Together, Jews loyal to Jesus and those who are not corporately embody Israel's historic difficulty in maintaining fidelity to God.

To make this claim, I first examine Luke's use and portrait of οἱ Ἰουδαῖοι. I outline Luke's general use of the phrase using the taxonomy proposed by Eric Barreto.[10] Next, I demonstrate that three Jewish groups emerge in the conflict scenes of Acts: those who are persuaded, those who remain unpersuaded and persecute the Way, and those who remain unpersuaded yet do not persecute the Way. I then outline how Luke depicts several venerable—or at least neutral—non-Jesus-following Jewish characters. "The Jews" are neither a monolith nor does this phrase function as a wholly negative rhetorical category. Second, I explore bumps along the Way to show that the *ecclesia* is not "ideal" and "unified." The Way has less-than-savory characters in its midst, internal conflicts and divisions, and struggles to understand and obey Jesus. Third, I explore the picture of the imperfect Paul. After his encounter with Jesus, Paul still stumbles along the way. He constantly stands in the center of divisive conflicts, his temperament often gets him into trouble, and sometimes he struggles to interpret and follow the leading of Jesus and the Spirit.

---

[8] To reiterate, this is not to say that all Jews *will* repent or will become faithful according to Acts. The threat of being cut off is not an idle one (e.g., Luke 3:9; Acts 3:23; 13:41; 18:6).

[9] Complex portraits should be expected since Luke's main influence, Israel's Scriptures, portrays Israel and its heroes as flawed, of ambiguous character, and in need of maturation. Still, God uses imperfect characters to achieve God's purposes (e.g., Jacob, Joseph, David, Elijah—discussed in Kaminsky, *Yet I Loved*, 15–80). Scholars have recognized the flaws of Jesus' disciples in Luke's Gospel, so one should expect this trend to continue in Acts (e.g., Smith, "Politics," 187–266).

[10] Barreto, *Ethnic Negotiations*, 73–98.

3.1 Luke's Mixed Picture of the Jews

To begin, I challenge claims that Luke uses "the Jews" as a wholly negative category, a rhetorical other, or paints them monolithically. Acts, I contend, observes and maintains Jewish diversity.[11] Luke specifies particular Jews within the narrative. Where "the Jews" seem generic and rhetorically charged, specifically in conflicts about Paul's preaching, Luke still differentiates groups of Jews based on their responses to Jesus. Three groups emerge: (1) persuaded Jews, (2) unpersuaded and hostile Jews, and (3) unpersuaded, dispassionate Jews. This final category contains non-believing Jews who are portrayed in a positive, or at least neutral, light. "The Jews," then, are a mixed group.

3.1.1 Differentiating among Jews

Barreto's relatively brief survey of the Lukan use of Ἰουδαῖος/Ἰουδαῖοι provides a helpful starting point. For Barreto, claims that the articular plural οἱ Ἰουδαῖοι refers to an "amorphous" or uniformly negative group in Acts flounder for three primary reasons.[12] First, prior studies fail to place Luke's portrait of the Jews within Luke's broader ethnic reasoning in antiquity. Acts navigates a multiethnic imperial world and, as such, its characterization of Jews must be taken alongside how it portrays other people groups. Second, some examinations treat the articular plural οἱ Ἰουδαῖοι apart from Luke's use of the singular Ἰουδαῖος. Acts' depictions of Jews in general must consider portraits of individual Jews and Jewishness in general, including when the phrase οἱ Ἰουδαῖοι is not used explicitly. Third, many scholars neglect how Lukan style adapts to narrative setting. Barreto observes, "only when the orbit of Luke's narrative extends beyond the confines of Judea does Luke feel compelled to specify this people with ethnic terminology."[13] Οἱ Ἰουδαῖοι, Barreto concludes, is mostly an ethnographic descriptor, often used to identify Jews when other people groups are present (e.g., Luke 7:3; 23:3, 37–38, 51). Thus, it appears far more frequently in the diaspora contexts of Acts.[14]

Barreto posits seven contextual uses of Ἰουδαῖος/Ἰουδαῖοι in Acts.[15] First, it can be a simple ethnic identifier for individual Jews. The neutral value of the label is evinced by its application to an array of characters—a negative character like Elymas (13:6; cf. 19:13–14), neutral ones like Alexander (19:33) and Drusilla (24:24), and positive ones like Timothy's mother (16:1), Aquila (18:2), Apollos (18:24), and Paul (22:3). Second, the term identifies Jews from or in specific locales (e.g., 2:14; 11:19; 16:3; 17:13;

---

[11] "In much the same way any invocation of Black folk implies some specific particularity Luke's 'the Jews' are actually Cyrenian, Cypriot, Asiatic, Pharisaic, Herodian, Priestly, Scribal, or members of the Sadducees. Though Luke frequently uses the general term 'Jews', he consistently reminds his audience that the narrative setting is always in context and aware of Jewish particularity" (Carter, "Diaspora Acts," 102).

[12] Barreto, *Ethnic Negotiations*, 80, see 73–98.

[13] Barreto, *Ethnic Negotiations*, 85. Luke's alterations between names based on setting and rhetorical emphasis reinforces this observation (e.g., Saul/Paul; Simon/Peter; Tabitha/Dorcas). One wonders if it is safe to assume all believers in Acts whose ethnicity are not specified are Jews (e.g., the Ephesian disciples; 18:24–27).

[14] Barreto, *Ethnic Negotiations*, 85–87. Acts is similar to Josephus' *Antiquities* in this regard (cf. Staples, *Israel*, 44–48).

[15] Barreto, *Ethnic Negotiations*, 88–91. See also Carter, "Diaspora Acts," 459–534.

24:19; 25:7). Third, Ἰουδαῖοι can describe Jewish things like territory (10:39), synagogues (13:5; 14:1; 17:1, 10; 19), leadership (19:14; 25:2, 15; 28:17), or law (25:8). Fourth, it is a generic label paired with other groups like proselytes (2:11; 13:43), Greeks (14:1; 18:4; 19:10, 17; 20:21), gentiles (14:2, 5), Godfearers, (14:4; 17:17), or apostles (14:4). Fifth, it portrays the people group in relation to political powers (e.g., 12:3; 18:12, 14; 22:30; 24:5; 25:9–10; 26:21). Sixth, Ἰουδαῖοι can refer to the ethnicity in general (2:5; 10:22, 28; 26:4). Seventh, Luke uses the term in scenes of conflict, that is, when Jews contend with other Jews, typically members of the Way (12:11; 13:45, 50; 16:20; 17:5; 18:12; 19:33; 20:3, 19; 21:20, 21; 23:12, 20; 24:5, 9; 25:10; 26:2, 4, 7, 21; 28:19).

Acts' use of Ἰουδαῖος/Ἰουδαῖοι, Barreto shows, often says more about Lukan style than it does about Luke's view of Jews. Nevertheless, the frequency with which "the Jews" applies to those hostile to Paul must be considered. Barreto's classification provides a helpful aid in considering the Lukan use of Ἰουδαῖος/Ἰουδαῖοι. Still, each instance, even in apparent generalized uses in sites of contention, must be taken in context to examine if and how the Jews in scenes of conflict are also particularized.

3.1.2 Differentiating Jewish Responses

Throughout the book, Acts differentiates between Jews based on their responses to the Way and to Paul. Luke repeatedly highlights Jewish *division* to the Way's message (cf. Luke 2:34–35; 12:49–53).[16] Narrative context specifies which Jews are in view. When "the Jews" appears after a divided response, it often functions as shorthand for "unpersuaded Jews" (14:2), that is, Jews who do not accept the message of Jesus. Since not all Jews who do not believe are hostile, context further suggests that "the unpersuaded Jews" are those who vocally (and sometimes violently) oppose the Way.[17] Three Jewish groups thus emerge: those who join the Way, those who do not and are hostile toward the Way, and those who neither join nor oppose it.

3.1.2.1 Jewish Division in Acts 1–8

Although the term "the Jews" is infrequent in the early portions of Acts, Jewish division appears frequently. In these sections, the Jewish people in Jerusalem—primarily labeled "the people" or "Israelites" since the setting remains in Judea, that is, among Jews—respond in various ways to the Way's message. As successful as the Way's early mission is, Luke refrains from idealizing Jerusalem's initial response to the message as uniformly positive. From the beginning, reception is mixed.[18]

The divided response emerges the first time the Way's message goes public (2:1–13). Tellingly, the initial occurrence of Ἰουδαῖοι in Acts demonstrates Jewish specificity, hybridity, and differing reactions to the Way. These Jews residing in Jerusalem are "pious men (ἄνδρες εὐλαβεῖς) from every nation (ἀπὸ παντὸς ἔθνους) under heaven" (2:5;

---

[16] Jervell, *People*, 41–74.
[17] Boesenberg, "Negotiating Identity," 59.
[18] For Jewish division in the Luke's Gospel, see Smith, "Politics," 124–380.

cf. Luke 2:25). Acts delineates the ethnic origins of these devout Jews and proselytes (2:9–11) and then highlights how these Galilean Jews of the Way (2:7) speak of God's deeds of power in the native languages of their diverse Jewish listeners.[19] Although all of them respond with awe and confusion (ἐξίσταντο δὲ πάντες καὶ διηπόρουν), some respond with cynicism, jeering (διαχλευάζοντες) that the disciples are drunk (2:12–13). The first image of non-Jesus-following Jews is mixed: They are pious yet ignorant, with some disparaging the disciples. The acts of God in Jesus on behalf of Israel are not self-evident; they must be explained and received.[20] Ultimately, most of Peter's listeners respond positively to his message (2:37). Luke stops short of saying that *all* of Peter's audience receives the message of Jesus, however. Only those who receive (οἱ ἀποδεξάμενοι) the message among the multitude (τὸ πλῆθος; 2:6) are baptized (2:41). Three thousand is a great number (2:41), but it does not seem to be the entire multitude of Jews listening to Peter (2:6), let alone all those dwelling in Jerusalem (cf. 2:43–44; 3:12; 5:13–14).

Peter and John further precipitate division after they heal a man unable to walk (3:1–10). Like the Pentecost observers, all the people (πᾶς ὁ λαός) who witness this healing are amazed yet fail to comprehend its significance (3:10, 12).[21] Peter explains that "in Jesus is the resurrection of the dead" (4:2; cf. 3:10–26). This message receives three different responses (4:1–4). First, one group responds with hostility. The priests, the temple captain, and the Sadducees become vexed, arrest Peter and John, and bring them to trial (4:1–22). Because of the sign done before the people who look favorably on the apostles (4:2, 21), Israel's leadership does not punish them. They merely command them to stop preaching in the name of Jesus and threaten them if they do not cease (4:18–21). The high priests and the Sadducees continue to oppose, arrest, and eventually beat the apostles—as an alternative to killing them (5:33–38)—for preaching the message (5:17–41). Second, many Jewish-Israelites (cf. 3:12) who heard Peter's message (πολλοὶ δὲ τῶν ἀκουσάντων), five thousand Luke says, believe (ἐπίστευσαν; 4:4). Many is not all, though (3:10). The third, unspoken group is the rest of the people who neither believe nor respond with hostility (4:2, 21). Indeed, the people of Jerusalem speak well of the Way, though many do not join it (5:13–14, 41).[22]

The burgeoning hostility toward the Way reaches its apex with Stephen's martyrdom. Stephen—like Peter and John before him, and Joseph, Moses, and Jesus whom he describes—is full of the Spirit, wisdom, grace, and power (6:3, 10; cf. 7:10, 22; Luke 21:15), and performs "wonders and signs" (6:8; cf. 2:43; 4:30; 5:12; 7:36). As with the apostles and these figures of Israel's history, Stephen's actions cause opposition: "some (τινες) of those from the so-called 'synagogue of the Freedmen,' also Cyrenians,

---

[19] On the table of nations and the centrality of Jerusalem in Acts 2, see Richard Bauckham, *The Jewish World around the New Testament* (Grand Rapids, MI: Baker Academic, 2010), 357–59.

[20] On the need for interpretation in Acts, see Michal Beth Dinkler, "Interpreting Pedagogical Acts: Acts 8.26–40 and Narrative Reflexivity as Pedagogy," *NTS* 63 (2017): 411–27; cf. Brigid C. Frein, "The Literary and Theological Significance of Misunderstanding in the Gospel of Luke," *Bib* 74 (1993): 328–48.

[21] On λαός in Luke-Acts, see Lohfink, *Sammlung*, 17–32; Brawley, *Jews*, 133–54.

[22] Daniel R. Schwartz, "Non-Joining Sympathizers (Acts 5:13–14)," *Bib* 64 (1983): 550–55.

Alexandrians, and of those from Cilicia and Asia, rose up disputing Stephen" (6:9).[23] Once again, Luke differentiates between Jews. Only *some* Cyrenian, Egyptian, Cilician, and Asian Jews—whose countrymen, including the Cilician Paul (21:39; 22:3; 23:34), respond positively to the Way elsewhere (2:9–11)—oppose Stephen.[24] These particular Jews eventually incite the people and Israel's leadership against Stephen (6:12–15), leading to his trial and execution (7:57–59).

Not all Jerusalem participates in Stephen's death, though. Some Jews mourn it: "Pious men (ἄνδρες εὐλαβεῖς; cf. 2:5) buried Stephen and made a loud lamentation (κοπετὸν μέγαν; cf. LXX Gen 5:10; 1 Macc 4:39; 9:20; 13:26) over him" (8:2; cf. Luke 23:48; *Ant.* 20.197–203).[25] These are not members of the *ecclesia*, which has already been scattered (διεσπάρησαν) from Jerusalem (8:1; cf. 5:37). Some Jews outside the Way maintain a positive outlook of it (cf. 5:13–14). Once again, Luke divides the Jewish community into Jewish members of the *ecclesia*, some diaspora Jews who oppose the *ecclesia* even through violence, and those Jews who neither join nor oppose it. Jews in Jerusalem simply are not a uniform category.

3.1.2.2 Jewish Division in Saul/Paul's Ministry

The pattern of Jewish division and differentiation persists in Saul's first ministerial excursion after his encounter with Jesus and continues throughout his ministry. After spending time with the very disciples in Damascus he sought to root out, Saul shocks those in the synagogue by proclaiming the message he once opposed (9:19–21; cf. 9:2).[26] He stirs up (συνέχυννεν) the Jews dwelling in Damascus with his arguments that "this one [Jesus] is the Messiah" (9:22; cf. 19:32; 21:27, 31; Luke 23:5). After some time, "the Jews" seek to kill Paul (Acts 9:23). Two observations nuance this use of "the Jews." First, Luke particularizes those in view: They are *Damascus* Jews (τοὺς Ἰουδαίους τοὺς κατοικοῦντας ἐν Δαμασκῷ; 9:22), specifically those not counted among the (Jewish) disciples in the synagogue.[27] Second, Luke notes that "his disciples (οἱ μαθηταὶ αὐτοῦ)" help Paul escape. The clearest antecedent for αὐτοῦ is "Saul" (9:24–25). This suggests that these are "Saul's disciples," that is, Jews who accepted Saul's message about Jesus and were added to "the disciples" in Damascus (9:19).[28] His oppressors, then, are a particular group of Damascus Jews, not all Damascus Jews. Saul's experience in Damascus inscribes a pattern: Saul finds some success among the Jewish community,

---

[23] Acts places Stephen in the line of rejected prophetic figures in Israel's history, with Zechariah son of Jehoida being the closest analogy (2 Chr 24:20–22). McWhirter, *Rejected*, 104–9.
[24] Given Luke's use of "many (πολλοί)" elsewhere, "some" does not refer to a majority.
[25] Tannehill suggests this is an act of protest since m. Sanh. 6:6 forbids lamenting over someone who was executed (*Narrative Unity*, 2:101). These men are analogous to the crowds who express remorse at Jesus' death and to Joseph of Arimathea (Luke 23:48–56; cf. 18:13; Acts 2:37).
[26] I alternate between *Saul* and *Paul* when Luke does. Saul/Paul's name changes based on setting; it is not a new name or a signal of his becoming a Christian (rather than a Jew). Isaac W. Oliver, "The Calling of Paul in the Acts of the Apostles," in *Early Reception*, 179–92.
[27] Contra claims that "they become 'the Jews'" (Conzelmann, *Theology*, 145; cf. Sanders, *Jews*, 81), they are οἱ Ἰουδαῖοι *before* hostility arises (9:22).
[28] Contra MacNamara, *Chosen Instrument*, 149–51, who contends that "disciples" coupled with a possessive pronoun always refer to Jesus' disciples in Luke-Acts. Saul's disciples are, of course, also (primarily) Jesus' disciples.

but then some Jews who reject him and persecute him (along some with gentiles) cause him to flee the region.²⁹

Saul encounters the same opposition in Jerusalem (9:26–30). After Barnabas vouches for him to the Jerusalem believers, Saul begins speaking with the Hellenists who then seek to kill him (9:29–30). This causes the brothers to send Paul back to Tarsus. Luke here refers to "the Hellenists" without any particular caveat or modifier, yet the reader knows that some Hellenists are members of the Way (6:1–6; cf. 11:19). "The Hellenists," then, must refer to specific Hellenistic Jews in Jerusalem, not to all of them. Luke, therefore, can refer to a group as "the X" without entailing the entirety of the group. Indeed, Luke will later refer seemingly wholesale to "the gentiles" as a group from whom Paul needs rescue (26:17; cf. 15:7, 12).³⁰ At this point, "the Jews" prove no more monolithic a category than "the Hellenists."

Particularizing Jewish division continues throughout Paul's endeavors in diaspora synagogues. At Salamis, they meet no resistance from the synagogue (13:5).³¹ It is not until after going through the entire island that, at Paphos, they encounter opposition, this time from an individual. The Jewish magician and false prophet (μάγον ψευδοπροφήτην Ἰουδαῖον) Bar-Jesus/Elymas attempts to dissuade Sergius Paulus, the proconsul, from the faith (13:6–8). The problem with Elymas, though, is not his Jewishness but his participation in magic and identification as a false prophet (cf. Deut 13:1–5; LXX Jer 6:13).³² Paul declares a judgment of blindness against Elymas. Luke contrasts the false prophet Elymas with the Spirit-filled prophetic Paul (13:9–11).³³ The contrast is not absolute, however. Paul experienced this same blindness and inability to find his way as part of his reorientation toward Jesus (9:8; 22:11).³⁴ These similarities with Paul suggest that, though Elymas is characterized uniformly negatively, his judgment is not final. It is only "for a time (ἄχρι καιροῦ)" (13:11; cf. 26:18). Though it is unclear what comes of him, the Jewish false prophet Elymas is an open character.

In Pisidian Antioch, the image of the differentiated Jewish community develops. Many Jews and proselytes followed (ἠκολούθησαν) Paul and Barnabas there; that is, many believed (13:43; cf. 13:16).³⁵ The "many of the Jews (πολλοὶ τῶν Ἰουδαίων)"

---

²⁹ This pattern has been long recognized (Bovon, *Luke the Theologian*, 364–86).
³⁰ Joseph of Arimathea illustrates how Luke can portray a group as seemingly uniform and still acknowledge exceptions (Luke 23:50–56). For an argument that Joseph is an honorable Pharisaic member of the council who is sympathetic to Jesus but not a follower, see Oliver, *Torah Praxis*, 148–49.
³¹ MacNamara, *Chosen Instrument*, 239, suggests some Jews at Salamis might already be believers due to the persecution spreading Jewish Jesus-followers to Cyprus (11:19).
³² Barreto, *Ethnic Negotiations*, 88. On Luke and magic, see Susan R. Garrett, *The Demise of the Devil: Magic and the Demonic in Luke's Writings* (Minneapolis, MN: Fortress, 1989).
³³ Blaire A. French, "The Completion of King Saul in Acts," *JSNT* 40 (2018): 424–33, suggests a contrast between King Saul and Saul/Paul in that King Saul died for consulting a sorcerer instead of God's word (1 Chr 10:13) whereas Paul rebukes one in defense of God's word.
³⁴ Hamm, "Paul's Blindness," 69–70.
³⁵ In Luke's Gospel, aside from mundane uses of literally following someone (e.g., 22:10, 39; 22:54; 23:27; cf. Acts 12:8–9; 21:36), ἀκολουθέω typically indicates a commitment or a call to loyalty to Jesus and his message (e.g., Luke 5:11, 27–28; 7:9; 9:11, 23, 49, 57–61; 18:22, 28, 43). The context of Acts 13 suggests that ἠκολούθησαν evokes similar notions of commitment to Paul and his message. The reference to μαθηταί (13:52) reinforces this claim since this term usually refers to Jesus-followers in a region (e.g., 6:1–2; 11:26; 14:20–22; 18:23).

restricts the scope of "the Jews" that become jealous. Only a minority among the Jewish community blasphemes, speaks against the message, and incites prominent gentiles against Paul and Barnabas (13:45, 50).[36] The message receives an overall positive response, although one that lacks uniformity.

"The same thing happened in Iconium (ἐγένετο δὲ ἐν Ἰκονίῳ κατὰ τὸ αὐτό)."[37] Many multitudes of Jews (πολὺ πλῆθος Ἰουδαίων) and also Greeks (τε καὶ Ἑλλήνων) believe (14:1). Paul's mission is initially successful. Luke further specifies Paul's opponents who emerge: They are *unpersuaded* Jews (οἱ δὲ ἀπειθήσαντες Ἰουδαῖοι; cf. LXX Isa 65:2). This group stands apart from the large numbers of Jews who believe. Thus, "the Jews" who oppose Paul are only a vocal, unbelieving portion of the larger community (14:4). Luke contrasts *groups* of Jews who believe, not merely individuals, with those Jews who are unpersuaded and act against Paul and Barnabas (cf. 28:24).[38] In direct response (οὖν) to this opposition, Paul and Barnabas remain in Iconium proclaiming and performing signs and wonders (14:3; cf. 5:12; 6:8; 7:36). As a result, "the multitude of the city was divided (ἐσχίσθη). Some were with the [unpersuaded] Jews, and some were with the apostles" (14:4). Paul's message does not merely divide Jews; it divides entire cities.

Paul's next conflict occurs in the "synagogue of the Jews (συναγωγὴ τῶν Ἰουδαίων)" in Thessalonica (17:1–9).[39] For three Sabbaths, Paul attempts to persuade them that Jesus is the Messiah (17:2–3). Once again, some Jews were persuaded (τινες ἐξ αὐτῶν ἐπείσθησαν) and join with Paul and Silas, along with numerous Greeks and prominent women (17:4; cf. 13:50; 14:1). Other Jews, that is, the antagonistic and unpersuaded, gather some wicked men against Paul (17:5). The hostile Jews in Thessalonica might comprise a larger group since only "some" Jews believed. This hostility forces Paul to flee the area (17:6–9).

The Berean synagogue community (τὴν συναγωγὴν τῶν Ἰουδαίων) stands in stark contrast. The Berean Jews are nobler (εὐγενέστεροι) than their Thessalonian counterparts. They eagerly receive and cross-examine the message with the Scriptures. As a result, many among them (πολλοὶ ἐξ αὐτῶν) and a number of reputable Greeks believe (17:11–12).[40] The Berean synagogue responds to Paul's preaching in a uniformly positive manner, but that does not mean that all of them accept the message. Many (πολλοί), not all, believe. Significantly, no Berean Jews persecute Paul. Rather, it is those Thessalonian Jews who were unpersuaded who pursue Paul (17:13–14). Once they

---

[36] Luke omits the object of their blasphemy (cf. 18:6; 26:11); they could be insulting the preachers, their message, or blaspheming God. These options are not exclusive since opposing God's servants is akin to opposing God in Acts (e.g., 5:39; 7:51–53; 9:4–5). Zhang, *Paul*, 114–15; Beers, *Followers*, 178.

[37] *Pace* Parsons, *Acts*, 197; Schnabel, *Acts*, 602, who translate κατὰ τὸ αὐτό as "as usual," taking it akin to κατὰ δὲ τὸ εἰωθὸς τῷ Παύλῳ (17:1; cf. Luke 4:16). The text emphasizes the similarities between the responses from the synagogues in these two cities more than Paul's ritual habits. Luke's Jesus similarly describes present analogies with past generations using κατὰ τὰ αὐτά (Luke 6:22, 26; 17:30).

[38] Contra Matthews, *Perfect Martyr*, 7; Sanders, *Jews*, 264, who claim Luke only distinguishes individual Jews. On ἀπειθέω as "unpersuaded," see Matthew D. Jensen, "Some Unpersuasive Glosses: The Meaning of ἀπείθεια, ἀπειθέω, and ἀπειθής in the New Testament," *JBL* 138 (2019): 391–412.

[39] Zhang reads ὅπου (17:1) as causal: Paul stops in Thessalonica instead of Amphipolis or Appolonia since there was a synagogue there (*Paul*, 169).

[40] The "many" (πολλοί) Jews who believe in Berea contrast with the "some" (τινες) in Thessalonica (Schnabel, *Acts*, 710n25).

hear of Paul's activities, those Thessalonian Jews hostile to Paul come to Berea and incite the crowds against him (17:13–14).[41] As in Berea, when Paul goes to the synagogue in Athens, he meets no hostility from the Athenian Jews (17:17).[42] Three groups of Jews emerge in Thessalonica, Berea, and Athens: Some or many join the Way, others do not and actively oppose it, and the rest remain neutral.

In Corinth, Jewish hostility initially seems more uniform. Luke writes, "the Jews with one accord (ὁμοθυμαδὸν οἱ Ἰουδαῖοι) seized Paul" and brought him before Gallio (18:12; cf. 19:28). Nevertheless, two things imply various groups of Jews are in view. First, Paul originally "was persuading (ἔπειθεν) Jews and Greeks" to believe his message that Jesus is the Messiah (18:3–5, 7–9). Most major translations render ἔπειθεν (18:4) as "he was *trying* to persuade," yet the typical usage of πείθω in Acts implies a modicum of success.[43] Second, the synagogue leader Crispus and his household come to faith, showing that some Jews in Corinth believed.[44] Third, many (πολλοί) Corinthians believe and are baptized. Nothing suggests that this group is uniformly gentile. In fact, the inclusion of Crispus prevents that conclusion (18:8–9). The hostile Jews in Corinth are not as uniform or representative of the Jewish community as they seem.

Paul then spends three months in Ephesus, a community that initially expressed interest in his message (18:19–21; cf. 18:24–28), persuading (πείθων) the synagogue about the kingdom (19:8–10). Eventually, some (τινες) were hardened (ἐσκληρύνοντο) and remain unpersuaded (ἠπείθουν).[45] They begin to speak evil (κακολογοῦντες) about the Way before the rest of the synagogue community (τοῦ πλήθους). Paul leaves those people (ἀπ' αὐτῶν) and marks off (ἀφώρισεν) the disciples in response, continuing his discussions (presumably with both Jews and gentiles) daily in the school

---

[41] Crowds outside of Jerusalem consist of Jews *and* gentiles (e.g., 13:45; 14:11, 13; 16:22; 19:26).

[42] The verb διαλέγομαι need not indicate hostility (17:17). It appears *before* conflict arises in Jewish settings (17:2; 18:4, 19; 19:8), among members of the Way (20:7, 9), and in neutral environs (19:9; 24:25). Strelan, *Ephesus*, 207–8, 246.

[43] People were persuaded (ἐπείθοντο) to follow Theudas and Judas the Galilean (5:36–37). The council was persuaded (ἐπείσθησαν) by Gamaliel's speech (5:39). The people of Tyre and Sidon persuade (πείσαντες) Blastus to join their cause (12:20). Jews from Antioch and Iconium persuade (πείσαντες) the crowd in Lystra, leading to them stoning Paul (14:19). Some Thessalonian Jews were persuaded (ἐπείσθησαν) by Paul and Silas (17:4). Demetrius bemoans that Paul persuaded (πείσας) people to abandon gods made by human hands (19:26). Paul persuades (πείθων, ἐπείθοντο) some Jewish leaders in Rome (28:23–24). Luke specifies when persuasion fails with ἀπειθέω (e.g., 14:2) or by negating the verb: Paul cannot be persuaded (μὴ πειθομένου) not to go to Jerusalem (21:14), and a centurion tells the tribune not to be persuaded (μὴ πεισθῇς) to bring Paul before the council (23:21). Two cases are more ambiguous (19:8; 26:28). Still, that "some were hardened and unpersuaded" (τινες ἐσκληρύνοντο καὶ ἠπείθουν, 19:9) implies others were persuaded (19:8). In 26:28, Agrippa sarcastically tells Paul that he has persuaded him to become a Christian (26:28). Such a comment parodies success.

[44] Stroup suggests Luke contrasts Crispus, a believing synagogue leader, with Sosthenes, an unpersuaded synagogue leader, to contrast *ecclesia* and synagogue (*Christians*, 125). It is not clear that Sosthenes represents the unbelieving portion of the synagogue, however (Mount, "Constructing Paul," 143–44). Crispus appears to be a leader in the same synagogue since the text only mentions one (18:7). As such, the contrast would be *internal* to the synagogue rather than between two different kinds of assemblies (cf. Stowers, "Synagogue," 141).

[45] The verb ἐσκληρύνοντο echoes LXX Ps 94:8, which warns readers not to be like the wilderness generation who failed to enter the land, God's rest, due to their hardened hearts (cf. Ezek 20:1–32). These Jews, Luke indicates, similarly risk failing to inherit the promise of the kingdom.

of Tyrannus (19:9). Notably, the synagogue does not expel him or the disciples. Moreover, no gentiles are explicitly mentioned in this scene. This is a schism *within* the synagogue.[46] Luke divides Ephesian Jews into three clear groups: the opposition (τινες), the disciples (τοὺς μαθητάς; cf. 19:1), and the rest of the community (τοῦ πλήθους).

Paul then faces a plot from "the Jews" in Syria (20:3). At first glance, this appears to be a uniform category that encompasses all Jews of Syria. However, these are likely the same group of Jews who have resisted Paul since his initial work in Damascus (9:23). Paul has repeatedly visited believing communities in Syria, which, given that the Antioch community precipitates the Jerusalem Council, contains Jews and gentiles (11:19-26; 14:21; 15:22-23, 41). Luke thus specifies that the oppressors are Jews, rather than gentiles, who are not part of the Way who threaten Paul. It is not all Damascus Jews, though. The term again serves as an ethnic-geographic identifier. The narrative progression dampens its rhetorical charge.

When Paul returns to Jerusalem, Luke continues to specify and divide groups of Jews. James informs Paul about "how many ten-thousands of those who have believed among the Jews (πόσαι μυριάδες εἰσὶν ἐν τοῖς Ἰουδαίοις τῶν πεπιστευκότων)" (21:21). The Jerusalem Jewish believing community has grown, though not all Jerusalem Jews have believed. James insinuates that there are at least (cf. 15:1-2) two Jewish groups in Jerusalem: those who believe and those who do not. A third group arises when Paul is in the temple: the Jews from Asia (οἱ ἀπὸ τῆς Ἀσίας Ἰουδαῖοι; 21:27; cf. 6:9; 20:18-19; 24:19).[47] These particular Jews stir up the second group, that is, the rest of the Jews (πάντα τὸν ὄχλον), by accusing Paul of bringing Trophimus, a gentile Ephesian, into the temple (21:28-29).[48] Furthermore, these Asian Jews are differentiated from Tychicus, an Asian Jew with Paul (20:4), as well as the (Jewish) Ephesian disciples (19:8-10; cf. 18:24-27).[49] Paul later reinforces this conclusion by clarifying that it was "*some* Jews from Asia (τινὲς δὲ ἀπὸ τῆς Ἀσίας Ἰουδαῖοι)" who roused the crowd against him (24:19). The three Jewish groups reappear. The number of Jewish Jesus-followers in Jerusalem has increased, but the city remains divided.

Finally, Luke's conclusion highlights this schism within the Jewish community in Rome. Many (πλείονες) Jews come to Paul where he proclaims Jesus and the kingdom of God to them from the Scriptures (28:23). Some were persuaded (οἱ μὲν ἐπείθοντο),

---

[46] The other use ἀφορίζω in Acts is when the Holy Spirit sets apart Paul and Barnabas (13:2). Its use in Luke's Gospel suggests being ostracized from the Jewish community (6:22). Still, Paul is the agent of this setting apart, not the synagogue. This phrasing suggests marking off some within the synagogue, not necessarily a mass departure. See also Brawley, *Jews*, 149-50; Strelan, *Ephesus*, 165-273.

[47] With the opposition of Asian Jews in the temple, Luke echoes the Stephen pericope, preparing the reader for the impending conflict and threat on Paul's life. The Miletus speech also anticipates the instigation of Asian Jews. Paul highlights his suffering at the hands of the Jews *in Asia* (20:18-19). The context of the seemingly generic usage geographically restricts how one understands "the Jews" here.

[48] On "the crowds" in Judea as a reference to the wider Jewish populace in Luke-Acts, see Lohfink, *Sammlung*, 33-46; Brawley, *Jews*, 133-54. This group often remains neutral but can be swayed between Jesus and his followers and their opposition. They are, in essence, the battleground of Luke-Acts. In this case, Paul's accusers, like Jesus', win over the crowd (21:36; 22:22; cf. Luke 23:4, 13, 48; Acts 21:11). Josephus likewise portrays the Jewish populace as the middle ground that can be persuaded one way or another by competing groups (Rajak, *Josephus*, 83).

[49] That Trophimus is the only gentile in Paul's cohort suggests that Tychichus is Jewish (21:17-36; Carter, "Diaspora Acts," 100n22).

but others did not believe (οἱ δὲ ἠπίστουν; 28:24). Notably, no Roman Jews show hostility toward Paul. They simply leave in disagreement with one another (ἀσύμφωνοι δὲ ὄντες πρὸς ἀλλήλους ἀπελύοντο; 28:25).[50] Acts' final image of the Jewish community is division, not uniform rejection. The debate about Jesus and the kingdom concludes in Acts as an internecine debate. From beginning to end, Luke depicts the Jewish world's response as mixed. Jesus truly brings division in Israel (cf. Luke 12:49–53).

3.1.2.3 *Summary*

This survey demonstrates that, in highlighting the division of the Jewish community over the message of Jesus, Luke differentiates between *groups* of Jews. Context reins in Luke's use of "the Jews"—from rhetorically charged to primarily descriptive. The positive responses of "some" or "many of the Jews/them" (e.g., 13:43; 14:1; 17:4) and other contextual markers restrain how one understands "the Jews" in conflict scenes. The clearest example is the conspiracy against Paul in Jerusalem (23:12–15, 20). Luke states that "the Jews" bind themselves under an oath or curse (ἀνεθεμάτισαν ἑαυτούς) to kill Paul (23:12, 14, 21).[51] Although this seems general and rhetorically charged, Luke specifies that "the Jews" refers narrowly to a group of "more than forty people" (23:13). Moreover, the reader already knows of the "many myriads" of Jewish believers in the city (21:20). A group of about forty people is miniscule by comparison.[52] It is likely, then, that Acts uses "the Jews" in this instance to differentiate these hostile Jews from the Roman centurions and tribune (23:10, 15, 17). Luke simply uses the term when one cannot assume the ethnic identity of characters. It reflects style more than hostile rhetoric.

Of course, specific Jews are characterized negatively. That Luke depicts individual Jews or groups of Jews adversely is indubitable. Such characterizations, though, are always contextualized and limited to particular Jews in particular locales. Οἱ Ἰουδαῖοι cannot refer to a uniform category any more than "the Hellenists" who oppose Paul in Jerusalem (9:29–30; cf. 6:1) or "the gentiles" who threaten Paul (14:3, 5; cf. 17:18–20). In certain regions, a third portion of the Jewish community emerges more noticeably: those who neither believe nor oppose the Way (17:10–14, 17; 19:9). This group operates in a more neutral, middle ground. As such, "the Jews," when used in these oppositional contexts, does not refer to all those who do not believe the Way's message.[53]

---

[50] Some manuscripts add that the Jews engage in intense debate with one another as they leave, highlighting the division *internal* to the Jewish people (cf. Epp, *Tendency*, 114–15; Richard I. Pervo, *Acts: A Commentary*, Hermeneia [Minneapolis, MN: Fortress, 2009], 686).

[51] In the LXX, αναθεματίζω often translates חָרַם (e.g., Num 21:1–3; Deut 13:15; 20:17) in the sense of "to devote to destruction" (cf. 1 Macc 5:5). In 2 Esd 10:8, Esdras declares that whoever does not come to Jerusalem within three days will have their possessions cut off and be banned from "the assembly of the colony" (cf. 1 Chr 4:41). In 1 En 6:4–5, angels bind themselves under a curse (ἀνεθεμάτισαν) to take wives from humans. Considering these uses and the reflexive pronoun (ἑαυτούς), Luke's description might entail a double entendre: in committing to Paul's destruction, these Jews bring judgment and exclusion (a curse) upon themselves (cf. Gal 1:8–9).

[52] The Jerusalem believing community and the immediately preceding reference to prophets and brothers from Judea and Jerusalem (11:27–32) similarly restrains how one perceives "the Jews" who are pleased by James' execution (12:1–3).

[53] Luke characterizes gentile responses to the Way in the same vein: some ignore (17:32), some join (17:34), and some violently oppose (16:16–24; 19:21–41).

3.1.3 Noble Non-Jesus-Following Jews

Beyond that, Luke positively characterizes certain Jewish individuals and groups. These characters embody Jesus' dictum that, even if that someone does not "follow with (ἀκολουθεῖ μεθ')" his disciples, "whoever is not against you is for you" (Luke 9:49–50; cf. 11:23). First, Luke depicts numerous Jews in Jerusalem favorably or at least neutrally. At Pentecost, Ἰουδαῖοι appears for the first time. Luke describes these Jews, who are not members of the Way, as "pious men (ἄνδρες εὐλαβεῖς)" (2:5). Despite this positive description, this crowd has a mixed reaction to the disciples' speaking in tongues (2:12–13) and is called to repent for their participation in Jesus' death (2:23, 36).[54] Though only a portion of them repent and are baptized, the entire group is pious. More pious men (ἄνδρες εὐλαβεῖς) bury Stephen and loudly lament his death (8:2). That they do so *after* the scattering of the assembly (8:1), save the apostles, suggests that those who bury Stephen are not Jesus-followers. These Jews are pious despite not being members of the Way. More neutrally, Luke notes how the general Jewish populace holds the apostles in high regard, even though only some join the *ecclesia* (5:13–14).

Second is Gamaliel (5:33–39). Some have argued that Gamaliel is an ironic or even negative character. Internal evidence suggests that Luke portrays him honorably, however. Gamaliel is introduced as a Torah teacher (cf. Luke 5:17), a Pharisee, and one "respected by all the people (παντὶ τῷ λαῷ)" (5:34). To be sure, all these descriptors are complicated, but none excludes reading Gamaliel as venerable. Torah teachers and Pharisees in Luke's Gospel are primarily characters who are intrigued by Jesus, respect him, yet frequently misunderstand him and, therefore, quarrel with him at times.[55] Nevertheless, they stay in close enough proximity to Jesus to debate with him, extend hospitality to him, and sometimes silently acknowledge the superiority of his *halakhic* reasoning (7:36–50; 11:37–51; 14:1–24).[56] They attempt to protect his life on two occasions, though in ways that show their misunderstanding of his mission (13:31; 19:39).[57] In Acts, Pharisees join

---

[54] On the Jewish people and Jesus' execution, see Jon A. Weatherly, *Jewish Responsibility for the Death of Jesus in Luke-Acts*, JSNTSup 106 (Sheffield: Sheffield Academic, 1995). In brief, Luke restricts culpability to the ignorant (and divinely ordained) actions of both Jews and gentiles in Jerusalem (Luke 24:20; Acts 2:23; 3:14–18; 4:23–28; 10:39 cf. 13:26–33).

[55] Their repeated use of "teacher" to address Jesus highlights their respect yet misunderstanding: "'Teacher' is an address used for Jesus by those outside the circle of his followers, by those who seek something from Jesus but have not fully formed their opinion of him" (Green, *Luke*, 688). For various readings on the Pharisees in Luke-Acts, Sanders, *Jews*, 123–31; Brawley, *Jews*, 84–106; Darr, *Character Building*, 85–126; David Gowler, *Host, Guest, Enemy, and Friend: Portraits of the Pharisees in Luke and Acts* (Eugene, OR: Wipf and Stock, 2008); Raimo Hakola, "'Friendly' Pharisees and Social Identity in the Book of Acts," in *Contemporary Studies*, 181–200; Josep Rius-Camps, "El Mesianismo de Jesús Investigado por el Rabino Lucas a Partir de sus Fuentes Judías y Cristianas: Un Escrito a Modo de 'Demonstración' (ἐπίδειξις) Dirigido al Sumo Sacerdote Teófilo," *EstB* 63 (2005): 527–57 (esp. 543–45); Mary Marshall, *The Portrayals of the Pharisees in the Gospels and Acts*, FRLANT 254 (Göttingen: Vandenhoeck & Ruprecht, 2014). On Gamaliel, see Osvaldo Padilla, *The Speeches of Outsiders in Acts: Poetics, Theology and Historiography*, SNTSMS 144 (Cambridge: Cambridge University Press, 2008), 106–34; cf. Robert C. Tannehill, *The Shape of Luke's Story: Essays on Luke-Acts* (Eugene, OR: Cascade, 2005), 257–70.

[56] Michal Beth Dinkler, "Silence as Rhetorical Technique in Luke 14:1–6," *PRSt* 40 (2013): 337–48.

[57] Nothing suggests the Pharisees fabricate Herod's plot (cf. Luke 3:20). The political overtones of the triumphal entry indicate that they tell Jesus to silence his disciples out of fear of Roman retribution. The Pharisees in these scenes play an analogous role to those who warn Paul about going to Jerusalem (Acts 21:12–14). Green, *Luke*, 535–38, 687–88.

the Way (15:1–2) and declare Paul innocent before the high priests and Sadducees (23:9). Of course, Pharisees participate in *stasis* in both instances, one of which occurs in the Way itself. Still, these two instances simply reiterate that Pharisees continue to struggle to understand. Misunderstanding, though, is not unique to Pharisees.[58] They too are mixed characters. Luke's identification of Gamaliel as a Torah teacher and a Pharisee, then, does not preclude respectability.

Luke paints the general Jewish populace, who hold Gamaliel in high regard, as a mixed bag. In general, the people are fickle. Sometimes they view Jesus and his followers favorably (Luke 21:38; 23:48; Acts 2:47; 5:13), occasionally providing a buffer between them and Israel's leadership (Luke 22:3; Acts 4:21; 5:26). Other times, they are persuaded to oppose Jesus and his followers (e.g., Luke 23:13–25; Acts 6:12; 21:27; 22:22). The crowds are an inconsistent group that struggles to understand the identity and significance of Jesus and his followers. Nevertheless, certain characters, including Paul, appeal to a person's standing before the people to establish their credibility (e.g., Luke 7:4–5; 10:22; 22:12; cf. Luke 24:19; Acts 5:13). That Gamaliel is well respected among all the people suggests that one should view him with respect rather than cynicism.

Most significant for establishing Gamaliel as an honorable character is that Luke links him to Paul (22:3). Paul's affiliation with Gamaliel does double duty. On the one hand, within the narrative world, it establishes Paul's credibility in the eyes of his audience in Jerusalem. On the other hand, the connection with Paul establishes Gamaliel's credibility in the eyes of the reader. One might object that Gamaliel's student Paul spearheads violence against the Way, harming Gamaliel's credibility. Yet, Paul's behavior ironically contradicts his master's teachings (5:33–37).[59] Paul all but explicitly confirms Gamaliel's fundamental point: Despite thinking he was serving God, Paul was actually fighting against God (22:3–11; 26:4–18). Gamaliel, though he does not join the Way, emerges as a commendable character (5:35; cf. 10:2, 22).

Gamaliel's honorability emerges most obviously in his speech when he defends the apostles from the hostility of the rest of the council (5:33–37). Gamaliel likely voices the perspective of the narrative that the Way, without God's help, would fail. Comparing the Jesus movement to failed rebellions, he exhorts the council to let the apostles be since, if the Way is a human movement, it will die. If it is from God, the council will be found fighting against God (cf. Josephus, *J.W.* 5.378; *Ant.* 14.310).[60] To be sure, the comparisons with Judas and Theudas demonstrate that Gamaliel, like other Pharisees, misunderstands Jesus and his followers, perceiving them as a messianic revolutionary group.[61] Though he lacks full understanding, Gamaliel perceives the Way better than his Sanhedrin compatriots. He deters them from killing the apostles. Gamaliel's advice

---

[58] Smith, "Politics," 206–266.

[59] Moreover, Paul persecutes with instructions from the high priest, rather than from a Pharisee (9:1). The chief priests and Sadducees drive hostility against the Way in Acts (e.g., 4:1; 5:17; 7:1).

[60] Padilla argues that Acts, like other Second Temple Jewish writings, uses speeches of "outsiders," like Gamaliel, to legitimate the narrative's aim (*Speeches*, 113–34, esp. 126; similarly, Lohfink, *Sammlung*, 85–87). Codex Bezae strengthens Gamaliel's advice and respectability. In it, Gamaliel adds that the apostles "are brothers (εισιν αδελφοι)" and tells the council to release them "without staining the hands (μη μιαναντες τας χειρας)" (Rius-Camps, "Mesianismo," 543).

[61] Gamaliel is not alone in this perception (e.g., 21:38; 24:5; Rowe, *World*, 53–89).

is scarcely heeded beyond this scene—the council will soon turn against Stephen and the Way (7:53–8:3)—the advice stands as wise and as an interpretive guide, nevertheless.[62] Gamaliel informs the council and the reader that God will bring about the failure or success of this movement. He does not join the Way, but he still protects it and provides an interpretive lens for the subsequent characters and events of Acts, including Paul and his ministry.

The third group of venerable Jews is the Berean synagogue (συναγωγὴν τῶν Ἰουδαίων; 17:10). Luke describes its members uniformly positively. These Jews (οὗτοι) are more noble (εὐγενέστεροι) than the Thessalonians. Luke specifies that the nobility of their response lies in their eager reception of the word (ἐδέξαντο τὸν λόγον; 17:11; cf. Luke 9:5; 10:8; Acts 8:14; 11:1). This response, though, does not entail complete acceptance; they consider the veracity of Paul's claims based on Israel's Scripture. As with other regions, only a portion of Berean Jews (πολλοὶ ἐξ αὐτῶν) believe the message (17:12). Nevertheless, their character and receptive posture toward Paul and the Way is commendable. The Berean Jews as a whole are applauded for their openness, though not all join the Way. Furthermore, no Berean commits violence against Paul. It is the Thessalonian Jews who drive Paul from the region. To be sure, Luke contrasts the Bereans with the more violent Thessalonians, but the comparison shows Luke's ability to differentiate between Jewish communities within the narrative. Luke can paint an entire diaspora Jewish community with uniform favor.

3.1.4 Summary: The Jews "in Disagreement with One Another"

Acts' portrait of the Jewish world is not monolithic. "The Jews" are not a uniformly antagonistic group that rejects the message of Jesus and stands against the Way. Rather, Luke's portrayal is nuanced. Acts tends to identify "the Jews" as such when other groups or ethnicities (i.e., gentiles) are involved and often specifies Jews based on geographic origins. The book subdivides the Jewish world based on their responses to the word. Some Jews are persuaded, others are unpersuaded and hostile, and others who are unpersuaded remain neutral. In this final group, some are honorable, pious, respectable Jews who refrain from joining the Way. As Gamaliel and the Bereans indicate, Jews have different degrees of perception regarding God's role in the Way and the veracity of their message. The Jewish community debates how to engage this new movement in its midst during the entirety of the narrative. Up until the end, the Jewish world divides over Jesus as it internally discusses about his identity and the message about him (Acts 28:23). Levels of fidelity and understanding vary in Israel, as has been the case throughout the people's history.

3.2 Bumps along the Way

Even the Way is not monolithic. Just like he abstains from a uniform portrait of "the Jews" as hostile, Luke refrains from idealizing the Jesus-following community. It, too,

---

[62] Matthews, *Perfect Martyr*, 64; Tannehill, *Narrative Unity*, 2:67; Fernández Ubiña, "Razones," 37.

struggles with obedience and understanding in Acts. The supposedly faithful Jesus-followers are more analogous to those typically considered the unfaithful in Israel. The Way needs to be made increasingly straight. All Israel, including Jesus-followers, must be brought into greater alignment with God's will. Indeed, the bumbling along the Way embodies Gamaliel's declaration that, were God not involved, the movement would fail. As God did through Jesus' death, so Israel's God uses Israel's errors and its imperfect heroes for God's purposes (3:17-18).

Three overlapping observations evince this claim. First, although they are described as uniform in thought at points, the Way, like other Jewish groups, faces internal conflicts, including its own *stasis*. When unity appears, it falls apart shortly thereafter, whether for external or internal reasons. Second, the believing community, like the wider Jewish world, has unsavory characters in its midst. These are the antitheses of the noble among the unbelieving Jewish community. Third, they have made strides since the resurrection, but the apostles and believing community still struggle to be faithful and understand Jesus' leadings. The disciples continue to mature as the narrative progresses, and the Way often falls short of its calling. They are slow to understand and obey Jesus, to be faithful to Israel's God. Therefore, they are akin to their non-believing kin. The Way in Acts is not an idealized community. It perpetuates Israel's difficulties with fidelity.

3.2.1 Divergences in the Way

After Peter's first two sermons, Luke paints a beautiful community that embodies how Israel was supposed to live (2:43-47). The believers, Luke says, were of "one heart and life (καρδία καὶ ψυχὴ μία)" as they shared their possessions so that "there was not anyone who was poor among them" (4:32-35; cf. LXX Deut 15:4, 7). This idyllic picture falls apart quickly. As it continues to grow, the Way begins to violate its sharing standards. Hellenist widows are being overlooked (παρεθεωροῦντο) in the daily table-service (6:1).[63] There appears to be unfair treatment in the community, against widows all the more. Some might consider this a blip on the radar or a natural result of a diverse community's rapid expansion, but this represents a serious failure.[64] It violates a core tenet of justice practices in Israel, namely, to protect the vulnerable, widows especially (e.g., Exod 22:22; Deut 10:14; 16:11; 27:19; Sir 4:10; 35:14-19; cf. Luke 2:36-38; 4:25-26). Disregarding widows is a grave offense that reintroduces needy persons among the community (cf. Acts 4:34). Additionally, this injustice and subsequent response of the Hellenists against the Hebrews disrupts the Holy Spirit-generated unity (ὁμοθυμαδόν; 1:14; 2:46; 4:24; 5:12). If the community's unity derives from the Spirit,

---

[63] On τῇ διακονίᾳ τῇ καθημερινῇ as the regular table fellowship rather than just daily food distribution, see David W Pao, "Waiters or Preachers: Acts 6:1-7 and the Lukan Table Fellowship Motif," *JBL* 130 (2011): 127-44. Specifics aside, widows are being excluded from a core practice of the community. Cf. Jorge Pantelis, "Etnias e Iglesias en Hechos de los Apóstoles," *Apuntes* 24 (2004): 109-18.

[64] Cf. Jervell, *Apostelgeschichte*, 215-23; Darrell L. Bock, *Acts* (Grand Rapids, MI: Baker Academic, 2007), 256-57; Keener, *Acts*, 2:1253-89; Mauricio Acuña, "'No Había entre Ellos Ningún Necesitado': La Normatividad de la Comunidad de Bienes en Hechos 2-6," *Kairós* 48 (2011): 35-53.

violation of said unity contravenes the Spirit.⁶⁵ A rift based on ethno-linguistic and socioeconomic lines has emerged under the apostles' oversight.

Grumbling occurs (ἐγένετο γογγυσμός) among the Hellenists against the Hebrews as a result (Acts 6:1). The Hellenists' grievance appears reasonable and justified. That they raise a γογγυσμός gives their response a less than honorable coloring, however (cf. Luke 5:30; 15:2; 19:7). The LXX uses this word group to refer to complaining against God directly (Wis 1:10–11; Isa 58:9–10; Ps. Sol. 16:11) and/or via God's appointed leaders (Num 17:5, 10). The most noteworthy example is when the wilderness generation complains (γογγυσμός) against Moses, Aaron, and God about their desire to return to Egypt because they want meat and bread (Exod 16:1–12, esp. 7–8; cf. Sir 46:7). Initially, Israel responds to God's act of liberating them from Egypt with belief and praise (Exod 14:31–15:1). The people grumble (διαγογγύζω) shortly thereafter because they lack water (15:23–24).⁶⁶ The Way, those within Israel responding to God's new exodus, reenacts this problematic behavior.⁶⁷ Like their ancestors, the Hellenists' grumbling occurs after an act of deliverance—in this case, the apostles being freed from Israel's leadership—and subsequent rejoicing at God's saving actions (5:41–42). Luke recounts a twofold problem shortly after the period of Spirit-generated harmonious fellowship: Seemingly biased prioritization in communal fellowship causes improper, even if justified, grumbling, likely directed at the Jesus-appointed apostolic leadership under whose watch such injustice and division emerged.⁶⁸ All are implicated in the dissolution of unity.

Of course, the council reaches a community-approved solution by appointing the seven for table-service (διακονεῖν τραπέζαις; 6:2–6). Whether this solution is entirely faithful to Jesus' teaching and the Spirit's leading is dubious for three reasons.⁶⁹ First and foremost, Luke intertwines serving (διακονέω) Jesus, the singular service of the apostolate (1:17, 25; cf. 20:45; 21:19), with tangible service (e.g., Luke 8:3; 12:37; 17:7–10; Acts 11:29–30; 12:25). In fact, Jesus, the one who brings good news to the poor (Luke 4:18), embodies this expectation by being among the apostles as one who serves at the table (ἐν μέσῳ ὑμῶν εἰμι ὡς ὁ διακονῶν)—and he expects his disciples to follow

---

⁶⁵ F. Scott Spencer, "Neglected Widows in Acts 6:1–7," *CBQ* 56 (1994): 715–33; Joel B. Green, "Neglecting Widows and Serving the Word? Acts 6:1–7 as a Test Case for a Missional Hermeneutic," in *New Testament Theology in Light of the Church's Mission: Essays in Honor of I. Howard Marshall*, ed. Jon Laansma, Grant R. Osborne, and Ray Van Neste (Eugene, OR: Cascade, 2011), 151–60.

⁶⁶ After departing from Sinai, the people grumbled wickedly before the Lord (ἦν ὁ λαὸς γογγύζων πονηρὰ ἔναντι Κυρίου) and against Moses again because of food, leading to the appointment of the seventy elders (LXX Num 11:1–17; Pao, "Waiters," 137). A key difference is that, while God instructs Moses to appoint the seventy, the apostles establish the seven of their own accord.

⁶⁷ On the new exodus motif in Acts, see Pao, *New Exodus*.

⁶⁸ Green, "Widows," 157–58; Pao, "Waiters," 142–43; Justo L. González, *Hechos*, CsB (Minneapolis, MN: Augsburg Fortress, 2006), 37–40.

⁶⁹ The standard interpretation that the apostles are in the right "assumes without warrant that Luke presents the apostles as authorized representatives of the narrator's perspective (and, thus, of the divine perspective, which the narrator represents and mediates in Luke-Acts) ... Rather than presuming that the apostles are above reproach we ought to wonder about the opposite. After all, was it not under their watch that the disciples had digressed from their idyllic state of unity and violated the character of their own community as one in which there was no needy person?" (Green, "Widows," 157).

suit as a part of their role as judges of the twelve tribes (Luke 22:24–30). Separating serving the word and prayer runs contrary to Jesus' teachings and actions. The apostles do not appear to be in alignment with him. Ironically, two of the seven appointed table-servers, Stephen and Philip, demonstrate the absurdity of bifurcated service. Both proclaim the message of Jesus. Stephen even performs apostle-like signs and wonders (cf. 5:12). These two, not the apostles, precipitate the spread of the word beyond Judea in accordance with Jesus' words (6:8–8:40; cf. 1:7–8).[70] Stephen and Philip serve table *and* word.

Second, the apostles say that the prospect of serving tables instead of the word "is not pleasing (οὐκ ἀρεστόν ἐστιν)" (6:2). To *whom* this is not pleasing is troublingly ambiguous. In the LXX, ἀρεστός and the related verb ἀρέσκω (6:5) can carry positive or negative connotations depending on who is pleased (cf. Gal 1:10)—God (Deut 6:18; Dan 4:34; Mal 3:4) or humans (Deut 12:8; Jer 9:14; 16:12)—and whether the pleasing thing is dishonorable (e.g., Gen 19:8; Judg 21:14; Esth 1:21) or honorable (e.g., Deut 23:16; Josh 22:33; 24:15; 3 Kgdms 3:10; Jdt 7:16; cf. Mark 6:22//Matt 14:6). Humans seeking their own pleasure, more often than not, runs contrary to what pleases God. Notably, the other use of ἀρεστός in Luke-Acts occurs when Herod's execution of James pleases some Jews (12:3). If the apostles are the ones who do not find the prospect of serving tables pleasing, their motivation seems suspect. Of course, their decision to appoint the seven pleases the multitude (ἤρεσεν ὁ λόγος ἐνώπιον παντὸς τοῦ πλήθους; 6:5). But, in light of the aforementioned echoes of the wilderness generation and the fickle nature of the multitudes in Luke-Acts (e.g., Luke 8:37; 23:1; Acts 14:4; 21:36; 23:7), communal consent need not amount to divine approval.[71] Given Luke's emphasis on serving the impoverished, including widows, the Lord Jesus might be less than pleased with the apostolic decision to pawn table-service onto others.

Third, casting further doubt, the Spirit rests on the seven and the apostles pray over them (6:3, 6), but the Spirit and prayer play no direct role in the decision itself. This omission is glaring. Luke tends to mention the influence of prayer and the Spirit in a decision or action, marking the subsequent act or words as a wise and faithful (e.g., 1:14, 24–26; 4:31; 8:29; 11:12; 13:1–4; 14:23; 15:28; 19:21; cf. 16:6–7; 21:4). Altogether, the apostles' motivation and decision to appoint the seven appear ambiguous at best. At worst, they betray a Jesus-given vocation (Luke 22:24–30).

Nevertheless, as God is wont to do, God uses ambiguous, even unfaithful actions in Israel to advance the word in the world. The Way grows (6:7). Immediately after, the Spirit-filled Stephen is killed (6:8–7:60), and the *ecclesia*, save the apostles, is scattered (διεσπάρησαν) due to severe persecution (διωγμὸς μέγας; 8:1). Diaspora typically is judgment for infidelity in the Scriptures and early Jewish literature (e.g., LXX Lev 26:33; Deut 4:27; 28:64; 32:28; Jer 13:24; 39:37; Ezek 12:15; Joel 3:2; Bar 2:29; 3:8; cf. Ps.

---

[70] Green, "Widows," 158; Spencer, "Widows," 729–32; Carter, "Diaspora Acts," 101. Paul, too, serves table (11:29–30; 12:25) and word (20:45; 21:19).

[71] This is not to say that the seven are problematic characters. On the contrary, Stephen and Philip are exemplary. It is to reiterate that God uses flawed, mistaken people and less-than-faithful actions to carry out God's will (e.g., Luke 6:16; 10:17–20; 24:36–39; Acts 2:23–24; 3:17–18).

Sol. 9:1–2; 4 Ezra 1:31). In an ironic twist, the Way's dispersion leads to expansion beyond Jerusalem. Persecution, not the direct action of the apostles, advances the word's spread in accordance with Jesus' teaching (8:4; 11:19; cf. 1:8; Luke 24:47–49). These results affirm Gamaliel's words that nothing, not even its own shortcomings, can stop the Way if it is God-ordained. Unlike the human-led movements of Judas and Theudas, whose scattering entailed their failure, the scattering of the Way leads to its growth (5:36–39). God's plans are achieved even when Jesus' followers misunderstand their calling and make less than faithful decisions.

The Way's initial idealistic sheen dims quickly. The justice and unity generated by the Spirit fray. The Way perpetuates Israel's struggle to maintain justice for widows (cf. Isa 1:23; Jer 22:2–5; Ezek 22:7). Such actions propagate division between Greek and Hebrew-speaking Jewish brothers and sisters within the renewed core of Israel. The *ecclesia* experiences division comparable to the wider Jewish world in Acts. Israel's future judges, the apostles, continue to misunderstand their Lord-given vocation by separating serving the word from serving the table. Like Israel historically, they struggle to respond faithfully to their calling to be the Lord's faithful witnesses in proclaiming the word to the ends of the earth (1:8; 10:39–41; cf. Isa 42:18–19; 43:13–28). The apostles have grown since receiving the Spirit, but they still need to grow in understanding their vocation. Nevertheless, God uses these imperfect followers to spread the word.

The next conflict internal to the Way is quite severe. When certain individuals come from Judea to Antioch, claiming circumcision—becoming Jewish—is required for salvation, "no small factionalism and debate (στάσεως καὶ ζητήσεως οὐκ ὀλίγης)" arises between them and Paul and Barnabas (15:1–2). That Luke uses litotes and repeats the motif of *stasis*, internecine strife often associated with sedition and potential violence in Luke-Acts (Luke 23:19, 25; Acts 19:40; 23:7, 10; 24:5) and Josephus (e.g., *J.W.* 2.466; 4.502, 545–548; 5.5–20; cf. Thuc. *P.W.* 3.82.6; 3.81.5), demonstrates the dispute's severity.[72] The argument pits the Way against itself, threatening to tear it apart at the seams. As with the Hellenists and the Hebrews, this division appears after a period of encouragement and fellowship in Antioch (14:21–28). This dissension precipitates the Jerusalem Council. Even after Paul and Barnabas, on the way to Jerusalem, report all God has done among them in reaching the gentiles, certain Pharisaic believers reiterate the need for circumcision and Torah observance for gentiles (15:2–5).[73] Ultimately, the leadership sides with Barnabas and Paul (15:12, 19–21). They blame the "certain people who went out from us (τινὲς ἐξ ἡμῶν ἐξελθόντες) without being instructed" for unsettling the gentile believers with their erroneous teaching (15:24).

Two points merit attention. First, the divergent teaching emerges *within* the mother community in Jerusalem (τινὲς ἐξ ἡμῶν), not from external influence (15:24; cf. 15:1).

---

[72] Rowe, *World*, 53–89; Wills, "Depiction," 635. Josephus uses *stasis* for internal discord and factionalism, Jewish and Roman alike (Rajak, *Josephus*, 78–104; Mader, *Josephus*, 55–104; Mason, *Christian Origins*, 78–87).

[73] Thiessen, *Contesting*, 111–47; Oliver, *Torah Praxis*, 445–82.

Diversity of praxis—it is *Pharisaic* believers who defend the gentile-circumcision position (15:5)—and thought persisted in the Way, as with the broader Jewish world, causing disagreement.[74] To be sure, Luke rejects the views and authority of these individuals, but he retains their place among the Way. They are still "believers (πεπιστευκότες)" and "brothers" (15:5, 13; cf. Gal 2:4). The Jerusalem Council expunges no one from the community. These incorrect believers, along with the entire assembly, are simply silenced; their views have been undermined and realigned (15:12, 22).[75] Second, that the Jerusalem Council must deliberate at all and needs to hear Barnabas, Paul, and Peter's testimonies *after* the initial reports of God's acts among the gentiles and "much debate (πολλῆς ζητήσεως)" before James' decision is made demonstrates that the conclusion was not self-evident (Acts 15:3–12). It needs the witness of leading figures, a reminder of the explicit affirmation of the Spirit, which the apostles and Jewish believers in Judea *already heard* from Peter (11:1–18), and scriptural warrant.[76] The Way still labors to discern God's activity in the world.

One expects that the Way is cohesive again. The unity dissipates instantly, however. Luke places Paul and Barnabas' separation from one another *immediately* after bringing the Jerusalem Council's encouraging word to Antioch (15:36–41). The "unanimity (ὁμοθυμαδόν)" by which the Council decided to send these beloved companions together soon becomes "irritation (παροξυσμός)" between the pair, causing a schism (15:25, 39). Large scale factionalism is prevented, but a partnership generated by the Holy Spirit dissolves (13:1–3).

Once the narrative shifts beyond Judea and Samaria, the presence of internal threats diminishes. Yet, as Paul's diaspora ministry nears its end, at Miletus, he warns the elders of the Ephesian assemblies that they will face external and internal threats that could cause division in the *ecclesia*. "After my departure," he states, "cruel wolves will come in among you (εἰσελεύσονται ... λύκοι βαρεῖς εἰς ὑμᾶς)" (20:29). Paul exhorts vigilance since some from the outside might intrude in the community to harm the flock. External influence will cause internal strife. Additional problems will emerge from the inside too. Paul warns that "people will arise from among you yourselves (καὶ ἐξ ὑμῶν αὐτῶν ἀναστήσονται), speaking crookedly in order to draw away the disciples after them" (20:30).[77] This threat emerges within the Way itself; fellow Jesus-followers will try to mislead the disciples. By "speaking crookedly (λαλοῦντες διεστραμμένα)," these believing individuals align themselves with the perverse generation that misunderstands Jesus and faces judgment (cf. Luke 9:41) and Paul's initial nemesis, Elymas (Acts 13:8–10).[78] They distort the intended smooth, straight way of the Lord (cf. Luke 3:4). These individuals pose an internal threat to unity.

---

[74] Carter, "Diaspora Acts," 101–2.
[75] Acts 11:18; 21:14; cf. Dinkler, "Silence," 346–48. That the decision is made and the letter sent with the consent of the entire *ecclesia* (ὅλῃ τῇ ἐκκλησίᾳ) further suggests the Pharisaic believers agree (15:22).
[76] Again, Pharisaic believers deserve a sympathetic reading. They are wrong from the vantage point of Acts, but Luke does not dismiss their view off-handedly. He preserves the debate.
[77] Jervell, *Apostelgeschichte*, 513; Brawley, *Jews*, 83.
[78] Indeed, the disciples are implicated in the wicked generation (Luke 9:37–41; cf. Ezek 20:1–32).

The presence of internal conflicts suggests that the Way is neither uniform in its views nor harmonious in its interactions (cf. 21:20–22). They face their own internecine divisions, akin to the wider Jewish world of Acts. Such threats will persist in the life of the community beyond the narrative (20:29–30). More problematic, though, is the presence of dishonorable figures within the *ecclesia*. These characters embody and provoke the internal strife and variances within the Way. They reiterate how the Way mirrors Israel's continued struggle with faithfulness. The Way is not an idealized, unified community.

3.2.2 Ignoble Jesus-Followers

Not only does the Way have its divergences, it has its blemishes. It has unsavory members. Three features among these ignoble figures link the Way to Israel at large. First, sinful (new) covenant members exist. Participation in God's people does not mean one maintains fidelity to Israel's Lord. Satan can lead Jesus-followers astray.[79] Second, infidelity does not preclude ongoing covenant membership. The unfaithful often have an opportunity to repent. If one steps off the Way, the opportunity to return to the straight and narrow usually remains. Though, the possibility of straying from the Way entirely and the threat of judgment, including exclusion from the people of God, persist. Third, God works despite and often through the infidelity and chastisement of covenant members. Israel remains God's servant even as Jewish-Israelites exhibit unfaithfulness.[80]

The first ignoble character counted among Jesus' followers in Acts is, of course, Judas. Judas embodies these three traits. First, one might be inclined to separate Judas from the Way, but Luke emphasizes that Judas was one of their own.[81] Judas, Peter states, "was counted among" the apostles (κατηριθμημένος ἦν ἐν ἡμῖν) "and received his portion of this service (καὶ ἔλαχεν τὸν κλῆρον τῆς διακονίας ταύτης)" (1:17). Similarly, Luke's Gospel refers to Judas as "being from the number of the Twelve (ὄντα ἐκ τοῦ ἀριθμοῦ τῶν δώδεκα)" even *as Satan enters him* (22:3). When Judas is again mentioned by name as he leads those who come to arrest Jesus, Judas remains "one of the Twelve (εἷς τῶν δώδεκα)" (22:47). Up until his removal from the Twelve and replacement by Matthias (Acts 1:20–26), the traitor is counted among Jesus' closest followers.

Notably, Judas is not the only apostle who faces satanic influence and risks betraying Jesus. Satan sifts Simon Peter with the result that he thrice denies Jesus (Luke 22:31–34, 54–62). The difference is that Simon Peter returns/repents (ἐπιστρέψας; 22:32), while Judas "went away (ἀπελθών)" never to return/repent (22:3; cf. Matt 27:3–5). Jesus' most

---

[79] In early Judaism, "the devil embodies the specific power that would mislead the people of God and hold them captive from the life to which God calls them" (Blumhofer, *Future*, 157; e.g., CD 4.13–21; 1QS 1.23–24; 2.4–19; Jub. 1:20–21; 12:20; 7:27; 11:1–16). Paolo Sacchi, *Jewish Apocalyptic and Its History*, trans. William J. Short, JSPSup 20 (Sheffield: Sheffield Academic Press, 1990), 211–32.
[80] Kaminsky, *Yet I Loved*, 137–58; Goldingay, *Israel's Faith*, 188–209.
[81] Contra Arie W. Zwiep, *Christ, the Spirit and the Community of God: Essays on the Acts of the Apostles*, WUNT 2/293 (Tübingen: Mohr Siebeck, 2010), 120.

intimate followers risk succumbing to the power of the adversary (cf. 22:31; Acts 26:18). Disciples, even apostles, can persist in or abandon fidelity to Jesus.[82]

Second, Judas, especially when compared with Peter, demonstrates how unfaithful Jewish-Israelites retain their covenantal identity, though can ultimately forfeit it and be removed from Israel. The traitor Judas participates in the establishment of the new covenant *after* Satan entered him and he departed from the Twelve (22:3–23). Judas shares the table with them (22:21). He is included in the new covenant community *and* later judged by God (Acts 1:17–20; cf. 1QS 1.21–2.17). Judas, then, embodies what it means to apostatize and be cut off from the people (Acts 3:23) as he forfeits his role as one of Israel's twelve future judges (Luke 22:30).[83] Judgment looms over all the unfaithful in Israel, including Jesus' followers.

Third, God still works through Judas' infidelity. Judas was instrumental in Jesus' Scripture-fulfilling death (Acts 1:16), which, of course, was integral to fulfilling the ancestral promises (e.g., 3:11–26). Moreover, Peter notes, Judas' own death and replacement also happen in accordance with the Scriptures (1:19–20; cf. Luke 22:22). God's plans for Israel persist even through the unfaithful in Israel, including the unfaithful of the Way. Indeed, the consummate figure of Israel's disloyalty to their Messiah in Luke-Acts *is an apostle*, one handpicked by Jesus himself (Luke 6:16).[84]

Lest one think that Judas was the only bad apple and the Way traverses a smooth road after the Spirit's advent (2:42–47), Luke incorporates other problematic Jesus-followers post-Pentecost. In fact, the oft-cited passage about the idealistic Way as a unified, generous group is undermined as soon as it appears. Ananias and Sapphira emerge *immediately* after the idyllic description of the community's Spirit-generated uniformity of "heart and life" and sharing possessions as exemplified in Barnabas (4:31–5:10). The couple parodies Barnabas' venerable act. They conspire in private and withhold from the community (5:1–2, 9), in contrast with Barnabas' openhandedness (4:32–34). Ananias and Sapphira's hearts run contrary to the community's "one heart." Their hearts, Peter states, have been filled by Satan to lie to the Spirit (5:3–4; cf. Luke 22:3). Ananias and Sapphira reiterate the fragility of the Way's unity. The ideal community does not last long.

Furthermore, this couple illustrates how Satan not only has power over those outside the Way (Acts 26:18; cf. 10:38; 13:10) but the accuser threatens the *ecclesia* itself. The Jerusalem Jesus-following community is not immune to falling prey to the one who tempts Israel away from its God. One can deviate from the Way of repentance and fidelity to Israel's God through Satan's influence. Even those among the Way risk being cut off from God's people. As a result of "testing the Spirit of the Lord (πειράσαι τὸ πνεῦμα κυρίου)," Ananias and Sapphira fall dead, judged for their deceitful imitation of

---

[82] Brawley, *Text*, 48–49, 63–64; Parsons, *Acts*, 31–33; Green, *Conversion*, 87–160; cf. Garrett, *Demise*, 37–60.

[83] B. J. Oropeza, "Judas' Death and Final Destiny in the Gospels and Earliest Christian Writings," *Neot* 44 (2010): 342–61; Matthew G. Whitlock, "Acts 1:15–26 and the Craft of New Testament Poetry," *CBQ* 77 (2015): 87–106. Judas' absence renders the Twelve, the representatives of Israel, incomplete. For additional parallels with Qumran, see Conzelmann, *Apostelgeschichte*, 28–29.

[84] On antisemitic tropes derived from Judas, see Zwiep, *Christ*, 77–99; Oropeza, "Judas' Death," 343–44.

Barnabas' generosity (4:9; cf. Luke 4:12).[85] In Israel's past such judgments warned about proper protocols for approaching God and call the people to honor Israel's appointed leaders (cf. Lev 10:8–11; Num 16:40).[86] Unsurprisingly, the Jerusalem *ecclesia* and all who hear about this event respond with great fear (5:6, 11), perhaps adversely causing some Jews who respect the Way not to join it (5:13).[87] In spite of the couple's infidelity and its fallout, God adds "a multitude (πλήθη)" to the number of believers (5:14). God's plans are still achieved.

Lest one contend that Ananias and Sapphira are the sole blemish on the Way's unity and picturesque generosity post-Pentecost, Simon the magician exhibits the persistence of wealth's allure, the presence of unrighteousness, and ongoing problems of the heart among members of the Way (5:3–4; 8:21; cf. 4:32).[88] Simon long amazed the people in Samaria with his magic, which they presumed was done by God's power (8:9–11).[89] Yet, Simon believes Philip's preaching of the good news about the kingdom and the name of Jesus along with the Samaritans (8:12–13). Luke highlights the surprising nature of Simon's inclusion: "*and even Simon himself believed* (ὁ δὲ Σίμων καὶ αὐτὸς ἐπίστευσεν)." Not only does the deceitful magician believe, he is baptized—perhaps signaling repentance (cf. Luke 3:3, 7–14; Acts 2:38)—and becomes utterly committed to Philip (βαπτισθεὶς ἦν προσκαρτερῶν τῷ Φιλίππῳ). Luke's description of the magician suggests that Simon is incorporated into the Way and loyal to its message about Jesus.[90]

Nevertheless, Simon remains flawed, deeply so. Seeing Peter and John conferring the Holy Spirit on the Samaritans by laying on hands, Simon attempts to purchase this power, treating it as magic (8:18–19). Peter, of course, rebukes him for attempting "to buy God's gift." Simon must repent (again) of "this wickedness of yours (τῆς κακίας σου ταύτης)" and beseech the Lord that he might be forgiven (8:21–22). Unlike Judas, Ananias, and Sapphira, Simon has the opportunity to repent and petition God to forgive him (if possible!) so as to avoid falling into destruction (εἰς ἀπώλειαν; 18:20; cf.

---

[85] Specific rationale for their deaths aside, suffice it to say that this episode reveals issues internal to and judgment against some among the Way. On early history of interpretation, see Ronald H. van der Bergh, "A Thematic and Chronological Analysis of the Reception of Ananias and Sapphira (Acts 5:1–11) in the First Five Centuries CE," *JECH* 7 (2017): 1–16. For recent proposals, see J. Albert Harrill, "Divine Judgement against Ananias and Sapphira (Acts 5:1–11): A Stock Scene of Perjury and Death," *JBL* 130 (2011): 351–69; David R. McCabe, *How to Kill Things with Words: Ananias and Sapphira under the Prophetic Speech-Act of Divine Judgement (Acts 4.32–5.11)*, LNTS 454 (London: T&T Clark, 2011); Anthony Le Donne, "The Improper Temple Offering of Ananias and Sapphira," *NTS* 59 (2013): 346–64.

[86] In Israel's Scriptures, "instant death by the hand of God is quite rare. When these two criteria are employed—(1) instantly, and (2) directly killed by God—such violence happens exclusively in proximity to the Lord's Shekinah presence: Nadab and Abihu (Lev 10.1–2); the sons of Korah (Num 16.31–35); and Uzzah (2 Sam 6.6–7)" (Le Donne, "Improper," 361). The Nadab-Abihu parallel seems strongest since Leviticus records the removal of their bodies (10:3–7; Acts 5:6, 9).

[87] Schwartz, "Sympathizers," 554.

[88] McWhirter, *Rejected*, 125.

[89] Simon parodies Jesus, whose great acts, though done by God's power, were attributed to Beelzebul (Luke 11:14–23). Garrett, *Demise*, 67.

[90] In Acts, προσκαρτερέω connotes habits or loyalty to people (1:14; 2:42, 46; 6:4; 10:7). Luke simply states that Simon believes, that is, has faith, without qualifying it as not "genuine" or "real" (*pace* Jervell, *Apostelgeschichte*, 265, 267; Garrett, *Demise*, 74; Parsons, *Acts*, 114–18) Simon might even receive the Spirit if he is counted among those upon whom the apostles lay hands (8:14–17).

LXX 1 Chr 21:17; Isa 33:2; Jer 51:12; Ps. Sol. 13:10; *Bar* 4:6; Rev 17:8).[91] Simon stands at a fork in the Way. He has believed, been baptized, and is a legitimate member of Jesus' followers (8:13). However, Simon exhibits his misuse of money, misunderstanding of the Spirit, and misguided desire for power (8:19). His connection to money and magic shows the continued influence of darkness, the realm of Satan, on him (cf. 5:3; 13:8–11; 26:18).[92] As such, he has "no portion or inheritance in this word (μερὶς οὐδὲ κλῆρος ἐν τῷ λόγῳ τούτῳ)" and remains bound by "the chains of unrighteousness (σύνδεσμον ἀδικίας)" (8:21, 23; cf. LXX Isa 58:6).[93] He must repent (again), lest he face judgment.

Simon disappears from the narrative as an open-ended character. Will he repent? Will he be forgiven? Will Peter's words of destruction against Simon come to pass (8:24)? Luke does not answer. Regardless, Simon demonstrates that the baptized, the *ecclesia* itself, face similar problems to the wider Jewish world. Jesus-followers are tempted by wealth, power, and esteem (5:1–10; cf. Luke 8:14; 9:46; 22:24–30). They can fail to comprehend God's actions, particularly the workings of God's Spirit. The Way, like all Israel, has an ongoing struggle with obedience (cf. Luke 11:14–22; Acts 13:6–11).

Though often underappreciated by those who think Acts idealizes the Way, Luke expressly includes these characters in the *ecclesia*.[94] Judas, the consummate traitor, was an apostle and initiated into the new covenant community (1:16–21; cf. Luke 22:14–23). Ananias and Sapphira conduct their deceit within the Jerusalem community, disturbing its idyllic fellowship (Acts 4:34–5:11). Simon Magus attempts to purchase the ability to confer the Holy Spirit after he believed and was baptized. Satan still seeks to lead Israelites, even those within the Way, away from Israel's Lord.[95] It is no surprise that Paul, as he recounts his own innocence, warns of unsavory individuals who will cause division (20:18–35). The Way faced internal threats, its own blemishes, since its infancy. The *ecclesia* can expect them to appear again.

3.2.3 Stumbling along the Way

Even the faithful among the Way, particularly the apostles, evince at several points that they can still be "slow of heart" (Luke 24:25).[96] They display continued maturation and ongoing growth in understanding. At times, they misunderstand and take missteps. The *ecclesia*'s need for enlightenment becomes particularly evident in regard to the gentile

---

[91] Since Simon's sin distorts the power and role of the Holy Spirit, it borders on blaspheming the Spirit (cf. Luke 12:10). Garrett notes that χολὴν πικρίας "alludes to LXX Deut 29:17 (MT 29:18), a curse against those who disobey the covenant by committing idolatry" (*Demise*, 71).

[92] Garrett, *Demise*, 67; Parsons, *Acts*, 117–18.

[93] LXX Deuteronomy uses μερὶς οὐδὲ κλῆρος to refer to the Levites' lack of territorial portion (12:12; 14:26, 28; 18:1; Bruce, *Acts*, 188; Jervell, *Apostelgeschichte*, 265). Simon could lose his allotment in the kingdom. Notably, God calls Israel to break all chains of unrighteousness (πάντα σύνδεσμον ἀδικίας; LXX Isa 58:6). Simon's release from these chains (and Satan; Luke 13:16) might be possible.

[94] Contra e.g., Haenchen, *Acts*, 239–4; Pervo, *Acts*, 132; Zwiep, *Christ*, 120–38.

[95] Green, *Conversion*, 143–60, explores how these characters map onto the parable of the soils (Luke 8:4–15).

[96] On the magnified imperfections of the apostles in the Bezan text, see Jenny Read-Heimerdinger, "The Apostles in the Bezan Text of Acts," in *The Book of Acts as Church History: Text, Textual Traditions and Ancient Interpretations*, ed. Tobias Nicklas and Michael Tilly, BZNW 120 (Berlin: de Gruyter, 2003), 262–80.

mission. Their reticence to accept the gentile mission stands alongside the wider Jewish population's apparent hesitation, even hostility, toward it (11:2–3, 18; 15:1–5; 22:21–22; cf. Luke 4:22–30). Like their unbelieving Jewish brethren, Jewish Jesus-followers, particularly in Jerusalem, sometimes stumble along the repentance-journey.

The apostles' need for enhanced understanding emerges at the beginning of Acts. After Jesus' resurrection and forty-day instruction about the kingdom of God, the apostles ask Jesus if he "will restore the kingdom to Israel at this time" (1:6). While not an invalid question, it is not the question Jesus thinks they should be asking at the time.[97] Instead, Jesus redirects their focus to their mission as witnesses "to Jerusalem, Samaria, and as far as the end of the earth" (1:5–8; cf. Luke 24:47–49). They need to focus on their role as envoys for Jesus.[98] The disciples first display a sluggish response to this calling as they continue to stare into the air. They do not move until two angelic figures question their (in)actions and interpret the ascension, reminding them of Jesus' future return (1:9–11).[99] The pre-Pentecost disciples need to realign their primary concerns with and act on the calling they received from Jesus.

The apostles' realignment seems complete after Pentecost. They testify boldly to Jesus in Jerusalem on several occasions, causing the community's growth and an initial idealistic state (2:43–47; 4:32–35; 5:12–16). Things take a turn for the worse with the appearance of the malfeasants, Ananias and Sapphira (5:1–12), and the Hellenists and Hebrews conflict (6:1–7). Such events disturb the community's Spirit-generated unity under the apostles' noses. The appointment of the seven further suggests that the apostles still need to be drawn into greater alignment with Jesus' expectations for their ministry (Luke 8:3; 12:37; 17:7–10; 22:24–30; Acts 11:29–30; 12:25). Post-Pentecost, the apostles retain some shortcomings in vision and action.

The subsequent dispersion further reveals the Way's, specifically the apostles' reticence to carry out Jesus' vision to be global witnesses. Persecution, not direct action motivated by obedience, initiates the movement of the word from Jerusalem into Samaria and beyond (Acts 8:1–4; 11:19–26; cf. 1:8; Luke 24:47–49). Furthermore, it is not Jesus' primary envoys, the Twelve who received this calling, who initially carry out this expansion. The apostles must be called to Samaria *after* Philip's successful ministry there (8:5–8, 14). While there, Peter and John take first steps toward obeying Jesus' instructions, and then take one step back. They "testify and speak the word of the Lord" in Samaria and proclaim the good news among Samaritan villages as they return to Jerusalem (8:25). They actively pursue the inclusion of and unity with the Samaritans

---

[97] Much ink has been spilt about the validity of the apostles' question. Five main reasons suggest their question is not misguided: (1) Luke 1–2 outline an Israel and Jerusalem-centered hope. (2) The question comes after Jesus has opened their minds to the Scriptures (Luke 24:45–49) and spoke with them about the kingdom for forty days (Acts 1:3–4). (3) Jesus does not reject the question but redirects their focus from timing to present vocation (1:7–8). (4) Linguistic parallels reappear at the Spirit-anointed Peter's second sermon (3:17–21), suggesting hope for a positive answer persists. (5) In Rome, Paul reiterates his commitment to "the hope of Israel" and preaches the kingdom of God (28:20, 30–31). The concluding scene of Acts echoes the initial question. Chance, *Jerusalem*, 132–34; Bauckham, "Restoration," 436–40; Kinzer, *Jerusalem*, 44–53; cf. Conzelmann, *Apostelgeschichte*, 26.

[98] Green, *Luke*, 258–59; Parsons, *Acts*, 28.

[99] Jervell, *Apostelgeschichte*, 117.

(cf. Luke 9:51–56).[100] Yet, they return to Jerusalem *instead of* joining Philip in advancing the mission to the end of the earth vis-à-vis the Ethiopian eunuch (8:26–40). Luke makes no explicit judgment on the actions (or lack thereof) of the apostles, but one can hear discrepancies with the commission they received from Jesus (1:8).[101] They are slow to adhere to their calling and sluggish to obey Jesus. As a result, the Spirit advances the word in the world through more faithful agents like Philip.

Peter eventually takes steps toward obeying the calling when he visits the communities in Judea, the Galilee, and Samaria (9:30–32). In Lydda and Joppa, respectively, Peter heals the paralyzed Aeneas and raises the faithful Tabitha from the dead (9:32–43). These actions demonstrate two areas of growth in Peter. First, he now evinces care for and provides support to widows (9:36–41). As Spencer observes, "Peter in Joppa brings back to life the widows' most cherished supporter and restores her to them. Unlike the Twelve in Jerusalem in Acts 6, Peter in Joppa closely combines prayer and service in an exemplary support system for needy widows. Put another way: supporting widows has been upgraded from secondary to priority status, on a par with prayer, in Peter's ministerial agenda."[102] He imitates Jesus (cf. Luke 5:17–26; 7:11–17). Second, Peter has moved beyond the confines of Jerusalem, as Jesus envisioned (1:8; cf. Luke 24:48–49). Even now, though, Peter does so not as a witness but as a visitor to established communities.

God is about to correct Peter, however. In the vision and interaction with Cornelius, the Lord moves Peter and the Jerusalem community from ignorance to greater understanding about God's character and activity in the world, Israel's Scriptures, and Jew-gentile interactions (10:1–11:18). In their interactions, Peter undergoes greater character development than Cornelius.[103] To begin, Cornelius obeys quicker than Peter. Cornelius immediately (ἐξαυτῆς) responds to his vision by sending messengers to Peter. When Peter arrives, Cornelius and his household stand alert to hear the Lord's message (10:7–8, 33). Peter, in contrast, initially resists God's instructions. He does not arise, kill, or eat (ἀναστὰς . . . θῦσον καὶ φάγε; 10:9–16). To be sure, Peter has a good reason not to eat, namely, *kashrut*. Significantly, the Lord corrects not Peter's reticence to obey but that Peter should not "call common (μὴ κοίνου)" things that "God purified (ὁ θεὸς ἐκαθάρισεν)" (10:15; 11:9; cf. 10:28). Peter's inaction is not the main problem. His inability to recognize God's cleansing acts is.[104]

---

[100] Tannehill, *Narrative Unity*, 2:104–5.

[101] Returning to Jerusalem is not the problem per se. The issue is the apostles' failure to travel beyond Jerusalem, Judea, and Samaria as Jesus told them to do (1:8).

[102] Spencer, "Widows," 732. Acts mentions widows only in the Hellenist-Hebrew conflict and Peter's raising of Tabitha, which nudges the reader to consider them together.

[103] My reading is indebted to Nicholas J. Schaser, "Unlawful for a Jew? Acts 10:28 and the Lukan View of Jewish-Gentile Relations," *BTB* 48 (2018): 188–201. I diverge in that I think Peter plays an important role in initiating the approval of the gentile mission and, therefore, helps catalyze full gentile inclusion (11:1–18). Furthermore, Peter seems impaired by ignorance, not "anti-Gentile convictions" (193). See also Gaventa, *Darkness*, 96–110; Green, *Conversion*, 98–99.

[104] Peter is not the first of God's servants to resist a food-related sign-act for purity concerns (Ezek 4:12–15). For arguments that the vision annuls neither *kashrut* nor the categories of clean-unclean and profane-holy, see Woods, "Peter's Vision," 171–214; Staples, "Rise," 9–14. Staples highlights the connection between animals/food and people groups in antiquity (cf. Jennings, *Acts*, 105–9).

Peter's gradual understanding that the vision pertains to God's cleansing of the gentiles is evinced by Peter's eventual obedience to the Spirit's follow-up commands. The Spirit renews the instruction for Peter to "arise (ἀναστάς)," telling him to "go down and go with (κατάβηθι καὶ πορεύου σὺν)" the three men sent by Cornelius "without making distinction (μηδὲν διακρινόμενος)" (10:19-20; cf. 11:12). That the Spirit speaks "as Peter was reflecting on the vision" suggests that these instructions aid Peter in interpretation. This conclusion is reinforced by the threefold structure, especially the repetition of "arise," and the command to not make a distinction—that is, not making predeterminations about God's relations to Jews versus gentiles (cf. 11:2, 12; 15:9 cf. 11:2, 12; 15:9).[105] The Spirit must guide Peter through the vision's meaning so he can understand that God has cleansed the gentiles, granting "them" the same salvation as "us" Jews (11:12-18; cf. 10:34, 44-48).

Peter learns more from the Spirit in this encounter than Cornelius. Cornelius merely receives correction after his attempt to worship Peter (10:25-26). This correction is significant, to be sure, but expected for a Roman centurion who likely participated in the imperial cult. Other than that, Cornelius appears to receive little to no new revelation. Peter states that Cornelius and his household know (ὑμεῖς οἴδατε) the message about Jesus, the Lord of all, and its spread throughout the world (10:36-43).[106] The Spirit's interruption of Peter without mention of action taken by Cornelius and his household reiterates this claim (10:44-47; cf. 11:12-18). The Spirit comes independently, signifying that God has cleansed the gentiles by God's own initiative.[107]

In contrast, Luke paints Peter's movement from cluelessness to comprehension in four ways. First, the text emphasizes Peter's ignorance about the vision by noting that "Peter was puzzling to himself (ἐν ἑαυτῷ διηπόρει ὁ Πέτρος)" (10:17; cf. 10:19, 21, 29). Being perplexed places Peter in the company of others who struggle to interpret Jesus and his actions in the world, like Herod (Luke 9:7), the Jerusalem Jews who witnessed the believers speaking in tongues (Acts 2:12), and the temple captain and the chief priests (5:24).[108] Peter, the leader of the twelve apostles, struggles to interpret the vision. The Lord must lead him to greater understanding.

Second, Peter states that "it is unlawful for a Jewish man to join with or visit a foreigner (ἀλλοφύλῳ)" (10:28).[109] Designating Cornelius a "foreigner"—a *hapax legomenon* in Luke-Acts and a term often reserved in the LXX for hostile outsiders,

---

[105] On διακρίνω and the continuation of Jewish and gentile identitiea, see Woods, "Acts 15:9," 109-23.
[106] Cornelius' repentance or Christological reorientation may be implicit (cf. 11:18). Gaventa concludes, "Cornelius appears to undergo alternation rather than conversion ... There is no rejection of the past required here, nor is Cornelius in need of a transformed world view of the world" (*Darkness*, 122).
[107] "Peter's interrupted speech about Cornelius' conversion (Acts 10:44) marks the culmination of his two previously interrupted speeches at the Transfiguration (Luke 9:28-36) and his denial of Jesus (22:54-62), which underscore Peter's lack of foresight and fortitude, respectively" (Schaser, "Unlawful," 189). On interrupted speech broadly, see Daniel L. Smith, *The Rhetoric of Interruption: Speech-Making, Turn-Taking, and Rule-Breaking in Luke-Acts and Ancient Greek Narrative*, BZNW 193 (Berlin: de Gruyter, 2012). Moffit contends that the Spirit's presence, which only inhabits holy spaces, confirms that God has cleansed the gentiles ("Atonement," 555-63).
[108] Schaser, "Unlawful," 192.
[109] See Schaser, "Unlawful," 188-91, for arguments why this statement neither reflects the Lukan perspective nor a common first-century Jewish outlook.

most notably Philistines (e.g., Exod 34:15; 1 Kgdms 4:1–7; Jer 29:4; Amos 1:8; Zeph 2:5)—conflicts with the narrator's description of Cornelius. Although he is a member of the Italian Cohort, he has a foot in the Jewish community. Cornelius is devout (εὐσεβής), fears God with his entire house (10:2), gives alms to the Jewish people (τῷ λαῷ; cf. 10:22), and prays at the proper Jewish times (10:4, 30; cf. 3:1). The entire Jewish nation (ὅλου τοῦ ἔθνους τῶν Ἰουδαίων) speaks highly of him (cf. Luke 7:3–5). The angelic visitation affirms Cornelius' piety. The angel informs Cornelius that his prayers and charity have ascended before God as a memorial offering (10:4, 31; cf. LXX Lev 2:2, 9, 16). Cornelius may be uncircumcised (11:3) but he is not a "foreigner."

Third, Peter learns "new" things. God teaches him "not to call any person common or unclean" (10:28), and that God "is not one who shows favoritism (οὐκ ἔστιν προσωπολήμπτης ὁ θεός)" but "among all the nations the one who fears him and works righteousness is acceptable to him" (10:34–35). These conclusions are not new, or at least not unprecedented. Peter's statement that Jews should not "associate with or visit" (κολλᾶσθαι ἢ προσέρχεσθαι; 10:28; cf. 8:29) gentiles and realization about God's lack of favoritism alludes to a lesson from Deuteronomy: Israel's God, whom Israel is called to fear and cling to (φοβηθήσῃ . . . κολληθήσῃ), "does not show favoritism (οὐ θαυμάζει πρόσωπον)" (10:17–19). God's character, along the experience of being strangers in Egypt, grounds Torah's instructions to love and protect strangers in Israel.[110] The Spirit guides Peter back to knowledge God gave Israel long ago.

Furthermore, Israel's Scriptures record gentile incorporation among God's people, God's ongoing relationships with other nations, and expectations for future gentile inclusion.[111] A few examples suffice. A mixed multitude leaves Egypt (Exod 12:37–38). Torah declares gentile sojourners in Israel should be treated like native-born Israelites (Lev 19:34; cf. Exod 12:49; Num 15:29). Ruth the Moabite, grandmother of Jesus' ancestor David, clings to Israel and its God (Ruth 1:13–18; 2:8, 21; cf. Isa 56:3–8; Jdt 14:10). God reminds Israel of his exodus-like dealings with the Philistines and the Arameans (Amos 9:7). Isaiah envisions the incorporation of former enemies Egypt and Assyria alongside Israel as God's people (19:18–25). One day, God will declare, "Happy are my people who are in Egypt and who are in Assyria (εὐλογημένος ὁ λαός μου ὁ ἐν Αἰγύπτῳ καὶ ὁ ἐν Ἀσσυρίοις), and the land of my inheritance, Israel" (LXX 19:25; 66:18–22).[112] Zechariah declares that one day many nations will seek the Lord in Jerusalem since they know God is with Israel (8:20–23). Indeed, God called Israel to be a light to the nations (Isa 42:6–7; 49:5–7; 55:4–5; cf. 51:4–7), witnesses for the world (43:8–13). Peter resembles all Israel in the Scriptures and Acts in that he too struggles to perceive and perform this role as a witness to the gentiles (cf. Acts 13:47).[113]

---

[110] Schaser, "Unlawful," 189, 196. Schaser notes parallels with the encounter between Philip and the Ethiopian eunuch (8:26–40). This link reinforces the contentions that Spirit uses the seven to spread the message because the Twelve are slow to act. Moreover, the Jerusalem community receives no report about the Ethiopian eunuch's baptism. Luke thus identifies Peter as integral to the acceptance and spread of the gentile mission, even if Peter too requires instruction before accepting it himself.

[111] Balch, *Contested Ethnicities*, 28–30; Fredriksen, *Paul*, 73–77; Simkovich, *Jewish Universalism*, 27–94.

[112] The MT states it stronger: "Blessed are my people Egypt, the work of my hand Assyria, and my inheritance Israel (בָּרוּךְ עַמִּי מִצְרַיִם וּמַעֲשֵׂה יָדַי אַשּׁוּר וְנַחֲלָתִי יִשְׂרָאֵל)." The LXX could insinuate Jews or Israelites dwelling in Egypt and Assyria instead of referring to Egyptians and Assyrians.

[113] Cf. Beers, *Followers*, 130–31, 161–64.

Beyond that, Luke-Acts builds to God's cleansing and incorporation of the gentiles. The righteous and pious (δίκαιος καὶ εὐλαβής; 2:25) Simeon, guided by the Spirit and echoing Isaiah, declares that Jesus would be "a light for revelation to the gentiles" (Luke 2:32; cf. Isa 49:6; Acts 15:14). In Nazareth, Jesus alludes to his ministry of healing to the gentiles through the stories of Elijah and Elisha (Luke 4:23–30). Jesus shows his willingness to interact with and reach out to gentiles by healing a centurion's servant (7:1–10). This nameless centurion, similar to Cornelius, is praised by the Jewish people because he built a synagogue out of love for them (7:4–5).[114] Jesus, with Jewish crowds— which would include Peter—following (7:9), agrees to enter the centurion's home with no qualms. Of course, Jesus does not actually enter the house. The centurion declares his unworthiness to have Jesus enter his home and acknowledges Jesus' authority (7:6). Still, Jesus is willing to associate with and bring healing to gentiles. Peter did not get the message. The Spirit must repeat the lesson.

Not only does Jesus enact the mission to the gentiles, but, after his resurrection, he expressly reminds the disciples of the scriptural expectation of gentile inclusion. Jesus opens their minds to comprehend that, "it has been written that ... repentance and forgiveness of sins are to be proclaimed *to all the nations* (εἰς πάντα τὰ ἔθνη), beginning in Jerusalem" (24:47). Moses, the prophets, and the psalms envision gentile-ingathering, just like they expect the Messiah's suffering and resurrection (24:44–45). Even after Scripture gave Israel these expectations, even after Jesus has opened their minds, and even after receiving the Spirit, Peter and the Jewish believers still need the Holy Spirit to teach them about gentile inclusion. Only when they witness the descent of the Spirit and hear the gentiles' speaking in tongues do they recognize God's acts among the gentiles (10:44–48; 11:17–18).

Fourth, Peter evinces growth by relaying this lesson to the other apostles and the rest of the community in Judea (11:1–18; cf. 15:6–12). After he returns to Jerusalem, circumcised believers differentiate themselves from Peter (διεκρίνοντο πρὸς αὐτόν; 11:2; cf. 10:20; 11:12) for his association with gentiles.[115] Peter, in response, recounts his conclusion that he should not distinguish "them from us." He tells these Jewish believers that, once the Spirit fell upon the gentiles, he recalled John's teaching about Jesus' being the one who baptizes with the Spirit. This connection caused Peter to recognize God's act and, therefore, not to hinder God (11:17). In retelling this experience, he persuades his believing interlocutors. The Jerusalem community now recognizes that "God has given the repentance into life even to the gentiles (καὶ τοῖς ἔθνεσιν)" (11:18). Of course, this issue reemerges before the Jerusalem Council, where Peter must reteach this lesson. Peter's journey toward understanding provides insight to the wider Jewish-believing world to God's acts. His growth aids theirs.

---

[114] "The notion that the centurion could build (or commission the building of) a synagogue without social interaction with Jews is, at best, improbable. Luke never hints at Jewish prejudice against the Gentile centurion; rather, Jews deem the centurion 'worthy'—citing his love of Israel—which shows positive, reciprocal relations between Jews and Gentiles" (Schaser, "Unlawful," 192). The centurion sends *Jewish* elders to Jesus (7:3), reiterating Jew–gentile interactions, at least engagements with Godfearers, contra Peter's statement (10:28).

[115] It is unclear whether οἱ ἐκ περιτομῆς is Jewish believers or a group who advocate circumcision (10:45; 11:2; cf. 15:1, 6; Gal 2:12; Titus 1:10). Although this impacts the scope of misunderstanding, it remains clear that they struggle to discern God's actions among the gentiles.

Peter and the Jewish-believing community have other instances when they are slow of heart in faith. When an angel delivers Peter from Herod's clutches, Peter initially thinks it is a vision (12:9). Only after the angel's departure does Peter realize that the Lord liberated him (12:11). Ironically, those praying for Peter (12:5, 12) "refuse to believe that their prayers have been answered."[116] These believers reenact the apostles' reticence to believe the female witnesses to Jesus' resurrections (Luke 24:10–11). They claim Rhoda is crazy (μαίνῃ) when she informs them that Peter was at the gate (12:15). The other occurrence of this accusation is when Festus calls Paul crazy (26:24–25). Like Festus, these believers mistake truth for insanity. After seeing Peter with their own eyes, they join the throngs of astonished (ἐξίστημι) people in Luke-Acts who are in the process of discerning God's activity through his agents (e.g., Luke 2:47; 8:56; 24:22; Acts 2:7, 12; 8:9, 11, 13; 9:21; 10:45). Even those engaged in prayer can be slow to perceive God's saving acts when the evidence lies before them (cf. Luke 24:16).[117]

The *ecclesia* is also slow to accept Saul, God's chosen instrument. This is unsurprising given Paul's spearheading persecution against the Way. It demonstrates their reticence to recognize God's transformation of their former persecutor, nonetheless. Ananias initially refuses the Lord's instructions to seek out Saul because of "how much evil (ὅσα κακά)" he has done against the Way (9:13). It takes an additional word from the Lord to convince Ananias to consider Saul a "brother" (9:15–16). When Saul attempts "to join with the disciples" (κολλᾶσθαι τοῖς μαθηταῖς; cf. 8:29; 10:28) in Jerusalem, all (πάντες) the disciples are afraid and disbelieve that he is a disciple. Barnabas, however, bridges the gap. He brings Saul to the apostles and recounts Saul's encounter with the Lord and subsequent preaching in Damascus (9:26–27). Although Luke does not record an explicit response from the apostles, they seemingly receive Paul, at least in part. Saul is now "with them (μετ' αὐτῶν)," moving about freely in Jerusalem (9:28). The brothers protect Paul's life by delivering him from the Hellenists and sending him back to Tarsus. In his returns to Jerusalem, the community welcomes him with open arms (15:4; 21:17; cf. 11:29; 12:25). Still, it took Barnabas' intervention to bring Paul into the fold.

Yet, the Jerusalem community's perception of Paul is never wholly favorable. Jesus-followers, like the broader Jewish world, remain divided over him. Some of these believers still consider Paul to be a threat. In Paul's final return to the city, James and the community elders inform Paul of a rumor about him circulating *among Jewish believers*. These brothers who are "zealous for the Torah" think Paul teaches against Torah and circumcision (21:19–21). Like some non-Jesus-following Jews, they think he teaches diaspora Jews to abandon their identity and ancestral customs (21:28). Therefore, the leaders instruct Paul to rebut this rumor by participating in the completion of a vow (21:22–26). Paul agrees that he must correct this misconception.

Unfortunately for Paul, Jews from Asia seize him and stir up the populace by reiterating this rumor (21:27–36; cf. 6:13–14). More jarring is that the Jerusalem community seemingly consigns Paul to the crowds in Jerusalem. They disappear even

---

[116] Parsons, *Acts*, 176. Similarly, Conzelmann, *Acts*, 385.
[117] "The church, too, experiences God ironically. New discoveries of the wonder of God are also discoveries of its own myopia" (Tannehill, *Narrative Unity*, 2:156).

though they sent him into the temple. Abandonment is more explicit in the Gospel account, but there are clear parallels to the disciples' desertion of Jesus at his arrest and trial.[118] Jesus' followers repeat their misstep. Beyond that, given the "myriads of myriads" of believers in Jerusalem who have heard similar rumors, zealous Jewish believers might participate in the hostile crowd (21:20–21; 22:3). Jewish believers, alongside the entire Jewish world, divide over Paul. Not only that, they repeat past mistakes by abandoning their brother to his fate.

Given the need for ongoing development among believers in Jerusalem and Judea, including the apostles, it is no surprise that diasporic Jesus-following Jews need further education in the Way. Of these, Apollos is the most well known. Luke introduces this Alexandrian with ringing praise. He is well spoken, learned in Scripture, instructed in the Way, excited in the Spirit (ζέων τῷ πνεύματι), and teaches accurately about Jesus (18:24–25). However, there is a gap in Apollos' knowledge. He knows only John's baptism.[119] Priscilla and Aquila explain things to him even more accurately (18:26). Paul similarly educates some twelve disciples who were ignorant of the Holy Spirit (19:1–6). They move from John's baptism into Jesus', receiving the Spirit when Paul lays his hands on them. Nevertheless, they were disciples prior to this knowledge and reception of the Spirit. These disciples must move into greater understanding, to take a new step on Israel's repentance-journey from John's water baptism of repentance to Jesus' Spirit baptism (cf. Ezek. 36:25–27). Moreover, these twelve echo the restored twelve apostles who receive the Spirit at Pentecost, who themselves represent Israel (Luke 6:12–13; 9:1; 22:30; Acts 7:8; 26:7).[120] These disciples stand in continuity with Israel's ongoing repentance that began with John in preparation of the Lord's coming (Luke 1:16, 76–77; 3:3–6, 16). Paul's mission continues God's work of restoring the penitent in Israel, including disciples who lack full understanding.

3.2.4 Summary: A Less-than-Ideal Jewish Community

The present analysis challenges claims that the Way is shown as an idealized Jewish group over and against the rest of Judaism. To be sure, Luke depicts it as possessing the proper understanding of Israel's Scriptures in its view that Jesus is the Messiah. But

---

[118] Parallels include being seized (Luke 22:54; Acts 21:27), a threefold accusation (Luke 23:2; Acts 21:28), being brought before the assembly (Luke 22:66–71; Acts 23:1–10), the crowds shouting "away with him" (Luke 23:18; Acts 21:36), trials in front of various leaders, including a Herod (23:6–12; Acts 26:13–26:32), and declarations of innocence by Roman leaders (Luke 23:13–17; Acts 26:32). David L. Tiede, "Contending with God: The Death of Jesus and the Trial of Israel in Luke-Acts," in *The Future of Early Christianity: Essays in Honor of Helmut Koester*, ed. Birger A. Pearson (Minneapolis, MN: Fortress, 1991), 301–8 (esp. 306). Paul and Jesus' temple-experiences contrast with Jeremiah's when some of Israel's leaders defend the prophet and his message (26:2–24).

[119] While this seems to link Apollos with the disciples who do not know there is a Holy Spirit (19:1–6), Luke does not say Apollos is ignorant of the Spirit or has not received it. In fact, ζέων τῷ πνεύματι suggests that Apollos, despite only knowing John's water baptism, is led by the Spirit. When referring to one's own spirit, Luke includes personal pronouns (Luke 1:47; 8:55; 23:46; Acts 7:59; 17:16). When referring to the Holy Spirit, Luke simply uses forms of ὁ πνεῦμα (e.g., Luke 2:27; 4:1, 14; Acts 2:4; 6:10; 10:19). On the subversion of ethnic stereotypes with Apollos and Aquila, Dulk, "Acts 18," 185–87.

[120] Johnson, *Acts*, 177. Pace Jervell, *Apostelgeschichte*, 477, there need not be competition between groups of twelve as Paul brings them into the single baptism of Jesus.

members of the Way, like all Israel, struggle to behave faithfully and to discern God's actions in the world. Unfaithful Jewish-Israelites exist among Jesus' followers. Luke's proclivity toward painting complex, mixed characters, including his heroes, is most evident in Peter. Since his initial calling (Luke 5:1–11), Peter has been in a process of growth.[121] It continues in Acts. Peter, the leader of the Twelve, has always struggled to see Jesus properly, to understand his own calling, and to act in obedience. These tendencies persist in Acts, even after the Spirit's advent. He remains a complex character. Luke's portrait of the rocky Way, exemplified in the apostles, affirms Gamaliel's words: if the Way was merely a human movement, it would have failed (5:38). God continues to straighten the Way in Israel.

To be clear, I am not denying that the apostles, especially Peter, are heroes in Acts. Luke generally portrays them positively. For the most part, they are reliable, faithful, venerable characters. Nevertheless, they, like all characters in Luke-Acts, should be measured against the narrative whole, especially the instructions and example of Jesus and the Holy Spirit, and Israel's Scriptures. When measured as such, Luke does not depict them as perfect or idealized. Their actions and perspectives are neither infallible nor inerrant. Like the heroes in Israel's history, Luke's heroes sometimes misunderstand God's instructions and make mistakes. They, like their Jewish siblings, need to grow as they continue along Israel's repentance-journey.

3.3 Paul's Rough Edges

There is no doubt that Paul is a hero, if not *the* hero of Acts. Luke's portrait of Paul is overwhelmingly positive. He is a faithful, reliable character. However, like all characters in Luke-Acts, Paul's words and acts must be tested against Israel's Scriptures, the character and words of Jesus, and the Holy Spirit. Under these lights, Paul is not infallible or idealized even after his experience with the risen Jesus. Luke retains some rough edges in his sketch of Paul. In particular, Luke paints Paul as a firebrand who causes and gets himself into trouble wherever he goes due to his apparent abrasiveness. Paul's rough edges, though, are not mere flaws. Acts' depiction of a coarse, stubborn Paul places him in good company with the Way, the Twelve, and Israel's prophets who struggle with their own people, and can stumble in following the Lord's calling (cf. Num 20:6–13; 1 Kgs 19:9–18). Indeed, God often sends obstinate prophets to the obstinate covenant people.

Four observations muddy Luke's portrait of Paul. First, Acts describes Paul's prophetic mission as exacerbating divisions and arousing animosity more than other preachers. Such is the result of his prophetic mission, to be sure. Yet, hostility against Paul in Acts often goes qualitatively and quantitatively beyond the mistreatment of other prophets and apostles in the book. It is unclear if it is something about the Lukan Paul's past, his mission, his personality, or a combination of factors that elicits such antagonism. Moreover, Paul's activities occasionally bring threats of violence to local

---

[121] Green, *Conversion*, 88–99.

believing communities, endangering those outside his prophetic vocation. Second, Luke's Paul encounters trouble for reasons other than preaching Jesus or going to the gentiles. Certain actions sparked by Paul's irritation or impatience bring him seemingly gratuitous harm. Third, Paul's separation from Barnabas in Acts is placed immediately after the account highlighting the unity of the Jerusalem Council. Luke refrains from explicitly assigning blame to either character, but their separation ends a Holy Spirit-ordained partnership sans guidance from prayer or the Spirit. Fourth, Luke's Paul at times appears at odds with the Spirit or other Spirit-led characters. It seems that Luke presents Paul as struggling or needing to discern and follow the leading of the Spirit. Like all characters in Acts, Paul needs further alignment with God's will. Nevertheless, like the inconsistent apostles, for Luke, Paul is an imperfect hero who stands in solidarity with all flawed Israel and whose occasional stumbling God uses to advance the kingdom.

3.3.1 The Divisive Paul

Most obviously like Israel's prophets (e.g., 1 Kgs 17–19; 22:7–28; Jer 26:1–24) and Jesus himself (Luke 12:49–53), Paul is a controversial, disputed figure in Acts. Of course, causing division and being abused are not necessarily character flaws but natural results of prophetic missions.[122] Such reactions and animosity toward Paul are by and large the inevitable result of his vocation (Acts 20:23). As Jesus' "chosen instrument" Paul "must suffer" for Jesus' name (9:16; cf. 14:21–23; 26:16–18). Nevertheless, repeated harsh reactions to Paul caution against viewing his mission as idealized, especially when contrasted with Jesus and the apostles who mainly arouse opposition from leadership alone (e.g., Luke 11:53; 19:47–48; 20;19 Acts 4:1–22; 5:17–41; cf. 12:1–4).[123] When Jesus sends out the Twelve and the seventy, he simply warns that some will receive them and others will not (Luke 9:1–6; 10:1–12). Indeed, the Son of Man himself has no place to lay his head (9:58). Jesus and his disciples, however, do not provoke violence almost everywhere they go (cf. 4:28–30). Paul does. He receives aggression beyond simply not being welcomed. He exacerbates division and hostility more than anyone else who proclaims Jesus. In Acts, people seem to take issue with *Paul* as much as, if not more than they take issue with his message.

Luke's Paul sows unparalleled discord and elicits unprecedented antagonism in most places he goes. He divides Jews, gentiles, and even Jesus' followers into factions (στάσις; 15:2; 19:40; 21:30; 23:7, 10). Although many have claimed the Jewish people are the source of such divisions, Mitzi Smith observes that "*stasis* occurs four times in Acts, but never to refer to *the Jews* as the instigators."[124] Paul, by contrast, stands at the center of every instance of *stasis* in Acts. Tertullus' accusation that Paul is "one who causes (κινοῦντα; cf. 21:30) *stasis* among all the Jews who dwell throughout the imperial

---

[122] Scott Cunningham, *Through Many Tribulations: The Theology of Persecution in Luke-Acts*, JSNTSup 142 (Sheffield: Sheffield Academic, 1997), 301–19; McWhirter, *Rejected*, 11–16.

[123] The persecution against the *ecclesia*—which overlooks the apostles (8:1–3)—derives from Israel's leaders, specifically the chief priests (9:2, 14, 21).

[124] Smith, *Literary Other*, 66.

world (οἰκουμένη)" has some basis in Luke's narrative world (24:5). Luke absolves Paul from charges of sedition (24:10–21; 26:30–32), yet this accusation links Paul with the insurrectionist and murderer Barabbas (Luke 23:19, 25; cf. Acts 9:1).[125] Tertullus tells a half-truth. On the one hand, Paul, unlike Barabbas, is neither a political threat nor a violator of Jewish tradition. On the other hand, Paul instigates Jews, all peoples for that matter, throughout the empire. "The overall effect of the whole narrative section from ch. 13 to ch. 19," Loveday Alexander observes, "is to leave the damaging impression that Paul's mission causes trouble wherever it goes (17.6): prudent magistrates might well conclude that any well-regulated city would be better off without it."[126]

Moreover, Paul is *the* primary target of animosity and violence in Acts. Jews and gentiles in various regions drive him and his partners away (13:51–14:7; 17:10, 40). His preaching prompts threats on his life (and *only his* life) in Damascus (9:23–25), Jerusalem (9:28–30; 22:22–23), and Lystra (14:19–20). Paul's stoning in Lystra is particularly odd since Barnabas, who is also a prophetic figure proclaiming the same message (13:1), is with Paul yet remains unharmed (cf. 14:6).[127] Similarly, the Thessalonian Jews, though they sought out Paul and Silas (17:5), mobilize to Berea when they hear of *Paul's* activity there. The community sends Paul alone away for his safety while Silas and Timothy remain (17:13–15). Though Aquila, Priscilla, Timothy, and Silas are all in Corinth, only Paul faces an attack from the Jewish community and is brought before Gallio (18:12–13). Of course, that Paul's ministry endangers his life places him in the line of the rejected prophets, Jesus, and the Twelve (e.g., Jer 26:2–24; Luke 13:31; Acts 5:33; cf. Luke 11:49). His sufferings imitate Jesus and fulfill his words (Acts 9:16).[128] Yet, Paul encounters consistent abuse that is unparalleled by any other faithful character in Acts. Rather than assuming this is Luke idealizing Paul and his mission, it is worth asking what about Paul incites such repeated aggressions while others around him remained untouched.[129]

On three occasions, these controversies around Paul endanger other individuals and/or communities, believing and/or Jewish. In Thessalonica, when the unpersuaded Jews cannot find Paul and Silas, Jason and his household are brought before the tribunal for their hospitality to Paul and Silas (17:5–9). In Corinth, the synagogue leader Sosthenes is beaten after Gallio refuses to arbitrate on intra-Jewish conflicts (18:12–17).[130] The silversmiths' grievance against Paul in Ephesus puts his companions Gaius and Aristarchus at risk. Furthermore, the mob threatens the entire Jewish community (19:21–41). Paul attempts to intervene, but the disciples prevent him, likely because they know that the mob's anger is directed toward him (19:26). In disrupting the entire world, Paul puts himself and others at risk, his Jewish brethren and fellow believers at

---

[125] Rowe, *World*, 73–78; Keener, "Paul," 209.
[126] Alexander, *Acts*, 199.
[127] This could be due to Paul's being the main speaker (14:12). Nevertheless, that Paul alone is targeted, despite others around him being faithful, is odd.
[128] Cunningham, *Tribulations*, 313–19.
[129] Compare Paul with Apollos. Apollos debates Jesus' messianic identity and preaches boldly in synagogues yet Luke mentions no aggression toward Apollos (18:24–28; cf. 9:27–30; 19:8–10).
[130] Whether Sosthenes is a Jesus-following Jew is unclear (cf. 1 Cor 1:1). Nor is it clear who is responsible for his beating (Mount, "Constructing Paul," 143–44; Stroup, *Christians*, 125–26).

that. Most prophets endanger only themselves (e.g., 1 Kgs 18:3–16; Jer 26:7–24; Dan 3:8–27; 6:1–24).

That conflicts in Acts center on Paul himself as much as, if not more than, his message is further evinced by two scenes in which Paul is forced to leave a region and the *ecclesia* experiences peace and growth immediately after his departure. After the believers send Paul to Tarsus when his life is threatened by the Hellenists, the *ecclesia* in Judea, Galilee, and Samaria experience peace and growth (9:31).[131] In Pisidian Antioch, the disciples in the region are filled with joy and the Holy Spirit once Paul and Barnabas move on to Iconium (13:52). These scenes suggest that those in the region who react with hostility are more agitated by Paul than the believing community at large (cf. 17:13–14). To be sure, believing communities welcome and protect Paul as their own. Regardless, he brings strife. Paul's presence, integral to the spread of the message of Jesus in the imperial world as it is, disrupts the peace of every group: Jews, gentiles, and other believers. While persecution in part displays Paul's prophetic mission, that many characters in Acts appear to take issue with Paul himself, not solely his message, suggests that his sufferings are not merely idealized.

3.3.2 The Temperamental Paul

Paul's sufferings seem related to Luke's depiction of Paul as somewhat cantankerous. Luke's Paul at times acts out of irritation in ways slightly incongruous with Jesus and the Spirit.[132] Like his scriptural namesake, Saul/Paul continues to do brash things after receiving a new heart (so to speak) and performs prophetic activities in the Spirit (cf. 1 Kgdms 10:9–13).[133] Unlike King Saul, Paul's frustrations are usually justified in Acts. Still, the resultant activities often get him into trouble with authorities, placing him in compromising situations for reasons other than proclaiming Jesus (cf. 1 Kgs 22:7–28; Jer 26:1–24). Paul twice gets irritated by foreign divinities and idols. Such a reaction is proper for a Jewish prophet, but his subsequent actions cause him to be arrested, abused, and tried (16:16–24; 17:16–21; cf. 14:15–17). Paul retorts—reasonably and prophetically so—to the high priest, causing him to speak against a leader of his people in ignorance (23:4–5). As usual, God uses these outbursts to advance God's purposes.

In Philippi, Paul becomes annoyed (διαπονηθείς; cf. 4:2) after being followed around by a slave-woman with a pythonic spirit who keeps crying out after them for many days (ἐπὶ πολλὰς ἡμέρας). Irritation leads him to cast out the spirit (16:18). This action, Paul's sole exorcism in Acts (cf. 19:11–12), bears some incongruities with his calling

---

[131] In Acts, μὲν οὖν often shifts the narrative focus in a way that develops from or at least links the new scene to the previous one (e.g., 1:6; 2:41; 5:41; 8:4; 11:19; 13:4; 15:3, 30; 16:5; 17:12, 17; 23:18, 31; 25:4). Though there may not be a direct causal relationship, Saul's leaving the region is linked to the peace of the *ecclesia*. The peace stems, at least in part, from the fact that Saul no longer leads the persecution against the community (8:1–3; 9:1).

[132] Outbursts of anger were a common antithesis "to the ideal of manly self-control in the ancient world" (Brittany E. Wilson, *Unmanly Men: Refigurations of Masculinity in Luke-Acts* [Oxford: Oxford University Press, 2015], 174–75). Acts avoids idealizing Paul along these particular social conventions.

[133] French, "Completion," 425–31.

and prior exorcisms in Luke-Acts.[134] Why did Paul wait "many days" to exorcise the spirit? Jesus and his disciples cast spirits out immediately upon encountering them (Luke 8:26–39; 9:37–43; 13:10–17; Acts 5:16; 8:7). Apparently, Paul could have cast out the spirit at any time since, once he decides to exorcise it, it comes out instantly (ἐξῆλθεν αὐτῇ τῇ ὥρᾳ). His delayed action seems inconsistent with his calling to facilitate people's turning from "the power of Satan" (26:18).[135] Paul's initial inaction becomes increasingly glaring since his cohort first encounters the woman on the way to the place of prayer (εἰς τὴν προσευχήν). Luke suggests, then, they initially meet the woman on the Sabbath (cf. 16:13). According to Jesus, the Sabbath is the ideal time to liberate people from Satan (Luke 13:16; cf. 6:5–10; 14:3–5).[136] Yet, Paul waits "many days" after the Sabbath to bring deliverance.

Why does Paul acknowledge only the spirit and not the slave-woman herself? Paul does not address the woman after the exorcism. Although this might be due to the response of the slave-woman's owners, Paul's silence toward her as an agent whom God has liberated is deafening. Jesus, in contrast, addresses both the spirit(s) and the human in his exorcisms (Luke 8:29–32, 35, 38–39; 9:42; 13:12). His acts liberate and heal the person in need, welcoming them back into the community. In contrast, Paul's annoyance—rather than a concern for the possessed enslaved woman or because she says something false—prompts him to drive out the spirit.[137] Irritation, it seems, is not an ideal reason to address a person in need of deliverance. Paul's exorcism falls short of Jesus' model (cf. Luke 9:37–41).

Paul's act borne from irritation leads to his and Silas being beaten and imprisoned by the city officials (16:19–24).[138] Of course, the greedy owners of the slave-woman bear direct responsibility for the unjust arrest. City officials (οἱ στρατηγοί) often assail Jesus and his followers for their preaching (cf. Luke 22:4, 52; Acts 4:1; 5:24, 26). And God uses Paul's impulsive act and subsequent imprisonment—as a result of which the jailor and his household receive salvation (16:25–34). Nevertheless, Paul's brash exorcism in Philippi, not his preaching about Jesus per se, exacerbates his suffering. It appears to be a misstep, albeit one God uses.

A similar thing occurs in Athens. As he waits for Silas and Timothy, Paul becomes "irritated (παρωξύνετο)" when he sees the city's rampant idolatry (17:16). Being a Jew and a prophet, Paul's irritation seems justified.[139] However, Luke emphasizes that Paul's agitation originates from "*his* spirit *in him* (τὸ πνεῦμα αὐτοῦ ἐν αὐτῷ)." This is the only instance in which Luke combines a possessive pronoun with πνεῦμα and a locative prepositional phrase like ἐν αὐτῷ (cf. Luke 1:47; 8:55; 23:46; Acts 7:59). The subsequent

---

[134] Cf. Todd Klutz, *The Exorcism Stories in Luke-Acts: A Sociostylistic Reading*, SNTSMS 129 (Cambridge: Cambridge University Press, 2004), 207–64, on similarities with prior exorcisms.

[135] Garrett, *Demise*, 37–45. For contrasts between Paul's encounter with Bar-Jesus and the encounter with the pythonic spirit, see John B. F. Miller, "Paul's Dream at Troas: Reconsidering the Interpretations of Characters and Commentators," in *Contemporary Studies*, 138–53 (esp. 148).

[136] Haenchen, *Acts*, 495; Klutz, *Exorcism*, 212–14.

[137] Parsons, *Acts*, 231–32; cf. Jervell, *Apostelgeschichte*, 423; Rowe, *World*, 24–27.

[138] The narrator ("we") is present yet not arrested or beaten with Paul and Silas (16:16–18).

[139] In the LXX, παροξύνω typically refers to wrath in response to infidelity to God, specifically idolatrous practices (e.g., Deut 1:34; 9:7; Isa 5:24–25; Jer 22:15; Hos 8:5; Zech 10:3).

actions that lead Paul into a precarious situation stem from irritation in his own spirit, not prompted by the Holy Spirit (or an angel; cf. 5:19–21).[140] Paul channels this irritation into his normal, responsible activities: discussing the good news in synagogues with Jews and Godfearers and with those present in the marketplace (17:17).[141] These faithful actions cause Paul to be put on trial before the Areopagus for proclaiming "foreign deities (ξένων δαιμονίων)" (18:18). As in Philippi, Paul's actions motivated from irritability, while still serving God's calling, lead him to trouble. They put his life at risk.[142] Granted, some pagan-gentiles in the Areopagus join (κολληθέντες; cf. 8:29; 10:28) with Paul and believe (17:34). Good comes of this, but one cannot overlook that his gut reaction, rather than the Spirit's clear leading, has again led Luke's Paul into a precarious situation.

Paul's final outburst occurs before the Sanhedrin (23:1–5). In all other trials in Jerusalem, the Sanhedrin invites defendants to respond to allegations (Luke 22:66–67; Acts 4:7; 5:27–28; 7:1). Paul, in contrast, speaks first, suggesting an impulsive or impatient response. After being struck on the mouth due to the high priest Ananias' orders, presumably for speaking out of turn, Paul retorts with a word of judgment (cf. Josephus, J.W. 2.427–429, 441–442).[143] Paul declares that God will strike the high priest (τύπτειν σε; cf. LXX Ezek 7:6), calls him a whitewashed wall (cf. Ezek 13:8–13), and accuses him, one supposed to judge according to Torah, of breaking Torah by having Paul struck (23:3; cf. LXX Deut 27:24). Again, Paul's outburst is justifiable and prophetic. Regardless, it gets him in further trouble. Those near him accuse him of "reviling (λοιδορέω)" God's high priest (23:4; cf. LXX Exod 17:2–3; Num 20:3, 13; Deut 33:8). In response, Paul does not explicitly retract or apologize for the comment but explains it. He spoke in ignorance. He would not knowingly speak evil of a leader in Israel since Torah prohibits it (23:5; cf. LXX Exod 22:27).[144] Although Paul's outburst stands as prophetic judgment against the high priest, this is the closest Paul comes to transgressing Torah in Acts. His words also do not help demonstrate his clear conscience to the court. In contrast with the apostles, Paul's response gets him into further trouble with Israel's leadership for reasons other than preaching Jesus.

---

[140] Paul's spirit and the Spirit's agencies are not mutually exclusive. Still, Luke emphasizes that irritation derives from inside Paul first and foremost. He is the primary agent.

[141] The marketplace-setting links the episodes in Philippi and Athens (16:19; 17:17).

[142] On reading this as a trial-scene reminiscent of Socrates' own, and thereby a genuine threat to Paul's life, see Rowe, *World*, 27–33.

[143] Luke notes that Peter is filled with the Holy Spirit before he speaks to the council (4:8; cf. Luke 12:11–12) and highlights the Spirit's presence with Stephen and his angelic appearance (Acts 6:5, 8, 15). To be sure, Paul is filled with the Spirit (9:17) and the Spirit's presence might be implied by Paul's "looking intently" (23:1; cf. 13:9), but that Luke does not say the Spirit prompts his speech is of note. Some consider Paul's retort to be a Jewish curse-formula (Conzelmann, *Apostelgeschichte*, 137; Jervell, *Apostelgeschichte*, 554–55; cf. Bruce, *Acts*, 409–10).

[144] The proposal that Paul is being ironic (cf. Jervell, *Apostelgeschichte*, 554–55; Tannehill, *Narrative Unity*, 2:286) suffers from a couple shortcomings. First, Paul speaks in a straightforward manner in Acts. Apart from one potential double entendre (17:22; cf. Joshua W. Jipp, "Paul's Areopagus Speech of Acts 17:16–34 as Both Critique and Propaganda," *JBL* 131 [2012]: 567–88), Paul does not speak ironically. Second, Acts 21–28 emphasizes Paul as a faithful Jew so it would make sense that Paul continues to rebut claims that he speaks against the Jewish people and their customs (cf. 21:28). Quoting from Torah reinforces this conclusion. Third, Paul's use of "brothers" suggests a conciliatory appeal (cf. 23:1, 6).

3.3.3 A Parting of the Ways

Paul's habit of causing divisions comes to a more clearly problematic head after the Jerusalem Council. Because of a heated dispute (παροξυσμός; cf. 17:16; LXX Deut 29:28; Jer 39:37) over whether they should bring John Mark with them on their visits to the diaspora communities, Paul and Barnabas part ways (15:36–41). On first glance, Paul appears justified. John Mark joined them on their initial Spirit-ordained mission after they brought famine relief to Jerusalem (12:25–13:5). After the incident with Elymas, John Mark withdrew from them (ἀποχωρήσας ἀπ' αὐτῶν), returning to Jerusalem (13:13). Luke harshly refers to John Mark as "the one who abandoned (τὸν ἀποστάντα) them and did not accompany them in the work" (15:38; cf. Luke 8:13).[145] Furthermore, the community commends Paul to the grace of God (παραδοθεὶς τῇ χάριτι τοῦ κυρίου) in his new mission. Paul then strengthens the communities in Syria and Cilicia (Acts 15:39–30; cf. 14:26). These details suggest Luke affirms Paul's decision to part from Barnabas.

Several factors complicate this instinct and indicate that Paul and Barnabas' separation is a suboptimal decision within the narrative world. First is Barnabas. To this point, Luke has portrayed Barnabas in uniformly positive terms. Luke introduces him as the exemplar of Spirit-generated unity and generosity in the Jerusalem community, earning the name "son of encouragement" (4:36–37). Luke later calls Barnabas "a good man, full of the Holy Spirit and faithfulness" (11:24). As such, he carries out the initial mission of exhorting the nascent Antioch community (11:22–25). Barnabas vouched for Saul before the Jerusalem community when they did not think he was a genuine disciple (9:26–27). Barnabas retrieved Saul from Tarsus in order to include him in the mission (11:25). In other words, Barnabas is responsible for Paul's reintroduction in the story. Barnabas enables and aids Paul in carrying out his calling (cf. 13:2).[146] If Acts idealizes any character, it is Barnabas, not Paul. Advocating for a second chance for John Mark, as he did for Paul, fits Barnabas' character. Luke's depiction of Barnabas cautions against assuming that Paul is right and Barnabas is wrong. Two of Luke's most faithful heroes are at odds; how can one adjudicate clearly between them?

Second, the timing of this separation is jarring. Paul and Barnabas depart from each other right after Spirit-generated unity emerged from the Jerusalem Council (15:25, 28; cf. 4:31–32). These two argued side by side in defense of God's full inclusion of the gentiles (15:2–4, 12). They were the ideal pair to bring the council's decision to their home community (15:22, 25, 35). Their parting is stunningly dissonant with the recent concord.

Third and most incriminating, this act divides a pair whom the Spirit brought together (13:1–4; cf. 14:26).[147] In the midst of prophets and teachers, during a time of

---

[145] Ironically, others accuse Paul of "teaching apostasy (ἀποστασίαν διδάσκεις)" (21:21; cf. 19:8).

[146] Paul does not flee his calling, but there remains a gap between Paul's commission and participation in ministry (9:15; 11:25; cf. Jon 1:3). See Bernhard Meininger, "Einmal Tarsus und zurück (Apg 9,30; 11,25–26): Paulus als Lehrer nach der Apostelgeschichte," MTZ 49 (1998): 125–43; MacNamara, *Chosen Instrument*, 183–236; Josep Rius-Camps, *El Camino de Pablo a la Misión de los Paganos: Comentario Lingüístico y Exegético a HCH 13-28*, LNT 2 (Madrid: Ediciones Cristiandad, 1984), 13–18.

[147] Miller observes that the particle δή only occurs in Acts during the Spirit's commissioning of Paul and Barnabas and their separation (13:2; 15:26), further linking these scenes ("Paul's Dream, 145).

worship and fasting, the Holy Spirit instructs the Antioch *ecclesia* to "set apart Barnabas and Saul for the work to which I have called them (εἰς τὸ ἔργον ὃ προσκέκλημαι αὐτούς)" (13:2). The Spirit brings them together for a singular commission. The community affirms it with prayer, fasting, and laying hands before sending them out. Paul and Barnabas' partnership and mission are ordained by the Spirit; the Holy Spirit sends them out (13:4). Any disbanding of the pair, therefore, should be initiated by the Spirit. However, the telltale signs of Holy Spirit influence—scriptural reasoning, prayer, fasting, or communal deliberation—are all absent when Paul and Barnabas separate.[148] The Spirit's voice is silent.

Fourth, Luke makes it clear that irritation (παροξυσμός) from the disagreement drives them apart: "a heated dispute occurred *with the result that* they were separated from one another (ὥστε ἀποχωρισθῆναι αὐτοὺς ἀπ' ἀλλήλων)" (15:39).[149] Of course, this is not the only time irritation motivated Paul to act in a problematic or at least ambiguous way (cf. παροξύνω in 17:16). Ultimately, they reenact John Mark's erroneous act. They separate (ἀποχωρίζω) from one another and go in opposing directions (15:39-40; cf. ἀποχωρέω in 13:13). The superfluous ἀπ' ἀλλήλων emphasizes the spatial dynamic: They go their separate ways, never to cross paths again in the story. Their single Spirit-motivated mission has become two.

To be sure, Luke abstains from openly assigning blame or making explicit comments about the division. God still uses Paul to advance the kingdom on his new journey. Nevertheless, this parting-within-the-Way is, at best, ambivalent.[150] More likely, it is tragic. Two of Luke's most faithful heroes, without the Holy Spirit's involvement, terminate their Spirit-generated partnership because of a dispute. They repeat Mark's problematic departure that sparked the argument. Regardless of whether Paul is not entirely at fault and one can understand his rationale, Luke portrays Paul front and center in another conflict. Akin to others in the Way, the Paul of Acts struggles to maintain the unity produced by the Spirit among Jesus' followers. Even with those closest to him, including the one with whom the Holy Spirit paired him, Luke's Paul appears to be a divisive, uncompromising figure. He exhibits comparable stubborn tendencies to historic Israel and his diaspora Jewish brethren.

3.3.4 Paul and the Holy Spirit

Casting further shadows on the partition with Barnabas, Paul experiences a newfound ambivalence in his relationship to the Spirit shortly after separating from Barnabas that persists throughout the rest of the narrative. While the Holy Spirit initially sent out Paul and Barnabas (13:4), the Spirit restricts Paul's movement. Paul and his party "were forbidden by the Holy Spirit to speak the word (κωλυθέντες ὑπὸ τοῦ ἁγίου πνεύματος

---

[148] Tannehill, *Narrative Unity*, 2:194.
[149] The passive ἀποχωρισθῆναι could be a divine passive, suggesting God enacts their separation. Lack of signs of the Spirit's influence mitigates this reading. Irritation drives the split. In this rendering, one can imagine people physically separating Paul and Barnabas from each other as they argue.
[150] Cf. Haenchen, *Acts*, 474; Bock, *Acts*, 519-20.

λαλῆσαι τὸν λόγον) in Asia" (16:6; cf. Luke 9:49–50).[151] Then, "the Spirit of Jesus did not permit (οὐκ εἴασεν) them" to pass through Bithynia (16:7). The Spirit frustrates Paul's movements; he does not seem fully aligned with the Spirit.[152] Of course, Paul is not entirely at odds with the Spirit. He carries out his calling faithfully under the Spirit's guidance (e.g., 19:21; 20:22–23). Nevertheless, the division between Paul and Barnabas disrupts Paul's accord with the Spirit, adding ambivalence to how wise some of his subsequent actions are. Akin to others in Israel (cf. 7:51), he experiences difficulties in following God's leading.

Eventually, a vision (ὅραμα) leads Paul and his party to Macedonia (16:9–10). Visions typically come from God and provide guidance in Acts (e.g., 7:31; 9:10, 12; 10:3, 17, 19; 11:5; 18:9). This vision, however, lacks a divine agent. It is the only vision in Acts without one.[153] Instead, Luke emphasizes human interpretation of and response to the vision: "immediately *we sought* (εὐθέως ἐζητήσαμεν) to depart to Macedonia, *concluding* (συμβιβάζοντες) that God had commissioned us (προσκέκληται ἡμᾶς; cf. 13:2) to preach good news to them" (16:10). It seems that the Spirit now commissions them to Macedonia but, by stressing human agency, Luke leaves room for ambiguity. The results foster further ambiguity. Paul experiences some success as well as imprisonment and abuse in Macedonia (16:11–17:15). However, his work in Thessalonica and Berea meets an "immediate (εὐθέως)" end due to persecution (17:10, 14).[154] The Macedonian mission ends as suddenly as it began with only moderate success. Paul, now leading his own mission apart from his more experienced partner Barnabas, must continue to develop his ability to align himself with the Spirit's leading. While God is using him to spread the word during this process, Paul must grow in discernment.

Additional ambivalences with the Spirit arise in Paul's final journeys to Jerusalem and Rome. He resolves "in the Spirit" to go to Jerusalem and tells himself that "it is necessary (δεῖ) for me to see Rome also" (19:21).[155] The Spirit prompts his return journey to Jerusalem, though Paul knows he will encounter imprisonment and persecution there (20:20–24). Paul seems aware that God intends for him to go to Rome (cf. 23:11).[156] The journey is met with some Spirit-informed challenges, though. Disciples at Tyre tell Paul "through the Spirit (διὰ τοῦ πνεύματος)" not to go to Jerusalem (21:4). At Philip's house in Caesarea, the prophet Agabus comes down from Judea to warn Paul that "the Holy Spirit says" that the Jewish people in Jerusalem will

---

[151] Given the repeated opposition from Asian Jews to the Way in Acts and that Paul starts a riot in Ephesus (6:9; 19:21–41; 21:27; 24:19), this restriction seems reasonable.

[152] Tannehill, *Narrative Unity*, 2:194.

[153] For an expanded reading of ambivalence surrounding the Macedonian vision and mission, see Miller, "Paul's Dream," 138–53.

[154] Miller, "Paul's Dream," 150. These are the *only* uses of εὐθέως in Paul's journeys.

[155] Paul seems slow to act on this Spirit-guided resolution. He sends his helpers to Macedonia yet remains in Asia (19:22). Around that time, a riot breaks out against the Way, Paul specifically (19:23–41). Inaction puts him at risk. Paul does not leave for Macedonia until the dust settles (20:1).

[156] Charles H. Cosgrove, "The Divine Δεῖ in Luke-Acts: Investigations into the Lukan Understanding of God's Providence," *NovT* 26 (1984): 168–90; Kylie Crabbe, *Luke/Acts and the End of History*, BZNW 238 (Berlin: de Gruyter, 2020), 157–64.

bind Paul and "give him into the hands of the gentiles" (21:10–11; cf. Luke 9:44; 18:32; 24:7). Hearing this, Paul's cohort and the locals, likely counting Philip the evangelist and his four daughters who are prophets (21:8–9), urge Paul not to go up to Jerusalem (21:12).[157] Reliable characters attempt to dissuade Paul. Spirit-influenced protests suggest that the directive for Paul's journey to Jerusalem is not entirely clear.[158] When they are unsuccessful, they simply ask that the Lord's will be done (21:14). The Lord's will requires discernment.

Paul's temple vision casts further ambiguity on Paul's visit to Jerusalem (22:17–21). After Paul returned to Jerusalem, he informs the crowd, the Lord visited him in the temple. The Lord tells him, "Hurry and *depart in haste from* Jerusalem because they will not receive your testimony about me" (22:18; cf. 5:19–20). During which of Paul's visits to Jerusalem this vision occurred in the narrative frame is unclear (9:26–27; 11:30; 12:25; 15:4). What seems clear is that this vision happened before Paul resolved to make his final trip to Jerusalem for Pentecost (20:16). Jesus has told Paul to leave Jerusalem since he will not be believed. And Paul still returns to Jerusalem. To be sure, he does so as a faithful Jew making pilgrimage and resolved in the Spirit (20:22). One still wonders why Paul is back in Jerusalem when Jesus told him to leave it.

Furthermore, Jesus has to tell Paul to leave Jerusalem twice. Like many prophets before him (e.g., Exod 3:11, 13; 4:1, 10, 13; Jer 1:5–10) and Peter (cf. Acts 10:9–48), Paul first objects. He seems to think that Jerusalem will be more receptive to his mission because of his past persecution of the Way and his participation in Stephen's execution (Acts 22:18–19; cf. 26:19). Jesus instead reiterates his command, informing Paul, "I will send you far away to the gentiles" (22:21). Paul was initially hesitant to obey the Lord's instructions.[159] Taken together, whether Paul should be in Jerusalem is ambiguous.

Of course, God uses Paul's Jerusalem experience as an opportunity to proclaim the word before kings, Jews, and gentiles in accordance with Paul's calling (23–26; cf. 9:15; 26:17, 23) and to bring him to testify in Rome (19:21; 23:11). Whether Paul must go to Rome *in chains* is uncertain, however. Agabus predicts Paul's arrest and being handed over to the gentiles in Jerusalem. Corrupt governors keep Paul in prison far longer than he should (24:22–27). Paul appeals to Caesar because, since he did nothing against the Jewish people, he should not be tried in Jerusalem, where some Jews hope to kill him (25:1–12). Yet, Luke includes a strange comment from Agrippa after Paul's defense speech: "This man *could have been set free* (ἀπολελύσθαι ἐδύνατο) *if he had not called upon Caesar* (εἰ μὴ ἐπεκέκλητο Καίσαρα)" (26:32). Luke highlights this statement by adding it after the conclusion that Paul does not deserve death or imprisonment (26:30–31). Agrippa's is the final judgment on Paul before he goes to Rome. Paul,

---

[157] Interestingly, this scene occurs in a "we-passage." The narrator appears included as one among Paul's cohort who cautions against (παρεκαλοῦμεν ἡμεῖς) his trip to Jerusalem.

[158] Cf. Kylie Crabbe, "Accepting Prophecy: Paul's Response to Agabus with Insights from Valerius Maximus and Josephus," *JSNT* 39 (2016): 188–208.

[159] Ananias, in Paul's recounting, asks, why Paul delays (νῦν τί μέλλεις) in response to the Lord's calling (22:16). Paul's defense to the Jerusalem Jews recounts his own sluggishness to respond to God, tying him closer to the Jerusalemites who struggle comparably. Paul is "as [they] are today" (22:3). Cf. Rius-Camps, *Camino, passim*.

Agrippa concludes, remains in chains *because of his own actions*. Jesus and the Spirit never told Paul his journey to Rome required chains.[160]

Beyond Agrippa's judgment, Paul's "calling upon (ἐπικαλέω) Caesar" (25:11-12, 21, 25; 26:32; 28:19) becomes increasingly dubious when one recalls that, according to Acts, calling on the Lord's name brings salvation (2:21; 15:17; cf. 7:59; 9:14, 21). All prior uses of ἐπικαλέω in the active or middle voice in Acts are connected with calling on the name of Israel's Lord (2:21; 7:59; 9:14, 21; 22:16; cf. 15:17). For Luke, as in Israel's Scriptures, the Lord's name is the only one that delivers, as Peter declares to the council: "*There is no other name* under heaven given among humanity by which we must be saved" (4:12).[161] Yet, in his time of trial, Paul calls on Caesar. This decision is, at best, bewildering. One might suspect that if Paul called on the Lord, he would have been set free. Paul seems to reenact Israel's tendency to call on others when they should appeal to the Lord (cf. 3 Kgdms 18:24-28; Hos 7:7, 11; Wis 13:17; cf. Jdt 3:8).[162]

3.3.5 Summary

In this section, my goal has been to shroud Paul in some ambiguity, not to make concrete judgments about which actions are entirely right or wrong. Rarely, if ever, does Luke intervene to tell the reader how to evaluate Paul and his actions. Yet, he depicts them in ambiguous ways. My point is that interpreters cannot assume Paul's infallibility in Acts. His actions must be weighed against the narrative whole, especially the person and words of Jesus and the leading of the Spirit. When this is done, Paul emerges as another in Israel who must learn how to (re)align with God and grow in faithfulness. The Paul of Acts, like Israel's heroes and the apostles before him, is a very human character. His portrait has rough edges. He continues along Israel's repentance-journey. Luke refrains from idealizing Paul after the Damascus Road. To be sure, Paul is Luke's hero whom God uses. But, like all Jewish-Israelite characters in Acts, his portrait contains shades of grey.

These rough edges make Luke's Paul a fitting prophetic figure in and representative of/to Israel (cf. 9:15). His obstinacy complements Israel's, making him unwilling to retreat from ministering to them when they refuse to listen. Paul in this regard seems reminiscent of Ezekiel: To a hardheaded people who refuse to listen, God sends the

---

[160] Paul's journey to Rome in chains seems emblematic of the Jewish people's exilic state at the hands of Rome after the temple's destruction. Still, his chains are, at least in part, due to his decision: "The divine plan does not force Paul into a situation of certain suffering; indeed, [21:4b] describes a divine longing for him to avoid it. But again, the focus lies on Paul's free choice to continue to Jerusalem, where he knows that affliction and imprisonment await him (20.22-23)" (Crabbe, "Accepting Prophecy," 202).

[161] In Acts, the passive voice of ἐπικαλέω is generally used for individuals with two names (1:23; 4:36; 10:5, 18, 32; 11:13; 12:12, 25). The LXX similarly uses ἐπικαλέω for names (e.g., Num 21:3; Judg 6:24; 15:19) and, more frequently, appealing to the Lord's name (e.g., Gen 4:26; 12:8; Exod 29:45; Deut 4:7) or (wrongly) to someone instead of the Lord (3 Kgdms 18:24-28; Hos 7:7, 11; Wis 13:17; Jdt 3:8).

[162] Paul says he "was compelled (ἠναγκάσθην) to call on Caesar" (28:18). The other use of ἀναγκάζω in Acts is Paul's statement that he compelled Jesus-followers "to blaspheme" (26:11; cf. 1 Macc 2:25; 2 Macc 6:1, 7, 18; 7:1; 4 Macc 4:26; 5:2, 27; 18:5). This admission renders Paul's appeal to Caesar more suspect.

hardheaded Paul to diaspora (exilic) Israel (cf. Ezek 3:4–11).[163] Moreover, his narrative arc and character development mimics the wider Jewish world's. In Paul's words to the Jerusalem Jews who oppose him, he is "just like all of you are today (καθὼς πάντες ὑμεῖς ἐστε σήμερον)" (22:3).

3.4 Conclusion

In this chapter, I have shown how Luke paints in various shades, not simply black and white.[164] Although Jesus divides the Way and the wider Jewish world, these groups are not depicted in contradistinction. Their images are not binaries of faithful–unfaithful, comprehending–ignorant, or idealized–demonized. Rather, alignment with and faithfulness to Israel's God are ongoing processes and, thus, spectrums in Acts. Characters and entire groups are mixed. Some Jews follow Jesus. Others vehemently reject his followers. Still others remain somewhat neutral. Certain non-Jesus-following Jews are commended for their piety, though still called to follow Jesus. The Way has its bad apples who, by betraying Jesus or the Spirit, exhibit comparable infidelity to Jews outside the nascent movement. Opportunities to repent remain for villains, and Jesus-followers demonstrate what it looks like to be cut off from Israel. Even the apostles, Israel's twelve judges appointed by the Messiah, and Paul, the Lord's chosen instrument, continually need to (re)align with God's purposes, discern the Spirit, and obey Jesus' instructions. Luke's characters remain in flux. Like Israel's past heroes, all occasionally stumble on Israel's repentance-journey.

To reiterate, Jesus is *the* dividing line within Israel. Jesus does not start a new way for Israel, though. Jesus, for Luke, is the primary orientating factor in Israel's repentance-journey jump-started by John the Baptist (Luke 3:3–17). Those who follow Jesus face the right direction on the repentance-journey. Luke makes an exclusivist call for all Israel to turn to Jesus. Nevertheless, the lines of understanding and faithfulness used to contrast Jewish believers from Jewish non-believers within Israel are quite blurry. The boundaries between these Jewish groups are porous. They are intertwined. The similarities between the Way, Paul, and the non-Jesus-following Jewish world run deeper than just ethnicity. Their struggles with fidelity reflect a deeper, common theological identity as Israel, God's elect, covenant people. Together, those Jewish-Israelites loyal to Jesus and those who are not reenact Israel's attempts to live faithfully their covenantal calling and identity. Some in Israel, though, are more aggressively unfaithful than others.

---

[163] On parallels between Paul's calling and Ezekiel, see Dale C. Allison, Jr., "Acts 9:1–9, 22:6–11, 26:12–18: Paul and Ezekiel," *JBL* 135 (2016): 807–26.
[164] Contra Zwiep, *Christ*, 120.

4

"I Persecuted this Way": Agents of Violence in Acts

In Acts, some Jews are violent, and the Way endures persecution.[1] That this is true is obvious. Jewish violence in Acts is often cited as a central piece of Luke's othering project. Matthews succinctly captures this notion: "the peaceful Christian and the violent *Ioudaioi* are constructed in tandem."[2] Luke's portrayal of the Jews, another form of the argument goes, gives "the impression that they are an *authentically ubiquitous group that acts harmoniously, homogeneously, and violently* to oppose the Gentile mission ... In Acts, Luke presents a *one-dimensional view* of *the Jews* as 'ringleaders' of baseless and violent opposition against the *ekklesia*." The Jews of Acts are "close-ended characters," stagnant and unable to change.[3] Because of their violent rejection of Jesus and his messengers, "the Jews" are decisively excluded from the people of God, solidified as God's enemies. They receive judgment, not salvation. For Matthews, Paul is central to Luke's othering project: "exemplified in the violent murder of Stephen and its connection to the persecuting-Saul-turned-persecuted-Paul, Acts constructs Jewish and Christian identity along a simple binary: to be a nonbelieving Jew is to be an agent of violence; to be a Christian is to suffer."[4] Some scholars have attempted to blunt the force of Jewish violence or certain aspects of it.[5] To date, no "pro-Jewish" or "within Judaism" interpreter has tackled the issue head on or at length.

The present chapter takes up this task. It contends that, while Acts portrays some Jews as violent and heralds repentance lest they face judgment and exclusion, Luke's rhetoric does not "other" the Jews. Luke does not portray Jews as uniformly, uniquely, or irredeemably violent in stark contrast to Jesus-followers. First, not all Jews are violent. Only *some* are. Others are entirely peaceful. Second, not only Jews are violent. Attacking the Way is not simply a Jewish phenomenon. Aggression arises from Jew and gentile alike in various locales to various degrees. Some gentiles perpetrate violence

---

[1] By *violent*, I mean actions that threaten or enact physical harm and/or death. I use *persecute* and *persecution* for violent opposition rather than general (verbal) opposition or disagreement.
[2] Matthews, *Perfect Martyr*, 9.
[3] Smith, *Literary Construction*, 64, 72, respectively; emphasis mine. Similarly, e.g., Conzelmann, *Theology*, 137–45; Sanders, *Jews*, 37–83; Wills, "Depiction," 646–47; Barbi, "*Ioudaioi*," 141; Pervo, *Dating Acts*, 324–27; Levine, "Luke," 399–401. To be sure, many of these interpreters think individual Jews can repent, but hope is abandoned for the corporate people. Carter provides an incisive analysis on the assumptions undergirding these readings ("Diaspora Poetics," 43–91).
[4] Matthews, *Perfect Martyr*, 9; cf. 56–57, 73–75; Smith, *Literary Construction*, 64–77.
[5] E.g., Brawley, *Jews*, 149–50; Weatherly, *Jewish Responsibility*; Moessner, *Luke*, 202.

against the Way without instigation from "the Jews." In fact, these gentiles persecute Paul *because he is Jewish*. Enduring gentile violence provides an ironic point of solidarity between the Way and the wider Jewish world. Third and most importantly, Acts uses violence to reinforce the *synkrisis* between Paul and the Jewish people, particularly those antagonistic toward the Way. Paul is the greatest single agent of violence in Acts, and he does not leave that fact in his past. Instead, Paul *self-identifies* with those acting as his enemies, his Jewish-Israelite siblings, by recounting his past violence in increasingly severe terms. As with ethnicity, the Lukan Paul's apologies *leverage* his violent past as a point of commonality with his fellow Jews. Jewish violence affords an opportunity to establish connection with non-Jesus-following Jews.

Of course, Acts expects Jews to cease persecuting Jesus and his followers and join the repentance-journey. Failure to abandon violence against God's messengers, as the prophets and Jesus warn, results in judgment, even destruction (e.g., Jer 7:1–15; Luke 13:34–35). Nevertheless, participation in violence does not entail de facto disqualification from the people of God or bar one from redemption.[6] Violent opposition to God's agents is, in fact, one of the historic hallmarks of God's people Israel. The risk of judgment and exclusion is ever present, certainly. But the opportunity for repentance continues. Indeed, the *synkrisis* between Saul/Paul, the prototypical Jewish God-fighter (cf. 5:39), and other violent Jews suggests that he personifies the ongoing potential for Jewish reorientation toward Jesus. If Israel's Lord can lead Paul away from violence to serve Israel's anointed one, there is hope for even the most violent and resistant among "the Jews." If God can reorient and forgive Saul, no Jew is too violent to be beyond redemption. God can change the ways and forgive those Jews who, like Paul, act like enemies by fighting against God.[7] Violence, then, does not signal immediate or permanent rejection in Acts.

To make this claim, I examine several Lukan texts that provide interpretive parameters for understanding Jewish violence in Acts. These texts frame it as a problem internal to and in continuity with Israel's history. Israel risks harsh judgment by reenacting the ancestral sins of rejecting and persecuting God's messengers. Still, some passages retain the possibility for repentance, transformation, or restoration even in

---

[6] The prophets reiterate that the righteous within Israel suffer alongside the disobedient. Israel together suffers for corporate wrongdoing, which causes the exclusion of some individuals (cf. Moessner, *Luke*, 282–301). Israel's corporate identity as God's people and hope for repentance remain (e.g., Ezek 18:1–32). As Strahan puts it, "forgiveness and impending punishment are compatible" (*Limits*, 86; contra Matthews, *Perfect Martyr*, 99–127). Bloodshed illustrates this well. On the one hand, it brings guilt and destruction (Luke 11:50). On the other, Jesus ratifies the new covenant and obtained the *ecclesia* by his blood (Luke 22:20; Acts 20:28). Space precludes extended comparison, but Luke's rationale is analogous to Jeremiah and Josephus who see violence and bloodshed as instrumental to the destruction of Jerusalem and the temple. On intertextual echoes with the prophets on the destruction of Jerusalem in conversation with early Judaism, see Chance, *Jerusalem*, 115–38; Schaefer, *Zukunft*, 33–384; McWhirter, *Rejected Prophets*, 58–86, 99–109; Smith, *Fate*. On Josephus, see Rajak, *Josephus*, 78–104; Per Bilde, *Flavius Josephus between Jerusalem and Rome: His Life, His Works and Their Importance* (Eugene, OR: Wipf and Stock, 2002), 71–73; Klawans, "Catastrophes," 290–303; Tucker S. Ferda, "Jeremiah 7 and Flavius Josephus on the First Jewish War," *JSJ* 44 (2013): 158–73.

[7] Strahan, *Limits*, 69–87; Aaron Kuecker, "'You Will Be Children of the Most High': An Inquiry into Luke's Narrative Account of Theosis," *JTI* 8 (2014): 213–28.

and/or through judgment. Next, I explore the variegated portrait of Jewish violence to show violence is not a uniformly Jewish phenomenon in Acts. I then turn to exclusively gentile violence to demonstrate that violence or inciting opposition to Paul is not a uniquely Jewish behavior. After that, I explore how Luke's Paul exemplifies how the risen Lord can make peace with the most stringent God-fighters in Israel. Luke constructs Paul's violence as archetypical of Jewish violence. When he persecuted the Way, Paul carried out many of the same violent acts he later endures. God transformed this representative opponent into a faithful servant, nevertheless. Finally, I explore how Paul uses his past to establish solidarity with Jerusalem Jews who oppose him and to recount his own transformative experience to them. Paul describes how he was like them to persuade them to become like him in serving Israel's Messiah.

4.1 Jewish Violence

4.1.1 Interpretive Guides

Luke has not left his readers without lenses for understanding violence and judgment in his two volumes. Proclamations from several reliable characters, including Jesus, provide four interpretive parameters. First, Jewish violence toward Jesus and his followers ironically reaffirms Jewish continuity with Israel. Second, Jewish violence is internecine fighting within Israel. As in Israel's past, Israelites target fellow Israelites whom God has sent as heralds of repentance to Israel in the face of divine judgment. Third, judgment follows violence against God's servants. In the present, the opportunity to repent stands (cf. Luke 13:1–5). Violence against God's messengers does not automatically or necessarily remove one from God's people, though that risk persists should one fail to change.[8] Fourth, some individuals might face destruction or removal from Israel, but hope appears to lie beyond (even through) judgment for the people. Luke's depiction of Jewish violence fits comfortably alongside other calls to repent or reform the ways of God's people Israel.

4.1.1.1 Simeon: The Fall and Rise of Many in Israel

The righteous and devout Simeon does not mention violence explicitly, but he provides the initial programmatic statement about the impending conflict in Israel sparked by Jesus (Luke 2:30–35). Simeon informs Mary that Jesus is "set for the fall and rise of many in Israel and as a sign to be spoken against (ἀντιλεγόμενον)" (2:34; cf. LXX Isa 65:2). As the conflict is internal to Israel (ἐν τῷ Ἰσραήλ), Jewish-Israelite antipathy toward Jesus and his followers does not preclude participation in the people of God.[9] Israel will become a house divided (cf. Luke 12:49–53). Mary—herself a representative

---

[8] Moessner, *Luke*, 292–301; Mitmann, "Polemik," 517–542; Schaefer, *Zukunft*, 365–70.
[9] François Bovon, *Luke*, 3 vols., *Hermeneia* (Minneapolis, MN: Fortress, 2002), 1:104.

of Israel—will not be exempt from the suffering that results from the impending conflict among the people. A sword (ῥομφαία) will pierce her as well (cf. 21:24).[10]

The terms and order of "fall and rise (πτῶσιν καὶ ἀνάστασιν)" deserve attention. The spatial imagery mirrors the status reversals outlined in Mary's speech, leading many to conclude that Simeon reuses the motif for divided Israel (1:51–53). Indeed, division emerges clearly in Luke-Acts as the humbled are exalted and the proud are humbled (e.g., 13:10–17). Other scholars have argued that "fall and rise" outlines a sequential pattern rather than just division. Many in Israel, they contend, experience falling first and then rising, akin to patterns of judgment and restoration outlined by the prophets (e.g., Amos 5:2; 7:2, 5; 8:12; 9:11–15).[11] Simeon's word order and word choice privilege the sequential reading. The noun πτῶσις occurs only here in Luke-Acts. It echoes the "well-known image of God as the stone that causes God's own people to stumble" (Isa 8:14–15; 28:13, 16; cf. Luke 20:17–18).[12] More precisely, πτῶσις in the LXX often functions as a euphemism for judgment and/or destruction, frequently against God's people due to disobedience (e.g., Exod 30:12; Ps 105:29; Isa 17:1; 51:17, 22; Jer 6:15; Ezek 27:27; 31:13; 32:10; Zech 14:12, 15, 18; cf. Judg 20:39; Nah 3:2). The verbal form, πίπτω, is used comparably (e.g., 1 Kgdms 2:33; Jer 8:4; Ezek 5:12; 6:11–12; Hos 10:8; 14:1; Amos 5:2). Acts uses the verbal form for judgment, including death (5:5, 10; 13:11; 20:9). The most significant of these appears in Jesus' declaration about Jerusalem's destruction and captivity (Luke 21:24; cf. 23:30; Acts 15:16). Simeon's language insinuates judgment.[13]

Furthermore, *all* other uses of the noun ἀνάστασις in Luke-Acts refer to resurrection of the dead (Luke 14:14; 20:27, 33–36; Acts 1:22; 2:31; 4:2, 33; 17:18, 32; 23:6, 8; 24:15,

---

[10] Luke Timothy Johnson, *The Gospel of Luke*, Sacra Pagina (Collegeville, MN: Liturgical Press, 1991), 72; Green, *Luke*, 149. In the LXX, ῥομφαία, which occurs only here in Luke-Acts, frequently serves as an instrument of judgment, often against God's people (e.g., Isa 66:16; Jer 50:11; Ezek 5:1–2; Hos 7:16; 14:1; Amos 7:9–11; Hag 1:11; Zech 13:7). Another sword (μάχαιρα) commonly used in judgment on Israel (e.g., Isa 1:20; Jer 4:10; Ezek 5:2) will strike Jerusalem (Luke 21:24). Oliver, *Eschatology*, 39.

[11] For a survey, see Alfonso Simón Muñoz, "La 'Permanencia' de Israel: Una Nueva Lectura de Lc 2,34a," *EstB* 50 (1992): 191–223 (esp. 192–96). For sequential readings, see, e.g., Jacques Winandy, "La Prophétie de Syméon (Lc 2,34–35)," *RevBib* 72 (1965): 321–51; Tiede, "Glory," 27–28; Kinzer, *Jerusalem*, 42–44. For division, see e.g., Johnson, *Luke*, 70; Green, *Luke*, 98–105. The two readings can coexist. Luke-Acts describes both division and characters who fall and rise. Moreover, the prophets hold these motifs in unison (e.g., Isa 28:13–22; Jer 32:26–44; Ezek 11:5–21; cf. Abraham Joshua Heschel, *The Prophets* [New York: HarperPerennial, 2001], 14–19).

[12] Green, *Luke*, 149; cf. Johnson, *Luke*, 70.

[13] *Judgment* is sometimes considered an on–off switch; it is punitive and utterly destructive against the wicked. However, judgment varies in degree and purpose in Israel's Scriptures and Luke-Acts. Judgment can entail removal from the people, but not all judgments carry such severe ramifications. Israel's corporate chastisement is *always* temporary in the prophets, despite some among the people experiencing utter destruction, and the people are called to repent if they are to experience restoration (Heschel, *Prophets*, *passim*; cf. Schaefer, *Zukunft*, 47–60, 100–1). For examples in Luke-Acts, the judgments of Judas, Ananias and Sapphira, and Herod are more punitive and permanent than those of Paul, Simon Magus, and Elymas, whose judgment seems transformative (or at least carries that potential). The spectrum of judgment lies along the lines of *severity* and *permanence*. Israel and its children can experience judgment without being utterly destroyed or cut off completely (cf. Tiede, "Glory," 34). And Israel remains God's chosen when some individuals are removed (Givens, *We the People*, 5).

21; 26:23; cf. 2 Macc 7:14; 12:43). The verbal form, ἀνίστημι, is used with a broader range (e.g., Luke 1:39; 4:16; 11:7–8; 17:19; 22:45–46; Acts 1:15; 5:17, 34–37; 20:30). Still, certain instances refer to resurrection (e.g., Luke 16:31; 18:33; 24:7, 46; Acts 2:24, 32; 13:33–34; 17:30; cf. Acts 9:40).[14] A few times ἀνίστημι insinuates a double entendre with physical movement and deliverance or new life (e.g., Luke 15:18, 20; 24:12; Acts 10:26; 12:7; 14:20; 22:16). In short, this term, especially the noun, is associated with the resurrection—which was connected to Israel's corporate restoration (Acts 4:1–2; 23:6; 24:15; 26:6–7; cf. Ezek 36–37; 4QPseudo-Ezekiel)—often enough to hear it resonate in Simeon's words.[15] His statement, then, could be paraphrased as "the judgment and the restoration of many in Israel." Simeon prefigures the conflict within Israel provoked by Jesus with prophetic connotations of calamity and subsequent consolation.[16]

Simeon's words, although not a direct prediction of Jewish violence, provide the initial hint for understanding Jewish opposition in Luke-Acts: God's people Israel will divide as many within it fall, experiencing judgment because of their resistance to Jesus and his followers. Judgment on the many, Simeon insinuates, is not the end of the story. The many antagonistic of Israel will experience a rising, a subsequent resurrection.[17] The people who resist God's saving acts in Jesus may yet experience salvation.

4.1.1.2 Jesus: Israel Persecuting the Prophets

As the most reliable character in the Lukan narrative, Jesus is essential to understanding violence in Luke's writings. Jesus models and outlines how his followers, like God's messengers to Israel past, will face opposition from their kin.[18] The Nazareth pericope enacts and prefigures this, including the first instance of intra-Jewish violence in Luke-Acts. When Jesus reminds his listeners of Elijah and Elisha's service to gentiles, animosity is ignited in his hearers (ἐπλήσθησαν πάντες θυμοῦ; cf. Acts 19:28). They attempt to "cast him out from the city" and kill him. Jesus leaves unscathed (4:23–30; cf. Acts 13:50). Jesus returns to Jewish communities after being rejected, rather than going to gentiles to the neglect of Jews (4:31; cf. Acts 14:1). Hostility from his kin in one

---

[14] Cf. Muñoz, "Permanencia," 211–16. In Acts, the "raising up" of Jesus also entails his enthronement (Anderson, *God Raised*, 234–60; David L. Tiede, "The Exaltation of Jesus and the Restoration of Israel in Acts 1," *HTR* 79 [1986]: 278–86).

[15] Anderson, *God Raised*, 118–260; Oliver, *Eschatology*, 127–31; cf. Charles H. Talbert, "The Place of the Resurrection in the Theology of Luke," *Int* 46 (1992): 19–30. On early Jewish perspectives on exile and restoration, see Staples, *Israel*, 85–348.

[16] Several characters embody this pattern of judgment and restoration, giving further credence to the sequential reading: the pious yet disbelieving Zechariah (1:5–22, 64–66; cf. Ezek 3:22–27; cf. Bovon, *Luke*, 1:37–38; Green, *Luke*, 79; Wilson, *Unmanly Men*, 79–112); Simon Peter (5:3–11; 22:31–34; 24:14); Jerusalem (13:34–35; 19:41–44; 21:20–24; see Chance, *Jerusalem*, 115–138; Schaefer, *Zukunft*, 130–85); Jesus in solidarity with Israel and Jerusalem (Kinzer, *Jerusalem*, 21–58, 129–59; cf. N. T. Wright, *Jesus and the Victory of God*, vol. 2 of COQG [Minneapolis: Fortress, 2008], 569–70); and Saul/Paul.

[17] Cf. Oliver, *Eschatology*, 39.

[18] Cunningham, *Tribulations*, 47–187; McWhirter, *Rejected Prophets*, 45–86; Moessner, *Luke*, 201–71.

region does not undermine his mission's priority to all Israel. In fact, cynicism and animosity are fairly standard responses to prophets in Israel.[19]

Jesus relays this point to his disciples when he informs them about the violence and opposition they will encounter (6:22–23; 12:4–12; 21:12–19). They will face the same things "their ancestors did to the prophets" (6:23; cf. 13:34–35; Neh 9:26; Ezek 2:1–7).[20] Their sufferings, though, provide opportunities to testify (ἀποβήσεται ὑμῖν εἰς μαρτύριον) to Jesus' name in Israel (21:13). Indeed, the Holy Spirit will guide their responses when people "drag you before synagogues, and rulers, and authorities (εἰσφέρωσιν ὑμᾶς ἐπὶ τὰς συναγωγὰς καὶ τὰς ἀρχὰς καὶ τὰς ἐξουσίας)" (12:11–12; cf. 21:12, 16–17).[21] Jesus' words, then, establish an evangelistic tenor to the apologies in Acts. Apologetic speeches are opportunities to persuade listeners about Jesus' messianic identity. When Jesus' followers are abused by their Jewish family, they will preach repentance for the forgiveness of sins.

Of course, the prophetic word comes with judgment. Jesus elaborates on this point in a Pharisee's house (11:37–52). In one of Jesus' woes, he declares that, by building the tombs of the prophets, the Torah experts (τοῖς νομικοῖς) are witnesses who affirm the murders of the prophets by their ancestors (11:47–48).[22] It will be no surprise that "this generation" similarly will "kill and persecute (ἀποκτενοῦσιν καὶ διώξουσιν)" the prophets and apostles sent by the Wisdom of God for Israel's sake (cf. 9:22; 13:34; 17:25; 20:14–15; Acts 7:52; 21:31; 23:12, 14).[23] The blood (τὸ αἷμα) of all the slain righteous in Israel's history will be required of this generation. They will be judged severely (Luke 11:49–51; cf. LXX Gen 42:22; 2 Kgdms 4:11; Ezek 3:18–20; 33:6–8; 4 Ezra 1:25–33; 2 Bar. 64:1–67:6). Those who oppose Jesus ironically conform to Israel's legacy of rejecting and even killing God's messengers, and face ruin as a result. Nothing moves these descriptions outside of Israel's story or beyond prophetic rhetoric about judgment that stems from violence (e.g., Isa 1:10–20; 59:1–8; Jer 7:1–15; 25:4; Ezek 9:9–10; cf. 2 Chr 24:19–22).

In further alignment with the prophetic pattern, Jesus' laments and proclamations over Jerusalem insinuate that hope for Israel's restoration lies beyond the judgment. Jesus grieves over the city for killing the prophets and stones those sent to her (13:34–35).[24]

---

[19] Brawley, *Jews*, 6–27; Koet, *Five Studies*, 44–52; Rebecca I. Denova, *The Things Accomplished among Us: Prophetic Tradition in the Structural Pattern of Luke-Acts*, JSNTSup 141 (Sheffield: Sheffield Academic, 1997), 138–46; McWhirter, *Rejected Prophets*, 34–49; contra Conzelmann, *Theology*, 32–38; Levine, "Luke," 400.

[20] Green, *Luke*, 268; cf., e.g., Jer 5:12–13; 6:13–15; Mic 2:11, on Israel celebrating false prophets.

[21] Notably, no one is brought to trial before a synagogue in Acts (Brawley, *Jews*, 149–50).

[22] The absence of a definitive object makes it unclear if this woe targets both Pharisees and Torah experts. The first two address "you Pharisees," and the third lacks clarification. In the following three, the first and third woes are against "you Torah experts," with the second ambiguous. The Pharisees are likely implicated, as the Torah experts felt when Jesus denounced the Pharisees (11:45).

[23] Green, *Luke*, 473–75; cf. Moessner, *Luke*, 294.

[24] Stoning was often for blasphemy (Lev 24:14, 16, 23) and apostasy (Lev 20:2; Deut 13:11). Jerusalem thus attributes "blasphemy or apostasy to the very ones whom God has sent" (Green, *Luke*, 538). Their opposition to God's messengers is ironically done out of loyalty to God. Nevertheless, Luke's Jesus mourns the city's destruction (Oliver, *Eschatology*, 83–89). On blasphemy in early Judaism, see Darrell L. Bock, *Blasphemy and Exaltation in Judaism: The Charge against Jesus in Mark 14:53–65* (Grand Rapids, MI: Baker, 2000).

Their violence and unwillingness to receive him causes the abandonment of their house (ἀφίεται ὑμῖν ὁ οἶκος ὑμῶν). Jerusalem and her children (τὰ τέκνα σου) will face destruction (cf. Jer 12:7; 22:5; 4 Ezra 1:33–34). They will not see Jesus again *until* (ἕως) they welcome him with the words of Ps 118:26. Jesus' conditional statement insinuates that judgment might not have the final word. Jesus might return to the city with healing.[25] Jesus' later comments about the city reinforce this reading (19:41–44; 21:20–24). Because of their violence and inability to perceive God's visitation which would bring peace, Jerusalem will be surrounded by enemies to be left desolate and exiled (19:42–44; 21:20; cf. Lev 26:32–35; Jer 22:5; Luke 1:68–75).[26] Echoing Simeon's words, Jesus states that "this people (τῷ λαῷ τούτῳ)" Israel "will fall by the mouth of the sword (πεσοῦνται στόματι μαχαίρης)" as the city is trampled by the gentiles (21:24; cf. Jer 21:7). This trampling has a limit. The "times of the gentiles" will be fulfilled (ἄχρι οὗ πληρωθῶσιν καιροὶ ἐθνῶν) one (undefined) day. Restoration lies beyond destruction. Indeed, the apostles will proclaim that the ignorant city can be forgiven for their violent rejection of Jesus— though that violence might bring judgment first—and receive times of refreshing (καιροὶ ἀναψύξεως; Acts 3:17–21; cf. 2:22–24, 38–40; Luke 21:24; 23:34; Acts 13:27). If Jerusalem stands as a figurehead for the Jewish people, then this pattern of falling and rising, of judgment and resurrection, remains possible for all Israel, even after violent behavior.[27]

4.1.1.3 *Gamaliel: Fighting against God*

Luke utilizes Gamaliel to voice the serious nature of violence against the Way: Those who fight against Jesus' followers fight against God (cf. Acts 9:4–5).[28] The respected Torah teacher prevents the council from fulfilling Jesus' words by killing the apostles, at least temporarily (5:33–40).[29] Gamaliel exhorts the council to "keep away from these people [the apostles] and leave them be" (5:38) because, he reasons (rightly according to Luke-Acts), messianic undertakings with human origins are doomed to fail. If the Way is like the movements of Theudas and Judas, it too will be overthrown (καταλυθήσεται; cf. Luke 21:6). However, Gamaliel continues, the council will be unable to overthrow (καταλῦσαι) the Way if it stems from God, and they (and all who fight against the Way) will "be found God-fighters (θεομάχοι εὑρεθῆτε)." Gamaliel does not explicate what happens to God-fighters, though. Absent from his comments is whether God-fighters can repent. Are they consigned to their fate, or can they change?

---

[25] Dale C. Allison, Jr., "Matt 23:39 = Luke 13:35b as a Conditional Prophecy," *JSNT* 5 (1983): 75–84; cf. Brawley, *Jews*, 123–26; Green, *Luke*, 538–39; Oliver, *Eschatology*, 85–89.

[26] Tannehill, *Shape*, 123, 134; Green, *Luke*, 689–91. "Even understanding the destruction of Jerusalem as a divine verdict on sinful Israel was commonplace before and after the Roman conquest. But the identification of Israel's sin and the definition of Israel's required repentance varied sharply" (Tiede, "Contending," 308).

[27] Stephen's speech notes that this pattern is common to Israel. Israel rejected two deliverers in the past, Joseph and Moses, only to be delivered by these same figures upon a second encounter (Acts 7:9–16, 23–39). On the interrelationship between Jerusalem and the Jewish people, see Bachmann, *Jerusalem*. For expositions of Jerusalem's fate in Luke-Acts, see Chance, *Jerusalem*, 115–138; Fusco, "Future," 10–16; Schaefer, *Zukunft*, 130–85; McWhirter, *Rejected Prophets*, 68–74; Kinzer, *Jerusalem*, 21–58.

[28] Lohfink, *Sammlung*, 86–87; Padilla, *Speeches*, 106–34.

[29] Cf. Matthews, *Perfect Martyr*, 64.

One presumes that, sans repentance, they face destruction. This is possible, but it might not be the only answer.[30] Another answer is found in Gamaliel's pupil Paul (22:3), who, in failing to heed his teacher's advice, becomes the quintessential Jewish God-fighter. Paul illustrates that, according to Acts, the Lord can defeat God's enemies through love (cf. Luke 6:27, 35) and reorient God-fighters in Israel out of God's own initiative, that is, without them responding to a prior call to or carrying out prior acts of repentance.[31]

4.1.1.4 Stephen: Jealous Brothers and Unjust Israelites

Stephen's speech sparks the influx of Jewish violence and provides the final interpretive guide. His recounting of Israel's history further frames violence in Acts as internecine, in continuity with Israel's history, and as a source of judgment yet not to the exclusion of future redemption. In Stephen's retelling, the twelve patriarchs are the first descendants of Israel to persecute a member of their own family (7:8–16).[32] Motivated by jealousy (ζηλώσαντες), they sell Joseph to Egypt (7:9; cf. Gen 37:11). This is the sole time Luke applies the ζῆλος word group to characters outside the narrative arc of Luke-Acts. All other uses apply to Jewish characters (Acts 5:17; 13:45; 17:5; 21:20; 22:3; cf. Luke 6:15; Acts 1:13).[33] The patriarchs' jealousy further frames the subsequent conflicts as internecine: Jealousy provokes *fraternal* conflict (cf. 1 Clem 4:1–5:7).[34] Violence does not dissolve familial ties, though. Despite the misdeeds, time, and distance, the patriarchs remain Joseph's family (τὸ γένος Ἰωσήφ), his brothers (τοῖς ἀδελφοῖς αὐτοῦ; 7:13–14).

The wrongdoing of Joseph's brothers still leads to suffering. A contrast emerges between Joseph and his brothers. God delivered Joseph "from all his afflictions (πασῶν τῶν θλίψεων αὐτοῦ)" first caused by his brothers, elevating him as a ruler over Egypt (cf. 11:19; 14:22; 20:23). Conversely, famine and "great suffering (θλῖψις μεγάλη)" come upon all Egypt and Canaan such that "our ancestors did not find food" (7:10–11). The persecuting patriarchs suffer—are judged even—while Joseph prospers.[35] The contrast

---

[30] Kylie Crabbe, "Being Found Fighting against God: Luke's Gamaliel and Josephus on Human Responses to Divine Providence," *ZNW* 106 (2015): 21–39; cf. Beers, *Followers*, 178.

[31] Cf. Kuecker, "Theosis," 217–24.

[32] Contra Richard, Joseph is included in "the *twelve* patriarchs" *and* differentiated as the target of violence. Richard rightly notes that Stephen casts the patriarchs in a negative light. They are not abandoned, however. God vindicates Joseph *to preserve* his jealous brothers ("Polemical," 258–262; cf. Conzelmann, *Apostelgeschichte*, 52–53; Jervell, *Apostelgeschichte*, 234–35; Ravens, *Restoration*, 61).

[33] The patriarchs are descendants of Israel and, therefore, Jewish ancestors (7:11, 15). Still, "Jewish" is a misnomer for the patriarchs since the term derives from affiliation with one patriarch, Judah. On the usage of the ζῆλος word group in the first century, see Benjamin J. Lappenga, *Paul's Language of Ζῆλος: Monosemy and the Rhetoric of Identity and Practice*, BibInt 137 (Leiden: Brill, 2015), 68–117.

[34] Contra Pervo, *Acts*, 141–42; Matthews, *Perfect Martyr*, 9; cf. Deutschmann, *Synagoge*, 184–85. Stephen distinguishes between familial conflict and oppression by a foreign power like Egypt (7:6–7, 17–19). First Clement similarly depicts jealousy-driven conflict among Jewish Jesus-followers as a cause of Rome's execution of Peter and Paul, as demonstrated by David L. Eastman, "Jealousy, Internal Strife, and the Deaths of Peter and Paul: A Reassessment of 1 Clement," *ZAC* 18 (2014): 34–53.

[35] There is no clear causal statement between their sin and the famine and suffering in Genesis or Stephen's speech, but the brothers think their suffering results from their sin in Gen 42:21–22.

is not absolute, however. Israel finds deliverance through Joseph. On their second visit, Joseph's identity is revealed (ἐν τῷ δευτέρῳ ἀνεγνωρίσθη Ἰωσήφ) and he welcomes Jacob "and all their kinsfolk (πᾶσαν τὴν συγγένειαν)" (7:13–14). Joseph receives and sustains the family that rejected him. Joseph is the first example of Israel's abusing and rejecting its deliverer whom God vindicates and still uses to redeem his people.[36]

The Moses narrative evinces a similar pattern (7:23–44). Moses "visits his brothers, the children of Israel (ἐπισκέψασθαι τοὺς ἀδελφοὺς αὐτοῦ τοὺς υἱοὺς Ἰσραήλ)" (cf. Luke 1:68, 78; 7:16; Acts 15:34). He strikes down an Egyptian to rectify an injustice (ἐκδίκησις; cf. Luke 18:7–8; 21:22), presuming his brothers would recognize him as God's agent of salvation (7:25). In his first appearance to Israel, Moses expected they would receive him. They did not. When Moses attempts to reconcile two quarreling Israelites, "the one treating his neighbor unjustly" (cf. Luke 10:27–36) pushes him (ἀπώσατο αὐτόν), denying him as their "ruler and judge" (7:27, 35). Moses, therefore, flees the people, his family, consigning them to forty additional years of slavery.[37] Moses eventually delivers Israel when he returns at God's behest (7:30–38). As with Joseph, Israelite opposition against God's agents might exacerbate judgment and suffering, but it does not preclude future redemption. Of course, Israel turns recalcitrant in the wilderness and "pushes Moses aside" again (7:35, 39–43). As a result, God redeems then judges the same wicked generation. Judgment and deliverance coincide.

4.1.1.5 Summary

These texts establish a fourfold guide for understanding Luke's depiction of Jewish violence and warnings of resultant judgment. First, Jewish oppressors ironically affirm their Israelite identities through violence against God's messengers. Second, Jewish violence in Acts is familial (cf. Luke 21:16). Israelites oppress their Israelite siblings who are sent to bring (the message of) redemption. Third, judgment looms overhead should the people fail to repent. Fourth, redemption lies beyond (or even through) judgment. Indeed, Israel's deliverers have a history of redeeming those who denied and oppressed them. Many might be judged for rejecting God's agents, but these messengers continue

---

[36] Jervell, *Apostelgeschichte*, 234–35; Tannehill, *Narrative Unity*, 2:97; Johnson, *Acts*, 118, 121–22. Jesus mirrors Joseph: handed over to a foreign power by his kin, vindicated by God as Israel's deliverer, and then hidden to be revealed on a later encounter (Brehm, "Vindicating," 279–84). Kaminsky observes that, "In the Joseph narrative one hears the brothers attribute the following statement to Joseph: 'You shall not see my face unless your brother is with you' (Gen 43:3, 5; 44:23). The very strong emphasis in these narratives on seeing, especially on seeing God's face, is too frequent to be coincidental. While the Joseph story lacks an explicit reference to seeing God, it may well imply it, inasmuch as Joseph himself often functions as a stand-in for the Deity ... if one hopes to see God's face and thus receive God's blessing, one must be reconciled with one's brother" (*Yet I loved*, 74). This bears striking resemblance to the Jesus' declaration that Jerusalem "will not see [him] until" they welcome him (Luke 13:35). As with Joseph and Moses, Israel's redemption may await Jesus' return.

[37] Jervell, *Apostelgeschichte*, 238–39. In Acts, Israel's response is what causes Moses to flee, not Pharaoh's desire to kill him (Exod 2:15; Haenchen, *Acts*, 282).

to call for repentance, intercede for, and provide hope to Israel amidst their sharp prophetic words.[38] Fallen Israel might rise anew.

4.1.2 Patterns of Jewish Violence

With this interpretive framework in place, I turn to evaluate the general patterns of Jewish violence (and occasional lack thereof) in Acts. This section demonstrates that violence in Acts is not uniform amid, ubiquitous among, or unique to Jews. Jewish violence is not monolithic in Acts. Only some Jewish people are violent. Others in certain regions oppose Paul in word only. Some Jewish people and communities are entirely peaceful. Moreover, Jews rarely commit violence without gentile participation. As with Jesus, Jews and gentiles—all peoples—come together to resist the word (4:24–27). Furthermore, hostility does not cause total social separation from Jews. Paul may leave a region due to violence, but he immediately returns to Jewish space in new places.

4.1.2.1 Violence against the Jerusalem Community

Violence emerges and escalates in the opening chapters of Acts in three scenes. First, the priests, Sadducees, and temple officers arrest Peter and John (4:1–31; cf. 8:3; 22:4; 26:10), threatens them (προσαπειλησάμενοι; cf. 4:29; 9:1), and ultimately releases them (4:1–31). This attempt fails, leading to the second, more abusive encounter. Full of jealousy (ἐπλήσθησαν ζήλου), the high priest and the Sadducees arrest the apostles twice due to angelic intervention. This latter arrest is done "without force" (οὐ μετὰ βίας; cf. 21:35) out of fear of being stoned by the people, who are positively inclined toward the nascent movement (5:13–26). Peter proceeds to infuriate (διεπρίοντο)—a passion Stephen reignites (7:54)—the council such that they want to kill him and the others (ἀνελεῖν αὐτούς; 5:33; cf. 22:20; 26:10).[39] Thanks to Gamaliel, the council only beats (δείραντες) the apostles—likely an internecine punishment for wayward Jews—before releasing them (5:40; cf. 16:37; 22:19).[40] Third, Stephen is not so fortunate. His accusers stir up the people and seize him (συνήρπασαν; 6:12; cf. 19:29). The council and those present drag him out of the city and stone him (ἐκβαλόντες ἔξω τῆς πόλεως ἐλιθοβόλουν) in response to his rebuke and heavenly vision (7:54–60), reenacting the behavior of their Israelite ancestors (cf. Luke 13:34; 20:12, 15). This sparks the scattering and persecution of the *ecclesia* in Jerusalem (8:1; 11:19).[41] Some pious Jews in Jerusalem outside the *ecclesia* protest Stephen's death (8:2). From the outset, Jewish violence lacks uniformity.

---

[38] Although a clear call to repent is absent, Stephen, like Jesus, requests that God not hold his death against his killers (7:56; cf. Luke 23:34). Stephen refrains from declaring a word of judgment, in stark contrast to Zechariah son of Jehoida (2 Chr. 24:20–22). Intercession is his final act (Keener, *Acts*, 2:1458–62; Strahan, *Limits*, 69–87; cf. Pervo, *Acts*, 195–96).

[39] "'Gnashing teeth' is a metonym for rage, often, in the LXX, for the fury of the unjust, e.g., Job 16:9; Pss 34:16; 36:12; 111:10; Lam 2:16" (Pervo, *Acts*, 197).

[40] Jervell, *Apostelgeschichte*, 208–12; Keener, *Acts*, 2:1241; cf. Luke 22:63.

[41] Bruce, *Acts*, 176–77; Jervell, *Apostelgeschichte*, 246–47; McWhirter, *Rejected Prophets*, 104–7.

4.1.2.2 Violence against Paul

Aside from these initial incidents, violence in Acts concentrates around Paul, whether it is precipitated by him or targets him.[42] In the diaspora, though, Jewish violence against Paul and his cohort lacks consistency. Numerous communities treat Paul peaceably, even if they do not accept his words. Others resist him in word alone. Notably, verbal opposition, not acts of violence, precipitates Paul's distancing himself from some Jewish communities. Paul continues to interact with the Jewish world after both verbal and physical antagonism. Significantly, diaspora violence stems from Jews and gentiles together. Diaspora Jews simply do not perpetuate violence sans gentile participation.[43] Paul's preaching divides every city and group, which provokes Jews and gentiles alike to treat him with hostility. Furthermore, aggression targets Paul and his immediate cohort primarily. Widespread acts of persecution against local diaspora assemblies of Jesus-followers are absent (cf. 8:1).

Paul's journeys, save his final trip to Rome in chains, are bracketed by threats on his life from Jews in Syria and Jerusalem.[44] These are the few places where Jews attack Paul without gentile involvement. In Damascus, Paul engages in his ministry for "many days" before the plot to kill him (ἀνελεῖν αὐτόν) arises (cf. 5:33).[45] As a result, the disciples in Damascus help him escape (9:23-25). When Paul returns to Syria on his last trip to Jerusalem, he encounters a renewed "plot (ἐπιβουλή) against him by the Jews" in the area (20:3; cf. 9:24). Nothing suggests that hostility against all members of the Way emerges in Damascus. Luke mentions no widespread persecution there (cf. 8:1; 11:19). The Damascus disciples do not flee the synagogue or city with Saul/Paul.

In Saul's first trip to Jerusalem, "the Hellenists" attempt to kill him, leading the Way to send him to Tarsus, his hometown. Ironically, the region experiences peace after his departure. Saul no longer poses a threat to the Way or brings threats against himself to them (9:28-31). When Paul returns to Jerusalem, an angry crowd sparked by some Asian Jews "lays hands on him" (ἐπέβαλον ἐπ' αὐτὸν τὰς χεῖρας; cf. Luke 21:12; Acts 4:3; 5:18; 12:1; συλλαμβάνω in 23:27; 26:21; cf. 12:3) and tries to kill him (21:27, 31; διαχειρίσασθαι in 26:21; cf. 5:30). In this latter case, echoing Jesus' trial (Luke 18:32; 20:20; 22:4-6; 24:20), gentiles get involved.[46] Agabus warned that "the Jews in Jerusalem

---

[42] Violence is also perpetrated by Herod. He kills James and arrests Peter (12:1-4). Herod, echoing Pharaoh's mistreatment (κακόω; ἐπέβαλεν ... τὰς χεῖρας; 7:6, 19) of the Israelites and prefiguring Paul's (14:2; 18:10; 21:27; cf. 4:3; 5:18), provides a consummate example of ruling powers persecuting God's people (cf. Luke 20:19; 21:12). Herod is notably struck down for usurping God's glory rather than for of his violent acts (12:20-23; cf. 2 Macc 9:5-9). Nevertheless, this king illustrates that some enemies of God are punished with death.
[43] See Deutschmann, *Synagoge*, 85-151, 227-32, for a comparable, more expansive overview.
[44] Smith overstates in saying that "'*the Jews*' plotting and conspiring frames or forms an *inclusio* around Paul's ministry in Acts" (*Literary Other*, 71-72; emphasis mine). Paul's ministry does not end in Jerusalem and Caesarea, where his life is threatened. It continues in Rome. The Jews there are peaceful.
[45] Luke's comments about durations of time indicate that Paul can engage in prolonged civil conversations before hostility arises (Parsons, *Acts*, 269).
[46] For parallels with Jesus' arrest and trial, see Marguerat, *Christian Historian*, 56-57; Rius-Camps, *Camino*, 264-69; Tannehill, *Narrative Unity*, 2:270-74; Moessner, *Luke*, 238-71.

would bind (δήσουσιν) [Paul] and hand him over *to the hands of the gentiles* (παραδώσουσιν εἰς χεῖρας ἐθνῶν)" (21:11; cf. 28:17). Interestingly, it is the Romans who "bind" Paul with chains (δεθῆναι ἁλύσεσι), and Felix and Festus who keep Paul bound, seeking favor with Paul's Jewish opponents (21:33; 22:29; 24:27; 25:9 cf. 12:6). To be sure, these gentiles preserve Paul's life from the Jewish crowd, the conflict within the Sanhedrin (22:22–23; 23:10), and the subsequent plot (ἐπιβουλή) from a Jewish group (23:12–22; 25:1–5). The Romans facilitate his incarceration and pervert justice nonetheless, almost abusing Paul themselves (22:24–25).[47] These last events in Jerusalem are the apex of Jewish violence in Acts. Even there, Paul's Jewish opposition is particularized, and gentile hands contribute (cf. 4:24–27).

In the diaspora, Paul often encounters joint Jew-gentile hostility. Jews in these regions *never* attack Paul and his cohort without some modicum of gentile involvement. Pisidian Antioch establishes a pattern with several pertinent parallels to earlier scenes. On seeing the crowds, the Jews who do not follow Paul and Barnabas are "filled with jealousy" (ἐπλήσθησαν ζήλου; cf. 7:9), speak against (ἀντέλεγον; cf. Luke 2:34; Isa 65:2) Paul's words, and blaspheme (13:45). Their contrarian posture and blasphemous words, according to Paul and Barnabas, indicate that these Jews "push aside (ἀπωθεῖσθε) [the word of God] and judge [themselves] unworthy of eternal life" (13:46). They align with the wilderness generation that ignored Moses, "turned in their hearts to Egypt" and failed to enter the Promised Land as a result (7:27, 39). Mimicking God's response to that generation, Paul and Barnabas "turn to the gentiles" (13:47; cf. 7:42).[48] These unpersuaded Jews incite gentiles, prominent devout women, and leading men in the city, who "stir up persecution (ἐπήγειραν διωγμόν)" against Paul and Barnabas and drive them (ἐξέβαλον αὐτούς) from the region (cf. Luke 4:29).[49] They respond by shaking the dust from their feet as a witness to the city, not just the Jewish community, about impending judgment (Acts 13:50–51; cf. Luke 9:5; 10:10–12). Nevertheless, this act, like other prophetic sign-acts, is a tacit call to repentance (e.g., Jer 27:2–22; Ezek 4:1–5:17; cf. Acts 13:41; 18:6).[50] Jewish violence and turning to the gentiles does not dismiss the covenantal identity of all Jews everywhere, though some risk excluding themselves from Israel's inheritance (cf. 3:17–23). Strikingly, the disciples in Pisidian

---

[47] On Roman perversions of justice in Acts, see Rowe, *World*, 53–87; Steve Walton, "Trying Paul or Trying Rome? Judges and Accused in the Roman Trials of Paul in Acts," in *Luke-Acts and Empire*, 122–41. If Acts postdates Paul's death, Rome's role becomes increasingly conspicuous and analogous to Jesus since, according to Eusebius, Rome kills him (*Hist. eccl.* 3.1.2).

[48] Tannehill, *Narrative Unity*, 2:172–75; Koet, *Five Studies*, 114–15; Beers, *Followers*, 130–31. God responded to the wilderness generation's turning with another: "God turned (ἔστρεψεν) from them and handed them over to the worship the host of heaven" (7:42). God, of course, did not abandon Israel. Neither do Paul and Barnabas abandon the Jewish people. Luke makes no mention if Paul and Barnabas leave Jewish space prior to departing the region, and they immediately return to the synagogue in Iconium.

[49] "Devout women" and "leading men" are groups that elsewhere respond positively to Paul (e.g., 13:12, 43; 16:14; 17:4). *All* groups divide over Paul's message (Jervell, *Apostelgeschichte*, 365). Paul's mission cannot simply be described as "Jewish rejection resulting in gentiles' acceptance" (contra Pervo, *Acts*, 341; cf. Ray, *Narrative Irony*, 103).

[50] Deutschmann, *Synagoge*, 128–37; Brawley, *Jews*, 71–76; Keener, *Acts*, 2:2105–6; contra Haenchen, *Acts*, 415.

Antioch are filled with joy and the Holy Spirit following Paul's and Barnabas' departure (13:52). The Jewish community does not oppress all Jesus-followers in the region.

Despite their first turn to the gentiles and brush with persecution, Paul and Barnabas immediately return to Jewish space in Iconium (14:1-7). Unpersuaded Jews again turn some gentiles against Paul and Barnabas yet do not drive them from the region or even the synagogue (14:2). Indeed (μὲν οὖν), they are able "to stay for a long time (ἱκανὸν μὲν οὖν χρόνον διέτριψαν)," proclaiming the word and performing signs and wonders (14:3).[51] It is not until after the entire city divides that a joint effort of gentiles and unpersuaded Jews emerges. This mixed crowd, "gentiles and also Jews with their rulers," make an attempt (ὁρμή) to mistreat and stone Paul and Barnabas (ὑβρίσαι καὶ λιθοβολῆσαι αὐτούς; cf. 4:25-27; 7:58-59) that forces them to flee the region (14:5).[52] This trend immediately repeats in the gentile region of Lystra (14:8-20). After some Jews from Pisidian Antioch and Iconium manage to turn the gentile crowds against Paul, they—presumably both these Jews and the gentile crowds—stone (λιθάσαντες) Paul and drag (ἔσυρον) him out of the city (14:19; cf. 8:3; 17:6).

This pattern recurs to varying degrees throughout Paul's later journeys. In Thessalonica, unpersuaded Jews become jealous (ζηλώσαντες) and recruit "some bad men" to find Paul (17:5-10).[53] Given their presence in the marketplace, these men likely are (or at least include) gentiles (cf. 16:19; 17:17; 19:38).[54] The mixed mob drags (ἔσυρον) Jason and some Jesus-followers who housed Paul before the city rulers since they cannot find Paul and Silas. This is the full extent of the violence in the city. Jason and his household are released on bail, and Paul and Silas are sent away.[55] Even the more united Jewish opposition (κατεπέστησαν ὁμοθυμαδὸν οἱ Ἰουδαῖοι) in Corinth includes gentiles (18:5-17). Preceding this attack, Paul makes his second "turn to the gentiles" after some local Jews oppose him and blaspheme. He issues a prophetic warning of impending judgment, declaring his innocence for their blood (cf. Ezek 33:2-9; Luke 9:5; 10:10-12; Acts 20:25-26).[56] Yet, Paul does not go far. He moves next door to the house of the Godfearer Titus Justus, and the (Jewish) synagogue leader

---

[51] In Acts, διατρίβω refers to remaining in a particular place (12:19; 14:28; 15:35; 16:12; 20:6; 25:6, 14). The absence of a direct locative reference makes it unclear if Paul and Barnabas stay in the city or, more specifically, in "the synagogue of the Jews" (14:1). Luke's silence should restrain the impulse to assume that the opposition forces them to leave Jewish space.

[52] Tannehill, *Narrative Unity*, 2:177. That Luke lists gentiles first, in contrast to the normal pattern (e.g., 13:50; 14:2, 19; 17:5, 13), might suggest that they initiate the attack.

[53] Codex D specifies that it is "the unpersuaded" Jews (Rius-Camps, *Camino*, 108).

[54] The scenes with a marketplace—Philippi, Athens, and Ephesus—depict gentile persecution of Paul and his ilk. In Athens, Luke notes that Paul argued "in the synagogues with the Jews and Godfearers and to those present in the marketplace" (17:17). This phrasing suggests an audience in the marketplace other than Jews and Godfearers; it is at least a partly gentile crowd. It seems that Paul's presence there sparks his conversations with Epicureans and Stoics, leading to him being brought to the Areopagus.

[55] On the charges levied against them, see Rowe, *World*, 92-102.

[56] "The gesture ... hardly means a 'total negation of fellowship' ... Otherwise 20:26 ... would mean a total break from all people. But there, as in Luke 9:5, 10:10-11, the gesture means that Paul, since he has preached the Kingdom (20:25), is no longer responsible for their acceptance and rejection of the gospel. Only in this way does it make sense for him to go to the synagogue again in the next region" (Burfeind, "Paulus," 79; translation mine).

Crispus and his household become loyal to Jesus (18: 6–8). Paul remains in close proximity to the Jewish world, spending a year and a half preaching in Corinth before any violence arises.[57] At that point, the group of (unpersuaded) Jews brings Paul (ἤγαγον αὐτόν) before the gentile tribune, Gallio (18:12), who dismisses their accusations as an internecine Jewish dispute. Due to Gallio's eschewal of the case, Sosthenes, another synagogue leader, is beaten, possibly by a gentile crowd (18:17).[58] Paul remains unscathed. He stays in Corinth for many days after that (ἔτι προσμείνας ἡμέρας ἱκανάς) before leaving on his own terms. No joint effort by Jews and gentiles drives Paul away. Aside from these incidents, Thessalonica and Corinth are relatively peaceful.

Importantly, the aforementioned areas where Paul encounters joint Jewish and gentile violence do not encompass all the places Paul visits. In several diaspora regions Paul encounters no violence from the local Jewish communities.[59] Some Jews in these areas reject his message and oppose him in word, but they inflict no physical abuse. Saul encounters no violence on his initial stop in the synagogues of Cyprus. Barnabas and Saul traverse the entire island before encountering resistance from one Jew alone, Elymas (13:4–12). Derbe is entirely peaceful, as is Paul's second trip to Lystra (14:20; 16:1–5). Paul encounters no violence from the Bereans. They are entirely receptive. It is not until the Thessalonian Jews come that threats emerge (17:10–14). No Athenian Jews oppose Paul (17:17). Only Athenian gentiles do (17:19–34). Some Jews in Ephesus who become hardened and unpersuaded by Paul's message speak evil of the Way, yet they commit no violent acts during his two-year span there (19:8–10). The Roman Jews peaceably hear Paul out to learn why the Way is spoken against everywhere (πανταχοῦ ἀντιλέγεται; cf. Luke 2:34). In fact, they received no condemning letters from Judea or evil words from their fellow Jews about Paul (28:21–22). These Roman Jews do not even argue with Paul after he preaches to them. They simply disagree with each other over his message (28:24–25). Violence from "the Jews" lacks uniformity or consistency in the diaspora.

4.1.3 Summary

Before his final journey to Jerusalem, Paul recounts his ministry in Asia where he endured "plots of the Jews (ταῖς ἐπιβουλαῖς τῶν Ἰουδαίων)" (20:19). Nevertheless, the depiction of Jewish violence in Acts lacks uniformity and ubiquity.[60] Luke's rhetoric about violent Jews is not *absolutizing* but *particularizing*. Paul encounters violence from certain members of the Jewish community—not the whole—in some cities.

---

[57] The mention of time insinuates that Paul found success before some Jewish people turned against him (Jervell, *Apostelgeschichte*, 461; Parsons, *Acts*, 269). Bart J. Koet, "As Close to the Synagogue as Can Be: Paul in Corinth (Acts 18, 1–18)," in *The Corinthian Correspondence*, ed. R. Bieringer, BETL 125 (Leuven: Peeters, 1996), 397–415; cf. Rius-Camps, *Camino*, 114–15.

[58] Rowe, *World*, 47–52. Who beats Sosthenes is ambiguous (cf. Jervell, *Apostelgeschichte*, 461–62; Stowers, "Synagogue," 141; Mount, "Constructing Paul," 143–44). Codex D identifies them as "the Greeks" (Parsons, *Acts*, 256). Regardless, Gallio's blind eye is another instance of Roman injustice.

[59] Cf. Marguerat, *Christian Historian*, 144.

[60] Contra e.g., Smith, *Literary Other*, 70–77.

Other Jewish communities treat him amicably. To be sure, the places where hostilities arise comprise more narrative space than the peaceful ones. But conflict drives narratives better than peace. Therefore, these nonviolent regions are often overlooked in considerations of Jewish violence in Acts, even though non-violent encounters encompass a substantial portion of Paul's journeys.

Moreover, violence generally centers on Paul. Violence in Acts does not target the Way at large, causing some split between *ecclesia* and synagogue. Only in Thessalonica, when the crowd cannot find Paul and Silas, are other Jesus-followers threatened (17:5–9). Even then, it is not the entire believing community that is targeted. As Pervo observes, "For Luke, Paul was the only threat to 'the Jews.' Once he had left a town, the believers were safe."[61] Beyond that, with the possible exception of Ephesus (19:9), Luke is silent as to whether all members of the Way leave Jewish spaces along with Paul and his immediate cohort (cf. 9:31; 13:52). Acts, in other words, does not seem to portray Paul's synagogue experiences as paradigmatic or exemplary for all members of the Way, or reflective of some supposed oppression of hypothetical Lukan communities faced from synagogues in Luke's day.[62] Paul's leaving synagogues does not require all Jewish Jesus-followers to do the same. Further, Paul never abandons the synagogue or the Jewish people entirely because of physical threats. Verbal opposition may cause him to leave synagogues in particular locales, and violence may drive him from areas, but Paul returns to Jewish space wherever he goes next. Acts abstains from allowing Jewish violence to establish a strong social separation between the Jewish people and the Way.

Lastly, Jews are not the sole perpetrators of violence in Acts. Violence, then, cannot be reduced to an attempt "to other" non-Jesus-following Jews. Save Syria and Jerusalem, Paul faces aggression from joint efforts from Jews and gentiles. Diaspora Jews simply do not attack Paul and his cohort without gentile involvement. In contrast, some gentiles treat Paul violently without Jewish participation. That gentile groups *actively* persecute Paul apart from Jews demonstrates (violent) gentile agency in Acts. Gentiles and Roman civil servants are not simply "instrumentalized by the Jews."[63] Paul divides and provokes gentiles as he does with Jews (cf. 20:23).

4.2 Gentile Violence

I now turn to instances in which gentiles perpetrate violence against Paul without Jewish participation. In his journeys with Silas and Timothy, Paul faces two purely gentile threats, one in Philippi and the other in Ephesus.[64] The apparent rationale driving this aggression toward Paul is his *Jewishness*, not necessarily his affiliation with Jesus. Gentile persecution of Paul in Acts appears to be run-of-the-mill Greco-Roman

---

[61] Pervo, *Acts*, 422.
[62] Schaefer, *Zukunft*, 362–65; contra Morgan-Wynne, *Pisidian Antioch*, 206–7.
[63] Contra Marguerat, *Christian Historian*, 144n51. Gallio *expressly refuses* instrumentalization (18:12–13). Rome and its agents are not merely passive in Acts (Rowe, *World*, 53–87).
[64] One might add Athens (Rowe, *World*, 27–41).

anti-Judaism.⁶⁵ In Ephesus, this anti-Jewish animosity threatens the entire Jewish community. Rather than using violence to differentiate the Way from "the Jews," Acts uses it to show how Jesus' followers face gentile threats *as part of* the Jewish world. Anti-Jewish violence provides an ironic point of solidarity.

4.2.1 Arrest and Abuse in Philippi

The first instance of abuse solely from gentiles occurs in Philippi (16:16-40). After Paul exorcises a pythonic spirit and ruins their chance for profit, the slave-woman's masters "take hold (ἐπιλαβόμενοι)" of Paul and Silas and bring them before the leaders in the marketplace (16:19; cf. 17:19; 18:17; 21:30, 33). The accusation is tied to Paul and Silas' ethnicity: "These men are disturbing (ἐκταράσσουσιν; cf. ταράσσω in 15:24; 17:8, 13) our city; *they are Jews* ('Ιουδαῖοι ὑπάρχοντες)."⁶⁶ These Jews, the pagan-gentile litigants continue, advocate customs (ἔθη) unlawful for Romans (16:20-21). Reminiscent of charges levied against Paul by Jews elsewhere (21:21; 26:3; 28:17; cf. 6:14), these Philippian gentiles perceive or at least portray Paul and Silas as threatening Roman customs (16:20-21). The accusers levy a common Roman anti-Jewish trope: Jews might lure Romans away from Rome's way of life (cf. 17:6-7).⁶⁷ This accusation of cultural destabilization would be particularly threatening in a Roman colony like Philippi where Roman control might be more tenuous.⁶⁸ In short, these gentiles accuse and abuse Paul and Silas because they are Jews whose Judaism is perceived as attacking Roman culture.

In response, the crowd attacks these two Jews (συνεπέστη ὁ ὄχλος κατ' αὐτῶν). The magistrates (οἱ στρατηγοί) have Paul and Silas stripped, beaten severely (ῥαβδίζειν πολλάς τε ἐπιθέντες αὐτοῖς πληγάς), then thrown into prison (εἰς φυλακήν; 16:23-24).⁶⁹ By not providing a trial the magistrates appear to have accepted the veracity of the anti-Jewish trope: These Jews (who must not be Romans) threaten Rome's ways. In doing so, Philippi wrongly abused Roman citizens. Paul drives this point home after being released: "They beat (δείραντες; cf. 5:40) us, men who are Romans (ἀνθρώπους Ῥωμαίους ὑπάρχοντας), publicly, without proper judgment, threw us into prison, now they release us secretly?"⁷⁰ These gentile leaders, not Paul and Silas, have violated

---

⁶⁵ On anti-Judaism in antiquity, see Gager, *Origins*, 35–112; Peter Schäfer, *Judeophobia: Attitudes toward the Jews in the Ancient World* (Cambridge, MA: Harvard University Press, 1997); Isaac, *Racism*, 481–500; cf. Gruen, *Constructs*, 265–80, 312–32.

⁶⁶ Barreto suggests reading the participle ὑπάρχοντες as causal: "*because* they are Jews" (*Ethnic Negotiations*, 163–64); cf. Rius-Camps, *Camino*, 103–6.

⁶⁷ Schäfer, *Judeophobia*, 180–97; cf. Strelan, *Ephesus*, 25–31.

⁶⁸ Conzelmann, *Apostelgeschichte*, 101; Bock, *Acts*, 533, 537–38; Rowe, *World*, 25–26; Barreto, *Ethnic Negotiations*, 158–64; cf. Jervell, *Apostelgeschichte*, 423–24.

⁶⁹ The magistrates' actions echo the robbers in the Good Samaritan parable, who strip and beat (πληγὰς ἐπιθέντες) the traveler (Luke 10:30). Furthermore, the στρατηγοί in Philippi are connected with the other στρατηγοί in Luke-Acts: those in the temple who arrest and abuse Jesus and the apostles in Jerusalem (Luke 22:4, 52; Acts 4:1; 5:24, 26). Of course, God uses Paul and Silas' unjust incarceration to bring their jailer and his house to salvation (16:25–34).

⁷⁰ These magistrates engage in the same behavior as the Sanhedrin (5:40). The main difference is that the Jewish leaders flog the apostles *after* a trial.

Roman custom. Paul demands that they rectify it publicly (16:37). The magistrates oblige from fear but still ask them to leave the city (16:39-40; cf. 22:25-29).[71] In Philippi, gentiles enact a similar pattern as diaspora Jewish communities. Actually, more harm is done to Paul and Silas than in most Jewish places Paul visits (cf. 14:19-20). Key is that, though Paul's exorcism of the girl, depriving her owners of profit, causes their accusations, the slave masters' stated rationale for having Paul and Silas abused and arrested in Philippi is that *"they are Jews"* who disrupt the Roman peace (16:20-21).

4.2.2 Riot in Ephesus

As Paul remains in Asia (19:22; cf. 16:6), he encounters uniquely gentile violence in Ephesus from the assembly (ἡ ἐκκλησία) led by angry silversmiths (19:21-41).[72] Anti-Jewish tropes again fuel the opposition. The silversmith Demetrius bemoans that Paul threatens not only their business but the goddess Artemis' reputation and temple. Implicit in their concern is that depriving Artemis, Ephesus' patron deity, of her glory would put the city, the region, and the empire (ὅλη ἡ Ἀσία καὶ ἡ οἰκουμένη) at risk of divine wrath (19:23-27).[73] For these gentiles, Paul is another Jew who threatens their city and way of life by leading people away from their patron deity (cf. 18:13-15). Demetrius' words enrage (πλήρεις θυμοῦ; cf. Luke 4:28) the guild, prompting chaos as people rush together (ὥρμησάν τε ὁμοθυμαδόν; cf. Acts 7:57; 18:12; 21:27, 31), dragging (συναρπάσαντες; cf. 6:12) Gaius and Aristarchus, Paul's Macedonian travel partners (19:28-34).[74] The Ephesian Jewish community (οἱ Ἰουδαῖοι) puts forth Alexander to make a defense (ἀπολογεῖσθαι). They seem to assume that the crowd is threatening *them* (19:33).[75] As far as they can tell, this is an anti-Jewish mob. The response affirms their assumption. Recognizing Alexander as a Jew, the crowd doubles down in their loud affirmations of Artemis' greatness (19:34).[76] Although a scribe disperses the crowd since they risk being accused of rioting (κινδυνεύομεν ἐγκαλεῖσθαι στάσεως), the pagan-gentile mob threatened Paul, his compatriots' lives, and the entire Ephesian Jewish community (19:35-41). These Ephesians gentiles target Paul in an act driven by anti-Jewish fears of cultural destabilization. Paul is threatened *for being a Jew*.

4.2.3 Summary

Disturbing the *Pax Romana* is not simply or solely a Jewish phenomenon in Acts. As a behavior not unique to or uniform among Jews, as well as something that targets Jews,

---

[71] Barreto, *Ethnic Negotiations*, 139-80; cf. González, *Hechos*, 105-7.
[72] On parallels between the riots in Ephesus and Jerusalem, see Rius-Camps, *Camino*, 166-83.
[73] Strelan, *Ephesus*, 126-65; Rowe, *World*, 41-49.
[74] The Ephesian crowd's behavior echoes the demon Legion, who seizes (συνηρπάκει) its host and causes a herd of pigs to rush (ὥρμησεν) headlong to their deaths (Luke 8:29, 33; cf. Acts 14:5).
[75] Conzelmann, *Apostelgeschichte*, 123; Jervell, *Apostelgeschichte*, 591-92. Nothing suggests that these Jews seek to differentiate themselves from the Way (Haenchen, *Acts*, 574-75; contra Marshall, *Acts*, 319; Bock, *Acts*, 611; cf. Strelan, *Ephesus*, 148-50; Rowe, *World*, 47). Since Paul meets no opposition in Ephesus or Asia prior to this, one wonders if the threat Paul brings to the Asian Jewish community sparks the subsequent animosity toward him among certain Asian Jews (20:18-19; 21:27; 24:19).
[76] Strelan proposes that they are chanting or singing rather than shouting (*Ephesus*, 143-44).

violence does not serve the purpose of "othering" Jews in contrast to the peaceable Way. Pagan-gentiles are comparably divided over and hostile toward Paul (and Jews in general). These reactions are, as Jesus predicated, normal responses to the gospel from Israel and the nations (cf. Luke 12:11, 49–53). Put in Acts' terms, "imprisonment and persecutions" await Paul in "every city," not only from "the Jews" (20:23). Beyond that, pagan-gentile violence puts Jewish Jesus-followers and unpersuaded Jews in the same boat threatened by the waves of Roman anti-Judaism. Pagan-gentiles oppress Paul because of the cultural threat he poses *as a Jew*. Israel suffers together at hands of empire. Furthermore, Paul stands in solidarity with his Jewish brethren *in perpetuating violence*, as he was the one at the original forefront of violence against the Way.

4.3 Paul's Violence

Often neglected from evaluations of Jewish violence in Acts is that Luke consistently counts Paul among violent Jews. Violence is central to the *synkrisis* between Paul and unpersuaded Jews. Three points evince this claim. First, Paul is one of, if not *the* greatest, single perpetrator of violence against Jesus and his followers in Acts. Luke introduces Saul as the "God-fighter (θεομάχος)" incarnate (5:39). As the embodiment of Jewish hostility, he tempers Luke's rhetoric about Jewish violence.[77] Paul's archetypical nature sets up how one understands his turning. Second, then, Paul's narrative arc affirms the potential for change among Luke's most violent characters. Jesus reorients Paul through direct confrontation, producing Paul's falling then rising (cf. Luke 2:34). Notably, Paul's transformation occurs apart from any clear call to repent in response to the message of Jesus. His election as the Lord's "chosen vessel" undergirds his transformation. Jesus alone enacts Paul's change. Paul can also be seen as archetypical of God's ability to "resurrect" the many in Israel who have fallen as a result of their violence; fighting against God is not a terminal condition. Third, reminders about Paul's violence continue throughout Acts. Rather than using Jewish violence to distance Paul from the Jewish people, Luke's Paul recounts his violent past with increasingly severe descriptions of violence in his apologies to Jews or those familiar with Judaism. As he did with his Jewishness, Paul leverages his violent past to establish commonality and repute with his audience. Moreover, he uses his past to gesture toward the message of repentance. Paul evinces Acts' ongoing hope for change among unpersuaded, violent Jews. He was like them in violence. They should (or one day might) become like him in turning (or being turned) from violence to allegiance to Israel's Messiah. In short, Paul embodies Luke's residing confidence that hostile Israel, God's chosen (cf. Isa 41:8; 43:20; 44:1–2), can be reoriented toward Jesus.

---

[77] In other words, Paul is the *subject* of many of the same violent actions he becomes the *object* of later (cf. Smith, *Literary Other*, 67–71, on "transitivity analysis").

4.3.1 The Quintessential God-fighter

In the first scenes in which Saul appears, Luke unveils Saul as the prototype of Jewish violence.[78] Saul's introduction is cryptic: Those who execute Stephen lay their coats at the feet of a young man named Saul (7:58). What role he has in Stephen's death is unclear. He could be a bystander who "should according to the law participate in the stoning but only after the witnesses (Deut 17:7). Saul's presence suggests a readiness to participate in the execution and a possible association with one of the groups mentioned at the beginning of the trial."[79] The act of "laying (something) at the feet" of another might be tacit recognition of Saul as a leader of Stephen's opposition.[80] Regardless of specifics, Saul is involved, and he "approved of Stephen's killing (ἦν συνευδοκῶν τῇ ἀναιρέσει αὐτοῦ)" (Acts 8:1; cf. 22:20).[81] He reenacts the behavior for which Jesus reproves the Torah experts, who "are witnesses and approve (μάρτυρές ἐστε καὶ συνευδοκεῖτε)" of their ancestors killing of the prophets. He participates in "the generation" that "will kill and persecute (ἀποκτενοῦσιν καὶ διώξουσιν)" Wisdom's prophets and apostles and, therefore, are subject to judgment for this shed blood (Luke 11:47–51; cf. Acts 22:20). Saul embodies Israel's long history of oppressing God's messengers and fighting against God (Acts 8:1, 3; 9:1–2; cf. 7:53–55).

Yet, in his introduction, Luke gestures toward a hopeful future for Saul and all of Stephen's executioners: "between the introduction of Saul and the description of his concurrence with the murder of Stephen, Luke describes Stephen's final words: 'Do not hold this sin against them.' While this cry first refers to those who have acted against Stephen, it also announced the 'forgiveness' of Saul which Luke portrays in Acts 9."[82] Stephen intercedes for the God-fighters in Jerusalem, including Saul, who, although he casts no stone, becomes emblematic of those who do.[83] Saul's foreshadowed (and later enacted) forgiveness gestures toward a comparable hope for all rebellious Israel. If Stephen's intercession proves efficacious for Saul, it might be for those like him.

Stephen's death triggers "a great persecution (διωγμὸς μέγας)" with Saul as the tip of the spear. Throughout Acts, Saul is the primary agent of "persecution (διώκω)" (9:4–5; 22:4; 22:7–8; 26:11–14; cf. 7:52; 13:50). He is persecutor *par excellence*.[84] Luke describes how Saul "was ravaging the *ecclesia* by entering (εἰσπορευόμενος) houses and, dragging (σύρων) men and women, handed them over to prison (παρεδίδου εἰς φυλακήν)" (8:3). Luke's descriptors align Saul with other violent actors, but also paint

---

[78] Saul's name recalls Israel's first king who persecuted Israel's archetypical king, David. For expanded expositions of this connection, see French, "Completion," 425–30; Michael Kochenash, "Better Call Paul 'Saul': Literary Models and a Lukan Innovation," *JBL* 138 (2019): 433–49.
[79] MacNamara, *Chosen Vessel*, 42–43. Cf. González, *Hechos*, 45.
[80] Jervell, *Apostelgeschichte*, 253; Johnson, *Acts*, 140; Keener, *Acts*, 2:1445–47; cf. 4:35, 37; 5:1. Saul, the reader later learns, originates from Cilicia (21:39; 22:3; 23:34), like some of the Jews who oppose Stephen (6:9), further connecting him to the situation.
[81] In stark contrast to Paul stand the pious Jews who bury and mourn over Stephen that break up the descriptions of Saul's response (8:1–3; Gaventa, *Darkness*, 55).
[82] Gaventa, *Darkness*, 55–56.
[83] In the following scenes, "Saul singlehandedly assumes their role" (Haenchen, *Acts*, 298; similarly, Moessner, *Luke*, 263–64).
[84] Gaventa, *Darkness*, 57–59.

Saul's extreme aggression as unique. He entered people's homes and dragged off believers like those in Lystra and Thessalonica (14:19; 17:5-6; cf. 22:4; 26:10). Saul's "handing over (παραδίδωμι)" places him in the company of the traitor Judas (Luke 22:4, 6, 21-22, 48) and others who betray the Son of Man (Luke 9:44; 18:32; 20:20; 24:7, 20; Acts 3:13; 7:52), Herod (12:4), and those who turn Paul over to Rome (21:11). He exhibits the same resistance to God's agents as the Sanhedrin, particularly the priests and Sadducees, who imprisoned the apostles (5:19, 22, 25; cf. 7:51-53). In short, Saul personifies the persecution about which Jesus warned his disciples (Luke 11:49; 21:12; cf. Acts 22:19). For his acts, he earns an NT *hapax legomenon* for his actions: he ravaged (ἐλυμαίνετο) the Way in Jerusalem.[85] Saul's extremism is in a class of its own.

When he reappears in the narrative, Saul is "still breathing threats and murder (ἔτι ἐμπνέων ἀπειλῆς καὶ φόνου) against the disciples of the Lord" (9:1). Saul's seething threats associate him with those Jews and gentiles in Jerusalem who opposed God's anointed and issued threats (τὰς ἀπειλὰς αὐτῶν) against the Lord's servants (4:27-29).[86] Saul's murderous intent links him to Jesus' "betrayers and murderers (προδόται καὶ φονεῖς)" (7:52). Luke, in other words, affiliates Saul with those in Jerusalem responsible for Jesus' death. Jesus will thus identify Saul as Jesus' own persecutor (9:4-5).[87] Perhaps more jarring, only one other individual character in Acts is affiliated with φόνος, the murderer (ἄνδρα φονέα) Barabbas (Acts 3:14; cf. Luke 23:19, 25). Although Luke abstains from explicitly portraying Saul's active participation in murder, murderous intent permeates Saul's breath. Seeking the execution of Jesus-followers infuses his character (cf. 26:10).[88] When the inhabitants of Malta assume that Paul must be a murderer (φονεύς ἐστιν) they are not entirely mistaken (28:4).[89]

Saul's murderous intent leads him to seek letters from the high priest(s), the leading agents of hostility prior to Saul (e.g., Luke 9:22; 19:47; 23:4; 24:20; Acts 4:5, 23; 5:17, 21, 24, 27; 7:1), to extend persecution. Three of Saul's particular actions prefigure the treatment he later receives from certain Jews in his travels. First, Saul pursues the *ecclesia* into the surrounding regions (9:2-3; cf. 14:19; 17:13). Second, should he find Jesus-followers, men and women alike, Saul will "bind and bring them to Jerusalem (δεδεμένους ἀγάγῃ εἰς Ἰερουσαλήμ)" (9:2, 14). Indeed, Saul is the first to bind (δέω) anyone in Acts (9:2, 14, 21; 22:5; cf. 12:6; 21:11, 13, 33; 22:29; 24:27). Third, Saul leads (ἄγω) his captives to trial in Jerusalem, repeating the council's treatment of Jesus and the apostles (Luke 22:54; 23:1, 32; Acts 5:21, 26-27; 6:12; cf. 17:19; 18:12; 19:37-38;

---

[85] Conzelmann, *Apostelgeschichte*, 59; Bruce, *Acts*, 182.
[86] Tannehill, *Narrative Unity*, 2:114. Interestingly, God is typically the one issuing ἀπειλή in the LXX (e.g., Job 23:6; Hab 3:12; Zech 9:14; Isa 54:9; Ps. Sol. 17:27; Odes Sol. 6:12; 8:5; cf. Ps 17:16; 3 Macc 2:24; esp. 4 Macc 4:1–14.). See also Keener, *Acts*, 2:1618–19; Johnson, *Acts*, 162.
[87] On the link between Jesus and his followers particularly in relation to the individual-corporate Servant Israel in Isaiah, see Michael A. Lyons, "Paul and the Servant(s): Isaiah 49,6 in Acts 13,47," *ETL* 89 (2013): 345–59; Beers, *Followers*, 154–75.
[88] Barrett, *Acts*, 1:445; MacNamara, *Chosen Instrument*, 57; Adam David Patrick Booth, "'A Death Like His': Saul's Privation and Restoration of Sight as Prophetic Formation in Acts 9," *JDR* 22 (2018): 42–62.
[89] Of course, the righteous Lord Jesus preserves Paul's life rather than Justice (ἡ δίκη) preventing him from living, as the inhabitants of Malta think. One might speak similarly about Barabbas. Barabbas' freedom and continued life results from the righteous Jesus' taking his place.

21:34; 25:6, 17, 23). Ananias' protest against the Lord's instructions to find Saul is, therefore, entirely reasonable. Ananias "has heard from many about this man, how much evil (ὅσα κακὰ ἐποίησεν) he has done to the holy ones in Jerusalem" (9:13).[90] To Ananias, Saul simply is an evildoer. Tellingly, the Lord does not deny the veracity of Ananias' comment. His assessment of Saul is correct, but it is also incomplete. This evildoer is simultaneously Jesus' "chosen instrument" who will bear his name to gentiles, kings, and the children of Israel in the diaspora, and suffer on its behalf (9:15–16; cf. Ps. Sol. 18:6).[91]

In short, Luke characterizes Saul as the definitive, extreme representative of Israel's traditional resistance to God through violence against God's messengers. Saul is Jewish violence personified. Nevertheless, this does not preclude Saul from salvation, from becoming Jesus' messenger. Perhaps Acts likewise depicts the encounter between the risen Lord and the embodiment of hostility toward God's agents might be emblematic for the potential forgiveness and change for other Jewish God-fighters in Israel.

4.3.2 Raising the Persecutor

To establish this link, Saul's transformative meeting with Jesus and calling on the Damascus Road must be examined (9:3–19). In this encounter, the Lord placates the prototypical God-fighter through a direct confrontation. How should Saul's "defeat" be understood?[92] Three verbal connections suggest that Simeon's words provide a key (Luke 2:30–35). The first verbal link to Simeon is light (φῶς). A heavenly light flashes around Saul, heralding the Lord's appearance (Acts 9:3; 22:6; 26:13; cf. Luke 2:30). Saul, though *still* a persecutor, receives a calling and commission from Israel's Lord, the object of his persecution (9:15–16). A direct, revelatory encounter with the risen Lord engenders Saul's transformation, bringing light to one in Israel who was in darkness (cf. Luke 1:79).[93] Saul witnesses the new light he will eventually proclaim to the nations and his people (Acts 26:23; cf. 9:15; Luke 2:32). Notably, the revelation is sudden (ἐξαίφνης) and unexpected (cf. Acts 22:6). Nothing save the Lord's decision and

---

[90] κακός is a relatively rare word in Luke-Acts. It often refers to harm or wrongdoing (Luke 16:25; Acts 16:28; 28:5). Pilate proclaims that Jesus is innocent of it (Luke 23:22), and Pharisees in the Sanhedrin exonerate Paul of it (Acts 23:9). The verb κακόω appears several times as well. Pharaoh "harms" the Israelites (7:6, 19), as Herod does against members of the Way. Other Jews "harm" gentile minds by turning them against the Way (14:2; 18:10). The phrase "to do evil" is unique to Saul in Luke-Acts. Analogous to him are the two κακοῦργοι crucified with Jesus (Luke 23:23–33, 39). Though one defends Jesus, both deserve condemnation for their conduct (23:41). Similar to Barabbas whose judgment Jesus takes upon himself, Jesus extends life, paradise, to the "worker of evil" (23:43). These analogies and Paul's sufferings reiterate that judgment, forgiveness, and salvation are not exclusive. To be sure, his trials derive in part from his vocation. That he endures the sufferings he inflicted upon others, though, suggests an element of (deuteronomistic) judgment (Moessner, *Luke*, 263–64).

[91] Gaventa argues that "the list moves from those who receive Paul's preaching (Gentiles) to those who hear without receiving (kings) to those who reject it (sons of Israel)" (*Darkness*, 63). Gentiles are divided over Paul's preaching like Jews and numerous sons of Israel accept the message, however.

[92] Gaventa, *Darkness*, 65; Kuecker, "Theosis," 220.

[93] Gaventa, *Darkness*, 85–87. On calling/commissioning language in these scenes, see Gaventa, *Darkness*, 58–59; Marguerat, *Christian Historian*, 179–204; Moessner, *Luke*, 302–14; Oliver, "Calling," 180–88; *pace* González, *Hechos*, 56–59.

election of Saul provokes this encounter, transformation, and calling, rather than any summons to or act of repentance by Saul (9:15–16; cf. Ps. Sol. 18:6). The Lord simply reveals himself to this God-fighter, and, in so doing, reorients him as a chosen vessel.

Second, Saul "falls (πεσών) to the ground" (Acts 9:4; 22:7; καταπίπτω in 26:14). "Falling" can denote bowing in Luke-Acts (e.g., Luke 5:12; 8:41), but associations with judgment (Luke 10:18; 11:17; 13:4; 17:16; 20:18; 21:24; 23:30; Acts 13:11; 15:16; 20:9), including death (5:5, 10), are more prevalent.[94] The extended phrase "falling to the ground" often appears in the LXX as a euphemism for death and/or destruction (e.g., Judg 3:25; Amos 3:14; 2 Chr 20:24; 1 Macc 6:46). Saul, then, experiences a judgment. His subsequent inability to see further suggests a punitive dimension. Paul later will note that the light itself inhibited his vision, solidifying the judgmental element to his divine visitation (26:9).[95] Saul experiences a type of death and embodies the many in Israel who (will) fall.[96]

Third, Saul concomitantly personifies the many in Israel who rise. Jesus commands Saul to "rise" (ἀνάστηθι; 9:4; 26:16; ἀναστάς in 22:10), a word frequently associated with resurrection (e.g., Luke 16:31; 24:7, 46; Acts 2:24; 13:33–34). To be sure, this command echoes accounts of God commissioning servants in the LXX and in Acts itself (e.g., Gen. 21:18; Deut 18:15, 17; 3 Kgdms 17:9; Jer 1:17; Ezek 3:22; Jon 1:2; Acts 8:26; 10:26; 14:10), and Paul clearly emerges as a prophetic figure thereafter (cf. 13:1).[97] Nevertheless, the calling dimension need not override its frequent connections with resurrection in Luke-Acts. Spatial imagery further suggests a double or symbolic meaning. Saul falls "to the earth (ἐπὶ τὴν γῆν)," then he "is raised from the earth" (ἠγέρθη . . . ἀπὸ τῆς γῆς; 9:8). Indeed, ἐγείρω, especially in the passive voice, commonly refers to resurrection, particularly as an act of God (e.g., Luke 7:14, 22; 9:7, 22; 11:31; 20:37; 24:6, 34; Acts 3:15; 4:10; 5:30; 13:30, 37; 26:8; cf. Luke 13:25).[98] Saul the persecutor falls in judgment and is "resurrected" as Saul the messenger for Jesus (Acts 9:17–23).

In sum, Saul seems to typify "the fall and rise of many in Israel," that is, the judgment and subsequent redemption that Simeon sets forth as programmatic for Israel (2:34–35).[99] As Jewish-Israelite opposition embodied, he exemplifies the potential for the violent and rebellious in Israel to be restored. Striking is that, despite tendencies to call this "Paul's conversion," repentance language is absent from all three accounts of Paul's encounter with the risen Lord. Jesus affirms Saul identity as *the* persecutor, but Jesus gives Saul no rebuke, correction, or a call to repent (cf. Luke 23:34). Nowhere

---

[94] MacNamara, *Chosen Instrument*, 74.
[95] "In fact, 'light' has this double meaning in Scripture" of entailing both salvation (e.g., Exod 10:23; Job 12:22; Ps 4:6; Isa 2:5; 9:2) and judgment (e.g., Job 28:11; Isa 10:17; 51:4)" (Green, *Luke*, 149). Eyes also establish an ironic contrast between Saul and Simeon. Simeon's eyes—the first pair mentioned in Luke-Acts—see God's salvation (Luke 2:30), but Saul's open eyes were unable to see anything (9:8).
[96] For a similar argument about Saul's "death" that explores parallels between the Damascus Road and Jesus' passion, see Booth, "Death," 50–54; cf. Parsons, *Acts*, 128; *pace* Gaventa, *Darkness*, 59–61.
[97] On calling and election language in this encounter, see Marguerat, *Christian Historian*, 190–96; Allison, "Paul and Ezekiel," 812–24; Oliver, "Paul's Calling," 188.
[98] A mundane sense is possible (i.e., Saul's compatriots help him get up), but the passive voice remains evocative of resurrection nonetheless (cf. Haenchen, *Acts*, 323).
[99] See the discussion of Simeon in section 4.1.1.1, above.

does Saul/Paul explicitly repent of his violence in Acts. He is changed, reoriented, raised anew by divine initiative.[100]

Jesus' election of Saul—an illustrative member of the elect people of Israel (cf. Isa 41:8; 44:1-2)—alone initiated the encounter (9:15-16). Jesus simply introduces a disjuncture (ἀλλά) in Saul's purpose. Yet, Jesus does not change the direction of Saul's journey, simply its intent. Saul now goes to Damascus not to persecute Jesus but to obey him (9:3-6).[101] Violent acts have not excluded Saul from being chosen and redeemed, albeit in and through accompanying judgment, or from carrying out Israel's vocation as God's servant to the nations (cf. 13:47). The Lord's choice of Saul overcomes Saul's violence.[102] In Saul, Israel's Messiah demonstrates that the most violent in Israel can be reoriented. Saul's narrative arc cautions against seeing hostile Jews as de facto excluded from the covenant people or beyond forgiveness and salvation.

4.3.3 Apologizing with Violence

Despite his transformation, references to Paul's past violence never disappear. In fact, they continue with gusto. Luke's Paul twice recounts his past aggression, each with increasing intensity. Numerous scholars have noted that Luke gradually unveils the severity of Paul's violence toward the Way.[103] Few have attempted to explain this phenomenon, however.[104] Of all places, Paul's defense speeches are where it is revealed that he was worse than Luke's initial portrait insinuated. While interpreters have focused on the apologetic effect of Paul's Jewish credentials as the crux of his response to the charges against him (21:28; 22:1-3; 23:6; 24:14-21; 26:4-8), the bulk of his main apologetic speeches focus on his violent past, reorienting calling, and subsequent mission (22:4-21; 26:9-23). The placement of this material suggests that the increasingly dark descriptions of Paul's past violence function similarly to his Jewishness: Paul's story establishes solidarity with his Jewish opposition with an eye toward persuading them that Jesus is Israel's Messiah. His apologies have an evangelistic dimension (cf. Luke 21:13). Paul was like them in their violent opposition; they should be like him in turning from those ways toward Israel's Lord. Violence is an ironic means of fostering commonality with the Jewish people rather than a means by which Luke differentiates

---

[100] Nave, *Repentance*, 209. Two caveats: (1) Paul's abstention from food and drink might be signs of repentance (e.g., Pervo, *Acts*, 234, 237), but they could also be a sign of understanding (MacNamara, *Chosen Instrument*, 87; cf. Dan 2:18; 9:3; Acts 13:2-3; 14:23), preparation for a task (Luke 4:2; Acts 23:12, 21), or mourning (5:33-35; cf. 22:18, 30). (2) Ananias instructs Saul to "be baptized and have your sins washed" (22:16). Since baptism and forgiveness are linked at points to repentance it might be implicit (e.g., Luke 3:3; Acts 2:38). Regardless, Paul's fasting and baptism—like his overall change in behavior—*result from* the reorienting encounter with Jesus and Paul's symbolic death and resurrection; they do not precipitate his transformation.

[101] Gaventa, *Darkness*, 58; Conzelmann, *Apostelgeschichte*, 65; Jervell, *Apostelgeschichte*, 280-81.

[102] To be sure, Jesus does so in a non-coercive manner. The encounter with the risen Jesus engenders Saul's obedient response. See also Kuecker, "Theosis," 219-24.

[103] E.g., Gerhard Lohfink, *The Conversion of St. Paul: Narrative and History in Acts*, trans. Bruce J. Malina (Chicago, IL: Franciscan Herald Press, 1976), 93; Pervo, *Acts*, 630.

[104] James A. Kelhoffer, "The Gradual Disclosure of Paul's Violence against Christians in the Acts of the Apostles as an Apology for the Standing of the Lukan Paul," *BR* 54 (2009): 25-35.

Jews and Jesus-followers. Paul's past provides Israel with an invitation for repentance and salvation.[105]

Paul first uses his violent past as a rhetorical appeal to the crowd in Jerusalem that beat and attempted to kill him (21:30–35). He informs them of his "being jealous (ζηλωτὴς ὑπάρχων) for God, just like all of you are today" (22:3). Although one might be inclined to perceive Paul's ζῆλος as honorable (cf. 21:20), it is likely linked to Paul's violence. First, ζῆλος was frequently associated with violence for God, most notably in the persons of Phinehas and Judah Maccabee (LXX Num 25:11–13; 2 Macc 4:2–3; 4 Macc 18:12; cf. 4 Kgdms 10:16–28). Paul's letters similarly connect his ζῆλος with his persecution of the *ecclesia* (Gal 1:14; Phil 3:6; cf. Rom 10:2; 1 Tim 1:13).[106] Second, the ζῆλος-word group typically drives hostility in Acts, particularly among the family of Israel (5:17; 7:9; 13:45; 17:5). Third, the revelation that Paul studied under Gamaliel, who repudiated violence against the Way (5:37–41), recalls the concept of "God-fighting." The Gamaliel reference reminds the reader that those Jews fighting against Paul are opposing God *and* that Paul himself was a God-fighter who ignored his teacher's wisdom.[107] Fourth, Paul's recollection of persecuting the Way continues his self-description as a "zealot (ζηλωτής)" with a masculine singular relative pronoun (ὅς).[108] Sandwiched between Paul's self-identification as a "zealot" and a persecutor is his point of contact with his audience: "I am a zealot for God—*just like you all are today*—who persecuted this Way" (22:4). These identifiers link him to his audience as much as his Jewishness. They all share (misdirected) ζῆλος for God that caused them to oppress God's messengers. In an apologetic setting, for Luke's Paul, these common traits should garner favor and a fair hearing from his audience.

The ensuing narrative arc Paul tells extends this purpose. He reminds his listeners that he stood at the forefront of Jewish God-fighting efforts. Two additional details arise in this new account. First, Paul states, "I persecuted this Way *until death* (ἄχρι θανάτου)." Not only does he reiterate that he bound, imprisoned, and punished men and women of the Way "in every synagogue" (22:19; cf. 8:3; 9:2), Paul informs those trying to kill him that he, like them, sought to kill members of the Way. Later, he reiterates to Agrippa that he voted in favor of their deaths (ἀναιρουμένων αὐτῶν; 26:10). Beyond murderous intent (9:1), Paul's goal was the destruction of the Way and the death of its members. The Jerusalem crowd might seek his death for his rumored teachings (21:28), but Paul sought the elimination of the entire movement. Indeed, the high priest and the council—those who initiated hostility toward the Way—can attest to how Paul "took upon himself the responsibility of annihilating" the Way (22:4–5; cf.

---

[105] Similarly, Gaventa, *Darkness*, 92; González, *Hechos*, 141.

[106] Lappenga, *Paul's Language*, 68–117.

[107] Bruce, *Acts*, 400; Jervell, *Apostelgeschichte*, 542–43; Kochenash, "Better Call," 440. Moreover, the new information that Paul originates from "Tarsus in Cilicia" recalls the group of Jews who opposed Stephen (6:9).

[108] Gaventa, *Darkness*, 68–70. To be clear, by *zealot* I do not mean a member of the "Fourth Philosophy." I simply mean one zealous for God, Torah, and Israel (cf. Luke 6:15; Acts 1:13; Bruce, *Acts*, 73; Green, *Luke*, 260).

9:1).¹⁰⁹ Second, Paul specifies that he sought to bring those in Damascus back to Jerusalem "so that they might be punished (ἵνα τιμωρηθῶσιν)." Paul later states that these many punishments (πολλάκις τιμωρῶν) were intended "to compel them to blaspheme (ἠνάγκαζον βλασφημεῖν)" (26:11; cf. 13:45; 18:6). Notably, punishment (τιμωρέω) is twice used in Acts, and it only appears in relation to Paul's persecution of the Way (22:5; cf. δέρω in 5:40; 22:19; 16:37; Luke 22:63). The extent of Paul's God-fighting, the scope of his violence, was greater than previously described. Essentially, Paul tells his audience that his behavior was *worse* than theirs; he fought against God more than they do today.

Nevertheless, the Lord changed, raised, and commissioned Paul as his witness (22:6–21). God reoriented Paul on Israel's way. Additional details in Paul's retelling suggest that, while the story functions as an apologetic explanation of his transformation, it carries a persuasive dimension. To this end, Ananias' greater role in this recounting is central. In the first Damascus Road story, Ananias merely states that Jesus sent him so Saul might regain his sight and be filled by the Spirit (9:17). In Paul's recounting, Ananias exhorts him to "rise (ἀναστάς), be baptized (βάπτισαι), and be washed from your sins by calling (ἐπικαλεσάμενος) on [the Righteous One's] name" (22:16; cf. 9:18). These verbs echo past contexts where repentance is proclaimed to Israel, particularly Peter's Pentecost proclamation. Rising carries connotations of Israel's new life in conjunction with Jesus' resurrection (2:24, 32; cf. 3:22, 26; 4:1–2). Baptism and the resultant washing of sins constitute proper response to and outcome of the call for repentance (Acts 2:38; cf. Luke 3:7; Acts 8:12–13, 36–38; 10:47–48; 16:15, 33; 18:8; 19:3–5), echoing Israel's promised cleansing and restoration by God's own initiative (e.g., Ezek 36:22–37:28).¹¹⁰ Calling upon (ἐπικαλέω) the Lord's name brings salvation (Acts 2:21; cf. 7:59; 9:13, 21; 15:17). An explicit exhortation to repentance is absent—the Lord alone reoriented Paul—but Ananias still calls Paul to respond to the Lord's acts and initiation (cf. Deut 4:26–31). In expanding Ananias' role, Paul (and Luke) seems to redirect these exhortations to Paul's listeners. As his zealous persecution links him with them, so he implicitly calls them to become like him in responding to Jesus as he did, receiving Israel's promised washing and salvation in the Lord.¹¹¹

---

[109] Raúl Caballero Yoccou, *Hechos*, 3 vols., CBCN (Miami: Editorial Unilit, 1998), 2:167 (translation mine).

[110] Paul's reorientation, which happens at God's prerogative, resonates with Ezekiel. According to the prophet, God will cleanse and restore Israel from God's initiative alone, apart from any repentance or action from Israel. On Luke's use of Ezekiel, see Reed Metcalf, "Fire and Water, Shepherds and Sentinals: Echoes of Ezekiel in Luke-Acts" (PhD diss., Fuller Theological Seminary, Pasadena, CA, 2022).

[111] Based on the ignorance of Saul's companions, one might object that Paul receives a unique call from Ananias (e.g., Gaventa, *Darkness*, 64). While true, Saul's unique experience can still be emblematic of others like him. He would be analogous to Jesus whose death and resurrection, while unique, prefigures *the* resurrection of the dead and of Israel as a whole (cf. 3:17–21; 4:1–2). Gaventa has made a similar argument about how Paul's depicts his experiences as paradigmatic for his audience ("Galatians 1 and 2: Autobiography as Paradigm," *NovT* 28 [1986]: 309–26; similarly, Susan G. Eastman, "Israel and the Mercy of God: A Re-Reading of Galatians 6.16 and Romans 9–11," *NTS* 56 [2010]: 367–95. I posit that this argument applies or is at least analogous to the Paul of Acts' relationship to the Jewish people. Indeed, Paul's vocation, which is reminiscent of the Servant Israel's in Isaiah 40–66 (see Beers, *Followers*, 168–73), is a particularization of Israel's corporate calling, which is encapsulated in Jesus.

Paul's temple vision confirms that, at least according to the Paul of Acts, his past should persuade those Jews in Jerusalem who threaten him. In response to Jesus' exhortation to leave the city "because they will not accept your witness," Paul protests by again repeating his past aggression (22:17–21). Jerusalem knows how he imprisoned and abused people everywhere, and how he oversaw the coats and approved the shedding of Stephen's blood (ἐξεχύννετο τὸ αἷμα Στεφάνου; cf. 8:1). The use of ἐκχέω reinforces the connection between Paul and the generation on whom falls all the blood shed of God's prophets. It connects him to Jerusalem, the city that kills the prophets (Luke 11:50; cf. 13:34–35). Paul insinuates that his engagement in violence grants him a strong platform to be heard and received in the city. His concurrent speech belies that he still perceives this is the case. Jerusalem should listen to his witness because he was like them in practicing violence toward God's messengers.

Jesus is right, of course. The Jerusalem crowd turns on Paul. Nevertheless, Paul leverages his violent past twice in the apology to garner favor from his audience. Instead of distancing himself from them, he uses their common zealous antagonism toward the Way as a way to proclaim Jesus to them via his own reorienting encounter with Israel's Lord. To echo the historical Paul, to those who are violent Luke's Paul presents himself as violent so that he might bring salvation to some of them (1 Cor 9:19–23; cf. Gal 1:13–15; 1 Tim 1:13). Though they may not listen, he calls them to be like him by turning from their violence and having their sins cleansed by calling upon Jesus' name nonetheless (cf. Acts 26:20–21).

Before Agrippa, Paul again recounts his violent past and transformative encounter with Jesus to defend himself "against all the accusations from Jews" (26:2). His acts of persecution and subsequent transformation provide as much of a defense against the charges levied against him as his loyalty to Israel's tradition does. In fact, his redemptive arc is *intertwined* with his Jewishness, his identification with the people and their way of life. After recounting his Jewish credentials (26:4–8), Paul insinuates that what he considered the logical conclusion of his ancestral hopes was opposition to the Way: "Indeed, I myself was therefore convinced (ἐγὼ μὲν οὖν ἔδοξα ἐμαυτῷ) that it was necessary to act in many ways against (δεῖν πολλὰ ἐναντία πρᾶξαι) the name of Jesus of Nazareth" (26:9). Paul's Jewishness and ancestral beliefs funded his exceedingly maniacal (περισσῶς ἐμμαινόμενος) maltreatment of Jesus' followers.[112] This animosity led him, like some Jews he encountered in diaspora, to pursue members of the Way to foreign cities (26:11; cf. 14:19; 17:13). These hostile activities (ἐν οἷς) motivate the journey to Damascus where he has his transformative encounter with Jesus (26:12–20).[113]

According to this third account, Jesus himself instructs Paul to reach Jews and gentiles alike so they might turn, obtain forgiveness, and receive an inheritance among

---

[112] The turn to Jesus turns Paul's "mania" to "sound-mindedness" (σωφροσύνη; 26:24–25). One might note the parody between what Paul deems necessary (δεῖ) and what God deems necessary in Luke-Acts, which includes the suffering and violent death of God's anointed (cf. Cosgrove, "Divine Δεῖ," 179–83; Crabbe, *End of History*, 161–64.).

[113] On "kicking against the goads" and Paul's role as a "God-fighter" (cf. *Bacch.* 794–95), see Conzelmann, *Apostelgeschichte*, 149; Pervo, *Acts*, 631–32; Kochenash, "Better Call," 443–44.

those who have been sanctified by fidelity to Jesus. Paul was obedient to this vision. He proclaimed this message to Jews in Damascus, Jerusalem, and Judea before sharing it with gentiles (20:17–21; cf. Jer 1:7–8; Ezek 2:3–6).[114] He now calls Jews and gentiles alike to repent and receive forgiveness through Jesus. His past violence, Paul reiterates, facilitates his proclamation of Jesus. Indeed, he proclaims this same message about the Messiah's death, resurrection, and light in accordance with the prophets and Moses to Herod and to "the people [of Israel] and to the gentiles" up to "this present day" (26:22–23). Herein lies the apologetic and persuasive function: Paul was like those Jews who accuse him and now he calls them to be like him by changing their ways by seeing Israel's Messiah anew (cf. 26:2–3). In fact, Paul tells Agrippa, who recognizes the persuasive purpose of Paul's apology, he prays that "all who are listening to me today *also become like I am*, except for these chains (26:28–29). Once again, Luke's Paul uses violence to establish a connection with his fellow Jews and reiterates the hope that they become like him by turning (or being turned) to their Messiah.

4.3.4 Summary

Acts' rhetoric about Jewish violence is ultimately tempered by Luke's repeated reminders about Paul's violence and transformation, particularly by leveraging his past in his apologetic speeches. Luke's Paul, rather than distancing himself from Jewish violence, uses it to establish connections with the Jewish people. Violence in Acts, then, functions more as *synkrisis*, establishing parallels between Paul and the Jewish people at large, than as an "othering" technique. Saul's violence and God-fighting typifies Jewish violence and God-fighting. He is paradigmatic of Israel's historic opposition to the Lord and his messengers. This is illustrated in the following table, which captures the overlap between his violence and Jewish violence he experiences in his diaspora journeys.

Action	Saul/Paul in Acts	Jews/Israel in Luke-Acts
Association with Killing/Murder	8:1; 22:20; 9:1; 22:4; 26:10	Luke 11:47–49; 13:34; 22:2; Acts 3:15; 5:33; 9:23–24, 29; 7:52; 21:12, 14; 27:42
Persecuting	8:1; 9:4–5; 22:4, 7–8; 26:14–15	Luke 11:49; 21:12; Acts 7:52; 13:50
Handing Over	8:3; 9:3; 22:4	Luke 9:44; 18:32; 20:20; 21:12; 22:48 (Judas); Acts 12:4 (Herod); 21:11; 28:17
Ravaging	8:3	
Entering Homes	8:3	cf. Acts 17:5
Dragging	8:3	Acts 7:58; 17:6
Threats	9:1	Acts 4:21, 29
Imprisoning or Binding	9:2, 14; 22:4–5, 19; 26:10	Luke 21:12; Acts 4:3; 5:18; 12:1 (Herod); 21:27

(*continued*)

[114] οὕς refers to both "the [Jewish] people" and "the gentiles" (Acts 26:17; cf. 9:15; 22:17; Jervell, *Apostelgeschichte*, 594–95; Conzelmann, *Apostelgeschichte*, 149; Caballero Yoccou, *Hechos*, 2:202).

(continued)

Action	Saul/Paul in Acts	Jews/Israel in Luke-Acts
Pursuing	9:2, 14; 22:5; 26:11	14:19; 17:13
Bringing to Trial	9:2, 21, 27; 22:5	Acts 5:21, 26–27; 6:12; 18:12
Doing Evil	9:13; cf. 26:9	Acts 12:1 (Herod); 14:2
Jealousy/Zeal	22:3–4	Acts 5:17; 7:9; 13:45; 17:5
Beating or Punishing	22:5, 19; 26:11	Luke 22:63; Acts 5:40; 21:32; 23:2
(Forcing to) Blaspheme	26:11	Acts 13:45; 18:6
Enraged	26:11	Luke 4:28; Acts 4:25; 5:33; 7:54

To be sure, Acts through Paul (implicitly) calls all Jewish-Israelites to abandon violent hostility. As he was like them, they should become like him (26:29). In violently oppressing Jesus' followers, they—as he did—reenact the sins of their ancestors. As with all calls to repent in Acts there is a looming threat of judgment (cf. 2:40; 3:23; 13:41). Nevertheless, Acts uses Paul's narrative arc to relay how a violent past, present, or future, and even the experience of judgment itself does not place someone beyond the reach of Israel's God. If God can transform a one as savage as Paul simply because he is chosen by God, then any member of God's chosen covenant people can repent or can be reoriented by the Lord. The chance continues for Israel and even its violent members to reorient themselves or be reoriented by God.

4.4 Conclusion

This chapter sought to refute claims that Luke paints "the Jews" as uniformly, ubiquitously, or uniquely violent. Positively, it showed that only some Jews oppose the Way, and entire regions of Jews are completely peaceful. Diaspora Jewish violence is variegated. Most diaspora Jewish violence also occurs with gentile participation, both Godfearing (13:50) and pagan-gentile (14:19). Gentiles, at least twice, persecute Paul without Jewish participation. Beyond that, their violence against him, at least in his opponents' ostensible charges, is tied to Paul's Jewishness and the perceived threat his Jewish identity and practices have on Roman identity and custom. Paul, in short, suffers fairly standard Roman anti-Judaism. Rather than being an "othering" technique, Luke's nuanced portrait of violent behaviors places Paul more firmly within the Jewish world.

Moreover, violence, though it may lead to judgment, does not automatically exclude one from the covenant people of Israel or preclude salvation. Paul's narrative arc exemplifies this. The Lord Jesus reorients Paul, the epitome of Jewish violence, on the road to Damascus, notably without any preceding act of repentance from or call to repent given. The Lord simply reorients his chosen vessel out of his own initiative. That the Paul of Acts repeats this story in apologetic, rhetorically charged speeches suggests that his transformation is emblematic of Israel's (potential or future) transformation through direct encounter with the risen Lord. Paul, then, is not just a representative figure of God's relationship to and ability to redeem rebellious Israel. One sees in Paul how God can transform the most ferocious God-fighters. In other words, Luke through Paul exhorts all to become like Paul by being reoriented toward Israel's Lord Jesus (26:29). Luke's Paul enacts and prefigures the "fall and rise of many in Israel," their judgment and restoration. Indeed, if Saul's participation in violence against Jesus and Stephen can be forgiven (Luke 23:34; Acts 7:60), violence against Paul can be. The door for repentance and hope for "resurrection" for Israel remains open, even for the violent.

5

"I Could Not See": Israel's Blindness, Paul, and the End of Acts

The most obvious stumbling block to my thesis that Acts' depiction of Jewish people should be read within Judaism is the book's final scene. Quoting Isaiah, Paul's concluding words describe ongoing blindness and unbelief toward the message about Jesus among the Jewish people as salvation goes to the gentiles (28:17–31; cf. Isa 6:9–10). While some scholars maintain that Luke retains ongoing hope for Jewish repentance, likely at the parousia, and read Paul's concluding words as another prophetic call to reform, numerous others argue that the final scene ends in condemnation or tragedy for the Jewish people at large.[1] Paul's quotation from Isaiah seals Jewish opposition to Jesus, terminates the Jewish mission with his third and final "turn to the gentiles," and, therefore, closes the door for salvation for the people. The *ecclesia*, so the logic goes, abandons the Jews and supplants them as God's people. Individual Jews may repent, but an *en masse* hope for Jews ends. Jerry Lynn Ray's comments are illustrative:

> [A]lthough [Luke] delights in the stories of individual conversions of Jews, and is, no doubt, hopeful of their continuance, these are ultimately inadequate as far as Judaism's status as the people of God is concerned. Judaism, as represented by its official leaders and the majority of Jews who have followed them, has rejected the claims of Jesus and the church. It has gone its separate way in rebelling against the plan of God for his people. The Jews have therefore reached the point of no return. *Their deafness, blindness, and hardness of heart have caused them to miss the salvation of God at work in Jesus and the gospel.* The Jewish rejection is thus final in the sense that Judaism as an organized religious system has cut itself off from the blessings of God. Through its rejection of Jesus and the gospel, Judaism has forfeited its own status as the people of God, while ironically it has enabled that privilege to be conferred upon people from every nation.[2]

---

[1] Karl L. Armstrong, "The End of Acts and the Jewish Response: Condemnation, Tragedy, or Hope?:" *CBR* 17 (2019): 209–30.
[2] Ray, *Narrative Irony*, 128, emphasis mine; cf., e.g., Conzelmann, *Apostelgeschichte*, 159–60; Lohfink, *Sammlung*, 55; Jervell, *Apostelgeschichte*, 631; Rius-Camps, *Camino*, 305.

Whether emphasis lies on the tragic or condemnatory tenor of Paul's final words, the result is the same: The blind opposition of the Jewish people to Jesus is finalized; they move beyond salvation, and the *ecclesia* conclusively distances itself from Judaism.

To date, much of the debate about Acts' cryptic conclusion has focused on the function of the LXX Isaiah citation in its context, its reception in early Judaism, and Paul's threefold turn to the gentiles.[3] Less attention has been given to how the ubiquitous motif of blindness and sight in Luke-Acts, particularly as it is formed by Isaiah, might shape how one reads Paul's quotation of Isa 6 at the narrative's conclusion. Interpreters tend to treat the final quotation from Isaiah independently from how Luke depicts lack of sight, its role as judgment, and its healing elsewhere in his narrative, even when the motif echoes or explicitly quotes Isaiah (e.g., Luke 4:16–21; cf. Isa 61:1–3; 58:6).[4] Exploring how Luke utilizes images of blindness and sight throughout the narrative would illumine how this motif culminates in Acts' conclusion.

The present chapter takes up this task. I argue that, rather than signaling the rejection of Judaism or the exclusion of the Jewish people from salvation, Luke gives reasons for confident hope that the blindness Paul proclaims on divided Israel using Isaiah's words at the end of Acts can be healed. Moving from *blindness* to *sight* is an analogous metaphor for Israel's repentance-journey, one that suggests that divine intervention is required for Israel's healing to be accomplished. Throughout the entirety of Luke-Acts, Israel's blindness is a temporary condition.[5] As in Isaiah, corporate Israel for Luke remains God's blind servant whose blindness can (and likely will) be alleviated by the individual servant who personifies Israel. Blindness is not an unending state that permanently prohibits Israel's repentance-journey.[6] Indeed, granting renewed vision is integral to Jesus' and Paul's missions (Luke 4:18; 7:22; Acts 26:23). Even punitive blindness in Israel is "for a time" and serves a transformative function, facilitating the reorientation from darkness to light. Paul's final words, then, are not utter condemnation

---

[3] On the reception of Isa 6, see Craig A. Evans, *To See and Not Perceive: Isaiah 6.9–10 in Early Jewish and Christian Interpretation*, JSOTSup 64 (Sheffield: Sheffield Academic, 1989); Martin Vahrenhorst, "Gift oder Arznei? Perspektiven für das neutestamentliche Verständnis von Jes 6, 9f. im Rahmen der jüdischen Rezeptionsgeschichte," *ZNW* 92 (2001): 145–67.

[4] See e.g., Conzelmann, *Apostelgeschichte*, 159–60; Jervell, *Apostelgeschichte*, 627–29; Bock, *Acts*, 755–56; Caballero Yoccou, *Hechos*, 2:224. Pervo considers other instances of blindness and its healing but finds that Paul turns Jesus' message of healing into a word of judgment and rejection only (*Acts*, 685–86).

[5] By discussing *blindness* rather than, say, *sightlessness*, I seek to capture cultural, symbolic connotations associated with this condition in Luke's cultural encyclopedia (even if it can be problematic and disparaging) rather than medical neutrality. On these concerns, see Louise Joy Lawrence, *Sense and Stigma in the Gospels: Depictions of Sensory-Disabled Characters* (Oxford: Oxford University Press, 2013), 31–56; Booth, "Death," 43. I do not mean to repurpose *blindness* "as a tool of social rejection" or to perpetuate "essentialist labels" (Lawrence, *Sense*, 32, 39). Indeed, Luke often subverts cultural tropes about physical differences, including vision. See Mikeal C. Parsons, *Body and Character in Luke and Acts: The Subversion of Physiognomy in Early Christianity* (Waco, TX: Baylor University Press, 2011).

[6] On this motif in Isaiah specifically, see Philip D. Stern, "The 'Blind Servant' Imagery of Deutero-Isaiah and Its Implications," *Bib* 75 (1994): 224–32; Robert P. Carroll, "Blindsight and the Vision Thing: Blindness and Insight in the Book of Isaiah," in *Writing and Reading the Scroll of Isaiah: Studies of an Interpretive Tradition*, ed. Craig C. Broyles and Craig A. Evans, VTSup 70 (Leiden: Brill, 1997), 79–94.

and complete rejection. They are another warning and, therefore, another call to repent. The Isaiah quotation recalls the expectation that lack of perception can be remedied, though it might require Jesus' direct intervention. Acts' ending is optimistic, even confident about Israel's future healing.[7]

As with his violent behavior, I contend that Luke's Paul, who was unable to see and now shares (in)sight with others, functions as a representative of and to Israel. Acts presents Paul's experience of blindness as an embodiment of God's interactions with the Jewish people who fail to perceive Jesus. Paul was blinded for oppressing God's Way, though his eyes were open. He was then granted new vision for his prophetic task (9:1–19; 22:6–21; 26:12–23; cf. 13:47). The divided Jewish people remain blind to God's actions in Jesus at the end of Acts, as Paul's story portends, but Jesus is quite capable of alleviating the inability to see (Luke 4:16–31; 7:22; 18:41–42; 24:25–32). Luke's motif of blindness provides sanguinity, even expectation, that, like all other cases of blindness in Luke-Acts, Israel's blindness is temporary, and God will one day alleviate their sight problems. God continues to reach out to the "unpersuaded and contrarian people (λαὸν ἀπειθοῦντα καὶ ἀντιλέγοντα)" at the end of the narrative and even beyond it (LXX Isa 65:2). Though Paul's words toward the Jewish leadership in Rome are harsh, his ministry persists for the sake of Israel. He (and Luke) retains solidarity with the Jewish people.[8]

To make this claim, I begin by discussing how Luke's Gospel adapts the Isaianic motif of Israel as God's blind servant and Jesus as the anointed Servant who alleviates this condition as part of the mission to restore the people. This section makes four salient points. First, *all Israel*, including Jesus' own followers, fail to see Jesus rightly. Few characters in Luke's Gospel recognize Jesus as they should. Second, inability to comprehend stems primarily from Israel's stubbornness and reticence to obey. Israel's, Jerusalem's, and the apostles' open eyes fail to perceive Jesus' identity due to their faithlessness. Third, as a result, many fall in judgment. Still, hope that Israel might move or be brought into light endures. Fourth, Jesus alleviates Israel's blindness. Most effective in opening unseeing eyes and uncomprehending minds is direct encounter with the risen Lord.

---

[7] Though I do not explore these connections here, similarities between the end of Acts and Rom 9–11 have long been recognized. E.g., Haacker, "Bekenntnis," 447; Ravens, *Restoration*, 173–211; Kenneth D. Litwak, "One or Two Views of Judaism: Paul in Acts 28 and Romans 11 on Jewish Unbelief," *TynBul* 57 (2006): 229–49; Simon Butticaz "'Has God Rejected His People?' (Romans 11.1): The Salvation of Israel in Acts: Narrative Claim of a Pauline Legacy," in *Paul and the Heritage of Israel: Paul's Claim upon Israel's Legacy in Luke and Acts in the Light of the Pauline Letters*, ed. David P. Moessner, Daniel Marguerat, Mikeal C. Parsons, and Michael Wolter, trans. Nicholas J. Zola (London: T&T Clark, 2012), 148–64; Schaefer, *Zukunft*, 385–440.

[8] Like Jesus and many of the prophets, Paul participates in Israel's fate. He goes into exile among the Jewish people in Rome. On exile as a type of national death and national restoration as a type of resurrection, see Andrew Chester, "Resurrection and Transformation," in *Auferstehung-Resurrection: Resurrection, Transfiguration, and Exaltation in Old Testament, Ancient Judaism, and Early Christianity*, ed. Friedrich Avemarie and Hermann Lichtenberger, WUNT 135 (Tübingen: Mohr Siebeck, 2001), 47–78; cf. Jon D. Levenson, *Resurrection and the Restoration of Israel: The Ultimate Victory of the God of Life* (New Haven, CT: Yale University Press, 2006); Haacker, "Bekenntnis," 444–48; Staples, *Israel*, 183–348.

I then explore how Luke's Paul is the epitome of Jewish imperception of Jesus. He experiences judgment and has his eyes opened to see properly thanks to an encounter with the risen Lord. Jesus commissions Paul to open the eyes of Israel and the nations to see the Lord (Acts 26:17–18, 23; cf. 13:47). Paul extends Jesus' work of bringing people from darkness to light. Nevertheless, Paul issues prophetic warnings and judgments to those who remain in their stubbornness. Amid critique and rebuke, he retains solidarity with Israel and expectation for renewed vision. This tension is most evident when Paul inflicts blindness on Elymas. Elymas evinces that the inability to see is not a permanent condition even for those most recalcitrant in Israel. The chapter culminates in an examination of Acts 28:17–31 that shows how the ending retains Isaianic confidence that Israel's eyes eventually will be opened and the people healed.

Before delving into the relevant texts, framing comments are in order. First, Isaiah and Luke-Acts share a cluster of images connected (though not equivalent) to *blindness*, *sight*, and *perception*. These include *eyes*, *death*, *hiddenness*, *light*, and *darkness*.[9] The cluster of images interplay with each other, most visible in how Saul's *eyes* that are open yet unable *to see* because of the *light* (9:8; 26:11), but not all will be present in each case. They are intertwined and mutually informative, nonetheless. Second, I presume that Luke uses the universal metaphor of blindness and sight to communicate characters' (in)ability to perceive and respond to God's activities in Jesus as they should. In light of conceptual metaphor theory, one cannot bifurcate *physical* blindness—corporeal inability to see—and *metaphorical* blindness. *Sight* functions as a physical and an epistemological category since the experience of sight is inseparable from notions of perception. These senses function concurrently. Put differently, moving from *blindness* to *sight* or from *light* to *darkness* are analogous to and interconnected with the metaphor of Israel's repentance-journey. I also presume Luke's awareness and use of ancient conceptions of *physiognomy*, that is, that physical features represent inner characteristics. Interplays and ironies between the various images and senses of blindness can be expected.[10]

---

[9] Parsons, *Acts*, 128–29. Loss of sight can be associated with death (e.g., Pss 49:19; 58:8; m. Šabb. 23:4–5; Lam 3:6; cf. Booth, 52–54). Sleep (cf. Acts 7:60; 13:36) could also be included. See Brawley, *Text*, 48; Parsons, *Acts*, 171, 287–89; Andrew Arterbury, "The Downfall of Eutychus," in *Contemporary Studies in Acts*, ed. Thomas E. Phillips (Macon, GA: Mercer University Press, 2009), 201–22. Auditory imagery often appears alongside the visual as part of Luke's use of sensory imagery in relation to perception. Nevertheless, given the frequent appeals to blindness as indicative of Israel's willful rejection of Jesus in Acts, I give it primacy in my investigation. For an investigation of the auditory-visual interplay, especially in Stephen's speech, see Brittany E. Wilson, "Hearing the Word and Seeing the Light: Voice and Vision in Acts," *JSNT* 38 (2016): 456–81. On the blindness motif in Israel's Scriptures and early Judaism more broadly, see Hartsock, *Sight and Blindness*, 83–124; see also Wilson, *Unmanly Men*, 162–69, on blindness in Greco-Roman sources.

[10] On conceptual metaphor theory, see George Lakoff and Mark Johnson, *Metaphors We Live By* (Chicago, IL: University of Chicago Press, 2003); Vyvyan Evans and Melanie Green, *Cognitive Linguistics: An Introduction* (Edinburgh: Edinburgh University Press, 2009), 286–309. On *physiognomy*, see Parsons, *Body and Character*; Chad Hartsock, *Sight and Blindness in Luke-Acts: The Use of Physical Features in Characterization*, BibInt 94 (Leiden: Brill, 2008), 7–51. See Ray, *Narrative Irony*, 40–49, on irony.

5.1 Blindness in Luke's Gospel

To understand the final declaration of blindness in Acts, it is necessary to explore how the motif functions in Luke's two volumes. Language of vision and perception permeates Luke-Acts. To some degree, the entirety of Luke-Acts is about Israel's (including the disciples') struggle to understand (i.e., to see) and respond to Jesus rightly. A full examination merits its own project.[11] Since Luke-Acts' conclusion quotes Isaiah regarding Israel's inability to perceive, I limit my scope to scenes where Isaianic influence on the Lukan blindness metaphor is evident through quotations, echoes, or common conceptual patterns. Isaiah is a well-known structuring guide to Luke-Acts.[12] The prophet proves particularly influential on Luke's depiction of blindness. Luke directly quotes Isaiah when describing Israel's imperceptions and Jesus' mission to heal this malady (e.g., Luke 4:16–21; 7:21–23; cf. Acts 13:47; 28:26–28). Numerous other Lukan scenes parrot Isaianic images of blindness/sight, light/darkness, and/or understanding/ignorance (e.g., Luke 1:8–23; 2: 30–35; 18:35–43; 24:13–35; cf. Acts 13:9–11). Examining Isaiah's influence on Luke-Acts regarding blindness establishes a framework for interpreting the final citation. In what follows, I seek to demonstrate that Luke mimics Isaiah in treating blindness as a temporary, albeit persistent and pernicious, problem in Israel that can itself be judgment and can result in further judgment. Still, recalcitrant Israel remains God's chosen corporate servant who can be healed and reoriented by the servant, Jesus, who proves quite capable at this task. In short, for Luke, Israel's blindness is a transient condition that Jesus is well able to rectify.

5.1.1 Establishing the Metaphor: Blindness and Sight in Luke 1–2

Motifs of sight and light saturated with Isaianic language emerge from the outset of Luke's writings. Reminiscent of Isaiah, Luke's Gospel opens with repetitious visual imagery in the temple, by the altar specifically, and the presence of prayer (1:8–23; cf. Isa 6:1–13; 56:7). Zechariah sees a vision (ὀπτασίαν ἑώρακεν) during his priestly service as the angel "appears (ὤφθη) to him" next to the incense altar (Luke 1:11, 22; cf. 24:23; Acts 26:19). Like Isaiah, this temple vision terrifies Zechariah (Luke 1:12;

---

[11] Smith, "Politics," 64–65; cf. Carroll, "Blindsight," 80. On the ubiquity of perception imagery in Luke-Acts, specifically sight and blindness, see Dennis Hamm, "Sight to the Blind: Vision as Metaphor in Luke," *Bib* 67 (1986): 457–77; idem, "Paul's Blindness," 64–70; Frein, "Misunderstanding," 328–48; Hartsock, *Sight and Blindness*, 167–205; Brittany E. Wilson, "The Blinding of Paul and the Power of God: Masculinity, Sight, and Self-Control," *JBL* 133 (2014): 367–87; idem, "Hearing," 460–75, esp. 460-64.

[12] E.g., Pao, *New Exodus*; Bart J. Koet, "Isaiah in Luke-Acts," in *Isaiah in the New Testament: The New Testament and the Scriptures of Israel*, ed. Steve Moyise and Maarten J. J. Menken (London: Bloomsbury Publishing, 2005), 79–100; Peter Mallen, *The Reading and Transformation of Isaiah in Luke-Acts*, LNTS 361 (London: T&T Clark, 2008); Jon Ruthven, "'This is My Covenant with Them': Isaiah 59.19-21 as the Programmatic Prophecy of the New Covenant in the Acts of the Apostles (Part I)," *JPT* 17 (2008): 32–47; idem. "'This is My Covenant with Them': Isaiah 59.19-21 as the Programmatic Prophecy of the New Covenant in the Acts of the Apostles (Part II)," *JPT* 17 (2008): 219–37.

Isa 6:5; cf. Dan 8:15–18; cf. Judg 13:6, 22; Ezek 1:28). Unlike Isaiah, Zechariah's response is less than faithful. His question, "How will I know this? (κατὰ τί γνώσομαι τοῦτο;)," amounts to disbelief (οὐκ ἐπίστευσας). In contrast with the Isaiah's purified lips, Zechariah is judged with muteness (1:18–20; cf. also Ezek 3:22–27). The righteous Zechariah sees a vision but cannot comprehend due to his unbelief. His encounter with Gabriel, the bearer of apocalyptic insight (Dan 8:16–18; 9:12; cf. 1 En. 9:1; 20:1–7; 40:1–10; Jub. 2:18; 1QH 6.13), fails to engender faith about God's coming one.[13] The first character introduced in Luke's writings is pious yet imperceptive of God's activity. Even the righteous in Israel may fail to perceive the light.

Of course, Zechariah's imperception is temporary. In a scene replete with Isaianic imagery, he affirms Gabriel's words in obedience and praise (1:59–79).[14] Zechariah declares that his prophet son will grant the same "knowledge of salvation (γνῶσιν σωτηρίας)" that Zechariah was hesitant to believe (1:77; cf. 1:19; Acts 28:28). Moreover, Zechariah introduces the language of *light* and *darkness*. John, declares the aged priest, will herald the emergence of dawn (ἀνατολή) on Israel (1:78; cf. 22:53; 23:44; Acts 13:11; 23:18). These words resonate with Isaiah's vision of a new day rising (ἀνατέλλω) on Israel at its salvation (Isa 45:6–8; 60:1–3; 61:11; cf. Num 24:17; Mal 4:2).[15] The echoes of the Isaianic program grow louder when Zechariah outlines that the new dawn will lead to the illumination (ἐπιφαίνω) of "those sitting in darkness and the shadow of death (ἐν σκότει καὶ σκιᾷ θανάτου καθημένοις)" (Luke 1:79; cf. Isa 8:19–9:6; 29:18–19; 42:6–7; 49:9).[16] Zechariah describes John as the forerunner of God's deliverance for Israel from exilic death, a program outlined most famously by Isaiah (e.g., 40:1–11; 43:1–13; 48:12–49:26; 60:1–62:12; cf. Deut 28:28–29; Ezek 34:12–16; Mic 7:8).[17] This vocation is confirmed by the extended quotation of Isaiah at the outset of John's ministry (Luke 3:4–6; Isa 40:3–5). Beyond Israel, the culmination of the work John begins will be that "all flesh will see the salvation of God (ὄψεται πᾶσα σὰρξ τὸ σωτήριον τοῦ θεοῦ)" (3:6; Isa 40:5; cf. Acts 26:23).

Motifs of seeing God's salvation permeate the introduction of the righteous and pious Simeon (2:25–35). To this man who anticipates the comfort of Israel (παράκλησιν τοῦ Ἰσραήλ; cf. LXX Isa 40:1–2) the Holy Spirit revealed that "he would not see death (μὴ ἰδεῖν θάνατον) before he saw the Messiah (ἴδῃ τὸν χριστόν)" (2:26). The elderly

---

[13] Green, *Luke*, 78.
[14] Koet, "Isaiah," 82–84; Mallen, *Isaiah*, 64–66.
[15] "Salvation" also echoes God's deliverance of his people in Isaiah (e.g., 45:17; 46:13; 49:6–8; 52:7–10).
[16] The shepherds who appear shortly after Zechariah's words personify this (2:8–20). They are the first to experience the emergence of God's glorious light (δόξα κυρίου περιέλαμψεν αὐτούς; cf. Acts 26:13) as they sit in the darkness of night (2:8). In contrast to Zechariah's disbelief, they respond with faithful vision, going to see the child, proclaiming the words that the child is Israel's savior, the Lord-Messiah (2:15–17; cf. 2:11–12), and glorifying and praising God "for all that they heard and saw" (2:20). Their encounter with the glory of the Lord in darkness reorients them toward praise and testimony of the new light on Israel.
[17] For additional echoes in Zechariah's words related to Israel's redemption, see Green, *Luke*, 116–20; Salvador Carrillo Alday, *El Evangelio según San Lucas* (Estella: Editorial Verbo Divino, 2009), 74–75; Hays, *Echoes*, 198–200; Du Toit, "Reconsidering," 348–53; Reardon, *Politics*, 33–64; cf. Hamm, "Tamid," 220–21; Kinzer, "Sacrifice," 463–75. On the links between death, darkness, and Satan in Luke-Acts, see Garret, *Demise*, 37–60 (e.g., Luke 22:53; 23:44; Acts 13:11; 23:18); cf. Green, *Conversion*, 100–1, on light.

Simeon who sits in the shadow of death (cf. 1:79) is the first in Jerusalem to recognize God's agent of salvation: "My eyes (οἱ ὀφθαλμοί μου) have seen (εἶδον) your salvation (τὸ σωτήριόν σου) … a light (φῶς) for revelation for the gentiles, and glory of your people Israel" (2:30–32). Peter Mallen observes that the pairing of *salvation* with *sight* "is rare in Scripture but occurs twice in Isaiah 40–55 LXX" (Isa 40:5; 52:10; cf. 49:6; 51:4; 62:1).[18] Jesus is central to the fruition of the Isaianic program of redemption for Israel. Simeon's eyes, the first pair mentioned in Luke's writings, perceive the light and glory of salvation for Zion and the nations that Isaiah envisioned.

Of course, Simeon makes explicit what was implicit with Zechariah and common to the sections of Isaiah to which Simeon alludes: Not all Israel will perceive rightly, at least not initially. Jesus will be a "sign that is spoken against (εἰς σημεῖον ἀντιλεγόμενον)" (cf. Isa 65:2), leading to the "fall and rise of many in Israel" (2:34–35). By introducing conflict with more Isaianic language, Luke's perception metaphors take on the darker side. Many in Israel will persist in the condition of blindness the prophet declared upon the people, inhibiting their ability to fulfill their vocation as God's servant and experience redemption (6:5–10; 42:18–19; 43:9).[19] Blindness, failure to perceive the light of deliverance, will continue to be a problem among Israel as it long has been. Many will fall into infidelity and darkness. Even some of the righteous in Israel will find it difficult to perceive properly.[20]

Nevertheless, one should not assume that, though they may encounter judgment, the imperceptive de facto lose their place among God's people or are consigned to darkness permanently. Zechariah stands in direct contrast to this idea. As Simeon insinuates, "falling" into disbelief and judgment can become "rising" to perceiving and proclaiming the salvific light.[21] These two aged righteous men suggest that Philip Stern's words about Isaiah will ring true for Luke's narrative as it progresses: "Deutero-Isaiah juxtaposes light and darkness. Israel dwells in darkness, but it will light up the nations. Indeed, the Second Isaiah seems to revel in dark images, because the prophet sees the darkness as temporary. If Israel is trapped in holes and dungeons, it will surely emerge to see the light. Salvation is to come because YHWH wills it."[22]

---

[18] Mallen, *Isaiah*, 65; similarly, Koet, "Isaiah," 82–84.

[19] Stern, "Blind Servant," 225–32; cf. Rikki E. Watts, "Consolation or Confrontation: Isaiah 40–55 and the Delay of the New Exodus," *TynBul* 41 (1990): 31–59.

[20] Illustrating this point is the boy Jesus in the temple and his parents (2:41–50). They see him (ἰδόντες αὐτόν) yet do not understand (οὐ συνῆκαν) his response about why he was in the temple. Jesus' pious parents are the first in Israel to fail to comprehend Jesus' words. In fact, the only time συνίημι is used to describe someone comprehending accurately is when Jesus opens the disciples' minds to understand the Scriptures (24:45; cf. 8:10; 18:34; 24:45; Acts 7:25; 28:26–27).

[21] Zechariah's and Simeon's words resonate strongly with LXX Micah 7:8, when Israel declares, "Do not rejoice over me, my enemy (ἡ ἐχθρά μου; cf. Luke 1:74), because I have fallen, and I will rise (πέπτωκα καὶ ἀναστήσομαι; cf. Luke 2:34). Because if I sit in darkness (καθίσω ἐν τῷ σκότει), the Lord will illumine (φωτιεῖ; cf. Luke 1:79) me" (cf. Du Toit, "Reconsidering," 352–53). Israel acknowledges its punishment results from its own sin but expects that God will "lead me into light, and I will see his righteousness (ἐξάξεις με εἰς τὸ φῶς, ὄψομαι τὴν δικαιοσύνην αὐτοῦ)" (Mic 7:9).

[22] Stern, "Blind Servant," 226. Carroll similarly observes, "Within the various clusters of seeing/not-seeing (blindness), perceiving/not perceiving images and *topoi* in Isaiah are included all the elements of transformation and reversal" ("Blindsight," 90).

5.1.2 Israel, God's Blind Servant

The subsequent narrative of Luke's Gospel outlines the struggle for Israel to recognize Jesus so as to respond properly with repentance. Difficulties in perception emerge at the outset of Jesus' ministry and continue to the conclusion. Drawing from Isaiah, Luke paints Israel as God's blind servant. This characterization appears most visible, ironically enough, in Jesus' disciples. A tension arises in their depiction. On the one hand, Jesus grants them privileged knowledge in Israel (10:23–24). When Jesus begins speaking in parables, they must ask him for explanations; they cannot hear them rightly without his interpretations. Jesus then quotes Isaiah to describe how his parables inhibit perception for the rest of Israel (8:9–10, 16–18; cf. Isa 6:9). His prophetic activity solidifies how the stubborn in Israel will fail to receive the word and bear fruit (Luke 8:4–8; cf. 3:8).[23] Yet, "Luke records no change of scene, no separation of Jesus and the disciples from the others, and the presence of the crowds is assumed throughout."[24] Jesus' illumination of the parables for the disciples occurs before the others in Israel; there is no hard line between these groups based on understanding.

On the other hand, Jesus' disciples, like the rest of Israel, fail to comprehend completely. They are among those in Israel who cannot see the Son of Man and his kingdom (cf. 17:20–37). The Twelve whom Jesus chose—the core of restored Israel and the people's future leaders (6:12–16; 22:30; Acts 1:12–26; 7:8; 26:7)—cannot understand (οὐδὲν τούτων συνῆκαν . . . οὐκ ἐγίνωσκον) that the prophets declare how the Son of Man will be killed and rise again on the third day. It "was hidden (παρακεκαλυμμένον) from them so that they did not perceive it (μὴ αἴσθωνται)" (Luke 9:44–45; cf. 24:16). The second time Luke makes this point, he emphasizes the hiddenness (κεκρυμμένον) of this message by bracketing it between two comments about the apostles' obliviousness (18:34). Luke's terms again echo the servant and his mission in Israel. The "hiddenness" of the messianic mission faintly echoes God's hiding (ἔκρυψέν) of the servant in his hand and quiver (Isa 49:2; cf. 44:8). Isaiah uses αἰσθάνομαι, which appears only here in Luke-Acts, to describe how Israel and the world will perceive God's glory as a result of Israel's liberation (33:11; 49:26). At this point in the narrative, however, perception remains hidden from those closest to Jesus and all Israel. Indeed, as Israel's new Jesus-appointed leadership, the apostles' blindness *is* Israel's blindness.[25] The disciples might be further on the journey from blindness to sight than the rest of Israel, but they have a ways to go before their eyes perceive Jesus' light in full (cf. Luke 9:27–36).

Jesus bemoans the same hiddenness and inability to perceive that inhibits the disciples and all Israel when he "comes near (ἤγγισεν)" to Jerusalem. The things that would bring the city peace "now have been hidden from [their] eyes (νῦν δὲ ἐκρύβη

---

[23] Carroll's words about Isaiah ring true for Jesus in Luke: "The role of the speaker in the blinding of the people (cf. the blindness of the servant in 42:19) makes the prophet complicit in the darkened state of the people. Whatever may be the causes of the condition of the people of Jerusalem (corrupt leadership, social injustice, etc.), in the book of Isaiah prophets (cf. Hos 6:5) and YHWH are deeply implicated in constructing that condition" ("Blindsight," 83). See also Evans, *To See*, 115–18.

[24] Green, *Luke*, 326.

[25] Cf. Hamm, "Sight," 466. On the Twelve as representatives and leaders of Israel, see Fuller, *Restoration*, 239–69; Lohfink, *Sammlung*, 63–94.

ἀπὸ ὀφθαλμῶν σου)" (19:42). Like the disciples, critical information about Jesus has been obscured from their sight due to moral failures (cf. 13:34). Unlike Simeon, their eyes cannot see the Lord's salvation. The city will be razed along with her children (ἐδαφιοῦσίν σε καὶ τὰ τέκνα; cf. LXX Hos 10:14) as a result of the failure to "recognize (ἀνθ᾽ ὧν οὐκ ἔγνως) the time of your visitation" (19:44; cf. 21:20–24; LXX Isa 29:3; 37:33; 39:6; Jer 6:15; 10:15; 22:8–9; 23:38; 38:20).[26] Once again, Israel will go into captivity (αἰχμαλωτισθήσονται; Luke 21:24) "because they did not know the Lord" (LXX Isa 5:13).

Of course, as Jesus' other words over Jerusalem reiterate, as for the prophets who describe its destruction and exile, the city's sufferings are temporary (cf. Isa 52:2; 61:1). God's visitation is hidden from them for now (νῦν) (19:42). Their present inability to see is tempered by Jesus' "until" (ἕως, ἄχρι) statements (13:35; 21:24; cf. Acts 3:21).[27] Expectation remains that Jerusalem will one day see Jesus rightly as the times of the gentiles are fulfilled. Their redemption (ἡ ἀπολύτρωσις; cf. LXX Isa 63:4; Luke 1:68; 2:38; 24:21) will come near (ἐγγίζει) with the Son of Man's advent in glory (21:28; cf. Isa 45:21; 46:13; 50:8; 56:1). Given the connection with the removal of blindness at Israel's restoration in Isaiah that Luke so frequently draws on (e.g., Isa 35:5–10; 42:5–44:8), it seems that Luke similarly insinuates that Jerusalem's fortunes will change when her lack of sight is cured. At that time, the people will see the light of God's salvation.[28] Within the narrative, though, Israel, Jerusalem, and Jesus' own disciples remain blind. They must be brought to new sight.

5.1.3 Jesus, God's Servant Who Opens Blind Eyes

Thankfully for blind Israel, as Jesus announces in Nazareth, bringing sight to the blind is central to his mission (Luke 4:16–21). Quoting from Isaiah, Jesus states the purposes of his Spirit-anointed undertaking: He has been sent "to bring good news to the poor (εὐαγγελίσασθαι πτωχοῖς), to proclaim release to the captives (αἰχμαλώτοις ἄφεσιν) and recovery of sight to the blind (τυφλοῖς ἀνάβλεψιν), to send out the oppressed in release (τεθραυσμένους ἐν ἀφέσει), to proclaim the year of the Lord's favor" (4:18–19; cf. Isa 58:6; 61:1–2). Several phrases highlight Jesus' Israel-centric purposes.[29] First, εὐαγγελίζω is well known for its connection with Isaiah's depiction of Israel's restoration

---

[26] David L. Tiede, *Prophecy and History in Luke-Acts* (Philadelphia, PA: Fortress, 1980), 82; Green, *Luke*, 690–91. An echo of Hos 10:14b is particularly strong and significant as it describes the destruction God brings on Israel for its unrighteousness (cf. Luke 19:45–46). Nevertheless, the forecast of destruction is followed by God's declaration of loyalty to his wayward children and promise to restore them (Hos 11:1–12).

[27] Schaefer, *Zukunft*, 143–46, 179–83, 215–18; Kinzer, *Jerusalem*, 29–35.

[28] Stern's words about Isaiah again are fitting for Luke: "When the God of Israel has turned everything topsy-turvy as Isa 41,19 prophesies, then Worm Israel will be transformed into a people of seeing individuals (Isa 41,20)" ("Blind Servant," 226).

[29] To be sure, Jesus' mission encapsulates the gentiles and "all flesh" (Luke 2:32; 3:6; cf. Isa 40:5), but Israel still is a centerpiece. On other ancient readings of Isa 61, see John J. Collins, "A Herald of Good Tidings: Isaiah 61:1–3 and Its Actualization in the Dead Sea Scrolls," in *The Quest for Context and Meaning*, ed. Craig A. Evans and Shemaryahu Talmon (Leiden: Brill, 1997), 225–40; Randall Heskett, *Messianism within the Scriptural Scroll of Isaiah* (New York: T&T Clark, 2007), 311–99.

when God returns to Zion (Isa 40:9–11; 52:7; 60:6; cf. Nah 1:15; Joel 2:32).[30] Second, αἰχμαλώτος and its related terms are used in the LXX for prisoners of war (e.g., Num 21:29; Isa 23:1; 46:2; Nah 3:10), most commonly for the exiles of Israel (e.g., Isa 1:27; 5:13; 14:2; 45:13; 52:2; Jer 1:3; 15:2; Ezek 1:1–2; Amos 6:7; 7:11, 17; Tob 7:3; 13:10) and Judah (Ezek 12:4; Esth 2:5–6; 1 Macc 2:9).[31] Third, oppression (θραύω) is one of the curses for Israel's disobedience (LXX Deut 28:33; 2 Chr 6:24; cf. 2 Kgdms 12:15). Other texts maintain that this state would be reversed as injustices are destroyed (Isa 58:6) and as God overthrows Israel's enemies (Isa 2:5–21; 42:4; Ps. Sol. 17:24; Odes 1:6). Fourth, release (ἄφεσις) echoes the freedom associated with the Jubilee year (Lev 25:10–55), which Isaiah (e.g., Isa 33:24; 55:7) and the other early Jewish literature redeployed "to signify the eschatological deliverance of God (with its profound social implications)."[32] Jesus' mission is for national Israel's restoration.

At the center of this mission stands the granting of new sight to the blind in Israel.[33] In Isaiah, blindness was representative of and resultant from Israel's recalcitrance, its infidelity. Israel's willful ignorance prompted judgment of destruction and exile (e.g., 6:9–10; 43:8; cf. 65:2). Isaiah describes Israel's blind, exilic state as being in the darkness of prison (42:7; 49:9).[34] It is unsurprising, then, that the anticipated restoration is linked with the renewal of sight. Remedying blindness is integral to the healing of the rebellious and exilic state of the people in the Isaianic program (e.g., 29:1–12; 32:3; 35:5–6; 59:9–60:5).[35] In citing the prophet, Jesus makes explicit two features of the blindness-sight motif. First, blindness continues to be an issue in Israel. More precisely, proper sight is now connected to perceiving Jesus rightly as the fulfillment of Israel's

---

[30] Kinzer, *Jerusalem*, 2–7; cf. Wright, *Jesus*, 600–604. Other early Jewish readings of Isa 40:1–11 describe eschatological salvation for Israel (e.g., Bar 5:7; 4Q176; Ps. Sol. 11:4; see Mallen, *Isaiah*, 70–71).

[31] Rebecca I. Denova, *The Things Accomplished among Us: Prophetic Tradition in the Structural Pattern of Luke-Acts*, JSNTSup 141 (Sheffield: Sheffield Academic, 1997), 137. Isaiah even calls Jerusalem "captive daughter Zion" (Isa 52:2).

[32] Green, *Luke*, 212; Bradley C. Gregory, "The Postexilic Exile in Third Isaiah: Isaiah 61:1–3 in Light of Second Temple Hermeneutics," *JBL* 126 (2007): 475–96, esp. 483–87; cf. 11QMelch; Jub. 1:21–25; Ps. Sol. 11; Dan 9:24–27. See also Koet, *Five Studies*, 31–35; Denova, *Things Accomplished*, 133–38; Fuller, *Restoration*, 236–39; Reardon, *Politics*, 65–98. Of course, Luke often uses ἄφεσις and ἀφίημι for release of sins (e.g., Luke 5:20–24; 7:47–49; 11:4; 12:10; 17:3–4; 24:47; Acts 10:43; 13:38; 26:18), which is intimately connected to Israel's restoration (1:77; 3:3; Acts 2:38; 5:31; cf. Ezek 36–37). A corporate dynamic remains in view. Reinforcing this point, see Mark Strauss, *The Davidic Messiah in Luke-Acts: The Promise and Its Fulfilment in Lukan Christology*, JSNTSup 110 (London: Bloomsbury, 1995), 199–260, on the Davidic overtones in the Nazareth pericope.

[33] "In the programmatic episode of Jesus' debut in the synagogue at Nazareth, the proclamation of recovering of sight to the blind [*typhlois anablepsin*] stands at the center of a chiasm constructed artificially from the LXX of Isa 61,1–2 and 58,6c, proclaiming sight to the blind is what Jesus will be about through the whole Luke-Acts narrative" (Hamm, "Paul's Blindness," 68; similarly, Hartsock, *Sight and Blindness*, 172–73).

[34] Stern, "Blind Servant," 226; Carroll, "Blindsight," 90.

[35] Gregory, "Postexilic," 475–496; Jacob Stromberg, *Isaiah after Exile: The Author of Third Isaiah as Reader and Redactor of the Book*, OTM (Oxford: Oxford University Press, 2011); cf. Bruce Chilton, *The Glory of Israel: The Theology and Provenience of the Isaiah Targum*, JSOTSup 23 (Sheffield: JSOT Press, 1983), 28–33; Stern, "Blind Servant," 224–25; Carroll, "Blindsight," 80–90; Hartsock, *Sight and Blindness*, 122–23. I am not suggesting all diaspora Jews considered exile as a death-like state or faced existential angst over not being in the land. My point is simply that numerous texts in Israel's Scriptures, Luke's primary sourcebook, depict exile as a form of national death.

hope. Yet, all eyes in the Nazareth synagogue (πάντων οἱ ὀφθαλμοὶ ἐν τῇ συναγωγῇ) fail to see Jesus in this light (4:20-30).[36] Second, Jesus is the one who restores Israel's sight (Luke 4:21; cf. Isa 42:6-7). The question as the narrative progresses is whether Jesus will remedy the imperceptiveness of his hometown and all Israel, or if Israel's blind leaders will guide the rest of the nation into destruction (cf. 6:39-40).[37]

Still, seeing Jesus rightly in Luke's Gospel comes in shades. The movement from *blindness* to *sight* is a journey. This is evident in John the Baptist's questioning Jesus (7:18-23). John sends his disciples to ask Jesus if he is "the coming one (ὁ ἐρχόμενος)" (7:19-20; cf. 3:15-16). Before recording Jesus' response, Luke highlights Jesus' healing activities, the last but not least of which is how Jesus "gave sight freely to many blind people (τυφλοῖς πολλοῖς ἐχαρίσατο βλέπειν)." Jesus recommissions John's disciples to report to John the things they have seen and heard. The "things" Jesus describes echo God's eschatological restoration of Israel outlined by Isaiah (26:19; 29:18-20; 35:5-6; 43:8-10; 61:1).[38] The first mentioned is that "the blind receive sight (τυφλοὶ ἀναβλέπουσιν)" (Luke 7:22). Luke juxtaposes the two references of blindness, once again giving it a central place in Jesus' activities and self-identification, even though a particular instance of Jesus healing blindness has yet to be narrated. The Lord Jesus is working to grant new sight to the people.[39] Restoring Israel's sight seems to be a gradual process that, in part, depends on the response of the people, including the righteous like John. Even for one as great as John who prepared the way for the light of revelation, the ability to perceive Jesus as "the coming one" might require direct intervention and explication (7:27-28).

Only once does Luke record Jesus' healing of someone physically blind. Notably, Luke juxtaposes the healing of the blind beggar near Jericho with the apostles' ignorance concerning Jesus' identity and mission (18:31-43). The blind beggar evinces greater sight than the apostles. He is the *only* character to recognize Jesus (accurately) as "Son of David" (Luke 1:32-33; 3:31; cf. 20:31).[40] Increasing the irony, those leading the crowd rebuke the man for his correct words. They are the ones who lack sight (18:39).[41] The ignorant disciples and the great crowds of Israel stand in contrast to the perceptive blind man. Despite opposition, the man persists in petitioning David's Son for mercy. Jesus obliges. The man's faithfulness, his acknowledgement of Jesus as "Lord," saves him

---

[36] In Acts, even among the apostles, ἀτενίζω can indicate lack of understanding (1:10; 3:12; 6:15; 11:6) or true sight (3:4; 7:55; 10:4; 13:9; 14:9; 23:1; cf. Luke 22:56).
[37] On Luke 6:39-40, see Hamm, "Sight," 465-66; Green, *Luke*, 277-78; Hartsock, *Sight and Blindness*, 179-80.
[38] Hartsock describes the healing of blindness in Isaiah "an apocalyptic sign" (*Blindness and Sight*, 123; similarly, Hamm, "Sight," 461). LXX Isaiah 29:18-19 links Jesus' response to John with Mary's and Zechariah's words: with Israel's restoration (cf. Isa 29:22-24), "the eyes of the blind in the darkness (ἐν τῷ σκότει; Luke 1:79) and in the fog will see, and the poor will rejoice (ἀγαλλιάσονται πτωχοὶ; cf. Luke 1:47) because of the Lord."
[39] Cf. Green, *Luke*, 296-97.
[40] Green, *Luke*, 661-65; Alday, *Evangelio*, 309; Strauss, *Davidic Messiah*, 306-7; *pace* Hartsock, *Sight and Blindness*, 183-84
[41] ἐπιτιμάω evinces different connotations depending on its subject. Jesus rebukes demons, illnesses, and nature, demonstrating his power (4:35, 49, 41; 8:24; 9:42; cf. 9:21). Rebukes from/to other characters often expose ignorance (9:55; 17:3; 18:15; 19:39; 34:40).

(ἡ πίστις σου σέσωκέν σε). Emphasized is how Jesus restores the man's physical sight—ἀναβλέπω is repeated three times—to match the man's faithful perception of Jesus (18:40-43). His fidelity enables the Isaianic healing activity for Israel that is central to Jesus' mission. When all the people see this (πᾶς ὁ λαὸς ἰδών), they respond in praise to God. They acknowledge God's activity in Jesus after the miracle rather than prior to it, as the beggar was able to do. The miracle brings them closer to sight, but, as the story progresses, they still lack the beggar's perception.[42] They need Jesus to open their eyes.

5.1.4 Revelation of the Risen Lord

This tension between the blind servant Israel and the servant Jesus who restores sight comes to a head in Luke's final chapter, particularly in the encounter on the Emmaus Road (Luke 24:13-35).[43] Here, Jesus climactically demonstrates his ability to overcome Israel's blindness as exemplified by the apostles, Cleopas, and his companion. Three details characterize them as emblematic of Israel's corporate condition of disbelief and ignorance and, concomitantly, representative of Jesus' power to overcome said inability to see (cf. Acts 3:17).[44] First, the disciples persist in imperceptions common to Israel and reinscribe the people's divided view of Jesus. The remaining eleven apostles disbelieve (ἠπίστουν) the testimony of Mary Magdalene, Joanna, and Mary, James' mother, about the risen Lord (24:9; cf. 24:41; Acts 28:24). In fact, these women's words seem nonsensical to the apostles (24:9-11). Cleopas similarly recounts how he and the other disciples were astonished (ἐξέστησαν) by the women's report that they had seen an angelic vision (ὀπτασίαν ἀγγέλων ἑωρακέναι) that Jesus was alive (24:23; cf. 1:11-22).[45] Some (τινες; cf. Acts 28:24), like Peter, do respond more positively, though, and go to the tomb. Still, these disciples "did not see him (αὐτὸν δὲ οὐκ εἶδον)" (24:12, 24). Even for the more faithful in the group, their sight is better but is still lacking. The disciples, like the Jewish leadership in Rome at the end of Acts, divide over the message about Jesus (Acts 28:23-25).

Second, Luke's terminology echoes Jesus' weeping over Jerusalem at the not-so-triumphal entry (19:41-44). As Cleopas and his companion journey from Jerusalem, Jesus draws near (ἐγγίσας; cf. 10:9-11; Isa 45:21; 46:13; 50:8; 56:1) to the pair, but "their eyes were prevented from recognizing them (οἱ δὲ ὀφθαλμοὶ αὐτῶν ἐκρατοῦντο τοῦ μὴ ἐπιγνῶναι αὐτόν)" (24:14-16).[46] The agent of Jerusalem's salvation, the one who

---

[42] On how the motif of sight extends from the rich ruler (18:18-30) and continues in the Zacchaeus pericope and the parable of the ten pounds that follow (19:1-27), see Hamm "Sight," 463-66.

[43] "Das Problem der Verstockung Israels beschäftigt Lukas nicht nur am Ende der Apostelgeschichte, sondern auch am Ende des Evangelium. Deshalb erzählt er die Emmausgeschichte Ohren durch die Schriftauslegung (als er redete auf dem Wege), läßt die trägen Herzen brennen; dass Öffnen der Augen läßt ihn selbst, den Herrn, erkennen" (Anna Maria Schwemer, "Der Auferstandene und die Emmausjünger," in *Auferstehung*, 95–117 [114]).

[44] Mittmann, "Polemik," 530.

[45] Astonishment usually entails interest yet lack of understanding or falling short of faith in Luke-Acts (Luke 2:47; 8:56; Acts 2:7, 12; 8:9, 11, 13; 9:21; 10:45; 12:16).

[46] The setting continues a common Lukan trope: Revelation of Jesus' identity often occurs when approaching cities (e.g., 7:12-17; 19:29-45; Acts 9:3; 10:9; 22:6), the most pertinent parallel being Jesus healing the blind man near Jericho (18:35-43).

brings the kingdom of God, has come near to these disciples yet, like the city, they fail to recognize (ἔγνως) him because things "were hidden from her eyes (ἐκρύβη ἀπὸ ὀφθαλμῶν σου)" (19:42-44; cf. Luke 9:44-45; 18:31-34). Once again, Luke repeats the Isaianic motif of Israel's inability to see salvation.[47] The connection with their ignorance and Jerusalem's is further reinforced by Cleopas' ironic comment to Jesus: "Are you the only outsider in Jerusalem (μόνος παροικεῖς Ιερουσαλήμ) that does not know (οὐκ ἔγνως) what has happened in her in these days?" (24:18). Jesus, of course, is the only one in Jerusalem who does know what has truly transpired.

Third, as Cleopas explains "the things about Jesus of Nazareth" to Jesus of Nazareth, he parrots Israel's incomplete perspective (24:19-24). Cleopas describes Jesus as "a mighty prophet in action and word before God and all the people" (24:19; cf. 7:16; 9:8, 19; 13:34), a description that is accurate but insufficient (cf. 2:11; 2:26; 9:18-22; Acts 2:36). Cleopas, like all Israel, misapprehends a central puzzle piece.[48] He mixes Jesus' own words with Israel's unbelief. "Our chief priests and leaders," Cleopas recounts in words similar to Jesus', "handed him over (παρέδωκαν) for a death sentence and crucified him" (cf. 9:44; 18:32; 24:7). Jesus' death is a tragedy for Cleopas and the people: "We were hoping (ἡμεῖς δὲ ἠλπίζομεν; cf. Acts 26:7) that he was the one who was going to redeem Israel (λυτροῦσθαι τὸν Ἰσραήλ; cf. Luke 1:68; 2:38). But (ἀλλά), even with all these things, this is the third day since these things happened" (24:21-22). With the adversative, Cleopas reveals that, as far as he can tell, the passing of three days terminates hope. Cleopas and his unnamed companion reify and vocalize the sadness (σκυθρωπός) from the belief that Israel's redemption has failed, embodied in apostles whose incomplete number evokes Israel's broken expectations (24:17-24; cf. 1:68; 2:38). Yet, they all fail to recall that Jesus said he would be raised on the third day (9:12; 18:33; 24:7). For Jesus (and Luke), Cleopas' words simply exhibit Israel's ignorance. They are "foolish (ἀνόητοι; cf. LXX Deut 32:30) and slow in heart to believe (πιστεύειν) in all that the prophets spoke" (24:25; cf. 16:29-31; Acts 28:24-25). Unlike the blind man whose faith (πίστις) saves him (18:42-43), Cleopas and the rest of Israel lack faith.[49]

As representatives of Israel, these disciples' journey from *blindness* to *sight* provides the culmination of Jesus' mission to remedy blindness in Israel in the Third Gospel. The Emmaus Road and Jesus' appearance to the disciples insinuate that scriptural arguments, testimony, and calls to repentance have their importance and persuade some, but direct encounter with the resurrected Jesus is the ultimate means by which Jesus rectifies the condition of blindness among those in Israel who are slow to believe

---

[47] Schwemer, "Auferstandene," 113; Mittmann, "Polemik," 523-30. Whether God, Satan, or human infidelity cause this condition is unclear. The passives could entail divine agency. Yet, Satan's is the realm of darkness and misunderstanding Scripture (Luke 4:1-13; 22:53; Acts 26:18). In Isaiah, blindness results from moral failure and prophetic activity (Carroll, "Blindsight," 83). Luke seems to maintain a comparable ambiguity (Schwemer, "Auferstandene," 102-4).

[48] Green, *Luke*, 846-47.

[49] Faith frequently precipitates healing in Luke's Gospel (7:50; 8:48, 50; 9:24; 17:19; Acts 2:21, 40; 4:13; 14:9; cf. Luke 8:12; 18:26-27).

or the unpersuaded, including his own disciples.[50] Jesus provides an interpretive guide to understand the Scriptures (24:27, 45–47). Opening Scripture is not what opens eyes or minds, though. Encountering Jesus does. With Cleopas and his compatriot, Jesus utilizes table fellowship to remedy their lack of sight (24:29–32; cf. 9:16; 22:19).[51] After he gives them the blessed and broken bread, "their eyes were open and they recognized him (αὐτῶν δὲ διηνοίχθησαν οἱ ὀφθαλμοὶ καὶ ἐπέγνωσαν αὐτόν)" (24:30–31, 35; cf. Acts 16:14).[52] He disappears (ἄφαντος ἐγένετο) from their sight physically, but their condition of blindness is reversed because of the risen Jesus' direct, intervening presence.

Similarly, Cleopas' and his compatriot's account of this encounter does not evoke new sight among the apostles (22:33–35). It simply provokes conversation (24:46; cf. 24:14–15; Acts 28:25). When Jesus appears to the apostles, doubts (διαλογισμοί; cf. 2:35; 5:22; 9:46–47) arise in their heart (24:38). They believe him to be a ghost (24:37). Jesus' subsequent bids for them to "look" and touch him so they might "see" that it truly is him in the flesh only generate more wonder (θαυμαζόντων; cf. 24:12) and disbelief (ἀπιστούντων; 24:38–41; cf. 24:41; Acts 28:24). These disciples too need Jesus to open their eyes so as to generate fidelity (cf. 8:25). Jesus, therefore, interprets the Scriptures and opens their minds to understand the message about his suffering and resurrection, which they had previously failed to grasp (24:44–49; cf. 18:34; Acts 28:26–27). Their sight and knowledge were better than others in Israel, yet they suffered from the same imperceptiveness. They too needed direct encounter with and intervention from the risen Jesus to remedy their blindness. Jesus had to reorient them, as must be done for all Israel, on the journey from darkness to light.

5.1.5 Summary

Four points arise from this survey of Isaianic blindness in the Third Gospel relevant to the conclusion of Acts. First, following Isaiah, Luke depicts Israel, including Jesus' most intimate followers, as God's blind servant.[53] Blindness stems from Israel's infidelity, as well as the prophet's obfuscating activity in response to their obstinacy (Luke 1:18–21; 8:9–10; 13:31–35; 24:25; cf. Isa 6:5–13; 56:9–12; 59:9–11; Acts 13:9–11). Persistent

---

[50] "Luke emphasizes that the correct interpretation of the scriptures required more than a simple exposition of them. *A revelation from Christ*, together with his exegetical instruction, *was essential* to their proper understanding of the true meaning of these sacred texts" (Wendel, *Scriptural Interpretation*, 93; emphasis mine). Luke raises the possibility that Jesus will depart Cleopas and his companion without their having recognized him (24:28). There is the chance that their blindness persists. What prevents this is their extension of hospitality, that is, their welcoming of Jesus (Green, *Luke*, 849). Notably, Saul only gets "a revelation from Christ" and his eyes opened in Acts. No one exposits Scripture or calls him to repent.

[51] The parallels between this fellowship and the feeding of the 5000 are particularly poignant when one recalls the twelve baskets recovered that highlight Jesus' ability to provide for all Israel (Luke 9:10–17).

[52] One might object that διηνοίχθησαν is a divine passive and, therefore, it takes divine intervention to alleviate blindness. However, Luke has described Jesus as the agent of God's healing Israel's blindness and, as God's agent of Israel's salvation, one cannot clearly separate their activities for Luke.

[53] Moreover, in Acts, ignorance is a human problem, not simply a Jewish one (cf. 14:15; 17:30).

blindness culminates in the further darkness of Israel's experience of death, exile, and delayed restoration (Luke 19:41–45).[54] Rectification of sight is part and parcel of Israel's repentance-journey and renewal (Isa 29:17–24; 32:2–4; 35:1–10; Luke 7:18–23; cf. Acts 3:27–26). Second, blindness does not negate covenantal identity. It paradoxically reinforces it by invoking judgment (Luke 19:41–44).[55] Israel, including Jesus' own, remains God's corporate servant, albeit God's *blind* servant in need of healing (Isa 42:8–10, 19; 43:8–13; Luke 18:31–42; 24:25–49; cf. LXX Lam 3:45). All Israel needs their eyes to be open to what is hidden, that is, the recognition of Jesus' identity as Israel's risen Lord who redeems Israel (Luke 24:15, 31, 37–41; Acts 28:26–27; cf. Luke 19:43). Third, thankfully for God's people, God's messianic servant and his community work to open Israel's shut eyes to bring about restoration and be a light to the nations (Isa 29:10; 33:15 42:6–7, 16–17; 49:6; 61:1–3; Luke 2:30–35; 4:16–21; Acts 13:47). Israel's blindness—its stubborn opposition and exilic state—can be overcome by the risen Jesus. Jesus evinces his ability to alleviate Israel's blindness most clearly among his unfaithful followers, especially the apostles. Fourth, direct encounter with the resurrected Jesus proves most effective in alleviating Israel's blindness. Indeed, a key difference between the conclusions of the Third Gospel and Acts is Jesus' physical presence and direct action to open Scripture, eyes, and minds.

5.2 Blindness in Acts

In Acts, the blindness-sight motif centers on Paul, whether it is his experience of blindness or his proclamation of it others. Oddly, rarely has Paul's blindness influenced interpretation of his declarations of blindness on others.[56] This section explores the relationship between Paul's narrative arc and his vocation to bring light to Israel and the nations (26:18), continuing to highlight Isaiah's influence along the way. I seek to demonstrate how Paul embodies Israel's movement from *blindness* to *sight* that is most clearly described in Isa 42. After the declaration that the servant will be a light to the nations and one who opens blind eyes (42:6–7) and before God declares his servants are blind (42:18–19), God proclaims, "I will lead the blind in a way (καὶ ἄξω τυφλοὺς ἐν ὁδῷ) they did not know ... I will turn darkness into light for them and the crooked things straight (42:16). Exemplified in Paul, blindness in Israel can be overcome by direct encounter with the risen Lord in a way that enables Israel to carry out its vocation of bringing light to the nations.[57]

5.2.1 Paul's Blindness as Israel's Blindness

Paul is introduced as the archetype of those in Israel who oppose God's purposes and the "many" who fall. It is fitting, then, that the repeated accounts of the Damascus Road

---
[54] Watts, "Consolation," 31–59; cf. Strauss, *Davidic Messiah*, 288–92, who contends that Ben Sira interprets the Isaianic new exodus as delayed (48:22–25).
[55] Schaefer, *Zukunft*, 47–76; Moessner, *Luke*, 292–94.
[56] Hamm, "Paul's Blindness," 64–70.
[57] Ibid., 69–70; Mallen, *Isaiah*, 83.

encounter portray Paul's experience of blindness as intertwined and representative of Israel's corporate lack of sight. Several details in the initial account connect Saul to earlier Isaianic portrayals of blindness in the Third Gospel. First, characters approaching cities provide common settings for blindness to be proclaimed and/or alleviated by Jesus in Luke-Acts. The journey to Damascus anticipates a revelatory confrontation as it aligns Paul with the ignorant disciples, the blind man near Jericho, and Jerusalem—whose eyes are unable to recognize their approaching deliverer (9:3; 22:6; Luke 18:35, 40; 19:41; 24:15, 28). Second, after the encounter with Jesus' light, Saul reflects a posture reminiscent of the disciples on the Emmaus road and Jerusalem, and comparable to what he declares on Israel at the end of Acts. His eyes are opened (ἀνεῳγμένων δὲ τῶν ὀφθαλμῶν αὐτοῦ; cf. Isa 35:5; 42:7), but he cannot see anything (οὐδὲν ἔβλεπεν; cf. 28:26–28).[58] Something prohibits his eyes from proper perception (9:18; cf. Luke 19:42; 24).[59] Therefore, he must be led by the hand (χειραγωγοῦντες) into Damascus (9:8; 22:11; cf. 13:11; Isa 42:16). He enters into a helpless, judged state (9:9). Third, Saul's inability to see, like all prior instances of blindness, is temporary. He experiences Jesus' promised restoration of sight through the mediation of Ananias (9:12, 17–18; 22:13–16; cf. Luke 4:18; 7:22; 18:41–43). The Lord leads Saul from darkness into light, as he promised to do for Israel (Isa 42:16).

Paul's apologetic recounting of this encounter before the Jews of Jerusalem is particularly revealing (22:6–11). Once again, Paul leverages his reorienting encounter with the risen Jesus to defend himself and to persuade them of the veracity of his message. New details paint Paul's experience as emblematic of Isa 59's description of Israel's corruption, judgment, and renewal.[60] Paul specifies that his fall and blindness happened at noon (μεσημβρία), echoing Isaiah's description of how Israel, because of its corruption, will "fall at noon (πεσοῦνται ἐν μεσημβρίᾳ)" as they grope about like the blind and eyeless (Isa 59:10; cf. Deut 28:28–29).[61] Paul notes that "the glory of the light (τῆς δόξης τοῦ φωτός)" caused his inability to see. Isaiah comparably recounts how, though Israel was awaiting light (φῶς), darkness came upon them because of their wrongdoing (Isa 59:9). "Glory" and "light" rarely appear in close proximity in Isaiah, but they do shortly after the aforementioned judgmental words. God promises to alleviate Israel's darkness as God intervenes in righteousness to rectify Israel's unrighteousness (Isa 59:16–60:1; cf. 40:5; 46:13; 49:6; Luke 2:32).[62] Isaiah's emphasis on

---

[58] Though, in some sense, Saul's insight has grown; in his inability to see, "he sees a man in a vision (εἶδεν ἄνδρα ἐν ὁράματι)" who will facilitate the alleviation of his blindness (9:12).
[59] Hamm, "Paul's Blindness," 65; cf. Jervell, *Apostelgeschichte*, 280–81. On λεπίς, see Wilson, *Unmanly Men*, 160; Booth, "Death," 47; cf. Tob 11:7–15; Hartsock, *Sight and Blindness*, 188–96.
[60] Echoes are strengthened when one recalls that Paul is driven by "murder (φόνος)" before his encounter with the Lord (Acts 9:1; cf. Isa 59:7).
[61] CD 1:8–11 similarly "pictures Israel's repentant remnant before the advent of the Teacher of Righteousness, as 'blind persons . . . who grope the way for twenty years'" (Lawrence, *Sense*, 33).
[62] Mallen, *Isaiah*, 66. The final account of this encounter provides additional links to Isaiah's vision for Jerusalem. Paul states that the light that appeared in "the middle of the day (ἡμέρας μέσης)" was "brighter than the sun (τὴν λαμπρότητα τοῦ ἡλίου)" (Acts 26:12–13). Isaiah uses λαμπρότης to describe Zion's future glory (60:3; cf. Bar 4:24; 5:23; Ps 109:3). In that same chapter, the prophet promises Jerusalem that "the sun will not be your light of day (οὐκ ἔσται σοι ἔτι ὁ ἥλιος εἰς φῶς ἡμέρας) . . . but the Lord will be an eternal light for you" (60:19–20).

God's righteous intervention might illumine Ananias' use of "the Righteous One," which is a rare title for Jesus in Luke's two volumes (Acts 3:14; 7:52). Paul, like all Israel, must "look up (ἀνάβλεψον)" to see the Righteous One, call on his name, and serve as witness of the things he "has seen and heard" (22:14–15; cf. 13:47; 17:31; Isa 40:26; 42:6, 18–19; 43:5–13).[63] In the Jewish capital, Paul paints his own experience as Israel's movement from corruption to judgment and then illumination as described by Isaiah. Paul opposed God's way with violence, was judged with blindness, but eventually saw the light and now serves as a witness, as Israel was called to be (cf. Isa 43:8–13; 44:8).[64]

Moreover, the Lord's justification for Saul's reorientation echoes the rationale for Israel's restoration in Isaiah. Saul is God's "chosen instrument" (σκεῦος ἐκλογῆς; cf. προχειρίζω in 22:14; 26:16; LXX Exod 4:13; Josh 3:12; Acts 3:20) to witness before Israel and the nations. For Isaiah as the rest of Israel's Scriptures, God is committed to Israel because God chose (ἐκλέγομαι; ὁ ἐκλεκτός) them to be God's people, servant, and witnesses (42:1; 43:20; 65:9).[65] Despite Israel's waywardness and blindness, God promises to reaffirm their election when they are restored (14:1–2; 41:8–10; 43:8–10; 44:1–2; 45:4; 49:3–10). In other words, God redeems Israel based on God's own prerogative simply because of their election. The same appears to be true for Saul. No other reason is given for his reorientation. Neither an act of repentance nor a response to a message about Jesus precipitates Saul's encounter with the Lord. God simply opens Saul's eyes from God's own initiative by revealing the risen Lord to him.[66] For Luke as for Isaiah, God's commitment to God's chosen people can overcome their infidelity and blindness.

Paul, then, personifies the movement of Israel from darkness to light. He stands in blind opposition to God's plans, experiences judgment, but his blindness is alleviated so that he can bear witness to the nations. Paul embodies the Isaianic principle that, "even though Israel is self-blinded and unfit to be redeemed, the Lord will rescue Israel out of his own compassion and pride and for his own purposes."[67] As it pertains to his eyes, Paul's "fall and rise" appears to be archetypical of the many in Israel who initially fail to see the Lord and the ongoing possibility for their redirection.

5.2.2 Paul's Vocation: "To Open Their Eyes"

The accounts of the Damascus Road encounter describe the relationship between Paul's experience of sightlessness and his subsequent calling and vocation as Jesus' "witness to all people about what you have seen and heard" (22:12–15; cf. 9:15–16).[68] The final reiteration is particularly significant. There, Paul transposes his optical

---

[63] Hamm, "Paul's Blindness," 65–66.
[64] Mallen, *Isaiah*, 81–83.
[65] Kaminsky, *Yet I Loved*, 137–58. Paul affirms Israel's election in Pisidian Antioch (Acts 13:17; cf. Luke 6:13). For other parallels to "chosen instrument," see Conzelmann, *Apostelgeschichte*, 65–66.
[66] Caballero Yoccou, *Hechos*, 2:166.
[67] Stern, "Blind Servant," 227.
[68] On Paul as prophet in Acts, see, e.g., Jervell, "Paulus," 379–86; Litwak, *Echoes*, 181–83; Zhang, *Paul*, 114–15; McWhirter, *Rejected Prophets*, 88; Moessner, *Luke*, 292–301.

transformation from his encounter with Jesus' light onto those with whom he interfaces during his travels (26:12–18).[69] In doing so, Paul most clearly connects his movement from ignorance to enlightenment with Israel and the nations; he continues the work of alleviating ignorance (13:27; 17:23, 30; cf. 3:17; Luke 9:45).[70] Jesus informs Paul that "I have been seen by you (ὤφθην σοι; cf. 9:17; 22:15)" so that Paul might testify to what he saw (εἶδες) and what Jesus will show him (ὀφθήσομαί σοι). Paul receives a calling reminiscent of Jesus' Isaianic vocation (26:17–18; cf. Luke 4:16–21). Jesus sends Paul (ἐγὼ ἀποστέλλω σε) to Israel and the nations with one task: "To open their eyes (ἀνοῖξαι ὀφθαλμοὺς αὐτῶν)" like his were opened (cf. 9:8).[71] This mission has two intended goals (22:18): (1) that they "turn (ἐπιστρέψαι) from darkness to light (ἀπὸ σκότους εἰς φῶς; Isa 42:16) and from the authority of Satan to God," so that (2) "they receive forgiveness of sins and an inheritance (κλῆρον) among those who have been made holy (ἐν τοῖς ἡγιασμένοις) by loyalty to me" (22:18; cf. Isa 49:7; 58:6; 61:1). The language of "darkness to light," shifts in domains of authority, and inheritance evoke Isaiah's second exodus (e.g., Isa 9:2–7; 42:16; 49:1–13; 60:21; 61:7; cf. Exod 6:8).[72] Blindness, then, is not a sign that God has abandoned people. *Instead, those who cannot see are the very people to whom Paul is sent in order to bring them to the domain of God.* He extends God's work of liberating Israel and illuminating the nations by alleviating their inability to perceive Jesus.

Paul reiterates his ongoing commitment to this "heavenly vision" (26:19–23). The reason he stands before Agrippa is for this message that aligns with the prophets and Moses (cf. Luke 16:29–31; 24:27, 44–47; Acts 3:22; 28:23). Paul frames the climactic summary of his mission and message of hope he believes (26:6–8) as a logical progression from the Scriptures: "if the Messiah suffers (εἰ παθητός), if he is the first from the resurrection of the dead (εἰ πρῶτος ἐξ ἀναστάσεως νεκρῶν), then he is going to proclaim light (φῶς μέλλει καταγγέλλειν) both to the people of Israel and to the nations (τῷ τε λαῷ καὶ τοῖς ἔθνεσιν)" (26:23; cf. Luke 17:25).[73] Notably, the proclamation or perception of this light follows the suffering and resurrection of the Messiah. This seems reminiscent of the Emmaus and Damascus roads where direct encounter with the risen Lord, not merely illumination of the Scriptures, leads to sight. Indeed, Paul's inability to persuade Festus and Agrippa suggests that, on its own, teaching this message

---

[69] Hamm, "Paul's Blindness," 67; Gaventa, *Darkness*, 85. The third account of the Damascus Road does not supplant the prior ones but must be read in light of them (Marguerat, *Christian Historian*, 187). On the echoes of prophetic callings, especially Ezekiel's, in Paul's defense before Agrippa, see Allison, "Paul and Ezekiel," 812–19; cf. Bruce, *Book of Acts*, 444. See also Denova, *Things Accomplished*, 178–84, on Paul as a "reluctant prophet."

[70] Again, blindness and ignorance are common to Jews and gentiles alike in Acts (22:18; 26:23).

[71] Contra Johnson, *Acts*, 436–37, εἰς οὕς likely refers to both the people of Israel and the nations, not the gentiles alone, for three main reasons (cf.). First, οὕς is masculine and τῶν ἐθνῶν is neuter. Syntactically, the relative pronoun cannot refer to gentiles alone. Second, Jesus states Paul will go to both Israel and the gentiles (9:15; so, Conzelmann, *Apostelgeschichte*, 149), and Paul informs Agrippa that faithfulness to this vision manifested in proclamation to Jews and gentiles alike (26:20). Third, the mission of opening eyes is intimately tied to the remedying of Israel's blindness in both Isaiah and Luke-Acts.

[72] Cf. 1 Pet 2:9; Philo, *Virtues*, 179; Jos. Asen. 8:10; 15:13; Ps. Sol. 14:18–19 (Gaventa, *Darkness*, 86–87).

[73] Bruce, *Acts*, 447.

from the Scriptures does not enable one to perceive it properly.[74] Nevertheless, Paul's being "a light to the nations" (13:47; cf. Isa 49:6) and his turning to the gentiles do not come at the expense of his ministry to Israel. He continues to work toward opening Jewish eyes even while under arrest and on trial (26:23).[75]

5.2.3 Paul and Elymas

Significantly, Paul never heals physical blindness in Acts. He does inflict it, however, on the Jewish false prophet and magician Bar-Jesus, also called Elymas (Acts 13:4–12). Nevertheless, this confrontation remains within Israel. It reinforces how blindness functions both as judgment and as means of bringing the recalcitrant among God's people to repentance. Elymas is another Jewish character who, like Paul, exemplifies the Isaianic program of moving Israel from darkness to light. Three points buttress this claim. First, Isaianic imagery, especially from Isa 42 and 59, saturates the conflict between Paul and Elymas.[76] Both sections of Isaiah describe Israel's present blindness and unrighteousness (42:18–25; 43:8; 59:8–14), as well as God's intention to heal their blindness and/or restore them to righteousness (42:6–7; 59:16–60:4; cf. 29:15–24; 49:3–10). Luke portrays Elymas with language evocative of Isaiah's description of unrighteous Israel who walks on crooked paths and, therefore, needs redemption. The false prophet "opposes (ἀνθίστατο)" Paul and Barnabas as he attempts to mislead (διαστρέψαι) Sergius Paulus from the faith (13:8; Isa 59:8, 12; cf. Deut 13:1–10). Elymas is an "enemy of all righteousness" who "distorts (διαστρέφων) the straight ways of the Lord." This description recalls Isaiah's declarations that righteousness departed from Israel as the people traveled on crooked paths (Isa 59:8–9, 14; cf. 26:7, 10; 40:3–4; 42:16; 45:13; 64:6). Jesus observed that the crooked and faithless generation continued in Israel during his own time (Luke 9:41; 13:8–10; 20:30; Acts 2:40). Elymas epitomizes this ongoing wickedness—specifically, false prophecy and association with cosmic powers other than Israel's God (idolatry, one might say; cf. Isa 42:8, 17–19)—in Israel and its failure to live up to the covenant vocation as God's servant.[77]

Therefore, Paul declares judgment common against Israel on Elymas. "The hand of the Lord is upon you," Paul asserts. "You will be blind (τυφλός), unable to see (μὴ βλέπων) the sun for a time."[78] Immediately, "mist and darkness fall" on Elymas, and he goes about seeking someone to lead him by the hand (Acts 13:10–11). Elymas reflects Israel's posture prior to the alleviation of blindness as he gropes around "in darkness and in a fog" (Isa 29:18; 59:9–10). Elymas, like Israel as a whole, stands under covenant

---

[74] Similarly, Paul "opens the Scriptures" with the Bereans yet not all of them join (Acts 17:3–4).
[75] Jervell, *Apostelgeschichte*, 543–44, 595–96.
[76] Hamm, "Paul's Blindness," 69–70. For other echoes in Paul's rebuke, see Conzelmann, *Apostelgeschichte*, 81–82; Haenchen, *Acts*, 397–400; Jervell, *Apostelgeschichte*, 346–47.
[77] Cf. Garrett, *Demise*, 79–88; Watts, "Consolation," 44–45.
[78] The hand of the Lord can bring deliverance (e.g., Exod 15:6; Num 11:23; Isa 59:1) or judgment (e.g., Exod 9:3; Josh 22:31; Judg 2:15; Isa 40:2; 51:17).

curses for his wickedness (Deut 28:28-29; cf. 1QS 2:11-19).[79] The allusions to Deuteronomy in Isaiah and Luke suggest that Elymas endures judgment because of his wickedness *as a member of the covenant people*. The punishment is not necessarily expulsion from the people or a consignment to damnation. Rather, wicked Elymas, like the people he participates in, requires liberation from this condition.

Second, the *synkrisis* between Paul and Elymas depicts Elymas as an open-ended, representative character.[80] Of course, Elymas stands in contrast to Paul. Paul is a prophet (13:1). Elymas is a false prophet (13:6). Paul encounters Jesus. Elymas encounters Paul, Jesus' instrument. Paul is led to a street called "Straight" (9:11). Elymas distorts the "straight ways" of the Lord (13:10). Paul is blinded by light. Elymas is blinded by mist and darkness.[81] Luke narrates Paul's healing. Elymas' story concludes with blindness. Elymas functions as a foil for Paul, at least to a degree. In other ways, these two are strikingly similar. Both are known by two names. Both are paradigmatic opponents of the Way of the Lord prior to their blinding encounter and emblematic of certain maladies within Israel. Paul embodies Jewish violence against God's messengers, and Elymas, as a false prophet and magician, reflects Israel's idolatrous tendencies (LXX Jer 33:7-16; 34:7; Zech 13:2; cf. Deut 13:1-5; Isa 42:17-20; 1QS 2:11-19). Both are rendered unable to see during the daytime (13:11; 26:13) and enter a death-like state.[82] Each requires someone to lead them by the hand (9:8; 13:11; 22:11). The key difference is that Paul has guides to interpret his encounter with Jesus, whereas Elymas has yet to find one.[83] Will Elymas' similarities to Paul extend into new sight out of the darkness and fog (Isa 29:18)? Luke refrains from answering.

Third, Luke nonetheless insinuates that, even as a punitive punishment, Elymas' blindness is temporary. The hand of the Lord opposes Elymas "now (νῦν)" and he is unable to see "for a time" (ἄχρι καιροῦ; 13:11; cf. Luke 4:13).[84] Even for a Jewish-Israelite as rebellious as Elymas, blindness is not necessarily an inexorable state. He joins others who have been temporarily judged in Israel and receive or expect a future renewal— figures like Zechariah, Jerusalem, and Paul (Luke 1:20; 13:35; 21:24; cf. 19:42; Acts 9:8-9, 17-18). The metalepsis established by the Isaianic echoes suggests that the wicked and punished Elymas has the potential for reorientation and restoration.[85]

---

[79] Moreover, "[t]he punishment closely recalls that prophesied for the impious and for false prophets (Hos 14:10; Jer 23:12 LXX) and Elymas, like them, becomes enfeebled and stumbles in the dark" (MacNamara, *Chosen Instrument*, 252). See also Conzelmann, *Apostelgeschichte*, 82-83; Barrett, *Acts*, 1:618; Garrett, *Demise*, 82; Hartsock, *Blindness and Sight*, 199.

[80] Hamm, "Paul's Blindness," 69-70; Rius-Camps, *Camino*, 43-49; MacNamara, *Chosen Instrument*, 252-55; Kochenash, "Better Call," 444-46.

[81] Garrett, *Demise*, 84; Parsons, *Acts*, 190.

[82] Homer often uses ἀχλύς to describe loss of sight at death (Barrett, *Acts*, 1:618; Hartsock, *Blindness and Sight*, 199; Booth, "Death," 52-54).

[83] Notably, *all* characters—except Jesus, the interpreter *par excellence*—need interpretive guides in Luke-Acts (Frein, "Misunderstanding," 429-48; Dinkler, "Interpreting," 423).

[84] There is no reason to see the time limit as "stylistically secondary" (contra Conzelmann, *Apostelgeschichte*, 82-83). Moreover, the limitation and *synkrisis* with Paul caution against reading Elymas' representative blindness in stark contrast with the perceptive representative gentile, Sergius Paulus (cf. Haenchen, *Acts*, 403). Gentiles, too, reside in darkness in Acts (14:14-18; 17:29-31; 26:17-18).

[85] *Metalepsis* is the theory that referring to another text brings the wider context of the cited text into the text that cites it (Hays, *Echoes*, 10-11). It brings an established figuration into a new figuration.

Elymas falls into the condition that God promises to alleviate for those despairing in Israel in Isaiah (Isa 29:18–20; 42:16). Especially through the echoes of Isaiah, the account of Elymas illumines the nature of judgment against Israel in Luke-Acts. On the one hand stands the judgment of God's enemies who oppose righteousness (e.g., Luke 19:27; 20:43; Acts 2:35). Elymas does not simply receive judgment. His judged state embodies Israel's current state, one that the Lord has promised to repair.[86] On the other stands Jesus' advocacy for overcoming opponents or the wayward in Israel through love, as God did with Paul (Luke 6:27–35).[87] In light of these parallels, Paul's judgment of Elymas likely involves a reorienting purpose analogous to what Paul experienced. That is, Luke gives reason to imagine that punitive blindness initiates movement toward light. Once again, there is possibility for redirection through temporary judgment for wayward Israel.

The identification of Elymas as a "son of the devil" ironically reinforces the possibility of his redemption, while still carrying the threat of utter removal from the people. Luke-Acts depicts both fates for those connected to Satan. On the one hand, the devil removes the word so people cannot be saved and misleads members of Israel and the Way into destruction (Luke 8:12; 22:3; Acts 5:3). On the other, many are freed from Satan's control (Luke 13:16; 22:31; Acts 10:38; 26:18). The strong man is being overpowered (Luke 11:20–21). Indeed, guiding Jews and gentiles from Satan's domain to God's by opening their eyes is central to Paul's calling (Acts 26:18). Moreover, Paul's words are analogous to John the Baptist's rebuke of the crowds who came to him (Luke 3:7–9; cf. 6:35; 20:36). John calls his audience "offspring of vipers" imperiled by future wrath. In doing so, he calls them to repent and behave like children of Abraham. The "descent" metaphor describes neither a stagnant nor an ontological category. Rather, it is another way of referring to Israel's repentance-journey. It calls the people to change their ways and behave like the people of God should. They ought to live like Abraham. Paul's statement need not be a description of Elymas' nature or permanent fate. It is a comment about his current behavior and posture toward God. Elymas behaves like the devil by distorting God's ways and leading people astray.[88] Additionally, Elymas' similarities with Simon Magus recall how Peter's damning remarks against the other magician were in pursuit of repentance and salvation (Acts 8:18–24). Like Simon, the possibility of being forgiven remains if Elymas responds with repentance. In summation, by rebuking Elymas as a "son of the devil" and (temporarily) consigning him to blindness, Paul implicitly calls Elymas to begin the journey of repentance to

---

[86] "In Isaiah ... a common theme includes God (or God's servants) figuratively blinding Israel (e.g., Isa 6:9–10; 29:10) and in turn offering sight (e.g., Isa 29:18; 35:5–6; 42:6–7). God also more explicitly 'blinds' a number of men due to their disobedience. Deuteronomy 28:28–29, for example, maintains that God inflicts blindness (and additional physical vulnerability) on those who fail to follow the Law. In such accounts, blinding points to a power differential and highlights a favorite theme found throughout Jewish Scripture, namely, the all-powerful nature of the God of Israel. God can both blind (e.g., Exod 4:11) and restore sight (e.g., Ps 146:8), and both these acts demonstrate God's power" (Wilson, *Unmanly Men*, 168–69).
[87] Kuecker, "Theosis," 219–24.
[88] Sacchi, *Jewish Apocalyptic*, 211–32; Blumhofer, *Future*, 157.

become the "son of Jesus" that his name portends.[89] Even in judgment against the most wicked in Israel, Paul acts for the sake of reorienting Israel toward Jesus' light.

5.2.4 Summary

Acts presents Paul's narrative as an embodiment of recalcitrant, blind Israel as described memorably by Isaiah. Paul personifies God's interactions with unseeing, stubborn Israel. He persecuted God's Way and, as a result, was blinded in judgment, though his eyes remained open. This punishment, though, facilitated Paul's movement to sight. A direct encounter with the risen Jesus (re)enabled his vision as Paul was raised anew for his prophetic task (9:1–19; 22:6–21; 26:12–23; cf. 13:47). Paul extends this reorienting movement to those he encounters in his ministry, Jews and gentiles alike, seeking to bring them from darkness to light. Even when he proclaims blindness on the disobedient Elymas, hope for deliverance reverberates. Paul's pronouncements of judgment on hostile Jews remain open-ended; they do not preclude repentance or the opening of blind eyes. If one as opposed to God's ways as Elymas has hope, similar expectations remain for those not as bad as him, including the divided Jewish leaders at the conclusion of Acts.

5.3 Blindness at the End of Acts

In light of Isaiah's formative influence on Luke's blind Israel motif, I now turn to examine the final scenes and Isaianic citation in Acts. I seek to demonstrate that, at the book's conclusion, anticipation that Israel's Lord will remedy of Israel's inability to see continues. Luke's use of Isaiah's blindness motif underscores that blindness is temporary. Jesus is quite capable of bringing Israel to light, although it might be complicated by Israel's infidelity. That is, restoration of sight might take Jesus' direct intervention, as was necessary with Paul. Israel might require an encounter with Jesus to see his light. In Rome, Paul uses Isaiah (and Ezekiel) to warn about the threat of judgment associated with ongoing blindness in divided Israel. Nevertheless, the ending of Acts remains optimistic, expectant even, about Israel's future healing. The potential that Israel is reoriented from blindness to sight, from darkness to light like Paul remains, as it was for Elymas. Moreover, to the end Paul continues to self-identify with the Jewish people. He is innocent of charges that he besmirches or eschews the people or their customs. For Paul, they are still "my nation." The enchained Paul continues to identify with the Jewish people in their exile in Rome. Therefore, Acts depicts Paul's use of Isaiah in

---

[89] The historical Paul provides an analogy when he exhorts the Corinthians to hand a person over to Satan so that he might be saved (1 Cor 5:5). I am not suggesting that Luke draws from this Pauline text; I simply note the analogy. For a comparable reading of the Johannine Jesus' infamous comments that "the Jews" are children of the devil (John 8:44), see Blumhofer, *Future*, 153–59. Blumhofer's bottom line is worth citing for its similarities to my claim about Elymas: "*inherent to the charges in John that a person or group acts under the power of the devil is an awareness that the primary role of the devil or a demon is to prevent Israel from embracing its identity as the people of God*" (158, original italics).

continuity with the prophetic tradition wherein proclamations of judgment are coupled with calls to repent and expectations for Israel's restoration.[90]

5.3.1 Paul's Prophetic Posture

In his initial meeting with the Jewish leadership in Rome, Paul mounts a preliminary defense (28:17-22). His apology frames their engagement as internecine. Paul's words demonstrate that his definition of *Israel* vis-à-vis the Jewish people and his relationship to this people and their ancestral customs are unchanged. The terms *brothers*, *Jews*, and *Israel* stand in parallel and in contrast to *Romans* (28:17-20).[91] The Jewish people for Paul remain "my nation," Israel, against whom he brings no charge, and for whose national hope he wears chains.[92] Moreover, Paul reiterates that he has done nothing against "the people or the ancestral customs" (cf. 21:28). Despite all he has faced from his brethren in his journeys, the Lukan Paul reaffirms that he neither speaks against nor acts against the Jewish people. This proclaimed commitment to Israel's hope, people, and customs should color how one reads his final words to these leaders. If Paul's claims are to be believed, his rebuke should not be read as an attack or rejection of the people. Interpreting it as such seems to run contrary to the entire preceding narrative.[93]

Indeed, the terse description of Paul's subsequent interaction aligns his preaching within Israel's history and casts him as a prophet who preaches judgment and consolation to foster reform among the Jewish people. To the many that gather three days later, Paul "was explaining (ἐξετίθετο) by testifying (διαμαρτυρόμενος) to the kingdom of God and persuading (πείθων) about Jesus from the Torah of Moses and the prophets from early morning until night" (28:23). Each verb merits brief comment. First, two of the four uses of ἐκτίθημι in Luke-Acts describe Jewish Jesus-followers explaining the acts of God in Jesus more accurately to other Jewish Jesus-followers (11:4; 18:26; cf. 7:21). This reaffirms an internecine conversation: Paul seeks to educate his brethren about Israel's hope to bring them to greater illumination on Israel's repentance-journey.

Second, διαμαρτύρομαι often summarizes preaching about Jesus and is usually accompanied by warnings about impending judgment (2:40; 8:25; 18:5; 20:21-24; 23:11; cf. Luke 16:28). Though oriented toward Jesus, such usage conforms to the LXX's use of this term to alert listeners to the consequences associated with ignoring a prophet's voice (e.g., Jer 6:10; Ezek 16:2; 20:4; Mal 2:14; cf. Pss 49:7; 80:9; 2 Chr 24:19; 2 Esd 9:26, 34). Third, πείθω typically refers to (successful) attempts to convince Jews about the message of Jesus (e.g., Acts 13:43; 17:4; 18:4; 19:8, 26; 26:28; cf. Luke 16:31; 20:6). This usage resonates with the LXX, especially Isaiah (e.g., Isa 8:17; 10:20; 12:2;

---

[90] Boesenberg, "Prophetic Rebuke," 7-11; Moessner, *Luke*, 301.
[91] Paul declares blindness on all the Jewish leaders, not just the "disbelieving" ones so as to identify "true Israel" from those now removed from the people (Fusco, "Israel," 6; *pace* Lohfink, *Sammlung*, 61). *All* Israel, persuaded and disbelieving, is God's people. Corporate Israel remains blind and suffers together. This includes Paul who bears chains in the empire's capital.
[92] Although he understands "the hope of Israel" through the lens of Jesus of Nazareth, unlike these Jewish leaders, Paul seems to assume some degree of mutual understanding and agreement about the content of Israel's hope (cf. Chance, *Jerusalem*, 127-38; Haacker, "Bekenntnis," 440-45).
[93] Cf., e.g., Conzelmann, *Apostelgeschichte*, 159-60; Haenchen, *Acts*, 722-24; Caballero Yoccou, *Hechoes*, 2:223.

20:5–6; 30:3, 12, 15; 33:2; 42:17; 50:10; 59:4), which uses this term to describe the source of Israel's confidence, either in Israel's God or something else (e.g., Deut 33:12; Pss 48:7; 56:2; Hab 2:18; Zeph 3:2; Tob 14:4).[94] Luke's verbiage reinforces how Paul speaks as a prophet who calls his people to reform by receiving God's recent actions in Jesus. Paul preaches the same twofold prophetic message common to Luke-Acts: He attests to the kingdom of God, which lies at the center of Israel's hopes (cf. 1:6; Luke 1:33; 24:21), and to Jesus, Israel's messianic king.

Paul's message receives divided results, as per usual. Some Jews are persuaded (οἱ ἐπείθοντο) and others disbelieve (οἱ ἠπίστουν). Notably, though, they disagree with one another (28:24–25; cf. 14:1–2).[95] Their posture is reminiscent of the disciples at the end of the Third Gospel. Three links establish this connection. First, Paul, like Jesus, has expounded on Jesus' messianic identity from the Torah and the prophets (28:23; cf. Luke 24:27, 44–47). Jesus' disciples constantly struggled to comprehend this notion prior to Jesus' act of opening their minds (cf. 9:44–45; 18:34).[96] It is unsurprising, then, that these Roman Jews who know little about the Way have a difficult time understanding as well (Acts 28:21–22). Second, the only other uses of ἀπιστέω in Luke-Acts refer to the apostles' failures to believe (Luke 24:11, 41; cf. ἄπιστος in Luke 9:41; 12:46; Acts 26:8). Third, Luke emphasizes internal disagreement. As with the disciples, some of the Jewish leaders respond more faithfully than others to the scriptural testimony about Jesus. Sans the direct presence of the risen Lord, Paul's exposition of Scripture is only semi-effective in persuading his audience. The parallels with the disciples suggest that, once again, this instance of Israel imperceptiveness can be remedied by intervention from Israel's Lord.[97]

5.3.2 Isaianic Expectation amidst Judgment

The mixed response leads to Paul's word (ῥῆμα) from Isaiah (28:26–27; Isa 6:9–10). His warning reiterates how Israel's blind obstinacy will lead to comparable judgment as in past generations.[98] Two salient observations about LXX Isaiah in its wider context

---

[94] Armstrong, "Jewish Response," 262. The reciprocal ἀπειθέω refers to lack of persuasion or obstinacy toward God's messengers (e.g., Isa 59:13; 63:10; 65:2; Acts 14:2; 19:9). See Jensen, "Some Unpersuasive Glosses," 397–401, 403.
[95] Marguerat, "Enigma," 288–89.
[96] Steyn, *Septuagint*, 213; Schwemer, "Auferstandene," 113–14. The mention of the gentiles as part of God's mission further links the two texts.
[97] Fusco, "Israel," 16.
[98] As Litwak observes, "There is nothing in this text, however, which points to fulfillment. Paul explicitly states that the quotation was directed to 'your fathers', while the message is directed to Paul's audience, as suggested by the phrase, 'be it known to you'. Paul treats the citation, not as prophecy directed towards his audience, but as characterization of them analogously" (*Echoes*, 184; cf. Koet, *Five Studies*, 133; Vahrenhorst, "Gift," 165; contra Haenchen, *Acts*, 724). Furthermore, by saying, "your fathers," Paul is not excluding himself from the Jewish people. Like Stephen, he states that they are (or risk being) the descendants (i.e., in the likeness of) of those who opposed Isaiah's message. Paul, in contrast, is not like those who rejected Isaiah's message. Thus, a call to repent is implicit (Boesenberg, "Prophetic Rebuke," 11; Troy M. Troftgruben, *A Conclusion Unhindered: A Study of the Ending of Acts within Its Literary Environment*, WUNT 2/280 [Tübingen: Mohr Siebeck, 2010], 127–30). Interestingly, some manuscripts read "our fathers" (Pervo, *Acts*, 680).

suggest ongoing hope for the healing of Israel's blindness and the restoration of the people.[99] First, Isaiah's mission—and therefore Paul's—is not as harsh in the LXX as in the MT. In the Hebrew, Isaiah preaches for the purpose of hardening Israel; in the Greek hardening (παχύνω; cf. Deut 32:15) is the result of Isaiah's preaching and the people's stubborn refusal to repent.[100] They have shut (ἐκάμμυσαν) their eyes (Isa 33:15; cf. 29:10). Nevertheless, the LXX hopes that Israel's Lord "will heal them (ἰάσομαι αὐτούς)" should their eyes see, their ears listen, and their hearts understand (Isa 6:10; Acts 28:27). The prophet still preaches in the expectation the people change their ways (or be changed) and be restored. As God contributes to Israel's blindness (Isa 29:10), so too God facilitates the opening of Israel's eyes (29:18).[101] Second, in context, God calls Isaiah to preach to a people who will be chastised for their imperceptions and infidelity (cf. Jer 5:21–24). Still, Israel's judgment, its blind state, is temporary: "right after proclaiming the blindness of the people, the text adds: 'until when, Lord?' (Is. 6:11a). The answer confirms the punishment, but also states that it will come to an end (Is. 6:11b–13)."[102] Israel's chastisement is not necessarily exclusionary but purifying. It facilitates the people's reorientation toward God (e.g., 42:1–44:28; cf. 19:22). The movement of Isaiah reinforces this point as blindness and exile are not the last words for Israel. Light and restoration are.[103]

Luke's reading and use of Isaiah in shaping the blindness-sight motif in the *Doppelwerk* suggests that Isaiah's expectation for Israel's renewal continues at the end of Acts. This is most visible in the similarities between the Jewish people in Rome as described by Paul's quotation of Isa 6:9–10 and wider Israel as depicted throughout Luke-Acts, including the disciples and Paul. Israel in Rome cannot understand, akin to the apostles prior to Jesus opening their minds (Luke 18:34; 24:45; cf. 2:50; 8:10). As with Moses, Israel under foreign rule cannot recognize God's agent of redemption (Acts 7:25). Israel's heart remains slow to believe (cf. Luke 24:25–26). Like the disciples who struggled to recognize the risen Jesus (Luke 24:12, 24, 39–41; cf. 7:22) and Paul prior to his reorientation (Acts 9:8–9; cf. 26:13), their eyes look but cannot see. This people have closed their eyes. Otherwise, they would repent in order to be healed (28:27). Yet, Israel's Lord can open closed eyes (24:31–32, 45), even without the prior repentance of rebellious Jewish-Israelites (Acts 9:7; cf. 26:18). As in Isaiah, God's initiative can bring healing of sight and renewal to the people despite stubborn

---

[99] For more in-depth explorations of the differences in the Greek and Hebrew versions of Isa 6:9–10 and their impact on reading the end of Acts, see Martin Karrer, "'Und ich werde sie heilen': Das Verstockungsmotiv aus Jes 6, 9f. in Apg 28, 26f.," in *Kirche und Volk Gottes, Festschrift für Jürgen Roloff zum 70. Geburtstag*, ed. Martin Karrer, Wolfgang Kraus, and Otto Merk (Neukirchen-Vluyn: Neukirchener, 2000), 255–71; Mittmann, "Polemik," 523–27; Koet, "Isaiah," 95–97; Boesenberg "Prophetic Rebuke," 8–11. Cf. Enno Edzard Popkes, "Die letzten Worte des lukanischen Paulus: Zur Bedeutung von Act 28, 25–28 für das Paulusbild der Apostelgeschichte," in *Die Apostelgeschichte im Kontext antiker und frühchristlicher Historiographie*, ed. Jörg Frey, Clare K. Rothschild, and Jens Schröter (Berlin: de Gruyter, 2009), 605–26.

[100] Fusco, "Israel," 7; cf. Isa 63:17–19; Mittmann, "Polemik," 524.

[101] Carroll, "Blindsight," 82–84; Hartsock, *Blindness and Sight*, 128.

[102] Fusco, "Israel," 7. God continues on to describe that new life will emerge from Israel's stump (Isa 6:13; Litwak, *Echoes*, 192; Boesenberg, "Prophetic Rebuke," 8–9).

[103] Gregory, "Postexilic Exile," 492–95; Kinzer, *Jerusalem*, 145–47.

opposition (Isa 35:5; 42:1–9; 49:5–6; cf. Ezek 37:12–13). For Luke, an encounter with Jesus can reorient from darkness to light, as it did with Paul. It seems that, like Jerusalem and Elymas, inability to see is again temporary (Luke 13:35; Acts 13:11; cf. Luke 18:43). The Jewish people continue in the same condition of blindness common to God's people. Therefore, the same potential for redirection toward the light of the Lord remains. Luke's use of Isa 6 corresponds well with early Jewish reception history of this prophetic text: Expectations for restoration persist for obstinate Israel, even in and through judgment.[104]

5.3.3 Paul's Last Word and Actions

The anticipated healing of Israel's blindness is reinforced by Paul's final words and activity in Rome. "Therefore," he declares, "let it be known to you that this salvation of God (τὸ σωτήριον τοῦ θεοῦ) was sent (ἀπεστάλη) to the gentiles; they also will hear (αὐτοὶ καὶ ἀκούσονται)" (28:28). Paul's words echo Isaiah and Ezekiel.[105] These prophets combine to reinforce Paul's warning as one of purifying judgment amidst ongoing proclamation and expectations for restoration. The immediate context of Isa 6 highlights how Israel heard but did not respond, much like Paul's mixed hearers in Rome (28:22–24). In a section similar to Isaiah's commission, God describes to Ezekiel Israel's continued obstinacy and refusal to hear and perceive God's words (Ezek 2:3–3:4). God informs Ezekiel that, if God sent (ἐξαποστέλλω) the prophet to foreigners, "they might have listened to you (οὗτοι ἂν εἰσήκουσάν σου)."[106] Israel, in contrast, will continue to refuse to listen to the prophet (LXX Ezek 3:6–7). Nevertheless, God still strengthens and commissions Ezekiel to continue to speak to "your people (τοῦ λαοῦ σου)," the house of Israel in the Babylonian exile, regardless of their receptivity (3:8–11). Israel remains obstinate throughout Ezekiel. Nevertheless, this people's redemption, the prophet describes, eventually will come by God's initiative, not due to Israel's acts of repentance. God will redeem Israel *in spite of* the people's infidelity and imperceptiveness.[107] The echoes of Ezekiel reiterate that, as was necessary for Paul, Israel might require a divine act to bring them from darkness to light. Moreover, Paul, akin to Ezekiel in Babylon, is in Rome, the capital of the new empire that again destroys

---

[104] For summaries, see Evans, *To See*, 163–66; Vahrenhorst, "Gift," 146–59.

[105] Litwak, *Echoes*, 188–92. For grammatical and contextual arguments for translating αὐτοὶ καὶ ἀκούσονται as "they also will hear," see John Nolland, "Luke's Readers – A Study of Luke 4.22–8; Acts 13.46; 18,6; 28.28 and Luke 21.5–36" (PhD diss., University of Cambridge, 1977), 106–13.

[106] The overarching narrative of Acts denies that gentiles inherently hear or receive the message better than Jews do. They are comparably divided by the message, that is, if they can even comprehend it at all (e.g., 13:50; 14:14–20; 17:30–32; 26:24). As Nolland observes, there is a consistent parallel between Jews and Gentiles hearing the message of salvation concomitantly (e.g., Acts 13:16, 26)—rather than merely sequentially (13:46)—in the cities Paul visits and that both groups divide over Paul's message ("Luke's Readers," 108–111). Gentile division throughout Acts, then, suggests hearing Paul's words as commenting more on Israel's continued contentious state than on gentile receptivity or a change in mission.

[107] Paul Joyce, *Divine Initiative and Human Response in Ezekiel*, JSOTSup 51 (Sheffield: Sheffield Academic, 1989), 128–39; Tova Ganzel, "The Descriptions of the Restoration of Israel in Ezekiel," VT 60 (2010): 197–211. I am indebted to Reed Metcalf for this point and directing me to these works. See also Oliver, *Eschatology*, 85–89.

Jerusalem and exiles Israel. The Lukan Paul's narrative ends in exile with his people, proclaiming a message of judgment and consolation.[108]

Further solidifying expectations for restoration and Paul's ongoing solidarity with the Jewish people, the phrase τὸ σωτήριον τοῦ θεοῦ recalls the programmatic citation of Isa 40 that introduced John's ministry of calling Israel to repentance (Isa 40:5; Luke 3:6; Acts 28:28), as well as Simeon's vision for Israel's and the nations' illumination (Luke 2:30–32).[109] The "all" whom Paul welcomes solidifies this echo (28:30–31). It is reminiscent of the "all flesh" that will see salvation as part of God's activity to "comfort" Israel (Isa 40:1–5). Paul's actions further reinforce how the salvation of the gentiles does not come at the expense of Israel since the "all" to whom Paul preaches includes Jews. As in Isaiah, salvation for the gentiles does not mean Israel's restoration is forsaken.[110] God, through Paul, continues to reach out to the contrarian people (Isa 65:1).

After declaring Isaiah's judgment and the impending punishment upon Israel, then, Paul alludes to Isaiah's declarations of comfort for Israel, which culminate in all flesh (Jewish and gentile) seeing the glory of God and salvation (cf. Isa 49:6). Salvation's movement to the gentiles warns Israel that the eschatological age has now dawned; hence, there is the risk of judgment but not to the exclusion of confidence for the Jewish people's restoration. Many in Israel are blind, yet blindness in Israel can be overcome by Jesus.[111] What Israel might need to accomplish this is an experience like Paul's, whereby the Lord acts decisively to reorient Israel from darkness to light.

Excursus: Turning to the Gentiles

A few remarks about the turns to the gentiles in Luke-Acts are in order. Much has been written on this topic, so my comments are brief.[112] To begin, Jesus's reference

---

[108] Seemingly representative of the nation's exilic experience after 70 CE, Paul bears Roman chains in the imperial capital. Observing the parallels between Paul at the end of Acts and the conclusion of the Deuteronomistic history, Litwak notes, "In both cases, we have Israelites, who are prisoners, far from home, under house arrest. Both texts end abruptly. In both cases, economic aspects are described. Jehoiachin is regularly in the king's presence, while Paul is waiting to appear before the emperor ... The ending of 4 Kingdoms is not just about Jehoiachin, but Jehoiachin as a representative of God's people in captivity in Babylon" (*Echoes*, 198–99; cf. Schmidt, "Abkehr," 421–24). Paul retains solidarity with Israel, even in the experience of exile. In this way, he is parallels Jesus' identification with the destruction of Jerusalem (cf. Kinzer, *Jerusalem*, 21–58).

[109] The phrase is rare in the LXX (Ps 49:23; 97:3; Isa 38:11; 40:5). For an expanded examination of these echoes and their intertextual effects, see Litwak, *Echoes*, 191–92.

[110] Blindness "has not led Paul or others to abandon the Jews before, any more than God stopped sending prophets after Isaiah because Israel rejected Isaiah's message. Rather, since Isaiah was told to go and speak to Israel this message at the start of his prophetic ministry, and went on to preach to Israel afterwards, Luke's audience would assume that preaching to Jews would go on. Paul had not failed any more than Isaiah had failed. The 'mission' to the Jews had not failed any more than Isaiah's mission to Israel" (Litwak, *Echoes*, 187–88; similarly, O'Toole, "Reflections," 447–48; Alexander, "Political Vision," 293; González, *Hechos*, 174–75; Troftgruben, *Conclusion*, 27–28; contra Jervell, *Apostelgeschichte*, 631).

[111] See Koet, *Five Studies*, 128–31; cf. Beers, *The Followers of Jesus*, 174–75. Once again, according to Acts, Jesus' remedying of blindness is non-coercive; it is healing and transformative.

[112] See Armstrong, "End of Acts," *passim*, for various readings of the turns to the gentiles in relation to the book's conclusion.

to Elijah and Elisha establishes the precedence of movement to the gentiles (Luke 4:24–29). The metaleptic effect of Jesus's appeal to Elijah and Elisha insinuates that infidelity in Israel is a central reason for God's sending these prophets to gentiles (cf. 1 Kgs 16:29–34; 2 Kgs 5:1–19). Israel stands in a state of unworthiness as they reject the prophets and risk judgment as a result.[113] Nevertheless, healing gentiles does not entail the abandonment of Israel. Elijah confronts Israel's idolatry immediately after caring for the widow of Zarephath (1 Kgs 18), and, prior to the healing of Naaman, Elisha raises the son of the Shunammite woman, an Israelite (2 Kgs 4:8–37). Jesus and Paul similarly return to or remain near Jewish space and continue to persuade Jewish people immediately after they declare turns to the gentiles (Luke 4:31; Acts 13:46; 14:1; 18:6–8; 19:9–10; 28:30–31).[114] Never do they leave Jews or Jewish space entirely or permanently.

Paul's turnings are particularly saturated with prophetic imagery. These echoes reiterate that these are warnings of judgment, not the desertion of Israel. In Pisidian Antioch, certain Jews embody Simeon's Isaianic words as they "speak against (ἀντέλεγον)" Paul's and Barnabas's words (cf. Isa 65:2; Luke 2:34; Acts 28:19, 22). Paul and Barnabas thus "turn (στρεφόμεθα; cf. Isa 63:10; Acts 7:42) to the gentiles" (13:46; 18:6; cf. 22:21). Reinforcing the notion that this is a prophetic warning of judgment, the phrase εἰς τὰ ἔθνη first appears in Jesus's predictions of Jerusalem's destruction and exile, which also has an expiration date (Luke 21:24). Paul's quotation from Isaiah also occurs in the context of Israel's restoration from exile as integral to the servant's mission (Isa 49:5–7; cf. 42:6–7; 62:1). The servant's outreach to the gentiles is connected to the service to Israel. The rest of the narrative, namely, that Paul repeatedly returns to Jewish spaces (e.g., 14:1), affirms that Paul's mission to the gentiles, as for Isaiah's servant Isaiah, does not come at Israel's expense.[115] That Paul omits Isaiah's phrase "a covenant for the nation" reiterates that these Jews risk excluding themselves from Israel's restoration to life should they persist in rebellion (13:46).[116] The Jew-gentile missions remain intertwined. Certain Jews in this city may face judgment (Acts 13:50–51; 18:6; cf. Luke 9:5; 10:10–12), but the

---

[113] In Elijah's day, judgment came in the form of drought (1 Kgs 17:1). In Elisha's is the destruction wrought by Hazael (2 Kgs 8:11–13). I am not suggesting the gentiles receive salvation *only* due to Jewish obstinacy toward the message of Jesus. Rather, the declarations about going to the gentiles concomitantly warn Israel that its members risk exclusion from restoration. This can stand alongside the claim that these passages justify the gentile mission.

[114] Brawley, *Jews*, 71–76; McWhirter, *Rejected Prophets*, 49; cf. Tannehill, *Shape*, 3–30. The implied indictment of Israel provides an alternative rationale for why Jews take offense to going to the gentiles than the common assumption that Jews simply were antagonistic to the gentile mission due to xenophobia.

[115] Acts 13:47 quotes Isa 49:6 LXX, "where the gentiles themselves are directly addressed and are invited to listen to the Servant. In a direct word from the Lord (49:6) a new explanation of the Servant's task is given: alongside his task for Israel, he has likewise a mission for the gentiles … It is important, however, to note that in Isaiah the Servant's being a light for the gentiles is not at the expense of his mission toward Israel, but an extension of that task (see also Isa 49:7–13)" (Koet, "Isaiah," 94).

[116] "Within those Jewish circles harsh words were not necessarily understood as a rejection. We have a clear-cut example in this text. As we saw above, the quotation from Habakkuk sounds quite negative (13:41), but the reaction is a positive one (13:42–43)" (Koet, "Isaiah," 94; cf. van de Sandt, "Quotations," 45–46).

mission to Israel as a whole persists.[117] Similarly, when Paul alludes to Ezekiel in Corinth to explain his movement to the gentiles (18:6; cf. Ezek 33:1–9), he casts himself as the watchman to Israel who warns the people who risk being judged for their sins.[118] Nevertheless, the warning remains for Israel and its repentance (cf. 18:7–8).

Moreover, four differences between the final turning and the first two (13:46-47; 18:6) highlight the open-ended nature of Paul's comments toward the Jewish leaders in Rome. First, opposition against or animosity toward Paul himself is absent the final scene. Jewish internal division is the focal point. Second, there is no negative statement or symbolic action given as a sign of judgment (cf. 13:46; 18:6).[119] Third, Paul himself does not turn to the gentiles. He informs them that salvation was sent (ἀπεστάλη) to the gentiles, something that has begun in the narrative itself. It seems more like a declarative statement or an apocalyptic warning than a change in mission. Fourth, Paul continues to preach to all people, which likely includes Jews and gentiles. That he does not enter Jewish space is easily explained by his being on house arrest. At the end of the narrative, Jews remain divided into various groups because of Paul's preaching. Despite this, Paul continues to reach out to them.

In short, like past prophets to Israel, the prophet Paul (Acts 13:1–2) turns to the gentiles as an implicit prophetic warning of judgments against Israel for its infidelity (cf. Ezek 3:5–7). However, these warnings and turnings do not entail abandonment of the Jewish people. Even after turning, the prophets continue to minister to Israel, never abandoning the people entirely. Like the Isaianic Servant, the additional mission to the gentiles does not come at the expense of Jews. Paul continues to minister in and to Israel, seeking repentance and warning of judgment. Like his predecessors, Paul calls for the people to repent and reform, specifically by receiving the message of Jesus. He brings words of judgment along with the message of repentance, hope, and consolation. Paul engenders a degree of social separation from (some) Jews in particular locales, but he continues his prophetic ministry to them as a whole in that region and others.

5.3.4 Summary

In the end, Acts again defends Paul (and, in so doing, insinuates the narrative's own perspective) from charges of repudiating the Jewish people or their customs, even in his final prophetic word from Isaiah. Luke's Paul continues to be a Jewish-Israelite

---

[117] Koet, "Isaiah," 94. Likewise, Paul in Ephesus continues to preach to "Jews and Greeks" after leaving the wider Jewish community (19:9–10). On shaking dust off oneself as prophetic warnings of judgment, as well as on the turnings, see Brawley, *Jews*, 74–81.

[118] Moessner, *Luke*, 300; Burfeind, "Paulus," 79. Boda similarly notes that Ezekiel's words help preserve the remnant of Israel after the destruction of Jerusalem (*Return*, 90–93).

[119] Luke also abstains from specifying Paul's tone or motives in the turns to the gentiles. This silence is notable since Luke records emotions in Paul's responses elsewhere, even in preaching (e.g., 16:18; 17:16). It is possible to read Paul speaking in frustration to the mixed Jewish response, but reading his tone as sorrowful seems equally plausible (cf. Luke 19:41–41).

speaking prophetically to other Jewish-Israelites about their ancestral custom, judgment and consolation, and the direction for God's people, Israel.[120] As has been the case throughout Luke-Acts, Israel continues to find it difficult to see Jesus' light. "This people" Israel at the end of Acts resembles Isaiah's blind Israel—especially as embodied by the disciples and Paul—whose lack of sight Jesus proleptically remedies. Israel continues to be God's blind servant in need of moving from darkness to light. Therefore, Paul's use of Isaiah and Ezekiel indicate that, although the threat of judgment lingers over unseeing Israel, confidence for the alleviation of blindness continues. Israel's healing might only come through direct intervention from the Lord's actions to reorient them, but Luke's narration of blindness in Israel gives good reasons to expect this will happen.

5.4 Conclusion

This chapter explored how Isaiah shapes Luke's depiction of Israel's blindness in order to demonstrate that expectant hope for the restoration of the Jewish people persists through the end of the book. Fusco provides an apt summary: for Luke, "the theologoumenon of blindness is the interpretative key to the scandal of Israel's unbelief, yet always with the additional note of final salvation."[121] Four primary points evince this, particularly as they were embodied in representative characters—the disciples, the blind beggar, Jerusalem, Elymas, and, most notably, Paul. First, all Israel is blind to a degree, including some of the righteous and those closest to Jesus. Yet, Luke's narrative conditions the reader to see blindness as a transient condition. Second, inability to see stems from disobedience, disbelief, as well as prophetic preaching. However, for Luke as for Isaiah, Israel remains God's people, even in blindness and as they are called to move from darkness to light as part of Israel's repentance-journey. Third, should they fail to respond rightly, blind obstinacy leads to judgment. Such judgment, however, is not necessarily exclusionary or condemnatory.[122] It often bears a reorienting, purifying function. Indeed, no character in Luke-Acts is consigned to blindness without the potential that they might see properly down the road. Fourth, Jesus demonstrates his ability to open Israel's eyes, even without the initial repentance of the recalcitrant. Jesus repeatedly evinces his ability to intervene as God's servant who restores God's blind servant Israel out of his own volition.

Nowhere is this more visible than in Paul. His narrative arc, which he proclaims to the Jewish world, evinces how God can reorient disobedient Israel to see the Lord's light. To the end of his two volumes, Luke continues to identify Paul and his story as intimately intertwined with wayward, divided Israel's, confirming Paul's (and Acts') innocence of the charges of repudiating the Jewish people. This deep connection,

---

[120] Boesenberg, "Prophetic Rebuke," 7–11; Moessner, *Luke*, 301.

[121] Fusco, "Israel," 16.

[122] To reiterate, the threat of exclusion still lingers and the risk of being cut off from Israel persists through the end of the narrative. Nevertheless, standing alongside these threats is the hope for renewed sight for the people as a whole and even for blind, obstinate individuals in Israel.

coupled with the motif of temporary blindness, implies that the expectation for Israel's restoration continues through Acts' conclusion. Luke's rhetoric of blindness thus can be read comfortably within Judaism. The Jewish people are neither "othered" nor rejected as blind forever in Acts. Rather, Acts retains the anticipation that, as he did for Paul, Israel's Lord will intervene on behalf of God's people to open Israel's eyes to see that which was previously hidden, thereby bringing them from darkness to light.

Conclusion

"Among My Own Nation": Reading the Way, Paul, and "the Jews" in Acts within Judaism

Through this study, I have sought to demonstrate that Paul's statements and actions at the end of Acts encapsulate the posture and perspective of Acts toward "the Jews." Acts, like its main character Paul, brings no charge against the Jewish people. Rather than repudiating them or constructing a "hermeneutical Jew"—that is, using Jews as a literary caricature and negative other—to construct Christian identity in contradistinction, Acts intimately intertwines the Way, Paul, and the Jewish people in a non-competitive identity as *Israel*, God's chosen people. Jesus-following Jewish-Israelites and non-Jesus-following Jewish-Israelites stumble along together through Israel's repentance-journey in this shared identity. Jesus' Jewish followers call their brothers and sisters to change directions on this path by professing allegiance to Israel's Messiah. This is most evidently portrayed in and through Paul's representative narrative arc. Paul embodies Luke's retention of the expectant hope that Israel, even those hostile and blind toward Jesus and his followers, can turn (or be brought) from darkness to light, even in and through judgment. Luke preserves confidence for Israel's reorientation and subsequent restoration. For Acts, then, Israel "is not constituted by Israel's faithfulness to the exclusion of its unfaithfulness, but by God's faithfully holding Israelite faithfulness and unfaithfulness together with hope and forgiveness."[1] Acts' ongoing identification with the Jewish people evinces a vantage point at home in the Jewish ancestral tradition.

To show this, I employed a narrative approach to examine how Acts constructs Jewish Jesus-followers vis-à-vis the Jewish people. My evaluation was guided by Donaldson's rubric for measuring *supersessionism—self-understanding, social proximity* or *distance*, and *rhetoric*. I examined how and to what degree Acts defined its characters in connection or contradistinction to the Jewish people as the people of God, the degree of interaction and/or separation maintained with/from Jews, and the effect of Luke's rhetoric. I contended that Luke uses *synkrisis* to connect the Way and Paul with the Jewish people in a common identity as Israel. The Way and Paul retain solidarity and various degrees of fellowship even with those who disbelieve their message. Along the way, I compared Luke's writings to Israel's Scriptures and early Jewish texts to

---

[1] Givens, *We the People*, 5; similarly, Tiede, "Glory," 34; Moessner, *Luke*, 289.

support my claim that Luke's rhetoric evinced a Jewish perspective comparable to others in pluriform Second Temple Judaism.

The foundational way Luke interconnects the Way and Paul with the Jewish people is through ethnicity. In the wider ethnic discourse of Mediterranean antiquity, it would be difficult, if not impossible, to perceive Jewish Jesus-followers as something other than Jewish or anything but a way of adhering to the Jewish ancestral custom. In Acts, the Way and Paul check the major boxes of ancient Jewishness—shared genealogy, history, land, language, cult, and custom. Numerous of Luke's characters, including Paul himself, are identified or self-identify not just with Jews but *as Jews*. Jesus' followers also continue to interact with other Jews, even ones with whom they disagree. They retain proximity with the wider Jewish world. Moreover, Luke leverages this common Jewish identity in scenes of conflict, when Paul's commitment to the people and their tradition is called into question by other Jews. Acts affirms Jewish kinship bonds in the very scenes that would be most conducive to severing them.[2] As a whole, the Way in Acts emerges as an exclusivist, reformist Jewish subgroup. They make truth claims about Jesus as Israel's Messiah and include gentiles, but they do so within and for the sake of the tradition and the people. At a fundamental level, Jesus' followers are bound to the Jewish people. They remain family. Given the deep-seated Jewishness of his core characters and how he leverages Jewish identity to foster commonality with non-Jesus-following Jews, it seems reasonable to describe the narrator's own perspective as Jewish. He seems to be part of the family as well.[3]

Luke's *synkrisis* between the Way, Paul, and the Jews runs deeper than blood, though. It permeates their characterization and narrative progressions. Acts depicts the Way, the Jews, and even Paul as members of Israel who continue to develop in faithfulness and understanding. Luke neither demonizes the Jews nor idealizes the Way and Paul. On the one hand, Jews who do not believe in Jesus retain their Israelite covenantal identity, even in disbelief, though the threat of exclusion is ever-present. Moreover, Luke depicts some non-Jesus-following Jews as perceptive and venerable, even aiding the Way, despite not turning to Jesus. These Jews embody the dictum that "whoever is not against you, is for you" (Luke 9:50). On the other hand, Jews who follow Jesus can fall off the Way entirely and be removed from Israel. Even heroes like Peter and Paul appear to stumble at times. To be sure, Jesus provides a dividing line between faithful and unfaithful, yet these categories are not mere binaries. Faithfulness is a spectrum, and repentance is a journey. Jesus provides its primary orienting factor. God continues to (re)orient and progress Israel—both the Way and the wider Jewish populace—along the repentance-journey. Luke's depiction of Jesus' Jewish followers continues to identify them with the wider Jewish world in their attempts to be faithful to Israel's God. Luke's portrait of divided Israel connects more than it "others."

---

[2] As Bovon asks rhetorically, "Why does the Lukan Paul so cling to Judaism if he must justify the actual rupture between the church and synagogue?" (*Luke the Theologian*, 403).

[3] "Luke's narrator uses the first person plural 'us' and 'we' in 21.17–36 to depict the narrator as one of Paul's travel companions to Jerusalem (21.17–19). By implying that Trophimus was Paul's lone Gentile companion in Jerusalem, the narrator suggests that he is Jewish" (Carter, "Diaspora Acts," 100n22).

Luke's variegated portrait of the Jews and their *synkrisis* with Paul comes into particular focus through violence. Contravening common conceptions, Jewish violence in Acts is not uniform, ubiquitous, or unique. Only some Jews in some regions persecute Paul. Others maintain peace with Paul and the Way, even if they do not join the movement. When aggression emerges against the Way, more often than not, it comes from joint efforts from Jews and gentiles together. These efforts engender some social separation from Paul and local Jewish assemblies, but not from the Jewish world as a whole. Whenever Paul is driven from a region, he immediately returns to Jewish space in the next place. He retains ongoing proximity to Jews. Moreover, gentiles sometimes persecute Paul sans Jewish motivation or participation. In two instances, gentiles levy common anti-Jewish tropes against Paul. They, in other words, attack Paul because he is a Jew who disturbs the stability of Roman society. Suffering violence affords Luke another way of identifying Paul with the wider Jewish world. Beyond that, Luke's Paul repeatedly self-identifies with his Jewish oppressors. He was like them, worse even, in his persecution of the Way. Nevertheless, this archetypical God-fighter and embodiment of Jewish violence typifies the Lord's ability to reorient Israel along the repentance-journey, even without any prior acts of repentance or a response to the preaching of Jesus. Even the most violent in Israel can change their way in Israel (or have it changed), even in and through judgment. If Paul can be forgiven his violence, others like him can be, too. Some Jews may experience judgment, destruction even, for their violence, yet the many in Israel who have fallen can rise (or be raised) again.

Similarly, rather than functioning as an "othering" technique that conclusively repudiates the Jewish people by the end of Acts, Luke's use of the motif of blindness and sight fosters further commonality and solidarity between the Way, Paul, and the Jewish people. In fact, they ironically extend expectations for Israel's restoration. In Luke-Acts as Isaiah, Israel, including Jesus' followers, is God's blind servant whose condition in the darkness of infidelity and exile must be remedied by the servant who brings salvation by restoring Israel and bringing light to the nations (Isa 49:1–9). Luke *identifies* Jesus' followers with the wider Jewish world as blind Israel. Thankfully, Luke highlights how remedying Israel's blindness is central to Jesus' mission to bring redemption to Israel (4:16–21; cf. Isa 61:1–3). Nowhere is Israel's inability to see better seen than in Jesus' own imperceptive apostles whose eyes Jesus must open. Notably, Jesus remedies their blindness by his direct manifestation to them. In Paul, Jesus reiterates that he can restore sight and grant redemption even to the wicked Jewish-Israelites from darkness to light apart from any prior penitence or response to the word about Jesus. Jesus reorients Paul on Israel's way solely of Jesus' own accord. Jesus reveals himself to Paul and opens his eyes simply because Jesus has chosen Paul. Indeed, all of God's people might need Jesus' direct presence and healing touch to bring them from darkness to light. When the reader hears Paul's final words from Isaiah, there is good reason to be confident that Israel's Lord will eventually act to heal blind Israel. Paul (and Luke) continues the prophet's message of judgment and consolation to Israel.

In sum, Acts neither replaces the Jewish people nor redefines Israel apart from them, even if it maintains that some might be cut off. Instead of othering the Jews, Luke's *rhetoric*, harsh as it might be at times, remains internal to Israel and for the sake of the Jewish people's reorientation and advancement on the repentance-journey. Acts, through its characters and narrative, continues to *identify* with the Jewish people, including the more faithful and the less faithful in Israel. This suggests ongoing *social proximity*. Acts participates in the renegotiation of the Jewish tradition-in-crisis. Of course, for Luke, all Israel must (be) turn(ed) toward Jesus on the Way. Acts maintains its exclusive call for Israel, and some might be cut off from the people. Yet, Acts indicates that God can restore Israel apart from Israel's active repentance, seen proleptically in Paul. Like Paul, the many that fall in Israel can rise; the people can be restored by Israel's Lord. To use Donaldson's taxonomy of supersessionism, Acts perspective is best described as a combined "relationship of solidarity and mission" and "a relationship of co-existence in anticipation of the final redemption."[4] The Way does not compete for or negate the Jewish nation's identification as God's people as it preaches repentance and awaits restoration in Israel. Instead, Acts evinces a perspective that, like its main character Paul (cf. 26:4), finds its home "among my own nation," that is, among "the Jews."

---

[4] Donaldson, "Supersessionism," 28–29. Donaldson only maps the Jerusalem community of Acts as "a relationship of solidarity and mission." The only NT text Donaldson includes in this latter category is Rom 11:25–27, one that has much in common with my reading of Acts. In general, he identifies Luke-Acts under the rubric of "continuity, redefinition and reconstitution ("Supersessionism," 26–28).

Bibliography

Acuña, Mauricio. "'No Había entre Ellos Ningún Necesitado': La Normatividad de la Comunidad de Bienes en Hechos 2–6." *Kairós* 48 (2011): 35–53.
Aland, Barbara, and Holger Strutwolf, eds. *The Acts of the Apostles*. 3 vols. ECM III. Stuttgart: Deutsche Bibelgesellschaft, 1997.
Alexander, Loveday. *Acts in Its Ancient Literary Context*. LNTS 298. London: T&T Clark, 2007.
Alexander, Loveday. "Luke's Political Vision." *Int* 66 (2012): 283–93.
Allison, Jr., Dale C. "Acts 9:1–9, 22:6–11, 26:12–18: Paul and Ezekiel." *JBL* 135 (2016): 807–26.
Allison, Jr., Dale C. "Matt 23:39 = Luke 13:35b as a Conditional Prophecy." *JSNT* 5 (1983): 75–84.
Almagor, Eran. "'This is What Herodotus Relates': The Presence of Herodotus' Histories in Josephus' Writings." In *The Reception of Herodotus in Antiquity and Beyond*. Edited by Jessica Priestley and Vasiliki Zali. BCCR 6, 83–100. Leiden: Brill, 2016.
Amaru, Betsy H. "Land Theology in Philo and Josephus." In *The Land of Israel: Jewish Perspectives*. Edited by Lawrence A. Hoffman. SJCA 6, 65–93. Notre Dame, IN: University of Notre Dame Press, 1986.
Anderson, Kevin L. *"But God Raised Him from the Dead": The Theology of Jesus' Resurrection in Luke-Acts*. Eugene, OR: Wipf and Stock, 2006.
Anson, Edward M. "Greek Ethnicity and the Greek Language." *Glo* 85 (2009): 5–30.
Armstrong, Karl L. "A New Plea for an Early Date of Acts." *JGRCJ* 13 (2017): 79–110.
Armstrong, Karl L. "The End of Acts and the Jewish Response: Condemnation, Tragedy, or Hope?" *CBR* 17 (2019): 209–30.
Arterbury, Andrew. "The Downfall of Eutychus." In *Contemporary Studies in Acts*. Edited by Thomas E. Phillips, 201–22. Macon, GA: Mercer University Press, 2009.
Avemarie, Friedrich, and Hermann Lichtenberger, eds. *Auferstehung – Resurrection: Resurrection, Transfiguration, and Exaltation in Old Testament, Ancient Judaism, and Early Christianity (Tübingen, September 1999)*. WUNT 135. Tübingen: Mohr Siebeck, 2001.
Bachmann, Michael. *Jerusalem und der Tempel: Die geographisch-theologischen Elemente in der lukanischen Sicht des jüdischen Kultzentrums*. BWANT 109. Stuttgart: Kohlhammer, 1980.
Backhaus, Knut. "Zur Datierung der Apostelgeschichte: Ein Ordnungsversuch im chronologischen Chaos." *ZNW* 108 (2017): 212–58.
Baker, Cynthia M. "'From Every Nation under Heaven': Jewish Ethnicities in the Greco-Roman World." In *Prejudice and Christian Beginnings: Investigating Race, Gender, and Ethnicity in Early Christian Studies*. Edited by Laura S. Nasrallah and Elisabeth Schüssler Fiorenza, 79–99. Minneapolis, MN: Fortress, 2009.
Baker, Cynthia M. *Jew*. KWJS 7. New Brunswick, NJ: Rutgers University Press, 2017.
Balch, David L. *Contested Ethnicities and Images: Studies in Acts and Art*. WUNT 345. Tübingen: Mohr Siebeck, 2015.

Barbi, Augusto. "The Use and Meaning of (*Hoi*) *Ioudaioi* in Acts." In *Luke and Acts*. Edited by Gerald O'Collins and Gilberto Marconi, translated by Matthew J. O'Connell, 123–42. New York: Paulist, 1993.

Barclay, John M. G. "Ἰουδαῖος: Ethnicity and Translation." In David G. Horrell and Katherine M. Hockey (eds.). *Ethnicity, Race, Religion: Identities and Ideologies in Early Jewish and Christian Texts, and in Modern Biblical Interpretation*, 46–58. London: Bloomsbury, 2018.

Barclay, John M. G. *Jews in the Mediterranean Diaspora: From Alexander to Trajan (323 BCE–117 CE)*. Edinburgh: T&T Clark, 1998.

Barreto, Eric D. *Ethnic Negotiations: The Function of Race and Ethnicity in Acts 16*. WUNT 2/294. Tübingen: Mohr Siebeck, 2010.

Barrett, Charles K. *Acts of the Apostles*. 2 vols. ICC 34. Edinburgh: T&T Clark, 1994.

Barton, Carlin A., and Daniel Boyarin. *Imagine No Religion: How Modern Abstractions Hide Ancient Realities*. New York: Fordham University Press, 2016.

Barton, Stephen C. "Can We Identify the Gospel Audiences?" In Richard Bauckham (ed.), *The Gospels for All Christians: Rethinking the Gospel Audiences*, 173–98. Grand Rapids, MI: Eerdmans, 1998.

Bauckham, Richard. "James and the Jerusalem Community." In Oskar Skarsaune and Reidar Hvalvik (eds.). *Jewish Believers in Jesus: The Early Centuries*, 55–95. Peabody, MA: Hendrickson, 2007.

Bauckham, Richard. *The Jewish World around the New Testament*. Grand Rapids, MI: Baker Academic, 2010.

Bauckham, Richard. "The Restoration of Israel in Luke-Acts." In James M. Scott (ed.), *Restoration: Old Testament, Jewish, and Christian Perspectives*. JSJSup 72 435–88. Leiden: Brill, 2001.

Baumann, Gerd. "Grammars of Identity/Alterity: A Structuralist Approach." In Gerd Baumann and André Gingrich (eds.), *Grammars of Identity/Alterity: A Structural Approach*, 18–51. New York: Berghahn Books, 2004.

Baumgarten, Albert I. "Josephus and the Jewish Sects." In Honora Howell Chapman and Zuleika Rodgers (eds.), *A Companion to Josephus*, BCAW 110, 261–72. Malden, MA: Wiley-Blackwell, 2015.

Baur, F. C. *The Church History of the First Three Centuries*. Translated by Allan Menzies. London: Williams and Norgate, 1878.

Bauspiess, Martin, Christof Landmesser, and David Lincicum, eds. *Ferdinand Christian Baur und die Geschichte des frühen Christentums*. Tübingen: Mohr Siebeck, 2014.

Becker, Adam H., and Annette Yoshiko Reed, eds. *The Ways That Never Parted: Jews and Christians in Late Antiquity and the Early Middle Ages*. TSAJ 95. Minneapolis, MN: Fortress, 2007.

Beers, Holly. *The Followers of Jesus as the "Servant": Luke's Model from Isaiah for the Disciples in Luke-Acts*. LNTS 535. London: T&T Clark, 2015.

Ben-Eliyahu, Eyal. "Josephus's Lands: Mining the Evolution in the Depiction of the Land of Israel in the Words of Josephus." *JSP* 26 (2017): 275–304.

Bennema, Cornelis. "Character Reconstruction in the New Testament (1): The Theory." *ExpTim* 127 (2016): 365–74.

Bennema, Cornelis. "Character Reconstruction in the New Testament (2): The Practice." *ExpTim* 127 (2016): 417–29.

Bergh, Ronald H. van der. "A Thematic and Chronological Analysis of the Reception of Ananias and Sapphira (Acts 5:1–11) in the First Five Centuries CE." *JECH* 7 (2017): 1–16.

Bergsma, John Sietze. "Qumran Self-Identity: 'Israel' or 'Judah'?" *DSD* 15 (2008): 172–89.
Bilde, Per. *Flavius Josephus between Jerusalem and Rome: His Life, His Works and Their Importance*. Eugene: Wipf and Stock, 2002.
Blumhofer, Christopher. *The Gospel of John and the Future of Israel*. SNTSMS 177. Cambridge: Cambridge University Press, 2020.
Boccaccini, Gabriele, and Isaac W. Oliver, eds. *The Early Reception of Paul the Second Temple Jew: Text, Narrative and Reception History*. LSTS 92. London: T&T Clark, 2018.
Bock, Darrell L. *Acts*. Grand Rapids, MI: Baker Academic, 2007.
Bock, Darrell L. *Blasphemy and Exaltation in Judaism: The Charge against Jesus in Mark 14:53-65*. Grand Rapids, MI: Baker, 2000.
Bockmuehl, Markus. *Jewish Law in Gentile Churches: Halakhah and the Beginning of Christian Public Ethics*. Grand Rapids, MI: Baker Academic, 2003.
Boda, Mark J. *Return to Me: A Biblical Theology of Repentance*. NSBT 35. Downers Grove, IL: InterVarsity Press, 2015.
Boesenberg, Dulcinea. "Negotiating Identity: The Jewish of the Way in Acts." In Ronald A. Simkins and Thomas M. Kelly (eds.), *Religion and Identity*, 58–75. RelSocSup 13. Omaha, NE: Kripke Center, 2016.
Boesenberg, Dulcinea. "Prophetic Rebuke in Acts: Calling for Reform Rather than Rejection of Israel." In Ronald A. Simkins and Zachary B. Smith (eds.), *Religion and Reform*, 5–19. RelSocSup 18. Omaha, NE: Kripke Center, 2019.
Booth, Adam David Patrick. "'A Death Like His': Saul's Privation and Restoration of Sight as Prophetic Formation in Acts 9." *JDR* 22 (2018): 42–62.
Böttrich, Christfried. "Das lukanische Doppelwerk im Kontext frühjüdischer Literatur." *ZNW* 106 (2015): 151–83.
Bovon, François. *Luke*. 3 vols. *Hermeneia*. Minneapolis, MN: Fortress, 2002.
Bovon, François. *Luke the Theologian: Fifty-Five Years of Research*. 2nd ed. Waco, TX: Baylor University Press, 2006.
Boyarin, Daniel. *Judaism: The Genealogy of a Modern Notion*. KWJS 9. New Brunswick, NJ: Rutgers University Press, 2018.
Boyarin, Daniel. "Semantic Differences; or, 'Judaism'/'Christianity.'" In Adam H. Becker and Annette Yoshiko Reed (eds.), *The Ways that Never Parted: Jews and Christians in Late Antiquity and the Early Middle Ages*, 65–85. TSAJ 95. Minneapolis, MN: Fortress, 2007.
Brawley, Robert L. *Luke-Acts and the Jews: Conflict, Apology, and Conciliation*. SBLMS 33. Atlanta, GA: Scholars Press, 1987.
Brawley, Robert L. *Text to Text Pours Forth Speech: Voices of Scripture in Luke-Acts*. Bloomington, IN: Indiana University Press, 1995.
Brehm, H. Alan. "Vindicating the Rejected One: Stephen's Speech as a Critique of the Jewish Leaders." *Early Christian Interpretation of the Scriptures of Israel: Investigations and Proposals*. Edited by Craig A. Evans and James A. Sanders. JSNTSup 148. Sheffield: Sheffield Academic, 1997.
Bruce, F. F. *The Acts of the Apostles: The Greek Text with Introduction and Commentary*. 3rd ed. Grand Rapids, MI: Eerdmans, 1990.
Bruce, F. F. *The Book of Acts*. 3rd ed. NICNT. Grand Rapids, MI: Eerdmans, 1988.
Burfeind, Carsten. "Paulus muß nach Rom: Zur politischen Dimension der Apostelgeschichte." *NTS* 46 (2000): 75–91.
Butticaz, Simon. "'Has God Rejected His People?' (Romans 11.1): The Salvation of Israel in Acts: Narrative Claim of a Pauline Legacy." In David P. Moessner, Daniel Marguerat, Mikeal C. Parsons, and Michael Wolter (eds.), translated by Nicholas J. Zola, *Paul and*

the Heritage of Israel: Paul's Claim upon Israel's Legacy in Luke and Acts in the Light of the Pauline Letters*, 148–64. London: T&T Clark, 2012.
Caballero Yoccou, Raúl. *Hechos*. 3 vols. CBCN. Miami: Editorial Unilit, 1998.
Carandini, Andrea. "Urban Landscapes and Ethnic Identity of Early Rome." In Gabriele Cifani, Simon Stoddart, and Skylar Neil (eds.). *Landscape, Ethnicity and Identity in the Archaic Mediterranean Area*, 5–23. Oxford: Oxbow, 2012.
Carras, George P. "Observant Jews in the Story of Luke-Acts." In Jozef Verheyden (ed.), *The Unity of Luke-Acts*. BETL 142, 693–708. Leuven: Peeters, 1999.
Carrillo Alday, Salvador. *El Evangelio según San Lucas*. Estella: Editorial Verbo Divino, 2009.
Carroll, James. *Constantine's Sword: The Church and the Jews*. Boston, MA: Houghton Mifflin, 2001.
Carroll, Robert P. "Blindsight and the Vision Thing: Blindness and Insight in the Book of Isaiah." In Craig C. Broyles and Craig A. Evans (eds.), *Writing and Reading the Scroll of Isaiah: Studies of an Interpretive Tradition*. VTSup 70, 79–94. Leiden: Brill, 1997.
Carter, Jr., Arthur Francis. "Diaspora Acts: Contextualizing a Metanarrative Syntacts." In James P. Grimshaw. TC (ed.), *Luke-Acts*, 74–103. London: Bloomsbury, 2018.
Carter, Jr., Arthur Francis. "Diaspora Poetics and (Re)Constructions of Differentness: Conceiving Acts 6.1–8.40 as Diaspora." PhD diss., Vanderbilt University, Nashville, TN, 2016.
Carter, J. Kameron. *Race: A Theological Account*. Oxford: Oxford University Press, 2008.
Chalmers, Matthew. "Rethinking Luke 10: The Parable of the Good Samaritan Israelite." *JBL* 139 (2020): 543–66.
Chance, J. Bradley. *Jerusalem, the Temple, and the New Age in Luke-Acts*. Macon, GA: Mercer University Press, 1988.
Chester, Andrew. "Resurrection and Transformation." In Friedrich Avemarie and Hermann Lichtenberger (eds.), *Auferstehung–Resurrection: Resurrection, Transfiguration, and Exaltation in Old Testament, Ancient Judaism, and Early Christianity (Tübingen, September 1999)*. WUNT 135, 47–78. Tübingen: Mohr Siebeck, 2001.
Chilton, Bruce. *The Glory of Israel: The Theology and Provenience of the Isaiah Targum*. JSOTSup 23. Sheffield: JSOT Press, 1983.
Chilton, Bruce. "The Godfearers: From the Gospels to Aphrodisias." In Hershel Shanks (ed.), *Partings: How Judaism and Christianity Became Two*, 55–72. Washington, DC: Biblical Archaeology Society, 2014.
Cifani, Gabriele, Simon Stoddart, and Skylar Neil, eds. *Landscape, Ethnicity and Identity in the Archaic Mediterranean Area*. Oxford: Oxbow, 2012.
Cohen, Jeremy. *Living Letters of the Law: Ideas of the Jew in Medieval Christianity*. SMTFIJS. Berkeley, CA: University of California Press, 1999.
Cohen, Shaye J. D. "The Significance of Yavneh: Pharisees, Rabbis, and the End of Jewish Sectarianism." *HUCA* 55 (1984): 27–53.
Collins, John J. "A Herald of Good Tidings: Isaiah 61:1–3 and Its Actualization in the Dead Sea Scrolls." In Craig A. Evans and Shemaryahu Talmon (eds.), *The Quest for Context and Meaning: Studies in Biblical Intertextuality in Honor of James A. Sanders*. BibInt 28, 225–40. Leiden: Brill, 1997.
Conzelmann, Hans. *Acts of the Apostles*. Hermeneia. Philadelphia, PA: Fortress, 1988.
Conzelmann, Hans. *The Theology of St. Luke*. Translated by Geoffrey Buswell. Philadelphia, PA: Fortress, 1982.
Cosgrove, Charles H. "The Divine Δεῖ in Luke-Acts: Investigations into the Lukan Understanding of God's Providence." *NovT* 26 (1984): 168–90.

Cowan, J. Andrew. *The Writings of Luke and the Jewish Roots of the Christian Way: An Examination of the Aims of the First Christian Historian in the Light of Ancient Politics, Ethnography, and Historiography.* LNTS 599. London: T&T Clark, 2019.
Crabbe, Kylie. "Accepting Prophecy: Paul's Response to Agabus with Insights from Valerius Maximus and Josephus." *JSNT* 39 (2016): 188–208.
Crabbe, Kylie. "Being Found Fighting against God: Luke's Gamaliel and Josephus on Human Responses to Divine Providence." *ZNW* 106 (2015): 21–39.
Crabbe, Kylie. *Luke/Acts and the End of History.* BZNW 238. Berlin: de Gruyter, 2020.
Crossley, James G. *The New Testament and Jewish Law: A Guide for the Perplexed.* London: T&T Clark, 2010.
Crowe, Brandon D. *The Hope of Israel: The Resurrection of Christ in the Acts of the Apostles.* Grand Rapids, MI: Baker Academic, 2020.
Cunningham, Scott. *Through Many Tribulations: The Theology of Persecution in Luke-Acts.* JSNTSup 142. Sheffield: Sheffield Academic, 1997.
Dahl, Nils A. "'A People for His Name' (Acts 15:14)." *NTS* 4 (1958): 319–27.
Darr, John A. *On Character Building: The Reader and the Rhetoric of Characterization in Luke-Acts.* LCBI. Louisville, KY: Westminster John Knox, 1992.
Denova, Rebecca I. *The Things Accomplished among Us: Prophetic Tradition in the Structural Pattern of Luke-Acts.* JSNTSup 141. Sheffield: Sheffield Academic, 1997.
Deutschmann, Anton. *Synagoge und Gemeindebildung: Christliche Gemeinde und Israel am Beispiel von Apg 13,42–52.* BU 30. Regensburg: Pustet, 2001.
Dinkler, Michal Beth. "Building Character on the Road to Emmaus: Lukan Characterization in Contemporary Literary Perspective." *JBL* 136 (2017): 687–706.
Dinkler, Michal Beth. "Interpreting Pedagogical Acts: Acts 8.26–40 and Narrative Reflexivity as Pedagogy." *NTS* 63 (2017): 411–27.
Dinkler, Michal Beth. *Literary Theory and the New Testament.* AYBRL. New Haven, CT: Yale University Press, 2019.
Dinkler, Michal Beth. "New Testament Rhetorical Narratology: An Invitation toward Integration." *BibInt* 24 (2016): 203–28.
Dinkler, Michal Beth. "Silence as Rhetorical Technique in Luke 14:1–6." *PRSt* 40 (2013): 337–48.
Donaldson, Terence L. *Jews and Anti-Judaism in the New Testament: Decision Points and Divergent Interpretations.* Waco, TX: Baylor University Press, 2010.
Donaldson, Terence L. "Moses Typology and the Sectarian Nature of Early Christian Anti-Judaism: A Study in Acts 7." *JSNT* 12 (1981): 27–52.
Donaldson, Terence L. "Supersessionism and Early Christian Self-Definition." *JJMJS* 3 (2016): 1–32.
Du Toit, Philip La G. "Reconsidering the Salvation of Israel in Luke-Acts." *JSNT* 43 (2021): 343–69.
Dulk, Matthijs den. "Aquila and Apollos: Acts 18 in Light of Ancient Ethnic Stereotypes." *JBL* 139 (2020): 177–89.
Eastman, David L. "Jealousy, Internal Strife, and the Deaths of Peter and Paul: A Reassessment of 1 Clement." *ZAC* 18 (2014): 34–53.
Eastman, Susan G. "Israel and the Mercy of God: A Re-Reading of Galatians 6.16 and Romans 9–11." *NTS* 56 (2010): 367–95.
Eisenbaum, Pamela M. "Paul, Polemics, and the Problem of Essentialism." *BibInt* 13 (2005): 224–38.
Ellens, J. Harold, Isaac W. Oliver, Jason von Ehrenkrook, James Waddell, and Jason M. Zurawski, eds. *Wisdom Poured out Like Water: Studies on Jewish and Christian Antiquity in Honor of Gabriele Boccaccini.* DCLS 38. Berlin: de Gruyter, 2018.

Epp, Eldon Jay. *The Theological Tendency of Codex Bezae Cantabrigiensis in Acts*. SNTSMS 3. Cambridge: Cambridge University Press, 1966.

Evans, Craig A. *To See and Not Perceive: Isaiah 6.9–10 in Early Jewish and Christian Interpretation*. JSOTSup 64. Sheffield: Sheffield Academic, 1989.

Evans, Vyvyan, and Melanie Green. *Cognitive Linguistics: An Introduction*. Edinburgh: Edinburgh University Press, 2009.

Feldman, Louis H., and Gōhei Hata, eds. *Josephus, the Bible and History*. Detroit, MI: Wayne State University Press, 1989.

Ferda, Tucker S. "Jeremiah 7 and Flavius Josephus on the First Jewish War." *JSJ* 44 (2013): 158–73.

Fernández Ubiña, José. "Razones, Contradicciones e Incógnitas de Las Persecuciones Anticristianas: El Testimonio de Lucas-Hechos." *'Ilu* 18 (2007): 27–60.

Figueira, Thomas J. "Language as a Marker of Ethnicity in Herodotus and Contemporaries." In Thomas J. Figueira and Carmen Soares (eds.), *Ethnicity and Identity in Herodotus*, 43–71. New York: Routledge, 2020.

Figueira, Thomas J., and Carmen Soares, eds. *Ethnicity and Identity in Herodotus*. New York: Routledge, 2020.

Fitzmyer, Joseph A. *The Acts of the Apostles*. AB 31. New York: Doubleday, 1998.

Fortin, Denis. "Paul's Observance of the Sabbath in Acts of the Apostles as a Marker of Continuity between Judaism and Early Christianity." *AUSS* 53 (2015): 321–35.

Fragoulaki, Maria. *Kinship in Thucydides: Intercommunal Ties and Historical Narrative*. Oxford: Oxford University Press, 2014.

Fredriksen, Paula. "God is Jewish, but Gentiles Don't Have to Be: Ethnicity and Eschatology in Paul's Gospel." In Frantisek Ábel (ed.), *The Message of Paul the Apostle within Second Temple Judaism*, 3–19. Minneapolis, MN: Fortress, 2020.

Fredriksen, Paula. "How Jewish is God? Divine Ethnicity in Paul's Theology." *JBL* 137 (2018): 193–212.

Fredriksen, Paula. "'If It Looks like a Duck, and It Quacks like a Duck . . .': On Not Giving Up the Godfearers." In Susan Ashbrook Harvey, Daniel P. DesRosier, Shira L. Landerr, Jacqueline Z. Pastis, and Daniel Ullucci (eds.), *A Most Reliable Witness: Essays in Honor of Ross Shepard Kraemer*. BJS 358, 25–33. Providence, RI: Brown Judaic Studies, 2015.

Fredriksen, Paula. "Mandatory Retirement: Ideas in the Study of Christian Origins Whose Time Has Come to Go." *SR* 35 (2006): 231–46.

Fredriksen, Paula. *Paul: The Pagans' Apostle*. New Haven, CT: Yale University Press, 2017.

Fredriksen, Paula. "What 'Parting of the Ways'? Jews, Gentiles, and the Ancient Mediterranean City." In Adam H. Becker and Annette Yoshiko Reed (eds.), *The Ways That Never Parted: Jews and Christians in Late Antiquity and the Early Middle Ages*. TSAJ 95, 35–63. Minneapolis, MN: Fortress, 2007.

Fredriksen, Paula. *When Christians Were Jews: The First Generation*. New Haven, CT: Yale University Press, 2018.

Frein, Brigid C. "The Literary and Theological Significance of Misunderstanding in the Gospel of Luke." *Bib* 74 (1993): 328–48.

French, Blaire A. "The Completion of King Saul in Acts." *JSNT* 40 (2018): 424–33.

Fuller, Michael E. *The Restoration of Israel: Israel's Re-Gathering and the Fate of the Nations in Early Jewish Literature and Luke-Acts*. BZNW 138. Berlin: de Gruyter, 2006.

Fusco, Vittorio. "Luke-Acts and the Future of Israel." *NovT* 38 (1996): 1–17.

Gabrielson, Timothy A. "Parting Ways or Rival Siblings? A Review and Analysis of Metaphors for the Separation of Jews and Christians in Antiquity." *CBR* 19 (2021): 178–204.

Gafni, Isaiah. *Land, Center and Diaspora: Jewish Constructs in Late Antiquity*. JSPSup 21. Sheffield: Sheffield Academic, 1997.
Gager, John G. "Jews, Gentiles, and Synagogues in the Book of Acts." *HTR* 79 (1986): 91–99.
Gager, John G. *The Origins of Anti-Semitism: Attitudes toward Judaism in Pagan and Christian Antiquity*. Oxford: Oxford University Press, 1983.
Gager, John G. "Where Does Luke's Anti-Judaism Come From?" *ASE* 24 (2007): 31–35.
Ganzel, Tova. "The Descriptions of the Restoration of Israel in Ezekiel." *VT* 60 (2010): 197–211.
García Serrano, Andrés. "The Jerusalem Temple According to Luke." *EstB* 71 (2013): 37–56.
Garrett, Susan R. *The Demise of the Devil: Magic and the Demonic in Luke's Writings*. Minneapolis, MN: Fortress, 1989.
Gasque, W. Ward. *A History of the Interpretation of the Acts of the Apostles*. 2nd ed. Eugene, OR: Wipf and Stock, 2000.
Gaventa, Beverly Roberts. *From Darkness to Light: Aspects of Conversion in the New Testament*. OBT 20. Philadelphia, PA: Fortress, 1986.
Gaventa, Beverly Roberts. "Galatians 1 and 2: Autobiography as Paradigm." *NovT* 28 (1986): 309–26.
Givens, G. Tommy. *We the People: Israel and the Catholicity of Jesus*. Minneapolis, MN: Fortress, 2014.
Glombitza, Otto. "Zur Charakterisierung des Stephanus in Act 6 und 7." *ZNW* 53 (1962): 238–44.
Glover, Daniel. "The Promises Fulfilled for Whose Children? The Problem of the Text of Acts 13:33 in Contemporary Debate." *JBL* 139 (2020): 789–807.
Goldingay, John. *Israel's Faith*. Old Testament Theology 2. Downers Grove, IL: InterVarsity Press, 2006.
González, Justo L. *Hechos*. CsB. Minneapolis, MN: Augsburg Fortress, 2006.
Goodblatt, David M. *Elements of Ancient Jewish Nationalism*. Cambridge: Cambridge University Press, 2009.
Gowler, David B. *Host, Guest, Enemy, and Friend: Portraits of the Pharisees in Luke and Acts*. Eugene, OR: Wipf and Stock, 2008.
Green, Joel B. *Conversion in Luke-Acts: Divine Action, Human Cognition, and the People of God*. Grand Rapids, MI: Baker Academic, 2015.
Green, Joel B. "Luke/Acts, or Luke and Acts? A Reaffirmation of Narrative Unity." In Steve Walton (ed.), *Reading Acts Today: Essays in Honour of Loveday C. A. Alexander*. LNTS 427, 101–19. London: Bloomsbury, 2011.
Green, Joel B. "Narrative Criticism." In Joel B. Green (ed.), *Methods for Luke*. MBI, 74–112. Cambridge: Cambridge University Press, 2010.
Green, Joel B. "Neglecting Widows and Serving the Word? Acts 6:1–7 as a Test Case for a Missional Hermeneutics." In Jon Laansma, Grant R. Osborne, and Ray Van Neste (eds.), *New Testament Theology in Light of the Church's Mission: Essays in Honor of I. Howard Marshall*, 151–60. Eugene, OR: Cascade, 2011.
Green, Joel B. "The Book of Acts as History/Writing." *LTQ* 37 (2002): 119–27.
Green, Joel B. *The Gospel of Luke*. NICNT. Grand Rapids, MI: Eerdmans, 1997.
Green, Joel B. "'They Made a Calf': Idolatry and Temple in Acts 7." In Eric F. Mason and Edmondo F. Lupieri (eds.), *Golden Calf Traditions in Early Judaism, Christianity, and Islam*, 132–41. Leiden: Brill, 2018.
Gregerman, Adam. "Israel as the 'Hermeneutical Jew' in Protestant Statements on the Land and State of Israel: Four Presbyterian Examples." *IA* 23 (2017): 773–93.

Gregory, Andrew F., and C. Kavin Rowe, eds. *Rethinking the Unity and Reception of Luke and Acts*. Columbia, SC: University of South Carolina Press, 2010.

Gregory, Bradley C. "The Postexilic Exile in Third Isaiah: Isaiah 61:1-3 in Light of Second Temple Hermeneutics." *JBL* 126 (2007): 475-96.

Gruen, Erich S. *The Constructs of Identity in Hellenistic Judaism: Essays on Early Jewish Literature and History*. DCLS 29. Berlin: de Gruyter, 2016.

Haacker, Klaus. "Das Bekenntnis des Paulus zur Hoffnung Israels nach der Apostelgeschichte des Lukas." *NTS* 31 (1985): 437-51.

Hadot, Pierre. *What is Ancient Philosophy?* Translated by Michael Chase. Cambridge, MA: Harvard University Press, 2004.

Haenchen, Ernst. *Acts of the Apostles: A Commentary*. Philadelphia PA: Westminster John Knox, 1971.

Hakola, Raimo. "'Friendly' Pharisees and Social Identity in the Book of Acts." In Thomas E. Phillips (ed.), *Contemporary Studies in Acts*, 181-200. Macon, GA: Mercer University Press, 2009.

Hall, Jonathan M. "Contested Ethnicities: Perceptions of Macedonia within Evolving Defintions of Greek Identity." In Irad Malkin (ed.), *Ancient Perceptions of Greek Ethnicity*. CHSC 5, 159-86. Cambridge, MA: Harvard University Press, 2001.

Hall, Jonathan M. *Ethnic Identity in Greek Antiquity*. Cambridge: Cambridge University Press, 1997.

Hamm, Dennis. "Paul's Blindness and Its Healing: Clues to Symbolic Intent (Acts 9; 22 and 26)." *Bib* 71 (1990): 63-72.

Hamm, Dennis. "Sight to the Blind: Vision as Metaphor in Luke." *Bib* 67 (1986): 457-77.

Hamm, Dennis. "The Tamid Service in Luke-Acts: The Cultic Background behind Luke's Theology of Worship (Luke 1:5-25; 18:9-14; 24:50-53; Acts 3:1; 10:3, 30)." *CBQ* 65 (2003): 215-31.

Hare, Douglas R. A. "The Rejection of the Jews in the Synoptic Gospels and Acts." In Alan T. Davies (ed.), *Antisemitism and the Foundations of Christianity*, 27-47. Mahweh, NJ: Paulist, 1979.

Harrill, J. Albert. "Divine Judgement against Ananias and Sapphira (Acts 5:1-11): A Stock Scene of Perjury and Death." *JBL* 130 (2011): 351-69.

Hartsock, Chad. *Sight and Blindness in Luke-Acts: The Use of Physical Features in Characterization*. BibInt 94. Leiden: Brill, 2008.

Hays, Richard B. *Echoes of Scripture in the Gospels*. Waco, TX: Baylor University Press, 2016.

Hedlun, Randy J. "Rethinking Luke's Purpose: The Effect of First-Century Social Conflict." *JPT* 22 (2013): 226-56.

Hedrick, Pamela. "Fewer Answers and Further Questions: Jews and Gentiles in Acts." *Int* 66 (2012): 294-305.

Henten, Jan Willem. "Josephus, Fifth Evangelist, and Jesus on the Temple." *HTS* 71 (2015): 1-11.

Herman, David. *Basic Elements of Narrative*. Malden, MA: Wiley-Blackwell, 2009.

Herodotus. *The Histories*. Edited by Carolyn Dewald. Translated by Robin Waterfield. OWC. Oxford: Oxford University Press, 2008.

Heschel, Abraham Joshua. *The Prophets*. New York: HarperPerennial, 2001.

Heskett, Randall. *Messianism within the Scriptural Scroll of Isaiah*. LHBOTS 456. New York: T&T Clark, 2007.

Hicks-Keeton, Jill. *Arguing with Aseneth: Gentile Access to Israel's "Living God" in Jewish Antiquity*. New York: Oxford University Press, 2018.

Hill, Brian. "Protocols of Ethnic Specification in Herodotus." In Thomas J. Figueira and Carmen Soares (eds.), *Ethnicity and Identity in Herodotus*, 72–83. New York: Routledge, 2020.
Hill, Craig C. *Hellenists and Hebrews: Reappraising Division within the Earliest Church*. Minneapolis, MN: Fortress, 1991.
Hill, Craig C. "Restoring the Kingdom to Israel: Luke-Acts and Christian Supersessionism." In Tod Linafelt (ed.), *A Shadow of Glory: Reading the New Testament after the Holocaust*, 185–200. New York: Routledge, 2002.
Hill, Craig C. "The Jerusalem Church." In Matt A. Jackson-McCabe (ed.), *Jewish Christianity Reconsidered: Rethinking Ancient Groups and Texts*, 39–56. Minneapolis, MN: Fortress, 2007.
Holladay, Carl R. *Acts: A Commentary*. NTL. Louisville, KY: Westminster John Knox, 2016.
Horn, Friedrich Wilhelm. "Paulus, das Nasiräat und die Nasiräer." *NovT* 39 (1997): 117–37.
Horst, Pieter W. van der. "*Philosophia Epeisaktos*: Some Notes on Josephus, *A.J.* 18.9." In Mladen Popovic (ed.), *The Jewish Revolt against Rome: Interdisciplinary Perspectives*, 311–22. Leiden: Brill, 2011.
Isaac, Benjamin. *The Invention of Racism in Classical Antiquity*. Princeton, NJ: Princeton University Press, 2004.
Jáuregui, José Antonio. "'Israel' y la Iglesia en la Teologia de Lucas." *EstEcl* 61 (1986): 129–49.
Jennings, Willie James. *Acts: A Theological Commentary on the Bible*. Belief. Louisville, KY: Westminster John Knox Press, 2017.
Jennings, Willie James. *The Christian Imagination: Theology and the Origins of Race*. New Haven, CT: Yale University Press, 2010.
Jensen, Matthew D. "Some Unpersuasive Glosses: The Meaning of ἀπείθεια, ἀπειθέω, and ἀπειθής in the New Testament." *JBL* 138 (2019): 391–412.
Jervell, Jacob. *Die Apostelgeschichte*. KEK 3. Göttingen: Vandenhoeck & Ruprecht, 1998.
Jervell, Jacob. *Luke and the People of God: A New Look at Luke-Acts*. Minneapolis, MN: Augsburg, 1979.
Jervell, Jacob. "Paulus in der Apostelgeschichte und die Geschichte des Urchristentums." *NTS* 32 (1986): 378–92.
Jervell, Jacob. *The Theology of the Acts of the Apostles*. NTT. Cambridge: Cambridge University Press, 1996.
Jervell, Jacob. *The Unknown Paul: Essays on Luke-Acts and Early Christian History*. Minneapolis, MN: Augsburg, 1984.
Jipp, Joshua W. "Paul's Areopagus Speech of Acts 17:16–34 as Both Critique and Propaganda." *JBL* 131 (2012): 567–88.
Jipp, Joshua W. "The Paul of Acts: Proclaimer of the Hope of Israel or Teacher of Apostasy from Moses?" *NovT* 62 (2020): 60–78.
Johnson, Luke Timothy. *The Acts of the Apostles*. Sacra Pagina. Collegeville, MN: Liturgical Press, 1992.
Johnson, Luke Timothy. *The Gospel of Luke*. Sacra Pagina. Collegeville, MN: Liturgical Press, 1991.
Jones, Christopher P. "Ἔθνος and Γένος in Herodotus." *ClQ* 46 (1996): 315–20.
Joyce, Paul M. *Divine Initiative and Human Response in Ezekiel*. JSOTSup 51. Sheffield: Sheffield Academic, 1989.
Kaminsky, Joel S. *Yet I Loved Jacob: Reclaiming the Biblical Concept of Election*. Nashville, TN: Abingdon, 2007.

Karrer, Martin. "'Und ich werde sie heilen': Das Verstockungsmotiv aus Jes 6, 9f. in Apg 28, 26f." In Martin Karrer, Wolfgang Kraus, and Otto Merk (eds.). *Kirche und Volk Gottes, Festschrift für Jürgen Roloff zum 70. Geburtstag*, 255–71. Neukirchen-Vluyn: Neukirchener Verlag, 2000.

Keener, Craig S. *Acts: An Exegetical Commentary*. 4 vols. Grand Rapids, MI: Baker Academic, 2012–2015.

Keener, Craig S. "Paul and Sedition: Pauline Apologetic in Acts." *BBR* 22 (2012): 201–24.

Kelhoffer, James A. "The Gradual Disclosure of Paul's Violence against Christians in the Acts of the Apostles as an Apology for the Standing of the Lukan Paul." *BR* 54 (2009): 25–35.

Kinzer, Mark S. *Jerusalem Crucified, Jerusalem Risen: The Resurrected Messiah, the Jewish People, and the Land of Promise*. Eugene, OR: Cascade, 2018.

Kinzer, Mark S. "Sacrifice, Prayer, and the Holy Spirit: The Tamid Offering in Luke-Acts." In J. Harold Ellens, Isaac W. Oliver, Jason von Ehrenkrook, James Waddell, and Jason M. Zurawski (eds.), *Wisdom Poured out Like Water: Studies on Jewish and Christian Antiquity in Honor of Gabriele Boccaccini*. DCLS 38, 463–75. Berlin: de Gruyter, 2018.

Klawans, Jonathan. "Josephus, the Rabbis, and Responses to Catastrophes Ancient and Modern." *JQR* 100 (2010): 278–309.

Klutz, Todd. *The Exorcism Stories in Luke-Acts: A Sociostylistic Reading*. SNTSMS 129. Cambridge: Cambridge University Press, 2004.

Kochenash, Michael. "Better Call Paul 'Saul': Literary Models and a Lukan Innovation." *JBL* 138 (2019): 433–49.

Koet, Bart J. "As Close to the Synagogue as Can Be: Paul in Corinth (Acts 18, 1–18)." In R. Bieringer (ed.), *The Corinthian Correspondence*. BETL 125, 397–415. Leuven: Peeters, 1996.

Koet, Bart J. *Five Studies on the Interpretation of Scripture in Luke-Acts*. SNTA 14. Leuven: Peeters, 1989.

Koet, Bart J. "Isaiah in Luke-Acts." In Steve Moyise and Maarten J. J. Menken (eds.), *Isaiah in the New Testament: The New Testament and the Scriptures of Israel*, 79–100. London: Bloomsbury Publishing, 2014.

Korner, Ralph J. *The Origin and Meaning of Ekklēsia in the Early Jesus Movement*. AJEC 98. Leiden: Brill, 2017.

Kraft, Robert A. "The Weighing of the Parts: Pivots and Pitfalls in the Study of Early Judaisms and Their Early Christian Offspring." In Adam H. Becker and Annette Yoshiko Reed (eds.), *The Ways that Never Parted: Jews and Christians in Late Antiquity and the Early Middle Ages*. TSAJ 95, 87–94. Minneapolis, MN: Fortress, 2007.

Kuecker, Aaron. "'You Will Be Children of the Most High': An Inquiry into Luke's Narrative Account of Theosis." *JTI* 8 (2014): 213–28.

Laansma, Jon, Grant R. Osborne, and Ray Van Neste, eds. *New Testament Theology in Light of the Church's Mission: Essays in Honor of I. Howard Marshall*. Eugene, OR: Cascade, 2011.

Lakoff, George, and Mark Johnson. *Metaphors We Live By*. Chicago, IL: University of Chicago Press, 2003.

Lambert, David A. *How Repentance Became Biblical: Judaism, Christianity, and the Interpretation of Scripture*. Oxford: Oxford University Press, 2016.

Lanier, Gregory R. "Luke's Distinctive Use of the Temple: Portraying the Divine Visitation." *JTS* 65 (2014): 433–62.

Lappenga, Benjamin J. *Paul's Language of Ζῆλος: Monosemy and the Rhetoric of Identity and Practice*. BibInt 137. Leiden: Brill, 2015.

Laurence, Ray, and Joanne Berry, eds. *Cultural Identity in the Roman Empire*. London: Routledge, 1998.
Lawrence, Louise Joy. *Sense and Stigma in the Gospels: Depictions of Sensory-Disabled Characters*. Oxford: Oxford University Press, 2013.
Le Donne, Anthony. "The Improper Temple Offering of Ananias and Sapphira." *NTS* 59 (2013): 346–64.
Lentz, Jr., John Clayton. *Luke's Portrait of Paul*. SNTSMS 77. Cambridge: Cambridge University Press, 2004.
Levenson, Jon D. *Resurrection and the Restoration of Israel: The Ultimate Victory of the God of Life*. New Haven, CT: Yale University Press, 2006.
Levenson, Jon D. "The Universal Horizon of Biblical Particularism." In Mark G. Brett (ed.). *Ethnicity and the Bible*. BibInt 19, 143–69. Leiden: Brill, 1996.
Levine, Amy-Jill. "Luke and the Jewish Religion." *Int* 68 (2014): 389–402.
Levine, Amy-Jill. "Review of *The Portrayals of the Pharisees in the Gospels and Acts*, by Mary Marshall." *SCJR* 11.1 (2016): 1–3.
Levine, Amy-Jill. *The Misunderstood Jew: The Church and the Scandal of the Jewish Jesus*. San Francisco, CA: HarperOne, 2006.
Levine, Lee I. "Josephus' Description of the Jerusalem Temple: *War*, *Antiquities*, and Other Sources." In Fausto Parente and Joseph Sievers (eds.), *Josephus and the History of the Greco-Roman Period: Essays in Memory of Morton Smith*, 233–46. Leiden: Brill, 1994.
Levinskaya, Irina A. *The Book of Acts in Its Diaspora Setting*. Vol. 5 of *BAFCS*. Grand Rapids, MI: Eerdmans, 1996.
Lincicum, David. "F. C. Baur's Place in the Study of Jewish Christianity." In Stanley Jones (ed.). *The Rediscovery of Jewish Christianity: From Toland to Baur*. F. HHBS, 137–66. Atlanta, GA: Society of Biblical Literature, 2012.
Litwak, Kenneth D. *Echoes of Scripture in Luke-Acts: Telling the History of God's People Intertextually*. JSNTSup 282. London: T&T Clark, 2005.
Litwak, Kenneth D. "One or Two Views of Judaism: Paul in Acts 28 and Romans 11 on Jewish Unbelief." *TynBul* 57 (2006): 229–49.
Lohfink, Gerhard. *Die Sammlung Israels: Eine Untersuchung zur lukanischen Ekklesiologie*. SANT 39. München: Kösel, 1975.
Lohfink, Gerhard. *The Conversion of St. Paul: Narrative and History in Acts*. Translated by Bruce J. Malina. Chicago, IL: Franciscan Herald Press, 1976.
Lyons, Michael A. "Paul and the Servant(s): Isaiah 49,6 in Acts 13,47." *ETL* 89 (2013): 345–59.
MacIntyre, Alasdair C. *Whose Justice? Which Rationality?* Notre Dame, IN: University of Notre Dame Press, 1988.
MacNamara, Luke. *My Chosen Instrument: The Characterisation of Paul in Acts 7:58–15:41*. AnBib Dissertationes 215. Roma: GBPress, 2016.
Mader, Gottfried. *Josephus and the Politics of Historiography: Apologetic and Impression Management in the* Bellum Judaicum. Leiden: Brill, 2000.
Malkin, Irad. "Greek Ambiguities: 'Ancient Hellas' and 'Barbarian Epirus.'" In Irad Malkin (ed.), *Ancient Perceptions of Greek Ethnicity*. CHSC 5, 187–212. Cambridge: Harvard University Press, 2001.
Malkin, Irad. "Introduction." In Irad Malkin (ed.), *Ancient Perceptions of Greek Ethnicity*. Irad Malkin. CHSC 5, 1–28. Cambridge, MA: Harvard University Press, 2001.
Malkin, Irad, ed. *Ancient Perceptions of Greek Ethnicity*. CHSC 5. Cambridge, CA: Harvard University Press, 2001.

Mallen, Peter. *The Reading and Transformation of Isaiah in Luke-Acts*. LNTS 361. London: T&T Clark, 2008.
Marguerat, Daniel. *The First Christian Historian: Writing the "Acts of the Apostles."* SNTSMS 121. Cambridge: Cambridge University Press, 2002.
Marshall, I. Howard. *The Acts of the Apostles: An Introduction and Commentary*. TNTC. Grand Rapids, MI: Eerdmans, 1996.
Marshall, Mary. *The Portrayals of the Pharisees in the Gospels and Acts*. FRLANT 254. Göttingen: Vandenhoeck & Ruprecht, 2014.
Mason, Steve. *Josephus and the New Testament*. 2nd ed. Peabody, MA: Hendrickson, 2002.
Mason, Steve. *Josephus, Judea, and Christian Origins: Methods and Categories*. Peabody, MA: Hendrickson Publishers, 2009.
Matthews, Shelly. *The Acts of the Apostles: An Introduction and Study Guide: Taming the Tongues of Fire*. SGNT 5. London: T&T Clark, 2017.
Matthews, Shelly. *Perfect Martyr: The Stoning of Stephen and the Construction of Christian Identity*. Oxford: Oxford University Press, 2010.
McCabe, David R. *How to Kill Things with Words: Ananias and Sapphira under the Prophetic Speech-Act of Divine Judgement (Acts 4.32–5.11)*. LNTS 454. London: T&T Clark, 2011.
McInerney, Jeremy. "Ethnos and Ethnicity in Early Greeks." *Ancient Perceptions of Greek Ethnicity*. Edited by Irad Malkin. CHSC 5. Cambridge, MA: Harvard University Press, 2001.
McWhirter, Jocelyn. *Rejected Prophets: Jesus and His Witnesses in Luke-Acts*. Minneapolis, MN: Fortress, 2014.
Meininger, Bernhard. "Einmal Tarsus und zurück (Apg 9,30; 11,25–26): Paulus als Lehrer nach der Apostelgeschichte." *MTZ* 49 (1998): 125–43.
Melito of Sardis. *On Pascha: With the Fragments of Melito and Other Material Related to the Quartodecimans*. Translated by Alistair Stewart-Sykes. PPS. Crestwood, NY: St. Vladimir's Seminary Press, 2001.
Metcalf, Reed. "Fire and Water, Shepherds and Sentinals: Echoes of Ezekiel in Luke-Acts." PhD diss., Fuller Theological Seminary, Pasadena, CA, 2022.
Miller, David M. "Ethnicity Comes of Age: An Overview of Twentieth-Century Terms for Ioudaios." *CBR* 10 (2012): 293–311.
Miller, David M. "Ethnicity, Religion and the Meaning of Ioudaios in Ancient 'Judaism.'" *CBR* 12 (2014): 216–65.
Miller, David M. "The Meaning of Ioudaios and Its Relationship to Other Group Labels in Ancient 'Judaism.'" *CBR* 9 (2010): 98–126.
Miller, John B. F. "Paul's Dream at Troas." In Thomas E. Phillips (ed.), *Contemporary Studies in Acts*, 138–53. Macon, GA: Mercer University Press, 2009.
Mittelstaedt, Alexander. *Lukas Als Historiker: Zur Datierung des lukanischen Doppelwerkes*. TANZ 43. Tübingen: Francke, 2006.
Mittmann, Ulrike. "Polemik im eschatologischen Kontext: Israel und die Heiden im lukanischen Doppelwerk." In Oda Wischmeyer and Lorenzo Scornaienchi (eds.), *Polemik in der frühchristlichen Literatur: Texte und Kontexte*. BZNW 170, 517–42. Berlin: de Gruyter, 2011.
Moessner, David P. *Luke the Historian of Israel's Legacy, Theologian of Israel's "Christ": A New Reading of the "Gospel Acts" of Luke*. BZNW 182. Berlin: de Gruyter, 2016.
Moffitt, David M. "Atonement at the Right Hand: The Sacrificial Significance of Jesus' Exaltation in Acts." *NTS* 62 (2016): 549–68.

Moore, Stewart Alden. *Jewish Ethnic Identity and Relations in Hellenistic Egypt: With Walls of Iron?* JSJSup 171. Leiden: Brill, 2015.

Moraff, Jason F. "Recent Trends in the Study of Jews and Judaism in Luke-Acts." *CBR* 19 (2020): 64–87.

Morgan, Catherine. "Ethne, Ethnicity, and Early Greek States, ca. 1200-480 B.C.: An Archaelogical Perspective." In Irad Malkin (ed.), *Ancient Perceptions of Greek Ethnicity*. CHSC 5, 75–112. Cambridge, MA: Harvard University Press, 2001.

Morgan, Teresa. "Society, Identity, and Ethnicity in the Hellenic World." In David G. Horrell and Katherine M. Hockey (eds.), *Ethnicity, Race, Religion: Identities and Ideologies in Early Jewish and Christian Texts, and in Modern Biblical Interpretation*, 23–45. London: Bloomsbury, 2018.

Morgan-Wynne, John Eifion. *Paul's Pisidian Antioch Speech (Acts 13)*. Eugene, OR: Wipf and Stock, 2014.

Morlan, David S. *Conversion in Luke and Paul: An Exegetical and Theological Exploration*. LNTS 464. London: T&T Clark, 2013.

Mount, Christopher. "Constructing Paul as a Christian in the Acts of the Apostles." In Ruben R. Dupertuis and Todd C. Penner (eds.), *Engaging Early Christian History: Reading Acts in the Second Century*, 141–52. London: Routledge, 2014.

Nagy, Viktor Kókai. "The Speech of Josephus at the Walls of Jerusalem." *BN* 161 (2014): 141–67.

Nave, Guy D. *The Role and Function of Repentance in Luke-Acts*. AcBib 4. Atlanta, GA: Society of Biblical Literature, 2002.

Neubrand, Maria. *Israel, die Völker und die Kirche: Eine exegetische Studie zu Apg. 15*. SBAB 55. Stuttgart: Katholisches Bibelwerk, 2006.

Nicklas, Tobias, and Michael Tilly, eds. *The Book of Acts as Church History: Text, Textual Traditions and Ancient Interpretations*. BZNW 120. Berlin: de Gruyter, 2003.

Nikiprowetzky, Valentin. "Josephus and the Revolutionary Parties." In Louis H. Feldman and Gōhei Hata (eds.), *Josephus, the Bible and History*, 216–36. Detroit, MI: Wayne State University Press, 1989.

Nolland, John. "Luke's Readers – A Study of Luke 4.22–8; Acts 13.46; 18,6; 28.28 and Luke 21.5–36." PhD diss., University of Cambridge, 1977.

Nongbri, Brent. *Before Religion: A History of a Modern Concept*. New Haven, CT: Yale University Press, 2015.

O'Toole, Robert F. "Reflections on Luke's Treatment of Jews in Luke-Acts." *Bib* 74 (1993): 529–55.

Oliver, Isaac W. "Are Luke and Acts Anti-Marcionite?" In J. Harold Ellens, Isaac W. Oliver, Jason von Ehrenkrook, James Waddell, and Jason M. Zurawski (eds.), *Wisdom Poured out Like Water: Studies on Jewish and Christian Antiquity in Honor of Gabriele Boccaccini*. DCLS 38, 499–525. Berlin: de Gruyter, 2018.

Oliver, Isaac W. *Luke's Jewish Eschatology: The National Restoration of Israel in Luke-Acts*. New York: Oxford University Press, 2021.

Oliver, Isaac W. "Simon Peter Meets Simon the Tanner: The Ritual Insignificance of Tanning in Ancient Judaism." *NTS* 59 (2013): 50–60.

Oliver, Isaac W. "The Calling of Paul in the Acts of the Apostles." In Gabriele Boccaccini and Isaac W. Oliver (eds.), *The Early Reception of Paul the Second Temple Jew: Text, Narrative and Reception History*. LSTS 92, 179–92. London: T&T Clark, 2018.

Oliver, Isaac W. *Torah Praxis after 70 CE: Reading Matthew and Luke-Acts as Jewish Texts*. WUNT 2/355. Tübingen: Mohr Siebeck, 2013.

Oropeza, B. J. "Judas' Death and Final Destiny in the Gospels and Earliest Christian Writings." *Neot* 44 (2010): 342–61.

Osborne, Robin. "Landscape, Ethnicity and the *Polis*." In Gabriele Cifani, Simon Stoddart, and Skylar Neil (eds.), *Landscape, Ethnicity and Identity in the Archaic Mediterranean Area*, 24–32. Oxford: Oxbow, 2012.
Overman, J. Andrew. "The God-Fearers: Some Neglected Features." *JSNT* 32 (1988): 17–26.
Padilla, Osvaldo. *The Speeches of Outsiders in Acts: Poetics, Theology and Historiography.* SNTSMS 144. Cambridge: Cambridge University Press, 2008.
Pantelis, Jorge. "Etnias e Iglesias en Hechos de los Apóstoles." *Apuntes* 24 (2004): 109–18.
Pao, David W. *Acts and the Isaianic New Exodus*. 2nd ed. Eugene, OR: Wipf and Stock, 2016.
Pao, David W. "Waiters or Preachers: Acts 6:1-7 and the Lukan Table Fellowship Motif." *JBL* 130 (2011): 127–44.
Parente, Fausto, and Joseph Sievers, eds. *Josephus and the History of the Greco-Roman Period: Essays in Memory of Morton Smith*. Leiden: Brill, 1994.
Parsons, Mikeal C. *Acts*. Paideia. Grand Rapids, MI: Baker Academic, 2008.
Parsons, Mikeal C. *Body and Character in Luke and Acts: The Subversion of Physiognomy in Early Christianity.* Waco, TX: Baylor University Press, 2011.
Parsons, Mikeal C., and Richard I. Pervo. *Rethinking the Unity of Luke and Acts*. Minneapolis, MN: Fortress, 1993.
Penner, Todd C. *In Praise of Christian Origins : Stephen and the Hellenists in Lukan Apologetic Historiography*. ESEC. New York: T&T Clark, 2004.
Pervo, Richard I. *Acts: A Commentary*. Hermeneia. Minneapolis, MN: Fortress, 2009.
Pervo, Richard I. *Dating Acts: Between the Evangelists and the Apologists*. Sonoma, CA: Polebridge, 2006.
Pervo, Richard I. *The Making of Paul: Constructions of the Apostle in Early Christianity*. Minneapolis, MN: Fortress, 2010.
Peterson, Brian K. "Stephen's Speech as a Modified Prophetic Rîḇ Formula." *JETS* 57 (2014): 351–69.
Phillips, Thomas E., ed. *Contemporary Studies in Acts*. Macon, GA: Mercer University Press, 2009.
Popkes, Enno Edzard. "Die letzten Worte des lukanischen Paulus: Zur Bedeutung von Act 28, 25–28 für das Paulusbild der Apostelgeschichte." In Jörg Frey, Clare K. Rothschild, and Jens Schröter (eds.), *Die Apostelgeschichte im Kontext antiker und frühchristlicher Historiographie*, 605–26. Berlin: de Gruyter, 2009.
Rajak, Tessa. *Josephus: The Historian and His Society*. Philadelphia, PA: Fortress, 1983.
Ravens, David A. *Luke and the Restoration of Israel*. JSNTSup 119. Sheffield: Sheffield Academic, 1995.
Ray, Jerry Lynn. *Narrative Irony in Luke-Acts: The Paradoxical Interaction of Prophetic Fulfillment and Jewish Rejection*. MBPS 28. Lewiston, NY: Mellen, 1996.
Read-Heimerdinger, Jenny. "The Apostles in the Bezan Text of Acts." In Tobias Nicklas and Michael Tilly (eds.), *The Book of Acts as Church History: Text, Textual Traditions and Ancient Interpretations*, 262–80. BZNW 120. Berlin: de Gruyter, 2003.
Reardon, Timothy W. *The Politics of Salvation: Lukan Soteriology, Atonement, and the Victory of Christ*. LNTS 642. London: T&T Clark, 2021.
Regev, Eyal. "Jewish Legal Practice and Piety in the Acts of the Apostles: Apologetics or Identity Marker?" In Alberdina Houtman, Tamar Kadari, Marcel Poorthuis, and Vered Tohar (eds.), *Religious Stories in Transformation: Conflict, Revision and Reception*, 126–43. Leiden: Brill, 2016.
Regev, Eyal. "Were the Early Christians Sectarians?" *JBL* 130 (2011): 771–93.

Rese, Martin. "The Jews in Luke-Acts: Some Second Thoughts." In Jozef Verheyden (eds.), *The Unity of Luke-Acts.* BETL 142, 185–201. Leuven: Peeters, 1999.

Revell, Louise. *Ways of Being Roman: Discourses of Identity in the Roman West.* Oxford: Oxbow, 2016.

Rhoads, David M., David Esterline, and Jae-won Lee, eds. *Luke-Acts and Empire: Essays in Honor of Robert L. Brawley.* PTMS 151. Eugene, OR: Pickwick, 2011.

Richard, Earl J. "The Polemical Character of the Joseph Episode in Acts 7." *JBL* 98 (1979): 255–67.

Richardson, Peter. *Israel in the Apostolic Church.* SNTSMS 10. Cambridge: Cambridge University Press, 1969.

Rius-Camps, Josep. *El Camino de Pablo a la Misión de los Paganos: Comentario Lingüístico y Exegético a HCH 13–28.* LNT 2. Madrid: Ediciones Cristiandad, 1984.

Rius-Camps, Josep. "El Mesianismo de Jesús Investigado por el Rabino Lucas a Partir de sus Fuentes Judías y Cristianas: Un Escrito a Modo de 'Demonstración' (ἐπίδειξις) Dirigido al Sumo Sacerdote Teófilo." *EstB* 63 (2005): 527–57.

Rowe, C. Kavin. *One True Life: The Stoics and Early Christians as Rival Traditions.* New Haven, CT: Yale University Press, 2016.

Rowe, C. Kavin. *World Upside Down: Reading Acts in the Graeco-Roman Age.* Oxford: Oxford University Press, 2009.

Rudolph, David J. "Luke's Portrait of Paul in Acts 21:17–26." In Gabriele Boccaccini and Isaac W. Oliver (eds.), *The Early Reception of Paul the Second Temple Jew: Text, Narrative and Reception History.* LSTS 92, 192–205. London: T&T Clark, 2018.

Ruthven, Jon. "'This is My Covenant with Them': Isaiah 59.19–21 as the Programmatic Prophecy of the New Covenant in the Acts of the Apostles (Part I)." *JPT* 17 (2008): 32–47.

Ruthven, Jon. "'This is My Covenant with Them': Isaiah 59.19–21 as the Programmatic Prophecy of the New Covenant in the Acts of the Apostles Part II." *JPT* 17 (2008): 219–37.

Sacchi, Paolo. *Jewish Apocalyptic and Its History.* Translated by William J. Short. JSPSup 20. Sheffield: Sheffield Academic Press, 1996.

Salmon, Marilyn. "Insider or Outsider? Luke's Relationship with Judaism." In Joseph B. Tyson (ed.), *Luke-Acts and the Jewish People: Eight Critical Perspectives,* 76–82. Minneapolis, MN: Augsburg, 1988.

Sanders, E. P. *Judaism: Practice and Belief, 63 BCE–66 CE.* 40th Anniversary Edition. Minneapolis, MN: Fortress, 2016.

Sanders, Jack T. *The Jews in Luke-Acts.* Philadelphia, PA: Fortress, 1987.

Sandt, Huub van de. "The Quotations in Acts 13,32–52 as a Reflection of Luke's LXX Interpretation." *Bib* 75 (1994): 26–58.

Satlow, Michael L. "Defining Judaism: Accounting for 'Religions' in the Study of Religion." *JAAR* 74 (2006): 837–60.

Saulnier, Stéphane. *Calendrical Variations in Second Temple Judaism: New Perspectives on the "Date of the Last Supper" Debate.* JSJSup 159. Leiden: Brill, 2012.

Schaefer, Christoph. *Die Zukunft Israels bei Lukas: Biblisch-frühjüdische Zukunftsvorstellungen im lukanischen Doppelwerk im Vergleich zu Röm 9–11.* BZNW 190. Berlin: de Gruyter, 2012.

Schäfer, Peter. *Judeophobia: Attitudes toward the Jews in the Ancient World.* Cambridge, MA: Harvard University Press, 1997.

Schaser, Nicholas J. "Unlawful for a Jew? Acts 10:28 and the Lukan View of Jewish-Gentile Relations." *BTB* 48 (2018): 188–201.

Schiffman, Lawrence H. "Qumran Temple? The Literary Evidence." *JAJ* 7 (2016): 71–85.
Schmidt, Karl Matthias. "Abkehr von der Rückkehr: Aufbau und Theologie der Apostelgeschichte im Kontext des lukanischen Diasporaverständnisses." *NTS* 53 (2007): 406–24.
Schnabel, Eckhard J. *Acts*. ZECNT. Grand Rapids, MI: Zondervan, 2012.
Schwartz, Daniel R. "Non-Joining Sympathizers (Acts 5:13–14)." *Bib* 64 (1983): 550–55.
Schwartz, Daniel R., and Zeev Weiss, eds. *Was 70 CE a Watershed in Jewish History?: On Jews and Judaism before and after the Destruction of the Second Temple*. AJEC 78. Leiden: Brill, 2012.
Schwartz, Seth. "How Many Judaisms Were There? A Critique of Neusner and Smith on Definition and Mason and Boyarin on Categorization." *JAJ* 2 (2011): 208–38.
Schwartz, Seth. *Imperialism and Jewish Society: 200 B.C.E. to 640 C.E.* Princeton, NJ: Princeton University Press, 2009.
Schwemer, Anna Maria. "Der Auferstandene und die Emmausjünger." In Friedrich Avemarie and Hermann Lichtenberger (eds.), *Auferstehung–Resurrection: Resurrection, Transfiguration, and Exaltation in Old Testament, Ancient Judaism, and Early Christianity (Tübingen, September 1999)*. WUNT 135, 95–117. Tübingen: Mohr Siebeck, 2001.
Selvatici, Monica. "'The Most High Does Not Dwell in Houses Made with Human Hands': A Study of Possible Hellenistic Jewish Parallels for the Jerusalem Temple as Idolatry in Acts 7:48." *Antí* 10 (2017): 1063–82.
Shin, W. Gil. "Integrated Stories and Israel's Contested Worship Space: Exod 15.17 and Stephen's Retelling of Heilsgeschichte (Acts 7)." *NTS* 64 (2018): 495–513.
Simkovich, Malka Z. *The Making of Jewish Universalism: From Exile to Alexandria*. Lanham, MD: Lexington Books, 2016.
Simón Muñoz, Alfonso. "La 'permanencia' de Israel: Una Nueva Lectura de Lc 2,34a." *EstB* 50 (1992): 191–223.
Skarsaune, Oskar. "Evidence for Jewish Believers in Greek and Latin Patristic Literature." In Oskar Skarsaune and Reidar Hvalvik (eds.), *Jewish Believers in Jesus: The Early Centuries*, 516–28. Peabody, MA: Hendrickson, 2007.
Skarsaune, Oskar, and Reidar Hvalvik, eds. *Jewish Believers in Jesus: The Early Centuries*. Peabody, MA: Hendrickson, 2007.
Sleeman, Matthew. *Geography and the Ascension Narrative in Acts*. SNTSMS 146. Cambridge: Cambridge University Press, 2009.
Slingerland, Dixon H. "'The Jews' in the Pauline Portion of Acts." *JAAR* 54 (1986): 305–21.
Smith, Daniel L. *The Rhetoric of Interruption: Speech-Making, Turn-Taking, and Rule-Breaking in Luke-Acts and Ancient Greek Narrative*. BZNW 193. Berlin: de Gruyter, 2012.
Smith, David A. "Luke, the Jews, and the Politics of Early Christian Identity." PhD diss., Duke University, Durham, NC, 2018.
Smith, Mitzi J. *Literary Construction of the Other in the Acts of the Apostles: Charismatics, the Jews, and Women*. PTMS 154. Eugene, OR: Pickwick, 2012.
Smith, Steve. *The Fate of the Jerusalem Temple in Luke-Acts: An Intertextual Approach to Jesus' Laments over Jerusalem and Stephen's Speech*. LNTS 553. London: T&T Clark, 2016.
Soulen, R. Kendall. *The God of Israel and Christian Theology*. Minneapolis, MN: Fortress, 1996.
Spencer, F. Scott. "Neglected Widows in Acts 6:1–7." *CBQ* 56 (1994): 715–33.

Spencer, Patrick E. "The Unity of Luke-Acts: A Four-Bolted Hermeneutical Hinge." *CBR* 5 (2007): 341–66.
Spilsbury, Paul. "God and Israel in Josephus: A Patron-Client Relationship." *Understanding Josephus: Seven Perspectives*. Edited by Steve Mason. Sheffield: Sheffield Academic, 1998.
Spilsbury, Paul. *The Image of the Jew in Flavius Josephus' Paraphrase of the Bible*. TSAJ 69. Tübingen: Mohr Siebeck, 1998.
Staples, Jason A. "'Rise, Kill, and Eat': Animals as Nations in Early Jewish Visionary Literature and Acts 10." *JSNT* 42 (2019): 3–17.
Staples, Jason A. *The Idea of "Israel" in Second Temple Judaism: A New Theory of People, Exile, and Jewish Identity*. Cambridge: Cambridge University Press, 2021.
Stendahl, Krister. "Qumran and Supersessionism—and the Road Not Taken." *PSB* 19 (1998): 134–42.
Stern, Philip D. "The 'Blind Servant' Imagery of Deutero-Isaiah and Its Implications." *Bib* 75 (1994): 224–32.
Steyn, Gert J. *Septuagint Quotations in the Context of the Petrine and Pauline Speeches of the Acta Apostolorum*. CBET 12. Kampen: Kok Pharos, 1995.
Stowers, Stanley K. "The Synagogue in the Theology of Acts." *RestQ* 17 (1974): 129–43.
Strahan, Joshua M. *The Limits of a Text: Luke 23:34a as a Case Study in Theological Interpretation*. JTISup 5. Winona Lake, IN: Eisenbrauns, 2012.
Strait, Drew J. *Hidden Criticism of the Angry Tyrant in Early Judaism and the Acts of the Apostles*. Lanham, MD: Lexington Books, 2019.
Strange, W. A. *The Problem of the Text of Acts*. SNTSMS 71. Cambridge: Cambridge University Press, 1991.
Strauss, Mark. *The Davidic Messiah in Luke-Acts: The Promise and Its Fulfilment in Lukan Christology*. JSNTSup 110. London: Bloomsbury, 1995.
Strelan, Rick. *Luke the Priest: The Authority of the Author of the Third Gospel*. London: Routledge, 2008.
Strelan, Rick. *Paul, Artemis, and the Jews in Ephesus*. BZNW 80. Berlin: de Gruyter, 1996.
Stromberg, Jake. *Isaiah after Exile: The Author of Third Isaiah as Reader and Redactor of the Book*. OTM. Oxford: Oxford University Press, 2011.
Stroup, Christopher. *The Christians Who Became Jews: Acts of the Apostles and Ethnicity in the Roman City*. Synkrisis. New Haven, CT: Yale University Press, 2020.
Talbert, Charles H. "The Place of the Resurrection in the Theology of Luke." *Int* 46 (1992): 19–30.
Talmon, Shemaryahu. "The Emergence of Jewish Sectarianism in the Early Second Temple Period." In Patrick D. Miller, Paul D. Hanson, and S. Dean McBride (eds.), *Ancient Israelite Religion: Essays in Honor of Frank Moore Cross*, 587–61. Philadelphia, PA: Fortress, 1987.
Tannehill, Robert C. "Israel in Luke-Acts: A Tragic Story." *JBL* 104 (1985): 69–85.
Tannehill, Robert C. *The Narrative Unity of Luke-Acts*. 2 vols. Minneapolis, MN: Fortress, 1986–1990.
Tannehill, Robert C. *The Shape of Luke's Story: Essays on Luke-Acts*. Eugene, OR: Wipf and Stock, 2005.
Taylor, Justin. "Why Were the Disciples First Called 'Christians' at Antioch? (Acts 11, 26)." *RB* 101 (1994): 75–94.
Taylor, Nicholas H. "Stephen, the Temple, and Early Christian Eschatology." *RB* 110 (2003): 62–85.
Thiessen, Matthew. *Contesting Conversion: Genealogy, Circumcision, and Identity in Ancient Judaism and Christianity*. Oxford: Oxford University Press, 2011.

Thiessen, Matthew. "Revisiting the Προσήλυτος in 'the LXX.'" *JBL* 132 (2013): 333–50.
Thoma, Clemens. "The High Priesthood in the Judgment of Josephus." In Louis H. Feldman and Gōhei Hata (eds.), *Josephus, the Bible and History*, 196–215. Detroit, MI: Wayne State University Press, 1989.
Thomas, Rosalind. "Ethnicity, Genealogy, and Hellenism in Herodotus." In Irad Malkin (ed.), *Ancient Perceptions of Greek Ethnicity*. CHSC 5, 213–33. Cambridge, MA: Harvard University Press, 2001.
Thompson, Marianne Meye. *The Promise of the Father: Jesus and God in the New Testament*. Louisville, KY: Westminster John Knox, 2000.
Tiede, David L. "Contending with God: The Death of Jesus and the Trial of Israel in Luke-Acts." In Birger A. Pearson (ed.), *The Future of Early Christianity: Essays in Honor of Helmut Koester*, 301–8. Minneapolis, MN: Fortress, 1991.
Tiede, David L. "'Glory to Thy People Israel': Luke-Acts and the Jews." In Joseph B. Tyson (ed.), *Luke-Acts and the Jewish People: Eight Critical Perspectives*, 21–34. Minneapolis, MN: Augsburg, 1988.
Tiede, David L. *Prophecy and History in Luke-Acts*. Philadelphia, PA: Fortress, 1980.
Tiede, David L. "The Exaltation of Jesus and the Restoration of Israel in Acts 1." *HTR* 79 (1986): 278–86.
Trebilco, Paul. *Self-Designations and Group Identity in the New Testament*. Cambridge: Cambridge University Press, 2014.
Troftgruben, Troy M. *A Conclusion Unhindered: A Study of the Ending of Acts within Its Literary Environment*. WUNT 2/280. Tübingen: Mohr Siebeck, 2010.
Troiaini, Lucio. "The Πολιτεία of Israel in the Greco-Roman Age." In Fausto Parente and Joseph Sievers (eds.), *Josephus and the History of the Greco-Roman Period: Essays in Memory of Morton Smith*. 11–22. Leiden: Brill, 1994.
Trotter, Jonathan Robert. *The Jerusalem Temple in Diaspora: Jewish Practice and Thought during the Second Temple Period*. JSJSup 192. Leiden: Brill, 2019.
Turner, Max. *Power from on High: The Spirit in Israel's Restoration and Witness in Luke-Acts*. JPTSup 9. Sheffield: Sheffield Academic, 1996.
Tyson, Joseph B. "Acts, the 'Parting of the Ways' and the Use of the Term 'Christians.'" In Isaac Kalimi (ed.), *Bridging between Sister Religions: Studies of Jewish and Christian Scriptures Offered in Honor of Prof. John T. Townsend*. BRLJ 51, 128–40. Leiden: Brill, 2016.
Tyson, Joseph B. *Images of Judaism in Luke-Acts*. Columbia, SC: University of South Carolina Press, 1992.
Tyson, Joseph B. *Luke, Judaism, and the Scholars: Critical Approaches to Luke-Acts*. Columbia, SC: University of South Carolina Press, 1999.
Tyson, Joseph B. *Marcion and Luke-Acts: A Defining Struggle*. Columbia, SC: University of South Carolina Press, 2006.
Tyson, Joseph B. "Wrestling with and for Paul." In Thomas E. Phillips (ed.), *Contemporary Studies in Acts*, 13–28. Macon, GA: Mercer University Press, 2009.
Tyson, Joseph B., ed. *Luke-Acts and the Jewish People: Eight Critical Perspectives*. Minneapolis, MN: Augsburg, 1988.
Unnik, Willem C. van. *Sparsa Collecta, Part 1: Evangelia, Paulina, Acta*. NovTSup 9. Leiden: Brill, 1973.
Vahrenhorst, Martin. "Gift oder Arznei? Perspektiven für das neutestamentliche Verständnis von Jes 6, 9f. im Rahmen der jüdischen Rezeptionsgeschichte." *ZNW* 92 (2001): 145–67.
Verheyden, Jozef, ed. *The Unity of Luke-Acts*. BETL 142. Leuven: Peeters, 1999.

Walters, Patricia. *The Assumed Authorial Unity of Luke and Acts: A Reassessment of the Evidence*. SNTSMS 145. Cambridge: Cambridge University Press, 2009.

Wardle, Timothy. "Samaritans, Jews, and Christians: Multiple Partings and Multiple Ways." In Lori Baron, Jill Hicks-Keeton, and Matthew Thiessen (eds.),= *The Ways that Often Parted: Essays in Honor of Joel Marcus*. ECL 24, 15–39. Atlanta, GA: SBL Press, 2018.

Wardle, Timothy. *The Jerusalem Temple and Early Christian Identity*. WUNT 2/191. Tübingen: Mohr Siebeck, 2010.

Wasserberg, Günter. *Aus Israels Mitte—Heil für die Welt: Eine narrativ-exegetische Studie zur Theologie des Lukas*. BZNW 92. Berlin: de Gruyter, 1998.

Watts, Rikki E. "Consolation or Confrontation: Isaiah 40–55 and the Delay of the New Exodus." *TynBul* 41 (1990): 31–59.

Weatherly, Jon A. *Jewish Responsibility for the Death of Jesus in Luke-Acts*. JSNTSup 106. Sheffield: Sheffield Academic, 1995.

Weatherly, Jon A. "The Jews in Luke-Acts." *TynBul* 40 (1989): 107–17.

Wendel, Susan J. *Scriptural Interpretation and Community Self-Definition in Luke-Acts and the Writings of Justin Martyr*. NovTSup 139. Leiden: Brill, 2011.

White, Aaron W. *The Prophets Agree: The Function of the Book of the Twelve Prophets in Acts*. BibInt 184. Leiden: Brill, 2020.

Whitlock, Matthew G. "Acts 1:15–26 and the Craft of New Testament Poetry." *CBQ* 77 (2015): 87–106.

Wills, Lawrence M. *Not God's People: Insiders and Outsiders in the Biblical World*. Lanham, MD: Rowman and Littlefield, 2008.

Wills, Lawrence M. "The Depiction of the Jews in Acts." *JBL* 110 (1991): 631–54.

Wilson, Brittany E. "Hearing the Word and Seeing the Light: Voice and Vision in Acts." *JSNT* 38 (2016): 456–81.

Wilson, Brittany E. "The Blinding of Paul and the Power of God: Masculinity, Sight, and Self-Control." *JBL* 133 (2014): 367–87.

Wilson, Brittany E. *Unmanly Men: Refigurations of Masculinity in Luke-Acts*. Oxford: Oxford University Press, 2015.

Wilson, Stephen G. *Luke and the Law*. SNTSMS 50. Cambridge: Cambridge University Press, 2005.

Winandy, Jacques. "La prophétie de Syméon (Lc 2:34–35)." *RevBib* 72 (1965): 321–51.

Wischmeyer, Oda. "Stephen's Speech before the Sanhedrin against the Background of the Summaries of the History of Israel (Acts 7)." In Núria Calduch-Benages and Jan Liesen (eds.), *History and Identity: How Israel's Later Authors Viewed Its Earlier History*. DCLS, 341–58. Berlin: de Gruyter, 2006.

Woods, David B. "Does Acts 15:9 Refute Intra-Ecclesial Jew-Gentile Distinction?" *Conspectus* 19 (2015): 105–45.

Woods, David B. "Interpreting Peter's Vision in Acts 10:9–16." *Conspectus* 12 (2012): 171–214.

Wright, N. T. *Jesus and the Victory of God*. Vol. 2 of *COQG*. Minneapolis, MN: Fortress, 2008.

Zhang, Wenxi. *Paul among Jews: A Study of the Meaning and Significance of Paul's Inaugural Sermon in the Synagogue of Antioch in Pisidia (Acts 13:16–41) for His Missionary Work among the Jews*. Eugene, OR: Wipf and Stock, 2011.

Zwiep, Arie W. *Christ, the Spirit and the Community of God: Essays on the Acts of the Apostles*. WUNT 2/293. Tübingen: Mohr Siebeck, 2010.